Albert Harkness

Second Latin Book; Comprising a Historical Latin Reader

With Notes and Rules for Translating; and an Exercise-Book....

Albert Harkness

Second Latin Book; Comprising a Historical Latin Reader
With Notes and Rules for Translating; and an Exercise-Book....

ISBN/EAN: 9783337157722

Printed in Europe, USA, Canada, Australia, Japan

Cover: Foto ©Thomas Meinert / pixelio.de

More available books at **www.hansebooks.com**

SECOND LATIN BOOK;

COMPRISING

A

HISTORICAL LATIN READER,

With Notes and Rules for Translating;

AND AN

EXERCISE-BOOK,

DEVELOPING A

COMPLETE ANALYTICAL SYNTAX,

IN A SERIES OF

LESSONS AND EXERCISES,

INVOLVING THE

CONSTRUCTION, ANALYSIS AND RECONSTRUCTION
OF LATIN SENTENCES.

BY

ALBERT HARKNESS, P. D.,

PROFESSOR OF THE GREEK LANGUAGE AND LITERATURE IN BROWN UNIVERSITY

NEW-YORK:
D. APPLETON & CO., 443 & 445 BROADWAY.
M.DCCC.LX.

PREFACE

THE volume now offered to the public is designed to be at once a Reader and an Exercise Book. It is in its plan and arrangement especially adapted to follow, in the course of classical study, the author's edition of Arnold's First Latin Book, and accordingly presupposes that the pupil has, by the use of that or some similar work, or at least by the study of Latin grammar, become familiar with the common forms and inflections of the language. Starting from this point, it aims to introduce the learner to a true knowledge and appreciation of the *structure* and *spirit* of the Latin tongue; and thus to prepare him to enter with success and pleasure upon the consecutive study of some Latin author.

It is a matter of regret that classes are often put upon the study of Cæsar or Virgil, before they have acquired sufficient knowledge of the structure and idioms of the language to prepare them for any just appreciation of those authors. Nothing tends more to lower the standard of true and accurate classical scholarship.

To explain more fully the plan of the present work, the author begs leave to specify the following points which are believed to be among its leading characteristics:

1. The Latin, which comprises the reading lessons, presents a brief epitome of Roman and Grecian history, and will furnish the pupil with a multitude of facts and incidents at once interesting and instructive.

2. The lessons and exercises, which are carefully adapted to the Latin text and are designed to be studied in connection with it, aim both to develop a complete analytical Syntax and to present a distinct picture of the Latin sentence in all the marked varieties of its form.

3. The analysis of the structure of the Latin sentence, is designed to be at once simple and symmetrical. While it aims to follow closely the growth of the simple sentence from its essential elements to its more expanded forms, while it marks the various ways in which these forms combine with each other, giving rise to a variety of complex and compound sentences, and yet further as it traces the combinations of these again with still others of any of the varieties just mentioned, it recognizes only a few well-defined and leading principles pervading and controlling all these changes—principles which the youngest pupil will readily understand and successfully apply.

4. The exercises consist of three distinct parts; viz.,

1st. A selection of Latin sentences, illustrative of the particular subject of the lesson. These are taken principally from the Latin text, and are designed to be carefully analyzed.

2d. An exercise in changing and reconstructing Latin sentences; in answering historical questions in Latin; or in forming new sentences on given models,—an exercise which the author has found eminently successful both in awakening interest and in giving the learner power and facility in the use of the language.

3d. Translations of English into Latin. The sentences here used are, as far as practicable, conversational, and relate to the historical facts and incidents learned from the reading lessons, thus securing to the pupil a degree of interest and profit which could scarcely be expected from any set exercises on miscellaneous subjects.

5. Rules designed to aid the pupil in recognizing the idioms of the language and in rendering them into good English

are inserted in the volume, and constantly used by means of reference in the notes. This, it is hoped, will not only save the teacher much labor, but will afford him the pleasure of listening to translations comparatively free from those foreign idioms which too often mar the beauty and correctness even of the early efforts of the young student in translating Latin and Greek.

In the preparation of the present work, the author has resorted freely to whatever sources of information were within his reach. He has had before him numerous Grammars of the Latin, Greek, and English languages, editions of Latin authors, works on the structure of language, and on the general subject of Philology. Among the Latin Grammars which have come under his notice, the German of Kritz and Berger deserves special mention, as having furnished important aid in the development of the structure and analysis of the Latin sentence.

The Latin has been selected from Arnold's Historiae Antiquae Epitome, founded on the Lateinisches Elementarbuch of Professors Jacobs and Döring. It consists, with a few unimportant exceptions, of selections from the Latin historians, Eutropius, Justin, and Cornelius Nepos. The work of Eutropius was really an abridgment, founded on "the best authorities, and is, in style, plain, concise, and simple:" Justin's history is made up mainly of selections from Trogus Pompeius, who lived and wrote in the Augustan age; while Nepos belongs to the same period, and was at once the contemporary and friend of Cicero.

In the arrangement of the volume, the Roman history is placed before the Grecian, not only because the former is more simple in style, but also because, in the study of Latin, the history of Rome justly claims an earlier attention than that of Greece.

The present volume is designed to be used in connection with some Latin grammar; for the purposes of those, however, who do not intend to pursue the study to any considerable extent, the summary of Grammar contained in the author's edition of Arnold's First Latin Book may be found sufficient. Accordingly in the preparation of the notes, such grammatical points as seemed to require notice have been explained mainly by appropriate references to the First Latin Book, to the Latin Grammar of Andrews and Stoddard, and to that of Zumpt; thus adapting the notes to the convenience of all who use either of the above works.

The author is happy in this connection to acknowledge his obligations to his friends who have aided him in this work; especially to Professors J. L. LINCOLN and S. S. GREENE of Brown University, for their generous interest in his efforts, and for the valuable suggestions with which they have kindly favored him.

With the above statement of the design and plan of the work, the author now commits it to classical teachers, and to the public generally, in the hope that it may not be found unworthy of a share, at least, of the marked favor with which they have been pleased to receive his former work.

A. HARKNESS.

Providence, April, 1851.

CONTENTS.

READING LESSONS.

ROMAN HISTORY.

Period.	Page.
I. Italian and Roman Kings	1
II. Roman Struggles and Conquests	7
III. Roman Triumphs	14
IV. Civil Dissensions	22
V. Roman Empire	32

GRECIAN HISTORY.

I. Traditionary Greece	37
II. Grecian Triumphs	40
III. Civil Wars in Greece	45
IV. Graeco-Macedonian Empire	54
V. Decline of Grecian Power	65

LESSONS AND EXERCISES IN SYNTAX.

INTRODUCTION 75

CHAPTER I.

SIMPLE SENTENCES.

Lesson.
I. Principal Elements of Sentences; Subject and Predicate.—
Declarative Sentences 78
II. Subordinate Elements; Modifiers . . . 80

CONTENTS.

Lesson.		Page.
III.	Elements of Sentences, continued.—Interrogative and Imperative Sentences	83
IV.	Simple Subject	85
V.	Complex Subject.—Modifier; Simple	87
VI.	Complex Subject.—Modifier; Complex	91
VII.	Simple Predicate	93
VIII.	Complex Predicate.—Direct Object; Simple	95
IX.	Complex Predicate.—Direct Object; Complex	97
X.	Complex Predicate.—Indirect Object; Simple or Complex	99
XI.	Complex Predicate.—Remote Object; Genitive	101
XII.	Complex Predicate.—Remote Object; Ablative	104
XIII.	Complex Predicate.—Direct Object with Attributive Accusative	106
XIV.	Complex Predicate.—Combined Objects; two Accusatives	109
XV.	Complex Predicate.—Combined Objects; Accusative and Dative	111
XVI.	Complex Predicate.—Combined Objects; Accusative and two Datives	113
XVII.	Complex Predicate.—Combined Objects; Accusative and Genitive	115
XVIII.	Complex Predicate.—Combined Objects; Accusative and Ablative	117
XIX.	Complex Predicate.—Combined Objects; two Datives	119
XX.	Complex Predicate.—Combined Objects; Dative and Ablative	121
XXI.	Complex Predicate.—Adverbial Attribute; Adverbs	122
XXII.	Complex Predicate.—Adverbial Expressions of *Manner, Means,* &c.	126
XXIII.	Complex Predicate.—Adverbial Expressions of *Time*	129
XXIV.	Complex Predicate.—Adverbial Expressions of *Place*	131
XXV.	Complex Predicate.—Oblique Cases with Prepositions as Adverbial Expressions	134

CONTENTS.

Lesson.		Page.
XXVI.	Complex Substantive-Predicate.—Modifier; Objective or Attributive	137
XXVII.	Complex Adjective-Predicate.—Modifier; Objective or Attributive	139
XXVIII.	Complex Adjective-Predicate.—Modifier; Complex	142
XXIX.	Elements of Sentences.—Recapitulation	144

CHAPTER II

COMPLEX SENTENCES.

§ 1.—COMPLEX SENTENCES; UNABRIDGED.

XXX.	Sentence as Subject	152
XXXI.	Sentence as Predicate	157
XXXII.	Sentence as Modifier of Subject or other Noun	160
XXXIII.	Accusative with Infinitive, or Sentence with *Quod* as Object	165
XXXIV.	Dependent Question as Object	168
XXXV.	Sentence with *ut* or *ne* as Object.—Indirect Object	170
XXXVI.	Adverbial Attributive-Sentences.—*Place*	174
XXXVII.	Adverbial Attributive-Sentences.—*Time*	177
XXXVIII.	Adverbial Attributive-Sentences.—*Cause*	182
XXXIX.	Adverbial Attributive-Sentences.—*Cause;* Condition and Concession	185
XL.	Adverbial Attributive-Sentences.—*Manner;* Consequence and Comparison	191
XLI.	Complex and Compound Sentences as Elements of other Sentences	194

§ 2.—COMPLEX SENTENCES; ABRIDGED.

XLII.	Principal Elements, Abridged	198
XLIII.	Modifier of Subject or other Noun, Abridged	202
XLIV.	Object of Predicate, Abridged	206
XLV.	Attribute of Predicate, Abridged.—*Comparison* and *Participles*	210

Lesson.		Page
XLVI.	Attribute of Predicate, Abridged; *Gerunds* and *Supines*	214

CHAPTER III.

COMPOUND SENTENCES.

§ 1.—COMPOUND SENTENCES; UNABRIDGED.

XLVII.	Classes of Compound Sentences	215
XLVIII.	Formation of Compound Sentences	221

§ 2. COMPOUND SENTENCES; ABRIDGED.

XLIX.	Compound Elements.—Subjects, United	224
L.	Compound Elements.—Predicates, United	228
LI.	Compound Elements.—Modifiers of Subject, United	231
LII.	Compound Elements.—Objects of Predicate, United	233
LIII.	Compound Elements.—Attributives of Predicate, United	235
LIV.	Elements Common to Different Members	237
LV.	Classification of Sentences.—Recapitulation	239
	RULES FOR TRANSLATING	245
	NOTES	257
	LATIN-ENGLISH VOCABULARY	287
	ENGLISH-LATIN VOCABULARY	327
	HISTORICAL AND GEOGRAPHICAL INDEX	343

EXPLANATIONS.

A. & S.	— Andrews & Stoddard's Latin Grammar.
Z.	— Zumpt's Latin Grammar, American edition.
F. B.	— Harkness' Arnold's First Latin Book.
P. C.	— Arnold's Latin Prose Composition, American edit.
Smith's Dict.	— Smith's Dictionary of Greek and Roman Antiquities.
Schmitz's Hist.	— Schmitz's History of Rome, Andover edition.

Numerals not preceded by any initials refer to articles in this work; and, in the Notes, those enclosed in parentheses refer to the *Rules for Translating.*

The enclosed numerals standing at the beginning of each lesson refer to the paragraphs in the Latin which this lesson is designed to accompany; thus, [1 & 2] at the beginning of the 1st and 2d lessons denotes that those lessons are designed to be learned in connection with the 1st and 2d paragraphs of the Latin.

SECOND LATIN BOOK.

ROMAN HISTORY.

PERIOD I.—*Italian and Roman Kings.*
FROM THE EARLIEST TIMES TO THE BANISHMENT OF TARQUIN,
510 B. C.

Early Italian Kings.—Aeneas in Italy.

1. ANTIQUISSĬMIS temporĭbus Saturnus in Italiam venisse dicĭtur. Ibi haud procul a Janicŭlo arcem condĭdit, eamque Saturniam appellāvit. Hic Itălos primus agricultūram docuit.

2. Poste Latīnus in illis regionĭbus imperāvit. Sub hoc rege Troja in Asia eversa est. Hinc Aenēas, Anchīsae filius, cum multis Trojānis, quibus ferrum Graecōrum pepercĕrat, aufūgit, et in Italiam pervēnit. Ibi Latīnus rex ei benigne recepto filiam Laviniam in matrimonium dedit. Aenēas urbem condĭdit, quam in honōrem conjŭgis Lavinium appellāvit.

Ascanius and the Kings of Alba.

3. Post Aenēae mortem Ascanius, Aenēae filius, regnum accēpit. Hic sedem regni in alium locum transtŭlit, urbemque condĭdit in monte Albāno, camque Albam Longam nuncupāvit. Eum secūtus est Silvius, qui post Aenēae mortem a Lavinia genĭtus erat.

Ejus postĕri omnes, usque ad Romam condĭtam, Albae regnavērunt.

4. Unus horum regum, Romŭlus Silvius, se Jovę majōrem esse dicēbat, et, quum tonāret, militĭbus imperāvit, ut clypeos hastis percutĕrent, dicebatque hunc sonum multo clariōrem esse quam tonĭtru. Fulmĭne ictus, et in Albānum lacum praecipitātus est.

5. Silvius Procas, rex Albanōrum, duos filios relīquit, Numitōrem et Amulium. Horum minor natu, Amulius, fratri optiōnem dedit, utrum regnum habēre vellet, an bona, quae pater reliquisset. Numĭtor paterna bona praetŭlit; Amulius regnum obtinuit.

Birth of Romulus and Remus.

6. Amulius, ut regnum firmissĭme possidēret, Numitōris filium per insidias interēmit, et filiam fratris, Rheam Silviam, Vestālem virgĭnem fecit. Nam his Vestae sacerdotĭbus non licet viro nubĕre. Sed haec a Marte gemĭnos filios, Romŭlum et Remum, pepĕrit. Hoc quum Amulius comperisset, matrem in vincŭla conjēcit, puĕros autem in Tibĕrim abjĭci jussit.

7. Forte Tibĕris aqua ultra ripam se effudĕrat, et, quum puĕri in vado essent posĭti, aqua refluens eos in sicco relīquit. Ad eōrum vagītum lupa accurrit, eosque uberĭbus suis aluit. Quod videns Faustŭlus quidam, pastor illīus regiōnis, puĕros sustŭlit, et uxōri Accae Laurentiae nutriendos dedit.

Rome founded, 753 B. C.

8. Sic Romŭlus et Remus pueritiam inter pastōres transegērunt. Quum adolevissent, et forte comperissent, quis ipsōrum avus, quae mater fuisset, Amulium inter-

fecērunt, et Numitōri avo regnum restituērunt. Tum urbem condidērunt in monte Aventīno, quam Romŭlus a suo nomĭne Romam vocāvit. Haec quum moenĭbus circumdarētur, Remus occīsus est, dum fratrem irrīdens moenia transiliēbat.

Seizure of the Sabine Women.

9. Romŭlus, ut civium numĕrum augēret, asylum patefēcit, ad quod multi ex civitatĭbus suis pulsi accurrērunt. Sed novae urbis civĭbus conjŭges deĕrant. Festum ităque Neptūni et ludos instituit. Ad hos quum multi ex finitĭmis popŭlis cum mulierĭbus et libĕris venissent, Romāni inter ipsos ludos spectantes virgĭnes rapuērunt.

10. Popŭli illi, quorum virgĭnes raptae erant, bellum adversus raptōres suscepērunt. Quum Romae appropinquārent, forte in Tarpēiam virgĭnem incidērunt, quae in arce sacra procurābat. Hanc rogābant, ut viam in arcem monstrāret, eīque permisērunt, ut munus sibi poscĕret. Illa petiit, ut sibi dárent, quod in sinistris manĭbus gerĕrent, annŭlos aureos et armillas signifĭcans. At hostes in arcem ab ea perducti scutis Tarpēiam obruērunt; nam et ea in sinistris manĭbus gerēbant.

The Sabines are received into the City.—Death of Romulus.

11. Tum Romŭlus cum hoste, qui montem Tarpēium tenēbat, pugnam conseruit in eo loco, ubi nunc forum Romānum est. In media caede raptae processērunt, et hinc patres, hinc conjŭges et socĕros complectebantur, et rogābant, ut caedis finem facĕrent. Utrīque his precĭbus commōti sunt. Romŭlus foedus icit, et Sabīnos in urbem recēpit

12. Postea civitātem descripsit. Centum senatōres legit, eosque cum ob aetātem, tum ob reverentiam iis debĭtam, Patres appellāvit. Plebem in triginta curias distribuit, easque raptārum nominĭbus nuncupāvit. Anno regni tricesĭmo septĭmo, quum exercĭtum lustrāret, inter tempestātem ortam repente ocŭlis homĭnum subductus est. Hinc alii eum a senatorĭbus interfectum, alii ad deos sublātum esse existimavērunt.

Numa Pompilius.

13. Post Romŭli mortem unīus anni interregnum fuit. Quo exacto, Numa Pompilius Curĭbus, urbe in agro Sabinōrum, natus rex creātus est. Hic vir bellum quidem nullum gessit; sed non minus civitāti profuit. Nam et leges dedit, et sacra plurĭma instituit, ut popŭli barbări et bellicōsi mores mollīret. Omnia autem, quae faciēbat, se nymphae Egeriae, conjŭgis suae, monĭtu facĕre dicēbat. Morbo decessit, quadragesĭmo tertio imperii anno.

Tullus Hostilius.

14. Numae successit Tullus Hostilius, cujus avus se in bello adversus Sabīnos fortem et strenuum virum praestitĕrat. Rex creātus bellum Albānis indixit, idque trigeminōrum, Horatiōrum et Curiatiōrum, certamĭne finīvit. Albam propter perfidiam Metii Suffetii diruit. Quum triginta duōbus annis regnasset, fulmĭne ictus cum domo sua arsit.

Ancus Marcius.

15. Post hunc Ancus Marcius, Numae ex filia nepos, suscēpit imperium. Hic vir aequitāte et religiōne

avo simĭlis, Latīnos bello domuit, urbem ampliāvit, et nova ei moenia circu'mdĕdit. Carcĕrem primus aedificūvit. Ad Tibĕris ostia urbem condĭdit, Ostiamque vocāvit. Vicesĭmo quarto anno imperii morbo obiit.

Lucius Tarquinius Priscus

16. Deinde regnum Lucius Tarquinius Priscus accēpit, Demarāti filius, qui tyrannos patriae Corinthi fugiens in Etruriam venĕrat. Ipse Tarquinius, qui nomen ab urbe Tarquiniis accēpit, aliquando Romam profectus erat. Advenienti aquĭla pĭleum abstŭlit, et, postquam alte evolavĕrat, reposuit. Hinc Tanăquil conjux, mulier auguriōrum perīta, regnum ei portendi intellexit.

17. Quum Romae commorarētur, Anci regis familiaritātem consecūtus est, qui eum filiōrum suōrum tutōrem relīquit. Sed is pupillis regnum intercēpit. Senatorĭbus, quos Romŭlus creavĕrat, centum alios addĭdit, qui minōrum gentium sunt appellāti. Plura bella felicĭter gessit, nec paucos agros, hostĭbus ademptos, urbis territorio adjunxit. Primus triumphans urbem intrāvit. Cloācas fecit; Capitolium inchoāvit. Tricesĭmo octāvo imperii anno per Anci filios, quibus regnum eripuĕrat, occīsus est.

Servius Tullius.

18. Post hunc Servius Tullius suscēpit imperium, genĭtus ex nŏbĭli femĭna, captīva tamen et famŭla. Quum in domo Tarquinii Prisci educarētur, flamma in ejus capĭte visa est. Hoc prodigio Tanăquil ei summam dignitātem portendi intellexit, et conjŭgi persuāsit, ut cum sicŭti libĕros suos educāret. Quum adolevisset, rex ei filiam in matrimonium dedit.

19. Quum Priscus Tarquinius occīsus esset, Tanăquil de superiōre parte domus popŭlum allocūta est, dicens: regem grave quidem, sed non letāle vulnus accepisse; eum petĕre, ut popŭlus, dum convaluisset, Servio Tullio obedīret. Sic Servius regnāre coepit, sed bene imperium administrāvit. Montes tres urbi adjunxit. Primus omnium censum ordināvit. Sub eo Roma habuit capĭtum oċtoginta tria millia civium Romanōrum cum his, qui in agris erant.

20. Hic rex interfectus est scelĕre filiae Tulliae et Tarquinii Superbi, filii ejus regis, cui Servius successĕrat. Nam ab ipso Tarquinio de gradĭbus curiae dejectus, quum domum fugĕret, interfectus est. Tullia in forum properāvit, et prima conjŭgem regem salutāvit. Quum domum redīret, aurīgam super patris corpus, in via jacens, carpentum agĕre jussit.

Banishment of Tarquinius Superbus, 510 B. C.

21. Tarquinius Superbus cognōmen morĭbus meruit. Bello tamen strenuus plures finitimōrum populōrum vicit. Templum Jovis in Capitolio aedificāvit. Postea, dum Ardeam oppugnābat, urbem Latii, imperium perdĭdit. Nam quum filius ejus Lucretiae, nobilissĭmae femĭnae, conjŭgi Tarquinii Collatīni, vim fecisset, haec se ipsa occīdit in conspectu marīti, patris et amicōrum, postquam eos obtestāta fuĕrat, ut hanc injuriam ulciscerentur.

22. Hanc ob causam L. Brutus, Collátīnus, aliīque nonnulli in exitium regis conjurārunt, populōque persuasērunt, ut ei portas urbis claudĕret. Exercĭtus quoque, qui civitātem Ardeam cum rege oppugnābat, eum relīquit. Fugit ităque cum uxōre et libĕris suis. Ita

Romae regnātum est per septem reges annos ducentos quadraginta tres.

Period II.—*Roman Struggles and Conquests.*

FROM THE ESTABLISHMENT OF THE COMMONWEALTH TO THE FIRST PUNIC WAR, 264 B. C.

Consuls at Rome, 509 *B. C.*—*War with Tarquin.*

23. Tarquinio expulso, consŭles coepēre pro uno rege duo creāri, ut, si unus malus esset, alter eum coërcēret. Annuum iis imperium tribūtum est, ne per diuturnitātem potestātis insolentiōres redderentur. Fuērunt igĭtur anno primo, expulsis regĭbus, consŭles L. Junius Brutus, acerrĭmus libertātis vindex, et Tarquinius Collatīnus, marītus Lucretiae. Sed Collatīno paulo post dignĭtas sublăta est. Placuĕrat enim, ne quis ex Tarquiniōrum familia Romae manēret. Ergo cum omni patrimonio suo ex urbe migrāvit, et in ejus locum Valerius Publicŏla consul factus est.

24. Commōvit bellum urbi rex Tarquinius. In prima pugna Brutus consul, et Aruns, Tarquinii filius, sese invĭcem occidērunt. Romāni tamen ex ea pugna victōres recessērunt. Brutum Romānae matrōnae, quasi commūnem patrem, per annum luxērunt. Valerius Publicŏla Sp. Lucretium, Lucretiae patrem, collēgam sibi fecit; qui quum morbo exstinctus esset, Horatium Pulvillum sibi collēgam sumpsit. Ita primus annus quinque consŭles habuit.

War with Porsena, 508 *B. C.*

25. Secundo quoque anno itĕrum Tarquinius bellum Romānis intŭlit, Porsĕna, rege Etruscōrum, auxi-

lium ei ferente. In illo bello Horatius Cocles solus pontem ligneum defendit, et hostes cohibuit, donec pons a tergo ruptus esset. Tum se cum armis in Tibĕrim conjēcit, et ad suos transnāvit.

26. Dum Porsĕna urbem obsidēbat, Qu. Mucius Scaevŏla, juvĕnis fortis anĭmi, in castra hostium se contŭlit eo consilio, ut regem occidĕret. At ibi scribam regis pro ipso rege interfēcit. Tum a regiis satellitĭbus comprehensus et ad regem deductus, quum Porsĕna eum ignĭbus allātis terrēret, dextram arae accensae imposuit, donec flammis consumpta esset. Hoc facĭnus rex mirātus juvĕnem dimīsit incolŭmem. Tum hic, quasi beneficium refĕrens, ait, trecentos alios juvĕnes in eum conjurasse. Hac re terrĭtus Porsĕna pacem cum Romānis fecit, Tarquinius autem Tuscŭlum se contŭlit, ibīque privātus cum uxōre consenuit.

Secession to the Mons Sacer, 494 B. C.

27. Sexto decĭmo anno post reges exactos, popŭlus Romae seditiōnem fecit, questus quod tribūtis et militia a senātu exhaurirētur. Magna pars plebis urbem relīquit, et in montem trans Aniēnem amnem secessit. Tum patres turbāti Menenium Agrippam misērunt ad plebem, qui eam senatui conciliāret. Hic iis inter alia fabŭlam narrāvit de ventre et membris humāni corpŏris; qua popŭlus commōtus est, ut in urbem redīret. Tum primum tribūni plebis creāti sunt, qui plebem adversum nobilitātis superbiam defendĕrent.

Banishment of Coriolanus, 491 B. C.

28. Octāvo decĭmo anno post exactos reges, Qu. Marcius, Coriolānus dictus ab urbe Volscōrum Coriŏlis,

quam bello cepĕrat, plebi invīsus fiĕri coepit. Quare urbe expulsus ad Volscos, acerrĭmos Romanōrum hostes, contendit, et ab iis dux exercĭtus factus Romānos saepe vicit. Jam usque ad quintum milliarium urbis accessĕrat, nec ullis civium suōrum legationĭbus flecti potĕrat, ut patriae parcĕret. Denĭque Veturia mater et Volumnia uxor ex urbe ad eum venērunt; quarum fletu et precĭbus commōtus est, ut exercĭtum removēret. Quo facto a Volscis ut prodĭtor occīsus esse dicĭtur.

The Fabii cut off at the Cremĕra, 477 B. C.

29. Romāni quum adversum Veientes bellum gerĕrent, familia Fabiōrum sola hoc bellum suscēpit. Profecti sunt trecenti sex nobilissĭmi homĭnes, duce Fabio consŭle. Quum saepe hostes vicissent, apud Cremĕram fluvium castra posuērunt. Ibi Veientes dolo usi eos in insidias pellexērunt. In proelio ibi exorto omnes periērunt. Unus superfuit ex tanta familia, qui propter aetātem puerīlem duci non potuĕrat ad pugnam. Hic genus propagāvit ad Qu. Fabium Maxĭmum illum, qui Hannibălem prudenti cunctatiōne debilitāvit.

The Decemviri.—Laws of the Twelve Tables, 451 B. C.

30. Anno trecentesĭmo et altĕro ab urbe condĭta decemvĭri creāti sunt, qui civitāti leges scribĕrent. Hi primo anno bene egērunt; secundo autem dominatiōnem exercēre coepērunt. Sed quum unus eōrum Appius Claudius virgĭnem ingenuam, Virginiam, Virginii centuriōnis filiam, corrumpĕre vellet, pater eam occīdit. Tum ad milĭtes profūgit, eosque ad seditiōnem commōvit. Sublāta est decemvĭris potestas, ipsīque omnes aut morte aut exilio punīti sunt.

Election of Military Tribunes, 444 B. C.

31. Anno trecentesĭmo decĭmo ab urbe condĭta dignitātes mutātae sunt, et pro duōbus consulĭbus facti tribūni militāres consulāri potestāte. Hinc jam coepit Romāna res crescĕre. Nam Camillus eo anno Volscōrum civitātem, quae per septuaginta annos bellum gessĕrat, vicit; et Aequōrum urbem et Sutrinōrum, omnibus delētis exercitĭbus, occupāvit, et tres simul triumphos egit.

Camillus and the Schoolmaster of Falerii.

32. In bello contra Veientānos Furius Camillus urbem Falerios obsidēbat. In qua obsidiōne quum ludi literarii magister princĭpum filios ex urbe in castra hostium duxisset, Camillus scelestum munus non accēpit, sed homĭnem denudātum, manĭbus post tergum illigātis, reducendum Falerios puĕris tradĭdit; virgasque iis dedit, quibus proditōrem in urbem agĕrent.

Veii taken, 396 B. C.—*Rome taken and burnt by the Gauls*, 390 B. C.

33. Hac tanta anĭmi nobilitāte commōti Falisci urbem Romānis tradidērunt. Camillo autem apud Romānos crimĭni datum est, quod albis equis triumphasset, et praedam inīque divisisset; damnatusque ob eam causam, et civitāte expulsus est. Paulo post Galli Senŏnes ad urbem venērunt, Romānos apud flumen Alliam vicērunt, et urbem etiam occupārunt. Jam nihil praeter Capitolium defendi potuit. Et jam praesidium fame laborābat, et in eo erant, ut pacem a Gallis auro emĕrent, quum Camillus cum manu milĭtum superveniens hostes magno proelio superāret.

ROMAN STRUGGLES AND CONQUESTS.

Valor of Titus Manlius Torquatus, 361 B. C.

34. Anno trecentesĭmo nonagesĭmo quarto post urbem condĭtam Galli itĕrum ad urbem accessĕrant, et quarto milliario trans Aniēnem fluvium consedĕrant. Contra eos missus est T. Quinctius. Ibi Gallus quidam eximia corpŏris magnitudĭne fortissĭmum Romanōrum ad certāmen singulāre provocāvit. T. Manlius, nobilissĭmus juvĕnis, provocatiōnem accepit, Gallum occīdit, eumque torque aureo spoliāvit, quo ornātus erat. Hinc et ipse et postĕri ejus Torquāti appellāti sunt. Galli fugam capessivērunt.

Valor of Valerius Corvus, 348 B. C.—The Gauls cease to trouble Rome.

35. Novo bello cum Gallis exorto, anno urbis quadringentesĭmo sexto, itĕrum Gallus processit robŏre atque armis insignis, et prŏvocāvit unum ex Romānis, ut secum armis decernĕret. Tum se M. Valerius, tribūnus milĭtum, obtŭlit; et, quum processisset armātus, corvus ei supra dextrum brachium sedit. Mox, commissa pugna, hic corvus alis et unguĭbus Galli ocŭlos verberāvit. Ita factum est, ut Gallus facĭli negotio a Valerio interficerētur, qui hinc Corvīni nomen accēpit.

Beginning of Samnite Wars, 343 B. C.

36. Postea Romāni bellum gessērunt cum Samnitĭbus, ad quod L. Papirius Cursor cum honōre dictatōris profectus est. Qui quum negotii cujusdam causa Romam redīret, praecēpit Q. Fabio Rulliāno, magistro equĭtum, quem apud exercĭtum relīquit, ne pugnam cum hoste committĕret. Sed ille occasiōnem nactus felicissĭme dimicāvit, Samnītes delēvit. Ob hanc rem

a dictatōre capĭtis damnātus est. At ille in urbem con fūgit, et ingenti favōre milĭtum et popŭli liberātus est; in Papirium autem tanta exorta est seditio, ut paene ipse interficerētur.

The Roman Army is made to pass under the yoke, 321 *B. C.—The Samnites are conquered,* 290 *B. C.*

37. Duōbus annis post T. Veturius et Spurius Postumius consŭles bellum adversum Samnītes gerēbant. Hi a Pontio Thelesīno, duce hostium, in insidias inducti sunt. Nam ad Furcŭlas Caudīnas Romānos pellexit in angustias, unde sese expedīre non potĕrant. Ibi Pontius patrem suum Herennĭum rogāvit, quid faciendum putāret. Ille respondit, aut omnes occidendos esse, ut Romanōrum vires frangerentur, aut omnes dimittendos, ut beneficio obligarentur. Pontius utrumque consilium improbāvit, omnesque sub jugum misit. Samnītes denĭque post bellum undequinquaginta annōrum superāti sunt.

War with Pyrrhus, 281 *B. C.*

38. Devictis Samnitĭbus, Tarentīnis bellum indictum est, quia legātis Romanōrum injuriam fecissent. Hi Pyrrhum, Epīri regem, contra Romānos auxilium poposcērunt. Is mox in Italiam venit, tumque primum Romāni cum transmarīno hoste pugnavērunt. Missus est contra eum consul P. Valerius Laevīnus. Hic, quum exploratōres Pyrrhi cepisset, jussit eos per castra duci, tumque dimitti, ut renuntiārent Pyrrho, quaecunque a Romānis agerentur.

39. Pugna commissa, Pyrrhus auxilio elephantōrum vicit. Nox proelio finem dedit. Laevīnus tamen per

noctem fugit. Pyrrhus Romānos mille octingentos cepit, eosque summo honōre tractāvit. Quum eos, qui in proelio interfecti fuĕrant, omnes adversis vulnerĭbus et truci vultu etiam mortuos jacēre vidēret, tulisse ad coelum manus dicĭtur cum hac voce: "Ego cum talĭbus viris brevi orbem terrārum subigĕrem."

40. Postea Pyrrhus Romam perrexit; omnia ferro ignĕque vastāvit; Campaniam depopŭlātus est, atque ad Praeneste venit milliario ab urbe octāvo decĭmo. Mox terrōre exercĭtus, qui cum consŭle sequebātur, in Campaniam se recēpit. Legāti ad Pyrrhum de captīvis redimendis missi honorifĭce ab eo suscepti sunt; captīvos sine pretio reddĭdit. Unum ex legātis, Fabricium, sic admirātus est, ut ei quartam partem regni sui promittĕret, si ad se transīret; sed a Fabricio contemptus est.

41. Quum jam Pyrrhus ingenti Romanōrum admiratiōne tenerētur, legātum misit Cineam, praestantissĭmum virum, qui pacem petĕret ea conditiōne, ut Pyrrhus eam partem Italiae, quam armis occupavĕrat, obtinēret. Romāni respondērunt, eum cum Romānis pacem habēre non posse, nisi ex Italia recessisset. Cineas quum rediisset, Pyrrho eum interroganti, qualis ipsi Roma visa esset; respondit, se regum patriam vidisse.

42. In altĕro proelio cum rege Epīri commisso Pyrrhus vulnerātus est, elephanti interfecti, viginti millia hostium caesa sunt. Pyrrhus Tarentum fugit. Interjecto anno, Fabricius contra eum missus est. Ad hunc medĭcus Pyrrhi nocte venit promittens, se Pyrrhum venēno occisūrum, si munus sibi darētur. Hunc Fabricius vinctum redūci jussit ad domĭnum. Tunc rex admirātus illum dixisse fertur: "Ille est Fabricius, qui

difficilius ab honestāte, quam sol a cursu suo averti potest." Paulo post Pyrrhus, tertio etiam proelio fusus, a Tarento recessit, et, quum in Graeciam rediisset, apud Argos, Peloponnēsi urbem, interfectus est.

Period III.—*Roman Triumphs.*
FROM THE FIRST PUNIC WAR TO THE CONQUEST OF GREECE, 146 B. C.

First Punic (Carthaginian) War, 264 B. C.

43. Anno quadringentesĭmo nonagesĭmo post urbem condĭtam Romanōrum exercĭtus primum in Siciliam trajecērunt, regemque Syracusārum Hierōnem, Poenosque, qui multas civitātes in ea insŭla occupavĕrant, superavērunt. Quinto anno hujus belli, quod contra Poenos gerebātur, primum Romāni, C. Duillio et Cn. Cornelio Asĭna consulĭbus, in mari dimicavērunt Duillius Carthaginienses vicit, trigintą, naves occupāvit, quatuordĕcim mersit, septem millia hostium cepit, tria millia occīdit. Nulla victoria Romānis gratior fuit. Duillio concessum est, ut, quum a coena redīret, puĕri funalia gestantes et tibīcen eum comitarentur.

First Punic War, continued.—Invasion of Africa, 256 B. C.

44. Paucis annis interjectis, bellum in Afrĭcam translātum est. Hamilcar, Carthaginiensium dux, pugna navāli superātur; nam perdĭtis sexaginta quatuor navĭbus se recēpit; Romāni viginti duas amisērunt. Quum in Afrĭcam venissent, Poenos in plurĭbus proeliis vicērunt, magnam vim homĭnum cepērunt, septua-

ginta quatuor civitātes in fidem accepērunt. Tum victi Carthaginienses pacem a Romānis petiērunt. Quam quum M. Atilius Regŭlus, Romanōrum dux, dare nollet nisi durissĭmis conditionĭbus, Carthaginienses auxilium petiērunt a Lacedaemoniis. Hi Xanthippum misērunt, qui Romānum exercĭtum magno proelio vicit. Regŭlus ipse captus et in vincŭla conjectus est.

45. Non tamen ubīque fortūna Carthaginiensĭbus favit. Quum alĭquot proeliis victi essent, Regŭlum rogavērunt, ut Romam proficiscerētur, et pacem captivorumque permutatiōnem a Romānis obtinēret. Ille quum Romam venisset, inductus in senātum dixit, se desiisse Romānum esse ex illa die, qua in potestātem Poenōrum venisset. Tum Romānis suasit, ne pacem cum Carthaginiensĭbus facĕrent: illos enim tot casĭbus fractos spem nullam nisi in pace habēre: tanti non esse, ut tot millia captivōrum propter se unum et paucos, qui ex Romānis capti essent, redderentur. Haec sententia obtinuit. Regressus igĭtur in Afrĭcam crudelissĭmis suppliciis exstinctus est.

End of the First Punic War, 241 *B. C.*

46. Tandem, C. Lutatio Catŭlo, A. Postumio consulĭbus, anno belli Punĭci vicesĭmo tertio magnum proelium navāle commissum est contra Lilybaeum, promontorium Siciliae. In eo proelio septuaginta tres Carthaginiensium naves captae, centum viginti quinque demersae, triginta duo millia hostium capta, tredĕcim millia occīsa sunt. Statim Carthaginienses pacem petiērunt, eisque pax tribūta est. Captīvi Romanōrum, qui tenebantur a Carthaginiensĭbus, reddĭti sunt. Poeni Sicilia, Sardinia, et cetĕris insŭlis, quae inter Italiam

Africamque jacent, decessērunt, omnemque Hispaniam, quae citra Ibērum est, Romānis permisērunt.

Siege of Saguntum.—The Second Punic War, 218 B. C.

47. Paulo post Punĭcum bellum renovātum est per Hannibălem, Carthaginiensium ducem, quem pater Hamilcar novem annos natum aris admovĕrat, ut odium perenne in Romānos jurāret. Hic annum agens vicesĭmum aetātis Saguntum, Hispaniae civitātem, Romānis amīcam, oppugnāre aggressus est. Huic Romāni per legātos denuntiavērunt, ut bello abstinēret. Qui quum legātos admittĕre nollet, Romāni Carthagĭnem misērunt, ut mandarētur Hannibāli, ne bellum contra socios popŭli Romāni gerĕret. Dura responsa a Carthaginiensĭbus reddĭta. Saguntīnis interea fame victis, Romāni Carthaginiensĭbus bellum indixērunt.

Hannibal crosses the Alps, 218 *B. C.—Battles of the Ticīnus, Trebia, and Lake Trasimēnus.—Battle of Cannae,* 216 *B. C.*

48. Hannĭbal, fratre Hasdrubăle in Hispania relicto, Pyrenaeum et Alpes transiit. Tradĭtur in Italiam octoginta millia pedĭtum, et viginti millia equĭtum, septem et triginta elephantos abduxisse. Interea multi Ligŭres et Galli Hannibāli se conjunxērunt. Primus ei occurrit P. Cornelius Scipio, qui, proelio ad Ticīnum commisso, superātus est, et, vulnĕre accepto, in castra rediit. Tum Sempronius Gracchus conflixit ad Trebiam amnem. Is quoque vincĭtur. Multi popŭli se Hannibāli dedidērunt. Inde in Tusciam progressus Flaminium consulem ad Trasimēnum lacum supĕrat. Ipse Flaminius interemptus, Romanōrum viginti quinque millia caesa sunt.

49. Quingentesĭmo et quadragesĭmo anno post urbem condĭtam L. Aemilius Paullus et P. Terentius Varro contra Hannibălem mittuntur. Quamquam intellectum erat, Hannibălem non alĭter vinci posse quam mora, Varro tamen, morae impatiens, apud vicum, qui Cannae appellātur, in Apulia pugnāvit; ambo consŭles victi, Paullus interemptus est. In ea pugna consulāres aut praetorii viginti, senatōres triginta capti aut occīsi; milĭtum quadraginta millia, equĭtum tria millia et quingenti periērunt. In his tantis malis nemo tamen pacis mentiōnem facĕre dignātus est. Servi, quod nunquam ante factum, manumissi et milĭtes facti sunt.

50. Post eam pugnam multae Italiae civitātes, quae Romānis paruĕrant, se ad Hannibălem transtulĕrunt. Hannĭbal Romānis obtŭlit, ut captīvos redimĕrent; responsumque est a senātu, eos cives non esse necessarios, qui armāti capi potuissent. Hos omnes ille postea variis suppliciis interfĕcit, et tres modios aureōrum annulōrum Carthagĭnem misit, quos manĭbus equĭtum Romanōrum, senatōrum, et milĭtum detraxĕrat. Interea in Hispania frater Hannibălis, Hasdrŭbal, qui ibi remansĕrat cum magno exercĭtu, a duōbus Scipionĭbus vincĭtur, perditque in pugna triginta quinque millia homĭnum.

51. Anno quarto postquam Hannĭbal in Italiam venĕrat, M. Claudius Marcellus consul apud Nolam, civitātem Campaniae, contra Hannibălem bene pugnāvit. Illo tempŏre Philippus, Demetrii filius, rex Macedoniae, ad Hannibălem legātos mittit, eīque auxilia contra Romānos pollicētur. Qui legāti quum a Romānis capti essent, M. Valerius Laevīnus cum navĭbus missus est, qui regem impedīret, quo minus copias in

Italiam trajicĕret. Idem in Macedoniam penĕtrans regem Philippum vicit.

52. In Sicilia quoque res prospĕre gesta est. Marcellus magnam hujus insŭlae partem cepit, quam Poeni occupaverant; Syracūsas, nobilissĭmam urbem, expugnāvit, et ingentem inde praedam Romam misit. Laevīnus in Macedonia cum Philippo et multis Graeciae popŭlis amicitiam fecit; et in Siciliam profectus Hannōnem, Poenōrum ducem, apud Agrigentum cepit; quadraginta civitātes in deditiōnem accēpit, viginti sex expugnāvit. Ita omni Sicilia recepta, cum ingenti gloria Romam regressus est.

53. Interea in Hispaniam, ubi duo Scipiōnes ab Hasdrubăle interfecti erant, missus est P. Cornelius Scipio, vir Romanōrum omnium fere primus. Hic, puer duodeviginti annōrum, in pugna ad Ticīnum, patrem singulāri virtūte servāvit. Deinde post cladem Cannensem multos nobilissimōrum juvĕnum Italiam deserĕre cupientium, auctoritāte sua ab hoc consilio deterruit. Viginti quatuor annōrum juvĕnis in Hispaniam missus, die, qua venit, Carthagĭnem Novam cepit, in qua omne aurum et argentum et belli apparātum Poeni habēbant, nobilissĭmos quoque obsĭdes, quos ab Hispānis accepĕrunt. Hos obsĭdes parentĭbus suis reddĭdit. Quare omnes fere Hispaniae civitātes ad eum uno animo transiērunt.

54. Ab eo inde tempŏre res Romanōrum in dies laetiōres factae sunt. Hasdrŭbal a fratre ex Hispania in Italiam evocātus, apud Senam, Picēni civitātem, in insidias incĭdit, et strenue pugnans occīsus est. Plurĭmae autem civitātes, quae in Bruttiis ab Hannibăle tenebantur, Romānis se tradidērunt.

55. Anno decĭmo quarto postquam in Italiam Hannĭbal venĕrat, Scipio consul creātus, et in Afrĭcam missus est. Ibi contra Hannōnem, ducem Carthaginiensium, prospĕre pugnat, totumque ejus exercĭtum delet. Secundo proelio undĕcim millia homĭnum occīdit, et castra cepit cum quatuor millĭbus et quingentis militĭbus. Syphācem, Numidiae regem, qui se cum Poenis conjunxĕrat, cepit, eumque cum nobilissĭmis Numĭdis et infinītis spoliis Romam misit. Qua re audīta, omnis fere Italia Hannibălem desĕrit. Ipse a Carthaginiensĭbus in Afrĭcam redīre jubētur. Ita anno decĭmo septĭmo Italia ab Hannibăle liberāta est.

Battle of Zama, 202 B. C.

56. Post plures pugnas et pacem plus semel frustra tentātam, pugna ad Zamam committĭtur, in qua peritissĭmi duces copias suas ad bellum educēbant. Scipio victor recēdit; Hannĭbal cum paucis equitĭbus evādit. Post hoc proelium pax cum Carthaginiensĭbus facta est. Scipio, quum Romam rediisset, ingenti gloria triumphāvit, atque Africānus appellātus est. Sic finem accēpit secundum Punĭcum bellum post annum undevicesĭmum quam coepĕrat.

War with Philip.—Cynoscephalae, 197 B. C.

57. Finīto Punĭco bello, secūtum est Macedonĭcum contra Philippum regem. Superātus est rex a T. Quinctio Flaminio apud Cynoscephălas, paxque ei data est his legĭbus: ne Graeciae civitatĭbus, quas Romāni contra eum defendĕrant, bellum inferret; ut captīvos et transfŭgas reddĕret; quinquaginta solum naves habēret; relĭquas Romānis daret; mille talenta praestā-

ret, et obsĭdem daret filium Demetrium. T. Quinctius etiam Lacedaemoniis intŭlit bellum, et ducem eōrum Nabĭdem vicit.

War with Antiochus, 192 *B. C.*

58. Finīto bello Macedonĭco, secūtum est bellum Syriăcum contra Antiŏchum regem, cum quo Hannĭbal se junxĕrat. Missus est contra eum L. Cornelius Scipio consul, cui frater ejus Scipio Africānus legātus est addĭtus. Hannĭbal navāli proelio victus, Antiŏchus autem ad Magnesiam, Asiae civitātem, a Cornelio Scipiōne consŭle ingenti proelio fusus est. Tum rex Antiŏchus pacem petit. Data est ei hac lege, ut ex Eurōpa et Asia recedĕret, atque intra Taurum se continēret, decem millia talentōrum et viginti obsĭdes praebēret, Hannibălem, concitōrem belli, dedĕret. Scipio Romam rediit, et ingenti gloria triumphāvit. Nomen et ipse, ad imitatiōnem fratris, Asiatĭci accēpit.

War with Perseus.—Pydna, 168 *B. C.*

59. Philippo, rege Macedoniae, mortuo, filius ejus Perseus rebellāvit, ingentĭbus copiis parātis. Dux Romanōrum, P. Licinius consul, contra eum missus, gravi proelio a rege victus est. Rex tamen pacem petēbat. Cui Romāni eam praestāre noluērunt, nisi his conditionĭbus, ut se et suos Romānis dedĕret. Mox Aemilius Paullus consul regem ad Pydnam superāvit, et viginti millia pedĭtum ejus occīdit. Equitātus cum rege fugit. Urbes Macedoniae omnes, quas rex tenuĕrat, Romānis se dedidērunt. Ipse Perseus ab amīcis desertus in Paulli potestātem venit. Hic, multis etiam aliis rebus gestis, cum ingenti pompa Romam rediit in nave Per-

sei, inusitātae magnitudĭnis; nam sedĕcim remōrum ordĭnes habuisse dicĭtur. Triumphāvit magnificentissĭme in curru aureo, duōbus filiis utrōque latĕre adstantĭbus. Ante currum inter captīvos duo regis filii et ipse Perseus ducti sunt.

Third Punic War, 149–6 B. C.

60. Tertium deinde bellum contra Carthagĭnem susceptum est sexcentesĭmo et altĕro anno ab urbe condĭta, anno quinquagesĭmo primo postquam secundum bellum Punĭcum transactum erat. L. Marcius Censorīnus et M. Manlius consūles in Afrĭcam trajecērunt, et oppugnavērunt Carthagĭnem. Multa ibi praeclāre gesta sunt per Scipiōnem, Scipiōnis Africāni nepōtem, qui tribūnus in Afrĭca militābat. Hujus apud omnes ingens metus et reverentia erat, neque quidquam magis Carthaginiensium duces vitābant, quam contra eum proelium committĕre.

61. Quum jam magnum esset Scipiōnis nomen, tertio anno postquam Romāni in Afrĭcam trajecērant, consul est creātus, et contra Carthagĭnem missus. Is hanc urbem a civĭbus acerrĭme defensam cepit ac diruit. Ingens ibi praeda facta, plurimăque inventa sunt, quae multārum civitātum excidiis Carthāgo collegĕrat. Haec omnia Scipio civitatĭbus Italiae, Siciliae, Afrĭcae reddĭdit, quae sua recognoscēbant. Ita Carthāgo septingentesĭmo anno, postquam condĭta erat, delēta est. Scipio nomen Africāni juniōris accēpit.

Corinth taken, 146 B. C.

62. Intĕrim in Macedonia quidam Pseudophilippus arma movit, et P. Juvencium, Romanōrum ducem, ad

internecionem vicit. Post eum Q. Caecilius Metellus dux a Romanis contra Pseudophilippum missus est, et, viginti quinque millĭbus ex militĭbus ejus occīsis, Macedoniam recēpit; ipsum etiam Pseudophilippum in potestātem suam redēgit. Corinthiis quoque bellum indictum est, nobilissĭmae Graeciae civitāti, propter injuriam Romānis legātis illātam. Hanc Mummius consul cepit ac diruit. Tres igĭtur Romae simul celeberrĭmi triumphi fuērunt; Scipiōnis ex Afrĭca, ante cujus currum ductus est Hasdrŭbal; Metelli ex Macedonia, cujus currum praecessit Andriscus, qui et Pseudophilippus dicĭtur; Mummii ex Corintho, ante quem signa aenea et pictae tabŭlae et alia urbis clarissĭmae ornamenta praelāta sunt.

Period IV.—*Civil Dissensions.*

FROM THE CONQUEST OF GREECE TO THE DISSOLUTION OF THE ROMAN COMMONWEALTH, 31 B. C.

War with the Lusitanians.—Viriathus, 149 B. C.

63. Anno sexcentesĭmo decĭmo post urbem condĭtam Viriāthus in Lusitania bellum contra Romānos excitāvit. Pastor primo fuit, mox latrōnum dux; postrēmo tantos ad bellum popŭlos concitāvit, ut vindex libertātis Hispaniae existimarētur. Denīque a suis interfectus est. Quum interfectōres ejus praemium a Caepiōne consŭle petĕrent, responsum est, nunquam Romānis placuisse, imperatōrem a militĭbus suis interfĭci.

Numantia taken, 133 *B. C.*

64. Deinde bellum exortum est cum Numantīnis, civitāte Hispaniae. Victus ab his Qu. Pompēius, et post eum C. Hostilius Mancīnus consul, qui pacem cum iis fecit infāmem, quam popŭlus et senātus jussit infringi, atque ipsum Mancīnum hostĭbus tradi. Tum P. Scipio Africānus in Hispaniam missus est. Is primum milĭtem ignāvum et corruptum correxit; tum multas Hispaniae civitātes partim bello cepit, partim in deditiōnem accēpit. Postrēmo ipsam Numantiam fame ad deditiōnem coëgit, urbemque evertit; relĭquam provinciam in fidem accēpit.

War with Jugurtha, 112 *B. C.*

65. P. Scipiōne Nasīca et L. Calpurnio Bestia consulĭbus, Jugurthae, Numidārum regi, bellum illātum est, quod Adherbălem et Hiempsălem, Micipsae filios, patruēles suos, interemisset. Missus adversus eum consul Calpurnius Bestia corruptus regis pecunia pacem cum eo flagitiosissĭmam fecit, quae a senātu improbāta est. Denĭque Qu. Caecilius Metellus consul Jugurtham variis proeliis vicit, elephantos ejus occīdit vel cepit, multas civitātes ipsīus in deditiōnem accēpit. Ei successit C. Marius, qui bello termĭnum posuit, ipsumque Jugurtham cepit. Ante currum triumphantis Marii Jugurtha cum duōbus filiis ductus est vinctus, et mox iussu consŭlis in carcĕre strangulātus.

Social or Marsian War, 91 *B. C.*

66. Sexcentesĭmo quinquagesĭmo nono anno ab urbe condĭta in Italia gravissĭmum bellum exarsit. Nam

Picentes, Marsi, Pelignīque, qui multos annos popŭlo Romāno obediĕrant, aequa cum illis jura sibi dari postulābant. Perniciōsum admŏdum hoc bellum fuit. P. Rutilius consul in eo occīsus est; plures exercĭtus fusi fugatīque. Tandem L. Cornelius Sulla cum alia egregie gessit, tum Cluentium, hostium ducem, cum magnis copiis, fudit. Per quadriennium cum gravi utriusque partis calamitāte hoc bellum tractum est. Quinto demum anno L. Cornelius Sulla ei imposuit finem. Romāni tamen, id quod prius negavĕrant, jus civitātis, bello finīto, sociis tribuērunt.

Mithridatic War.—First Civil War.—Marius, Sulla, 88 B. C.

67. Anno urbis condĭtae sexcentesĭmo sexagesĭmo sexto primum Romae bellum civīle exortum est; eōdem anno etiam Mithridatĭcum. Causam bello civīli C. Marius dedit. Nam quum Sullae bellum adversus Mithridātem, regem Ponti, decrētum esset, Marius ei hunc honōrem eripĕre conātus est. Sed Sulla, qui adhuc cum legionĭbus suis in Italia morabātur, cum exercĭtu Romam venit, et adversarios cum interfēcit, tum fugāvit. Tum rebus Romae utcunque composĭtis, in Asiam profectus est, pluribusque proeliis Mithridātem coëgit, ut pacem a Romānis petĕret, et Asia, quam invasĕrat, relicta, regni sui finĭbus contentus esset.

Civil War, continued.

68. Sed dum Sulla in Graecia et Asia Mithridātem vincit, Marius, qui fugātus fuĕrat, et Cornelius Cinna, unus ex consulĭbus, bellum in Italia reparārunt, et ingressi Romam nobilissĭmos ex senatu et consulāres viros interfecērunt; multos proscripsērunt; ipsīus Sullae

domo eversa, filios et uxōrem ad fugam compulērunt. Universus relĭquus senātus ex urbe fugiens ad Sullam in Graeciam venit, orans ut patriae subvenīret. Sulla in Italiam trajēcit, hostium exercĭtus vicit, mox etiam urbem ingressus est, quam caede et sanguĭne civium replēvit. Quatuor millia inermium, qui se dedidĕrant, interfĭci jussit; duo millia equĭtum et senatōrum proscripsit. Tum de Mithridāte triumphāvit. Duo haec bella funestissĭma, Italĭcum, quod et sociāle dictum est, et civīle, consumpsērunt ultra centum et quinquaginta millia homĭnum, viros consulāres viginti quatuor, praetorios septem, aedilitios sexaginta, senatōres fere ducentos.

Mithridatic War, continued.—Lucullus.

69. Anno urbis condĭtae sexcentesĭmo septuagesĭmo sexto, L. Licinĭo Lucullo et M. Aurelio Cotta consulĭbus, mortuus est Nicomēdes, rex Bithyniae, et testamento popŭlum Romānum fecit herēdem. Mithridātes, pace rupta, Asiam rursus voluit invadĕre. Adversus eum ambo consŭles missi variam habuēre fortūnam. Cotta apud Chalcedŏnem victus proelio, a rege etiam intra oppĭdum obsessus est. Sed quum se inde Mithridātes Cyzĭcum transtulisset, ut, hac urbe capta, totam Asiam invadĕret, Lucullus ei, alter consul, occurrit, ac dum Mithridātes in obsidiōne Cyzĭci commorātur, ipse eum a tergo obsēdit, famēque consumptum multis proeliis vicit. Postrēmo Byzantium fugāvit; navāli quoque proelio ejus duces oppressit. Ita una hiĕme et aestāte a Lucullo centum fere millia milĭtum regis exstincta sunt.

War of the Gladiators.—Spartacus, 78 B. C.   JV

70. Anno urbis sexcentesĭmo septuagesĭmo octāvo novum in Italia bellum commōtum est. Septuaginta enim quatuor gladiatōres, ducĭbus Spartăco, Crixo, et Oenomao, e ludo gladiatorio, qui Capuae erat, effugērunt, et per Italiam vagantes paene non levius bellum, quam Hannĭbal, movērunt. Nam contraxērunt exercĭtum fere sexaginta millium armatōrum, multosque duces et duos Romānos consŭles vicērunt. Ipsi victi sunt in Apulia a M. Licinio Crasso proconsŭle, et, post multas calamitātes Italiae, tertio anno huic bello finis est imposĭtus.

Successes of Lucullus against Mithridates.

71. Intĕrim L. Lucullus bellum Mithridatĭcum persecūtus regnum Mithridātis invāsit, ipsumque regem apud Cabīra civitātem, quo ingentes copias ex omni regno adduxĕrat Mithridātes, ingenti proelio superātum fugāvit, et castra ejus diripuit. Armenia quoque Minor, quam tenēbat, eīdem erepta est. Susceptus est Mithridātes a Tigrāne, Armeniae rege, qui tum ingenti gloria imperābat; sed hujus quoque regnum Lucullus est ingressus. Tigranocerta, nobilissĭmam Armeniae civitātem, cepit; ipsum regem, cum magno exercĭtu venientem, ita vicit, ut robur milĭtum Armeniōrum delēret. Sed quum Lucullus finem bello imponĕre parāret, successor ei missus est.

Pompey puts down the Pirates, 67 B. C.—Is appointed successor to Lucullus.—Death of Mithridates, 63 B. C.

72. Per illa tempŏra pirātae omnia maria infestābant ita, ut Romānis, toto orbe terrārum victorĭbus, sola

navigatio tuta non esset. Quare id bellum Cn. Pompēio decrētum est, quod intra paucos menses incredibĭli felicitāte et celeritāte confēcit. Mox ei delātum bellum contra regem Mithridātem et Tigrānem. Quo suscepto, Mithridātem in Armenia Minōre nocturno proelio vicit, castra diripuit, et quadraginta millĭbus ejus occīsis, viginti tantum de exercĭtu suo perdĭdit et duos centuriōnes. Mithridātes fugit cum uxōre et duōbus comitĭbus, neque multo post, Pharnăcis filii sui seditiōne coactus, venēnum hausit. Hunc vitae finem habuit Mithridātes, vir ingentis industriae atque consilii. Regnāvi annis sexaginta, vixit septuaginta duōbus: contra Romānos bellum habuit annis quadraginta.

Victories of Pompey over Tigranes: he takes Jerusalem, 63 B. C.

73. Tigrāni deinde Pompēius bellum intŭlit. Ille se ei dedĭdit, et in castra Pompēii venit, ac diadēma suum in ejus manĭbus collocāvit, quod ei Pompēius reposuit. Parte regni eum multāvit et grandi pecunia. Tum alios etiam reges et popŭlos superāvit. Armeniam Minōrem Deiotăro, Galatiae regi, donāvit, quia auxilium contra Mithridātem tulĕrat. Seleuciam, vicīnam Antiochīae civitātem, libertāte donāvit, quod regem Tigrānem non recepisset. Inde in Judaeam transgressus, Hierosolўmam, caput gentis, tertio mense cepit, duodĕcim millĭbus Judaeōrum occīsis, cetĕris in fidem receptis. His gestis finem antiquissĭmo bello imposuit. Ante triumphantis currum ducti sunt filii Mithridātis, filius Tigrānis, et Aristobūlus, rex Judaeōrum. Praelāta ingens pecunia, auri atque argenti infinītum. Hoc tempŏre nullum per orbem terrārum grave bellum erat.

Catiline's Conspiracy, 63 *B. C.*

74. M. Tullio Cicerōne oratōre et C. Antonio consulĭbus, anno ab urbe condĭta sexcentesĭmo undenonagesĭmo L. Sergius Catilīna, nobilissĭmi genĕris vir, sed ingenii pravissĭmi, ad delendam patriam conjurāvit cum quibusdam claris quidem sed audacĭbus viris. A Cicerōne urbe expulsus est, socii ejus deprehensi et in carcĕre strangulāti sunt. Ab Antonio, altĕro consŭle, Catilīna ipse proelio victus est et interfectus.

Caesar Consul, 59 *B. C.*: *in Gaul*, 58 *B. C.*

75. Anno urbis condĭtae sexcentesĭmo nonagesĭmo tertio C. Julius Caesar cum L. Bibŭlo consul est factus. Quum ei Gallia decrēta esset, semper vincendo usque ad Oceănum Britannĭcum processit. Domuit autem annis novem fere omnem Galliam, quae inter Alpes, flumen Rhodănum, Rhenum et Oceănum est. Britannis mox bellum intŭlit, quibus ante eum ne nomen quidem Romanōrum cognĭtum erat; Germānos quoque trans Rhenum aggressus, ingentĭbus proeliis vicit.

Crassus slain by the Parthians, 53 *B. C.*

76. Circa eădem tempŏra M. Licinius Crassus contra Parthos missus est. Et quum circa Carras contra omĭna et auspicia proelium commisisset, a Surēna, Orōdis regis duce, victus et interfectus est cum filio, clarissĭmo et praestantissĭmo juvĕne. Reliquiae exercĭtus per C. Cassium quaestōrem servātae sunt.

Civil War of Pompey and Caesar, 49 *B. C.*

77. Hinc jam bellum civīle successit, quo Romāni nomĭnis fortūna mutāta est. Caesar enim victor e Gal-

lia rediens, absens coepit poscĕre altĕrum consulātum;
quem quum alĭqui sine dubitatiōne deferrent, contradictum est a Pompēio et aliis, jussusque est, dimissis
exercitĭbus, in urbem redīre. Propter hanc injuriam
ab Arimĭno, ubi milĭtes congregātos habēbat, infesto
exercĭtu Romam contendit. Consŭles cum Pompēio,
senatusque omnis atque universa nobilĭtas ex urbe fugit, et in Graeciam transiit; et, dum senātus bellum
contra Caesărem parābat, hic vacuam urbem ingressus
dictatōrem se fecit.

Defeat of Pompey's party in Spain.—Battle of Pharsalia. 48
B. C.—Death of Pompey.

78. Inde Hispanias petit, ibĭque Pompēii legiōnes
superāvit; tum in Graecia adversum Pompēium ipsum
dimicāvit. Primo proelio victus est et fugātus; evāsit
tamen, quia nocte interveniente Pompēius sequi noluit;
dixitque Caesar, nec Pompēium scire vincĕre, et illo
tantum die se potuisse superāri. Deinde in Thessalia
apud Pharsālum ingentĭbus utrinque copiis commissis
dimicavērunt. Nunquam adhuc Romānae copiae majōres neque meliorĭbus ducĭbus convenĕrant. Pugnātum est ingenti contentiōne, victusque ad postrēmum
Pompēius, et castra ejus direpta sunt. Ipse fugātus
Alexandrīam petiit, ut a rege Aegypti, cui tutor a senātu datus fuĕrat, accipĕret auxilia. At hic fortūnam
magis quam amicitiam secūtus, occīdit Pompēium, caput ejus et annŭlum Caesări misit. Quo conspecto,
Caesar lacrўmas fudisse dicĭtur, tanti viri intuens caput,
et genĕri quondam sui.

Caesar assassinated in the Senate-House, 44 B. C.

79. Quum ad Alexandrīam venisset Caesar, Ptolemaeus ei insidias parāre voluit, qua de causa regi bellum illātum est. Rex victus in Nilo periit, inventumque est corpus ejus cum lorīca aurea. Caesar, Alexandrīa potītus, regnum Cleopātrae dedit. ✗Tum inde profectus Pompeianārum partium reliquias est persecūtus, bellisque civilĭbus toto terrārum orbe composĭtis, Romam rediit. Ubi quum insolentius agĕre coepisset, conjurātum est in eum a sexaginta vel amplius senatorĭbus, equitibusque Romānis. Praecipui fuērunt inter conjurātos Bruti duo ex genĕre illīus Bruti, qui, regĭbus expulsis, primus Romae consul fuĕrat, C. Cassius et Servilius Casca. Ergo Caesar, quum in curiam venisset, viginti tribus vulnerĭbus confossus est.

The Second Triumvirate, Octavius, Antony, and Lepidus, 43 B. C.
—Death of Cicero.

80. Interfecto Caesăre, anno urbis septingentesĭmo nono bella civilia reparāta sunt. Senātus favēbat Caesăris percussorĭbus, Antonius consul a Caesăris partĭbus stabat. Ergo turbāta republĭca, Antonius, multis scelerĭbus commissis, a senātu hostis judicātus est. Fusus fugatusque Antonius, amisso exercĭtu, confūgit ad Lepĭdum, qui Caesări magister equĭtum fuĕrat, et tum grandes copias milĭtum habēbat; a quo susceptus est. Mox Octaviānus cum Antonio pacem fecit, et quasi vindicatūrus patris sui mortem, a quo per testamentum fuĕrat adoptātus, Romam cum exercĭtu profectus extorsit, ut sibi juvĕni viginti annōrum consulātus darētur. Tum junctus cum Antonio et Lepĭdo rempublĭcam ar-

mis tenēre coepit, senatumque proscripsit. Per hos etiam Cicĕro orātor occīsus est, multīque alii nobĭles.

Battle of Philippi, 42 *B. C.*

81. Interea Brutus et Cassius, interfectōres Caesăris, ingens bellum movērunt. Profecti contra eos Caesar Octaviānus, qui postea Augustus est appellātus, et M. Antonius, apud Philippos, Macedoniae urbem, contra eos pugnavērunt. Primo proelio victi sunt Antonius et Caesar; periit tamen dux nobilitātis Cassius; secundo Brutum et infinītam nobilitātem, quae cum illis bellum suscepĕrat, victam interfecērunt. Tum victōres rempublĭcam ita inter se divisērunt, ut Octaviānus Caesar Hispanias, Gallias, Italiam tenēret; Antonius Orientem, Lepĭdus Afrĭcam accipĕret.

Battle of Actium, 31 *B. C.*

82. Paulo post Antonius, repudiāta sorōre Caesăris Octaviāni, Cleopātram, regīnam Aegypti, uxōrem duxit. Ab hac incitātus ingens bellum commōvit, dum Cleopātra cupiditāte muliĕbri optat Romae regnāre. Victus est ab Augusto navāli pugna clara et illustri apud Actium, qui locus in Epīro est. Hinc fugit in Aegyptum, et, desperātis rebus, quum omnes ad Augustum transīrent, se ipse interēmit. Cleopātra quoque aspĭdem sibi admīsit, et venēno ejus exstincta est. Ita bellis toto orbe confectis, Octaviānus Augustus Romam rediit anno duodecĭmo quam consul fuĕrat. Ex eo inde tempŏre rempublĭcam per quadraginta et quatuor annos solus obtinuit. Ante enim duodĕcim annis cum Antonio et Lepĭdo tenuĕrat. Ita ab initio principātus ejus usque ad finem quinquaginta sex anni fuēre.

Period V.—*Roman Empire.*

FROM THE DISSOLUTION OF THE COMMONWEALTH TO THE DEATH OF DOMITIAN, THE LAST OF THE CAESARS, 96 A. D.

Tiberius, 14 *A. D.*

83. Tiberius Nero, privīgnus idem ac gener heres que Augusti, totus ab illo diversus fuit; ingenio non solum arroganti trucīque, sed etiam occulto, fingendis que virtutĭbus subdŏlo. Principia ejus imperii moderāta, Germanĭci Caesăris metu. Quo exstincto, metu solūtus, mores solvit. Sed ejus petulantiae a Livia matre, quam reverebātur, non nihil obstĭtum. Rege Cappadociae, per speciem amicitiae, evocāto retentōque, ejus regnum in provinciam redēgit. Herōdem Agrippam, in custodiam tradĭdit, quia publĭce precātus erat, ut Caium, Germanĭci filium, vidēret Augustum. Inter haec, Livia matre demortua, in omne ruit crudelitātis genus. Drusum Caesărem, ex se genĭtum, affectāti regni suspectum, venēno sustŭlit. Nerōnem ac Drusum, Germanĭci filios, nepōtes suos, fame necāvit. Sejāni praefecti praetorii instinctu, Romam primōrum civitātis caedĭbus polluit. Sed tandem ira Princĭpis in ipsum vertit crudelitātis auctōrem. In Capream insŭlam quum secessisset, eam infāmem reddĭdit sua nequitia luxūque. Ad ultĭmum, deliciis confectus, ad Misēnum exstinguĭtur, principātus sui anno vicesĭmo tertio.

Caligula, 37 *A. D.*

84. Caius Caligŭla, Germanĭco et Agrippīna genĭtus, in castris militāri habĭtu educātus, ex eōque Caligŭla dictus est. Is primo quidem haud indīgnum se

Germanĭco patre, ac popŭli Romāni favōre, praebuit. Sed brevi tyrannus exstĭtit, Tiberio immanior. Quum plurĭma vesānae mentis deliria edidisset, et adversum cunctos ingenti avaritia, libidĭne, crudelitāte saevīret, interfectus in palatio est anno imperii tertio.

Claudius, 41 *A. D.*

85. Claudius Nero, Caligŭlae patruus, ab eo ad ludibrium reservātus, imperii successor fuit; bonus princeps magis, quam sapiens. Britanniam et Orcădas insŭlas, sine proelio ac sanguĭne, subēgit. In amīcos adeo effūsus, ut A. Plautium, ob res in Britannia prospĕre gestas triumphantem, Caesar ipse prosequerētur, eīque Capitolium conscendenti laevum tegĕret latus. Illud dementer, quod, praeterĭto Britannĭco filio, Nerōnem privīgnum herēdem imperii fecit. Ităque privīgni fraude pater cum filio exstinguĭtur. Tenet fama, venēnum Claudio ab Agrippīna conjŭge in bolēto datum. Annos imperāvit quatuordĕcim.

Nero, 54 *A. D.*

86. Nero, Germanĭci ex filia nepos, Caligŭlae avuncŭlo magis, quam avo, se simĭlem praebuit. Agrippīnam matrem, Octaviam conjŭgem, Antoniam amĭtam, aliosque cognatiōne proxĭmos, Senĕcam quoque praeceptōrem, Lucāni poētae patruum, ipsumque Lucānum, necāvit. Ad haec magnam urbis partem, obscūris aedĭbus informem, per ludum incendit, ut Trojae repraesentāret incendium: culpam poenamque in Christianos transtŭlit. In re militāri nihil omnīno ausus, Britanniam paene amīsit. A senātu hostis judicātus, e palatio fugit, et in suburbāno se liberti sui interfēcit,

trigesĭmo et altĕro aetātis anno, imperii quarto decĭmo; atque in eo omnis familia Augusti consumpta est.

Galba, 68 A. D., Otho and Vitellius, 69 A. D.

87. Sergius Galba, Caesar ab exercĭtu creātus, Nerōni successit. Sed nimia severĭtas breve ejus imperium fecit. Othōnis insidiis mense septĭmo jugulātur.

88. Otho Silvius, invāso imperio, haud diuturnior eo, quem sustulĕrat, Caesar fuit. Quippe, a Vitellio, qui a Germanĭcis legionĭbus imperium accepĕrat, ad Cremōnam levi proelio victus, voluntariam mortem oppetiit mense imperii quarto.

89. Vitellius, a Vespasiāni ducĭbus multo cum dedecōre captus, per urbem raptātur nudus. Tandem jugulātus, praecipitātur in Tibĕrim mense imperii octāvo.

Vespasian, 70 A. D.

90. Vespasiānus huic successit, factus apud Palaestīnam imperātor; princeps obscūre quidem natus, sed optĭmis comparandus. A Claudio in Germaniam, deinde in Britanniam missus, tricies et bis cum hoste conflixit, duas validissĭmas gentes, viginti oppĭda, insŭlam Vectam, Britanniae proxĭmam, imperio Romāno adjēcit. Romae se in imperio moderatissĭme gessit: pecuniae tantum avidior fuit, ita ut eam nulli injuste auferret; quam quum omni diligentia colligĕret, tamen studiosissĭme largiebātur, praecipue indigentĭbus. Placidissĭmae lenitātis, ut qui majestātis quoque contra se reos non facĭle punīret ultra exsilii poenam. Sub hoc Judaea Romāno accessit imperio, et Hierosolўma, quae fuit urbs nobilissĭma Palaestīnae. Achaiam, Lyciam, Rhodum, Byzantium, Samum, quae libĕrae ante hoc

tempus fuĕrant, item Thraciam, Ciliciam, Commagēnen, quae sub regĭbus amīcis egĕrant, in provinciārum formam redēgit.

91. Offensārum et inimicitiārum immĕmor fuit: convicia, a causidĭcis et philosŏphis in se dicta, lenĭter tulit: dilĭgens tamen coercĭtor disciplīnae militāris. Hic cum Tito filio de Hierosolўmis triumphāvit. Per haec quum senatui et popŭlo, postrēmo cunctis amabĭlis ac jucundus esset, exstinctus est in villa propria, circa Sabīnos, annum aetātis agens sexagesĭmum nonum, imperii nonum et diem septĭmum: atque inter Divos relātus est.

Titus, 79 A. D.

92. Huic Titus filius successit, qui et ipse Vespasiānus est dictus; vir omnium virtūtum genĕre mirabĭlis adeo, ut amor et deliciae humāni genĕris dicerētur. Romae tantae civilitātis in imperio fuit, ut nullum omnīno punīret, convictos adversum sese conjuratiōnis ita dimisĕrit, ut in eādem familiaritāte, qua antea, habuĕrit. Facilitātis et liberalitātis tantae fuit, ut negāret quemquam oportēre tristem a princĭpe discedĕre; praeterea quum quodam die in coena recordātus fuisset, nihil se illo die cuiquam praestitisse, dixĕrit: "Amīci, hodie diem perdĭdi." Hic Romae amphitheātrum aedificāvit, et quinque millia ferārum in dedicatiōne ejus occīdit.

93. Per haec inusitāto favōre dilectus, morbo periit in ea, qua pater, villa, post biennium, menses octo, dies viginti, quam imperātor erat factus, aetātis anno altĕro et quadragesĭmo. Tantus luctus eo mortuo publĭcus fuit, ut omnes tanquam in propria doluĕrint orbitāte.

Senātus, obĭtu ipsīus circa vespĕram nunciāto, nocte irrūpit in curiam, et tantas ei mortuo laudes gratiasque congessit, quantas nec vivo unquam egĕrat, nec prae senti. Inter Divos relātus est.

Domitian, 81 *A. D.*

94. Domitiānus mox accēpit imperium, frater ipsīus junior; Nerōni, aut Cāligŭlae, aut Tiberio similior, quam patri, vel fratri suo. Primis tamen annis moderātus in imperio fuit, mox ad ingentia vitia progressus, libidĭnis, iracundiae, crudelitātis, avaritiae, tantum in se odii concitāvit, ut merĭta et patris et fratris abolēret Interfēcit nobilissĭmos ex senātu : domĭnum se et deum primus appellāri jussit: nullam sibi nisi auream et argenteam statuam in Capitolio poni passus est: consobrīnos suos interfēcit : superbia quoque in eo exsecrabĭlis fuit. Expeditiōnes quatuor habuit : unam adversum Sarmătas ; altĕram adversum Cattos ; duas adversum Dacos. De Dacis Cattisque duplĭcem triumphum egit : de Sarmătis solam lauream usurpāvit. Multas tamen calamitātes iisdem bellis passus est. Quum ob scelĕra universis exōsus esse coepisset, interfectus est suōrum conjuratiōne in palatio, anno aetātis quadragesĭmo quinto, imperii quinto decĭmo. Funus ejus cum ingenti dedecŏre per vespillōnes exportātum, et ignobilĭter est sepultum.

GRECIAN HISTORY.

Period I.—*Traditionary Greece.*

FROM THE FOUNDING OF ATHENS BY CECROPS, 1556 B. C., TO THE PERSIAN INVASION, 490 B. C.

The Early Kings of Attica.

95. Ante Deucaliōnis tempŏra Athenienses regem habuēre Cecrŏpem Aegyptium; quem, ut omnis antiquĭtas fabulōsa est, biformem tradidēre, quia primus marem femĭnae matrimonio junxit. Huic successit Cranaus, cujus filia Atthis regiōni nomen dedit. Post hunc Amphictyon regnāvit, qui primus Minervae urbem sacrāvit, et nomen civitāti Athēnas dedit. Hujus temporĭbus aquārum illuvies majōrem partem populōrum Graeciae absumpsit. Superfuērunt, qui in montes se recepērunt, aut ad regem Thessaliae Deucaliōnem ratĭbus evecti sunt; a quo propterea genus humānum condĭtum dicĭtur. Per ordĭnem deinde successiōnis regnum ad Erectheum descendit, sub quo frumenti satio apud Eleusin a Triptolĕmo reperta est. In hujus munĕris honōrem noctes initiōrum sacrātae. Tenuit et Aegeus, Thesei pater, Athēnis regnum: cui quum Theseus successisset, Attĭcos demigrāre ex agris, et in astu, quod appellātur, omnes se conferre jussit.

The Founders and first Princes of other Cities.

96. Argivōrum rex primus Inăchus exstĭtit; cujus filius Phorōneus vagos homĭnes ac dispersos in unum coegisse locum, et moenĭbus legibusque sepsisse memorātur. Danăus, quinquaginta genĕris per totĭdem filias

contrucidātis, Argos occŭpat. Cadmus, Eurōpae frater, litĕras e Phoenicia deportāvit in Graeciam; Thebas in Boeotia condĭdit. Rhadamanthus in Lycia, Minos in Creta, summa cum severitātis laude regnārunt. Pelops quoque, Tantăli filius, Pisae rex, deductis colōnis, Peloponnēso nomen fecit.

Grecian Colonies.

97. Tum Graecia maxĭmis concussa est motĭbus. Achaei, ex Laconĭca pulsi, eas occupavēre sedes, quas nunc obtĭnent: Pelasgi Athēnas commigravēre; acerque belli juvĕnis, nomĭne Thessălus, natiōne Thesprotius cum magna civium manu eam regiōnem armis occupāvit, quae nunc ab ejus nomĭne Thessalia appellātur.

Lycurgus, 884 B. C.: Some of his Laws.

98. Ea tempestāte clarissĭmus Graii nomĭnis Lycurgus Lacedaemonius, vir genĕris regii, fuit severissimārum justissimarumque legum auctor, et disciplīnae convenientissĭmae viris: cujus quamdiu Sparta dilĭgens fuit, excelsissĭme floruit. Ac primum quidem popŭlum in obsequia princĭpum, princĭpes ad justitiam imperiōrum formāvit. Parsimoniam omnĭbus suasit. Emi singŭla non pecunia, sed compensatiōne mercium jussit. Auri argentīque usum, velut omnium scelĕrum materiam, sustŭlit. Fundos omnium aequalĭter inter omnes divīsit. Convivāri omnes publĭce jussit, ne cujus divitiae vel luxuria in occulto essent. Puĕros pubĕres in agrum dedūci praecēpit, ut primos annos non in luxuria, sed in opĕre et laborĭbus agĕrent. Virgĭnes sine dote nubĕre jussit, ut uxōres eligerentur non pecuniae. Maxĭmum honōrem senum esse voluit. Haec quoniam

primo, solūtis antea morĭbus, dura vidēbat esse, auctōrem eōrum Apollĭnem Delphĭcum fingit. Dein, ut aeternitātem legĭbus suis daret, jurejurando oblĭgat civitātem, nihil eos de ejus legĭbus mutatūros, priusquam reverterētur, et simŭlat, se ad oracŭlum Delphĭcum proficisci, consultūrum, quid addendum mutandumque legĭbus viderētur Deo. Proficiscĭtur autem Cretam, ibĭque perpetuum exsilium egit, abjicīque in mare ossa sua moriens jussit, ne, reliquiis suis Lacedaemŏnem relātis, Spartāni se religiōne jurisjurandi solūtos arbitrarentur.

Institution of the Olympic Games.—Decennial Archons at Athens. —Annual Archons.

99. Clarissĭmum deinde omnium ludĭcrum certāmen, et ad excitandam corpŏris animīque virtūtem efficacissĭmum, Olympiōrum initium habuit, auctōre Iphĭto Elio. Is eos ludos mercatumque instituit ante annos quam Roma conderētur septuaginta. Hoc sacrum eōdem loco instituisse fertur. Atreus, quum Pelŏpi patri funĕbres ludos facĕret. Quo quidem in ludĭcro, omnisque genĕris certamĭnum Hercŭles victor exstĭtit. Tum Athēnis perpetui Archontes esse desiērunt, quum fuisset ultĭmus Alcmaeon: coeperuntque in denos annos creāri; quae consuetūdo in annos septuagĭnta mansit: ac deinde annuis commissa est magistratĭbus respublĭca. Ex iis, qui denis annis praefuērunt, primus fuit Charops, ultĭmus Eryxias; ex annuis, primus Creon.

Legislation of Solon, 594 B. C.

100. Quum Dracōnis leges crudeliōres essent, quam ut possent observāri, legĭtur Solon, vir justitia insignis,

qui velut novam civitātem novis legĭbus condĕret. Quo munĕre ita functus est, ut et apud plebem et optimātes, diuturnis antea dissidiis agitātos, parem inīret gratiam. Hujus viri, inter multa egregia, illud quoque memorabĭle fuit. Inter Athenienses et Megarenses de Salamīne insŭla, quam sibi uterque popŭlus vindicābat, prope usque ad interĭtum dimicātum fuĕrat. Post multas clades acceptas, Athenienses legem tulērunt, ne quis illud bellum reparandum proponĕret. Solon igĭtur quum opportunitātem quandam vidisset insŭlae vindicandae, dementiam simŭlat; habitūque deformis, more vecordium, in publĭcum evŏlat; factōque concursu homĭnum, versĭbus suadēre popŭlo coepit, quod vetabātur; omniumque anĭmos ita inflammāvit, ut extemplo bellum adversus Megarenses decernerētur, et, devictis hostĭbus, insŭla Atheniensium fiĕret.

PERIOD II.—*Grecian Triumphs.*

FROM THE PERSIAN INVASION TO THE PELOPONNESIAN WAR, 481 B. C.

Darīus invades Scythia: prepares to invade Greece.

101. Multis in Asia felicĭter gestis, Darīus Scythis bellum intŭlit, et armātis septingentis millĭbus homĭnum, Scythiam ingressus, quum hostes ei pugnae potestātem non facĕrent, metuens, ne interrupto ponte Istri, redĭtus sibi intercluderētur, amissis octoginta millĭbus homĭnum, trepĭdus refūgit. Inde Macedoniam domuit: et quum ex Eurōpa in Asiam rediisset, hortantĭbus amīcis ut Graeciam redigĕret in suam potestātem, clas-

sem quingentārum navium comparāvit, eīque Datim praefēcit et Artaphernen; hisque ducenta pedĭtum millia, et decem equĭtum dedit, causam interserens, se hostem esse Atheniensĭbus, quod eōrum auxilio Iōnes Sardes expugnassent, suāque praesidia interfecissent.

Battle of Marathon, 490 B. C.

102. Praefecti regii, classe ad Euboeam appulsa, celerĭter Eretriam cepērunt, omnesque ejus gentis cives abreptos in Asiam ad regem misērunt. Inde ad Attĭcam accessērunt, ac suas copias in Campum Marathōna deduxērunt. Is abest ab oppĭdo circĭter millia passuum decĕm. Hoc in tempŏre nulla civĭtas Atheniensĭbus auxilio fuit, praeter Plataeenses; ea mille misit milĭtum. Ităque horum adventu decem millia armatōrum complēta sunt: quae manus mirabĭli flagrābat pugnandi cupiditāte: quo factum est, ut plus, quam collēgae, Miltiădes valuĕrit, qui unus maxĭme nitebātur, ut primo quoque tempŏre dimicārent. Ejus auctoritāte impulsi, Athenienses copias ex urbe eduxērunt, locōque idoneo castra fecērunt; deinde postĕro die, sub montis radicĭbus, vi summa proelium commisērunt. Datis etsi non aequum locum vidēbat suis, tamen, fretus numĕro copiārum suārum, conflĭgĕre cupiēbat; eōque magis, quod, priusquam Lacedaemonii subsidio venīrent, dimicāre utĭle arbitrabātur. Ităque in aciem pedĭtum centum, equĭtum decem millia produxit, proeliumque commīsit. In quo tanto plus virtūte valuērunt Athenienses, ut decemplĭcem numĕrum hostium profligārint; adeōque perterruērunt, ut Persae non castra, sed naves petiĕrint. Qua pugna nihil est nobilius; nulla enim unquam tam exigua manus tantas opes prostrāvit.

Xerxes invades Greece, 480 B. C.

103. Quum Darīus, bellum instauratūrus, in ipso apparātu decessisset, filius ejus Xerxes Eurōpam cum tantis copiis invāsit, quantas neque antea neque postea habuit quisquam: hujus enim classis mille et ducentārum navium longārum fuit, quam duo millia onerariārum sequebantur: terrestres autem exercĭtus septingentōrum millium pedĭtum, equĭtum quadringentōrum millium fuērunt. Cujus de adventu quum fama in Graeciam esset perlāta, et maxĭme Athenienses peti dicerentur, propter pugnam Marathoniam, misērunt Delphos consultum, quidnam facĕrent de rebus suis. Deliberantĭbus Pythia respondit, ut moenĭbus ligneis se munīrent. Id responsum quo valēret, quum intelligĕret nemo, Themistŏcles persuāsit, consilium esse Apollĭnis, ut in naves se suăque conferrent: eum enim a deo significāri murum ligneum. Tali consilio probāto, addunt ad superiōres totĭdem naves trirēmes: suāque omnia, quae movēri potĕrant, partim Salamīna, partim Troezēna, asportant; arcem sacerdotĭbus paucisque majorĭbus natu, ac sacra procuranda tradunt; reliquum oppĭdum relinquunt.

Actions at Thermopylae and Artemisium, 480 B. C.

104. Hujus consilium plerisque civitătibus displicēbat, et in terra dimicāri magis placēbat. Ităque missi sunt delecti cum Leonĭda, Lacedaemoniōrum rege, qui Thermopўlas occupārent, longiusque barbăros progrĕdi non paterentur. Hi vim hostium non sustinuērunt, eōque loco omnes interiērunt. At classis commūnis Graeciae trecentārum navium, in qua ducentae erant

Atheniensium, primum apud Artemisium, inter Euboeam continentemque terram, cum classiariis regiis conflixit: angustias enim Themistŏcles quaerēbat, ne multitudĭne circumirētur. Hinc etsi parį proelio discessērant, tamen eōdem loco non sunt ausi manēre, quod erat pericŭlum, ne, si pars navium adversariōrum Euboeam superasset, ancipĭti premerentur pericŭlo. Quo factum est, ut ab Artemisio discedĕrent, et exadversum Athēnas, apud Salamīna, classem suam constituĕrent.

Battle of Salamis, 480 *B. C.*

105. At Xerxes, Thermopȳlis expugnātis, protĭnus accessit astu;* idque, nullis defendentĭbus, interfectis sacerdotĭbus, quos in arce invenĕrat, incendio delēvit. Cujus fama perterrĭti classiarii quum manēre non audērent, et plurĭmi hortarentur, ut domos suas quisque discedĕrent, moenĭbusque se defendĕrent; Themistŏcles unus restĭtit, et, universos esse pares posse aiēbat, dispersos testabātur peritūros. Idque Eurybiădi, regi Lacedaemoniōrum, qui tum summae imperii praeĕrat, fore affirmābat. Quem quum minus, quam vèllet, movēret, noctu de servis suis, quem habuit fidelissĭmum, ad regem misit, ut ei nuntiāret suis verbís: adversarios ejus in fuga esse, qui si discessissent, majōre cum labōre, et longinquiōre tempŏre bellum confectūrum, quum singŭlos consectāri cogerētur; quos si statim aggiiredērētur, brevi universos oppressūrum. Hoc eo valēbat, ut ingratiis ad depugnandum omnes cogerentur. Hac re audīta, barbărus, nihil doli subesse credens, postridie alienissĭmo sibi loco, contra opportunissĭmo hostĭbus, adeo angusto mari conflixit, ut ejus multitūdo navium

explicāri non potuĕrit. Victus ergo est magis consilio Themistŏclis, quam armis Graeciae.

Xerxes flies back into Asia.

106. Hic etsi male rem gessĕrat, tamen tantas habēbat reliquias copiārum, ut etiam cum his opprimĕre posset hostes. Itĕrum ab eōdem gradu depulsus est. Nam Themistŏcles, verens ne bellāre perseverāret, certiōrem eum fecit, id agi, ut pons, quem ille in Hellesponto fecĕrat, dissolverētur, ac redĭtu in Asiam excluderētur; idque ei persuāsit. Ităque, qua sex mensĭbus iter fecĕrat, eādem minus diēbus triginta in Asiam reversus est, seque a Themistŏcle non superātum, sed conservātum judicāvit. Sic unīus viri prūdentia Graccia liberāta est, Europaeque succubuit Asia. Haec altĕra victoria, quae cum Marathonio possit comparāri tropaeo: nam pari modo apud Salamīna, parvo numĕro navium, maxĭma post homĭnum memoriam classis est devicta.

Battles of Plataea and Mycale, 479 *B. C.*

107. Postĕro anno quam Xerxes in Asiam refugĕrat, Graeci, duce Pausania, Mardonium, regis genĕrum, apud Plataeas fudērunt: quo proelio ipse dux cecĭdit, Barbarorumque exercĭtus interfectus est. Reprehensus Pausanias, quod ex praeda tripŏdem aureum Delphis posuit, epigrammăte scripto, in quo erat haec sententia: suo ductu Barbăros apud Plataeas esse delētos, ejusque victoriae ergo Apollĭni donum dedisse. Hos versus Lacedaemonii exsculpsērunt, neque aliud scripsērunt, quam nomĭna eārum civitātum, quārum auxilio Persae erant victi. Eōdem forte die, quo Mardonii

copiae delētae sunt, in Asia, ad montem Mycălen, Persae a Graecis navāli proelio superāti sunt. Jamque omnĭbus pacātis, Athenienses belli damna reparāre coepērunt. Quumque Phalerĭco portu neque magno neque bono uterentur, Themistŏclis consilio triplex Piraeei portus constitūtus est, isque moenĭbus circumdătus, ut ipsam urbem dignitāte aequiparāret, utilitāte superāret. Idem muros Athenārum restituit, non sine pericŭlo suo, quum Lacedaemonii legātos Athēnas misissent, qui id fiĕri vetārent.

PERIOD III.—*Civil Wars in Greece.*

FROM THE PELOPONNESIAN WAR TO THE ACCESSION OF PHILIP OF MACEDON, 360 B. C.

The Peloponnesian War, 431 B. C.—Pericles.

108. Quum Athenienses maris imperium non sine superbia sociorumque injuria exercērent, multīque, gravi eōrum jugo fatigāti, alios, qui se tuerentur, circumspicĕrent; tota Graecia, ducĭbus Lacedaemoniis, aemŭlae urbi magnitudĭnem et incrementa invidentĭbus, in duas partes divīsa, velut in viscĕra sua arma convertit. Hoc bellum, quo nullum aliud florentes Graeciae res gravius afflixit, saepius susceptum et deposĭtum est. Initio Spartāni fines Attĭcae populabantur, hostesque ad proelium provocābant. Sed Athenienses, Perĭclis consilio, ultiōnis tempus exspectantes intra moenia se continēbant. Deinde, paucis diēbus interjectis, naves conscendunt, et, nihil sentientĭbus Lacedaemoniis, totam Laconiam depraedantur. Clara quidem haec Perĭclis

expeditio est habĭta; sed multo clarior privāti patrimonii contemptus fuit. Nam in populatiōne ceterōrum agrōrum, Perĭclis agros hostes intactos reliquĕrant, ut aut invidiam ei apud cives concitārent, aut in proditiōnis suspiciōnem adducĕrent. Quod intellĭgens, Perĭcles agros reipublĭcae dono dedit. Post haec alĭquot diēbus interjectis, navāli proelio dimicātum est. Victi Lacedaemonii fugērunt. Post plures annos, fessi malis, pacem in annos quinquaginta fecēre, quam non nisi sex annos servavĕrunt. Nam inducias, quas proprio nomĭne pepigĕrant, ex sociōrum persōna rumpēbant. Hinc bellum in Siciliam translātum est.

Expedition of the Athenians against Sicily, 415 *B. C.*

109. Quum enim jam antea, bello inter Catinienses et Syracusānos exorto, Athenienses Catiniensĭbus opem tulissent, tempŏre interjecto, quum pacis conditiōnes a Syracusānis non servarentur, illi denuo legātos Athēnas misērunt, qui sordĭda veste, capillo barbāque promissa, conciōnem adeunt, populumque lacrўmis movent, ut, quamvis Peloponnesiăco bello districtus, auxilium illis mittendum censēret. Igĭtur classis ingens decernĭtur; creantur duces Nicias, Alcibiădes et Lamăchus; tantaeque vires in Siciliam effūsae sunt, ut iis ipsis terrōri essent, quibus auxilio venĕrant.

Sicilian Expedition, continued.

110. Brevi post, quum Alcibĭades revocātus esset, Nicias et Lamăchus duo proelia pedestria secundo Marte pugnant; munitionibusque urbi Syracusārum circumdătis, incŏlas etiam marīnis commeatĭbus intercludunt. Quibus rebus fracti Syracusāni, auxilium a

Lacedaemoniis petivērunt. Ab his mittĭtur Gylippus, qui, quum in itinĕre de belli jam inclināto statu audivisset, auxiliis partim in Graecia, partim in Sicilia contractis, opportūna bello loca occŭpat. Duōbus deinde proeliis victus, tertio hostes in fugam conjēcit, sociosque obsidiōne liberāvit. In eo proelio Lamăchus fortĭter pugnans occīsus est.

Fatal termination of the Expedition, 418 *B. C.*

111. Sed quum Athenienses, terrestri bello superāti, portum Syracusārum tenērent, Gylippus classem Lacedaemōne cum auxiliis arcessit. Quo cognĭto et ipsi Athenienses in locum amissi ducis Demosthĕnem et Eurymedonta cum supplemento copiārum mittunt; et, quasi Graeciae bellum in Siciliam translātum esset, ita ex utrāque parte summis virĭbus dimicabātur. Prima igĭtur congressiōne navālis certamĭnis Athenienses viñcuntur; castra quoque cum omni publĭca ac privāta pecunia amittunt. Inter haec mala quum etiam terrestri proelio victi essent, Demosthĕnes censēre coepit, ut abīrent Sicilia, dum res, quamvis afflictae, nondum tamen perdĭtae essent. Nicias autem, seu pudōre male actae rei, seu impellente fato, manēre contendit. Reparātur igĭtur navāle bellum; sed inscitia ducum, qui Syracusānos, inter angustias maris facĭle se tuentes, temĕre aggressi fuĕrant, Atheniensium copiae iterum vincuntur. Eurymĕdon dux in prima acie fortissĭme dimĭcans, primus cadit: triginta naves, quibus praefuĕrat, incenduntur; Demosthĕnes et Nicias autem cum reliquiis exercĭtus terrestri itinĕre fugiunt. Ab his relictas centum triginta naves Gylippus invāsit, ipsos de inde insequĭtur; fugientes partim capit, partim caedit

Demosthĕnes, amisso exercĭtu, a captivitāte gladio et voluntaria morte se vindĭcat: Nicias autem cladem suōrum auxit dedecŏre captivitātis.

Alcibiades negotiates with the Athenians at Samos.—The Four Hundred, 411 B. C.

112. Per-idem tempus Alcibiădes cum duce exercĭtus Atheniensium, qui apud Samum morabātur, per internuntios colloquĭtur, polliceturque his amicitiam, si respublĭca a popŭlo ad senātum translāta foret. Ităque, permittente popŭlo, imperium ad senātum transfertur. Qui quum crudelĭter in plebem consulĕret, ab exercĭtu Alcibiădes exsul revocātur, duxque classi constituĭtur. Statim igĭtur Athēnas scripsit, se cum exercĭtu ventūrum, recepturumque a quadringentis jura popŭli, nisi ipsi reddĕrent. Hac denuntiatiōne terrĭti senatōres, primo urbem prodĕre Lacedaemoniis tentavēre; dein, quum id nequissent, in exsilium profecti sunt. Ităque Alcibiădes, patria ab intestīno malo liberāta, summa cura classem instruit, atque ita in bellum adversus Lacedaemonios pefrexit.

Successes of Alcibiades against the Lacedaemonians.

113. Hac expeditiōne tanta subĭto rerum commutatio facta est, ut Lacedaemonii, qui paulo ante victōres viguĕrant, perterrĭti pacem petĕrent; victi enim erant quinque terrestrĭbus proeliis, tribus navalĭbus, in quibus trecentas trirēmes amisĕrant, quae captae in hostium venĕrant potestātem. Alcibiădes simul cum collēgis recepĕrat Ioniam, Hellespontum, multas praeterea urbes Graecas, quae in ora sitae sunt Asiae: quarum expugnavĕrant quam plurĭmas, in his Byzantium; ne-

que minus multas consilio ad amicitiam adjunxĕrant, quod in captos benevolentia fuĕrant usi. Inde praeda onusti, locupletāto exercĭtu, maxĭmis rebus gestis, Athēnas venērunt.

Cyrus (the Younger) favors Lysander and the Lacedaemonians, 407 B. C.

114. Dum haec geruntur, a Lacedaemoniis Lysander classi bellōque praeficĭtur; et in locum Tissaphernis Darīus, rex Persārum, filium suum, Cyrum, Ioniae Lydiaeque praeposuit, qui Lacedaemonios auxiliis opibusque ad spem fortūnae priōris erexit. Aucti igĭtur virĭbus Alcibiădem cum centum navĭbus in Asiam profectum, dum agros populātur, repentīno adventu oppressēre. Magnae et inopinātae cladis nuntius quum Athēnas venisset, tanta Atheniensium desperatio fuit, ut statim Conōnem in Alcibiădis locum mittĕrent, ducis se fraude magis quam belli fortūna victos arbitrantes. Alcibiădes autem, impĕtum multitudĭnis verĭtus, in voluntarium exsilium proficiscĭtur.

Fatal defeat of the Athenians at Aegospotamos, 405 B. C.

115. Ităque Conon, Alcibiădi suffectus, classem maxĭma industria adornat; sed navĭbus exercĭtus deĕrat. Nam, ut numĕrus milĭtum explerētur, senes et puĕri arma capĕre coacti sunt. Plurĭbus ităque proeliis adverso Marte pugnātis, tandem Lysander, Spartanōrum dux, Atheniensium exercĭtum, qui, navĭbus relictis, in terram praedātum exiĕrat, ad Aegos flumen oppressit, eōque impĕtu totum bellum delēvit. Hac enim clade res Atheniensium penĭtus inclināta est. Tributariae civitātes, quas metus in fide retinuĕrat,

Lysandro se tradiderunt; qui, ejectis iis, qui Atheniensium rebus studerent, decem in unaquaque civitate delegit viros, quibus summum imperium potestatemque omnium rerum commisit.

Athens surrenders to Lysander, 404 B. C.

116. Lysander Athenas navigavit, miseramque civitatem, obsidione circumdatam, fame urget. Sciebat enim, neque ex advectis copiis multum superesse, et, ne novae advehi possent, providebat. Quibus malis Athenienses fracti, multis fame et ferro amissis, pacem petivere; quae an dari deberet, diu inter Spartanos sociosque deliberatum est. Quum nonnulli nomen Atheniensium delendum, urbemque incendio consumendam censerent, Spartani negarunt, se passuros, ut ex duobus Graeciae oculis alter erueretur; pacemque Atheniensibus sunt polliciti, si longi muri brachia dejicerent, navesque, quae reliquae forent, traderent; denique si respublica triginta rectores, ex civibus deligendos, acciperet.

Tyranny of the Thirty.

117. His legibus acceptis, tota civitas subito mutari coepit. Triginta rectores reipublicae constituuntur, Lacedaemoniis et Lysandro dediti, qui brevi tyrannidem in cives exercere coeperunt. Quippe a principio tria millia satellitum sibi statuunt; et, quasi hic numerus ad continendam civitatem non sufficeret, septingentos milites a victoribus accipiunt. His copiis instructi exhaustam urbem caedibus et rapinis fatigant: quumque hoc uni ex numero suo Therameni displicere didicissent, ipsum quoque ad terrorem omnium interficiunt.

Quo factum est, ut multi, urbe relicta, exsilii miserias, quam domestĭcum terrōrem pati mallent.

Thrasybulus occupies Phyle, 404 B. C.

118. Quum triginta tyranni, praepositi a Lacedaemoniis, servitūte oppressas tenērent Athēnas, Thrasybūlus (cui nemó fere praeferendus fide, constantia, magnitudĭne anĭmi, in patriam amōre) Phylen confūgit, quod est castellum in Attica munitissĭmum, quum non plus secum habēret, quam triginta de suis. Contemptus est primo a tyrannis, ignorantĭbus, nihil in bello debēre contemni. Hinc, virĭbus paulātim auctis, in Piraeum transiit, Munychiamque munīvit. Hanc bis tyranni oppugnāre sunt adorti, ab eāque turpĭter repulsi protĭnus in urbem, armis impedimentisque amissis, refugērunt. Usus est Thrasybūlus non minus prudentia, quam fortitudĭne, nam cedentes violāri vetuit: cives enim civĭbus parcĕre aequum censēbat; neque quisquam est vulnerātus, nisi qui prior impugnāre voluit; nemĭnem jacentem veste spoliāvit; nihil attĭgit praeter arma, quorum indigēbat, et quae ad victum pertinēbant. In secundo proelio cecĭdit Critias, triginta tyrannōrum acerrĭmus.

The Expedition of Cyrus the Younger.—Retreat of the Ten Thousand, 401 B. C.

119. Eōdem fere tempŏre Darīus, rex Persārum, morĭtur, Artaxerxe et Cyro filiis relictis. Regnum Artaxerxi, Cyro urbes Lydiae, quibus praefectus fuit, testamento legāvit. Sed Cyro judicium patris injuria videbātur; ităque occulte adversus fratrem bellum parāvit. Quod quum nuntiātum esset Artaxerxi, Cyrum

ad se arcessītum compedĭbus aureis vinxit, interfecissetque, nisi mater prohibuisset. Quod perĭcŭlum quum effugisset, Cyrus jam non occulte bellum, sed palam parāre coepit; auxilium undĭque contrăhit. Sed quum in proelio commisso fratrem imprudentius aggredĭtur, hunc quidem equi fuga perīcŭlo subtraxit, Cyrus autem a cohorte regia circumventus interficĭtur. In eo proelio decem millia Graecōrum in auxilio Cyri fuere; quae et in cornu, in quo stetĕrant, vīcērunt, et post mortem Cyri neque armis a tanto exercĭtu vinci, neque dolo capi potuērunt, sed per indomĭtas natiōnes et gentes barbăras, virtūte sua confīsi, in patriam revertuntur.

Peace of Antalcidas, 387 B. C.—Phoebidas seizes the Cadmēa, 382 B. C.

120. Dum haec geruntur, Artaxerxes, rex Persārum, legātos in Graeciam mittit, per quos jubet omnes ab armis discedĕre; qui alĭter fecisset, eum se pro hoste habitūrum: civitatĭbus libertātem suāque omnia restituit. Fessi tot bellis Graeci cupĭde paruērunt. Paucis annis interjectis, Phoebĭdas Lacedaemonius, quum exercĭtum Olynthum ducēret, ităque per Thebas facēret, Cadmēam occupāvit impulsu perpaucōrum Thēbanōrum, qui, adversariae factiōni quo facilius resistĕrent, Lacōnum rebus studēbant. Quo facto, eum Lacedaemonii ab exercĭtu removērunt, pecuniāque multārunt; neque eo magis arcem Thebānis reddidērunt. Liberandae patriae propria laus est Pelopĭdae, qui, exsilio multātus, Athēnas se contulĕrat. Ille, quum tempus est visum rei gerendae, communĭter cum his, qui Thebis idem sentiēbant, diem delēgit, ad inimīcos op-

primendos civitatemque liberandam, eum, quo maxĭmi magistrātus simul consuevĕrant epulāri. Quum, vesperascente coelo, duodĕcim adolescentŭli Thebas pervenissent, magistratuum statim ad aures pervēnit, exsŭles in urbem devenisse. Id illi, vino epulisque dedĭti, usque eo despexērunt, ut ne quaerēre quidem de tanta re laborārint: qui omnes, quum jam nox processisset, vinolenti ab exsulĭbus, duce Pepolĭda, sunt interfecti. Quibus rebus confectis, vulgo ad arma libertatemque vocāto, non solum qui in urbe erant, sed etiam undīque ex agris concurrērunt; praesidium Lacedaemoniōrum ex arce pepulērunt; patriam obsidiōne liberavērunt.

Epaminondas.—Battle of Leuctra, 371 B. C.: of Mantinea, 362 B. C.

121. Paucis post annis, Epaminondas, dux Thebānus, apud Leuctra superāvit Lacedaemonios, eōque res utrorumque perduxit, ut Thebāni Spartam oppugnārent, Lacedaemonii satis habērent, si salvi esse possent. Idem imperātor apud Mantinēam, quum universi in unum hostes impĕtum fecissent, gravĭter vulnerātus concĭdit. Hujus casu aliquantum retardāti sunt Boeotii, neque tamen prius pugna excessērunt, quam repugnantes profligārunt. At Epaminondas quum animadvertĕret, mortifĕrum se vulnus accepisse, simulque, si ferrum, quod ex hastīli in corpŏre remansĕrat, extrax isset, animam statim emissūrum, usque eo retinuit, quoad renuntiātum est, vicisse Boeotios. Id postquam audīvit, "Satis," inquit, "vixi; invictus enim morior.' Tum, ferro extracto, confestim exanimātus est.

Period IV.—*Graeco-Macedonian Empire.*

FROM THE ACCESSION OF PHILIP TO THE DEATH OF ALEXANDER,
323 B. C.

Decline of the Grecian States.—Rise of the Macedonian Power.

122. Sine dubio post Leuctrĭcam pugnam Lacedaemonii se nunquam refecērunt; et Thebae, quod, quamdiu Epaminondas praefuit reipublĭcae, caput fuit totīus Graeciae, et ante eum natum, et post ejus interĭtum, perpetuo aliēno paruērunt imperio. Athenienses, non ut olim in classem et exercĭtum, sed in dies festos apparatusque ludōrum redĭtus publĭcos effundēbant, frequentiusque in theātris quam in castris versabantur. Quibus rebus effectum est, ut obscūrum antea Macedŏnum nomen emergĕret; et Philippus, obses triennio Thebis habĭtus in Epaminondae domo, hujus praestantissĭmi viri et Pelopĭdae virtutĭbus erudītus, Graeciae servitūtis jugum imponĕret.

Philip takes Amphipolis, 358 B. C.

123. Huic regi primum cum Atheniensĭbus certāmen ad Amphipŏlin fuit; quibus per insidias victis, quum interficĕre omnes posset, incolŭmes sine pretio dimīsit. Post haec, bello in Illyrios translāto, multa millia hostium caedit. Urbem nobilissĭmam Larissam capit in Thessalia, non praedae cupiditāte, sed quod exercitui suo robur Thessalōrum equĭtum adjungĕre gestiēbat.

Extension of Philip's power.

124. Philippus, quum magnam gloriam apud omnes natiōnes adeptus esset, Olynthios aggredĭtur. Rc-

cepĕrant enim per misericordiam, post caedem unīus, duos fratres ejus, quos Philippus ex noverca genĭtos, velut aemŭlos regni, interficĕre gestiēbat. Ob hanc igĭtur causam urbem antīquam et nobĭlem exscindit, et fratres olim destināto supplicio tradit, simulque praeda ingenti fruĭtur. Inde auraria in Thessalia, argenti metalla in Thracia occŭpat. His ita gestis, forte evēnit, ut eum fratres duo, reges Thraciae, disceptatiōnum suārum judĭcem eligĕrent. Sed Philippus ad judicium, velut ad bellum, instructo exercĭtu supervēnit, et regno utrumque spoliāvit.

Battle of Chæronea, 338 B. C.

125. Quum, in Scythiam praedandi causa profectus, virtūte et numĕro praestantes Scythas dolo vicisset, diu dissimulātum bellum Atheniensĭbus infert, quorum causae Thebāni se junxērunt. Facta igĭtur inter duas antea infestissĭmas civitātes societāte, legationĭbus Graeciam fatīgant. Commūnem hostem putant communĭbus virĭbus summovendum; neque enim cessatūrum Philippum, nisi omnem Graeciam domuĕrit. Motae quaedam civitātes Atheniensĭbus se jungunt; quasdam autem ad Philippum belli metus traxit. Proelio ad Chaeronēam commisso, quum Athenienses longe majōre milĭtum numĕro praestārent, tamen assiduis bellis indurāta Macedŏnum virtūte vincuntur. Non tamen immemŏres pristĭnae virtūtis cecidērunt; quippe adversis vulnerĭbus omnes loca, quae tuenda a ducĭbus accepĕrant, morientes corporĭbus texērunt. Hic dies universae Graeciae et gloriam dominatiōnis et vetustissĭmam libertātem finīvit.

Philip prepares to invade Persia.

126. Hujus victoriae callĭde dissimulāta laetitia est. Non solĭta sacra Philippus illa die fecit; non in convi‑ vio risit; non corōnas aut unguenta sumpsit; et, quan‑ tum in illo fuit, ita vicit, ut victōrem nemo seutīret. Atheniensĭbus, quos passus infestissĭmos fuĕrat, et cap‑ tīvos gratis remīsit, et bello consumptōrum corpŏra sepultūrae reddĭdit. Compositis in Graecia rebus, om‑ nium civitātum legātos ad formandum rerum praesen‑ tium statum evocāri Corinthum jubet. Ibi pacis leges universae Graeciae pro merĭtis singulārum civitātum statuit, conciliumque omnium, velŭti unum senātum, ex omnĭbus legit. Auxilia deinde singulārum civitātum describuntur; nec dubium erat, eum Persārum impe‑ ‑ium et suis et Graeciae virĭbus impugnatūrum esse.

Death of Philip, 836 *B. C.*

127. Interea dum auxilia a Graecia coeunt, nuptias Cleopātrae filiae, et Alexandri, quem regem Epīri fe‑ cĕrat, magno apparātu celĕbrat. Ubi quum Philippus ad ludos spectandos, medius inter duos Alexandros, et filium et genĕrum, contendĕret, Pausanias, nobĭlis ex Macedonĭbus adolescens, occupātis angustiis, Philippum in transĭtu obtruncat. Hic ab Attălo indīgno modo tractātus, quum saepe querēlam ad Philippum frustra detulisset, et honorātum insŭper adversarium vidĕret, iram in ipsum Philippum vertit, ultionemque, quam ab adversario non potĕrat, ab inīquo judĭce exēgit.

Alexander the Great succeeds to the Macedonian Throne, 836 *B. C.*

128. Philippo Alexander filius successit, et virtūte et vitiis patre major. Vincendi ratio utrīque diversa.

Hic aperte, ille artĭbus bella tractābat. Deceptis ille gaudēre hostĭbus, hic palam fusis. Prudentior ille consilio, hic anĭmo magnificentior. Iram pater dissimulāre, plerumque etiam vincĕre; hic ubi exarsisset, nec dilatio ultiōnis, nec modus erat. Vini uterque nimis avĭdus; sed ebrietātis diversa ratio. Pater de convivio in hostem procurrĕre, manum conserĕre, perīcŭlis se temĕre offerre; Alexander non in hostem, sed in suos saevīre. Regnāre ille cum amīcis volēbat; hic in amī cos regna exercēbat. Amāri pater malle, hic metui. Literārum cultus utrīque simĭlis. Solertiae pater majōris, hic fidĕi. Verbis atque oratiōne Philippus, hic rebus moderatior. Parcendi victis filio anĭmus promptior; ille nec sociis abstinēbat. Frugalitāti pater, luxuriae filius magis dedĭtus erat. Quibus artĭbus orbis imperii fundamenta pater jecit, opĕris totīus gloriam filius consummāvit.

Beginning of Alexander's Reign.

129. Imperio suscepto, prima Alexandro cura paternārum exsequiārum fuit; in quibus ante omnia caedis conscios ad tumŭlum patris occīdi jussit. Inter initia regni multas gentes rebellantes compescuit; orientes nonnullas seditiōnes exstinxit. Deinde ad Persĭcum bellum proficiscens, patrimonium omne suum, quod in Macedonia et Eurōpa habēbat, amīcis divīsit; sibi Asiam sufficĕre praefātus. Nec exercitui alius quam regi anĭmus fuit. Quippe omnes oblīti conjŭgum liberorumque, et longinquae a domo militiae, nihil nisi Orientis opes cogitābant. Quum delāti in Asiam essent, primus Alexander jacŭlum velut in hostīlem terram jecit; armatusque de navi tripudianti simĭlis pro-

siluit, atque ita hostias caedit, precātus, ne se regem illae terrae invītae accipiant. In Ilio quoque ad tumŭlos herōum, qui Trojāno bello cecidĕrant, parentāvit.

Battle of the Granīcus, 334 B. C.

130. Inde hostem petens milĭtes a populatiōne Asiae prohibuit parcendum suis rebus praefātus, nec perdenda ea, quae possessūri venĕrint. In exercĭtu ejus fuēre pedĭtum triginta duo millia, equĭtum quatuor millia quingenti, naves centum octoginta duae. Hac tam parva manu universum terrārum orbem vincĕre est aggressus. Quum ad tam periculōsum bellum exercĭtum legĕret, non juvĕnes robustos, sed veterānos, qui cum patre patruisque militavĕrant, elēgit: ut non tam milĭtes, quam magistros militiae electos putāres. Prima cum hoste congressio in campis Adrastīae fuit. In acie Persārum sexcenta millia milĭtum fuērunt, quae non minus arte quam virtūte Macedŏnum superāta, terga vertērunt. Magna ităque caedes Persārum fuit. De exercĭtu Alexandri novem pedĭtes, centum viginti equĭtes cecidēre; quos rex magnifĭce humātos statuis equestrĭbus donāvit; cognātis eōrum autem immunitātes a publĭcis munerĭbus dedit. Post victoriam major pars Asiae ad eum defēcit. Habuit et plura proelia cum praefectis Darīi, quos jam non tam armis, quam terrōre nomĭnis sui vicit.

Battle of Issus, 333 B. C.

131. Interea Darīus cum quadringentis millĭbus pedĭtum ac centum millĭbus equĭtum in aciem procēdit. Commisso proelio, Alexander non ducis magis quam milĭtis munia exsequebātur, optĭmum decus caeso rege

expĕtens. Quippe Darīus curru sublīmis eminēbat, et suis ad se tuendum, et hostĭbus ad incessendum, ingens incitamentum. Macedŏnes cum rege ipso in equĭtum agmen irrumpunt. Tum vero simĭlis ruīnae strages erat. Circa currum Darīi jacēbant nobilissĭmi duces, ante ocŭlos regis egregia morte defuncti. Macedŏnum quoque, non quidem multi, sed promptissĭmi tamen caesi sunt: inter quos Alexandri dextrum femur levĭter mucrōne perstrictum est. Jamque qui Darīum vehēbant equi, confossi hastis et dolōre efferāti, jugum quatĕre et regem curru excutĕre coepĕrant: quum ille, verĭtus ne vivus venīret in hostium potestātem, desĭlit, et in equum, qui ad hoc ipsum sequebātur, imponĭtur, insignĭbus quoque imperii, ne fugam prodĕrent, indecōre abjectis. Tum vero cetĕri dissipantur metu, et, qua cuīque patēbat via, erumpunt. Inter captīvos castrōrum mater et uxor et filiae duae Darīi fuēre: in quas Alexander ita se gessit, ut omnes ante eum reges et continentia et clementia vincĕret.

Tyre besieged and taken, 332 *B. C.*

132. Jam tota Syria, jam Phoenīce quoque Macedŏnum erat, excepta Tyro, cujus urbis incŏlae, fiducia loci, obsidiōnem ferre decrevĕrant. Alexander, quum et classem procul habēret, et longam obsidiōnem magno sibi ad cetera impedimento vidēret fore, caduceatōres, qui ad pacem eos compellĕrent, misit: quos Tyrii contra jus gentium occīsos praecipitavērunt in altum. Atque ille, tam indigna morte commōtus, urbem obsidēre statuit. Sed ante jacienda moles erat, quae continenti urbem committĕret: magna vis saxōrum ad manum erat, Tyro vetĕre praebente: materies ex Libăno

monte ratĭbus et turrĭbus faciendis advehebātur. Incepto opĕri et fretum ipsum, Afrĭco maxĭme objectum, obstābat; et Tyrii, quicquid ad impediendam molem excogitāri potĕrat, non segnĭter exsequebantur. Septĭmo demum mense capta est urbs et vetustāte origĭnis et crebra fortūnae varietāte ad memoriam posteritātis insīgnis. Alexander, exceptis qui in templa confugĕrant, omnes interfĭci, ignemque tectis injĭci jubet. His per praecōnem nuntiātis, nemo tamen armātus opem a diis petĕre sustinuit: puĕri virgĭnesque templa complevĕrant; viri in vestibŭlo suārum quisque aedium stabant, parāta saevientĭbus turba: quantumque sanguĭnis fusum sit, vel ex hoc aestimāri potest, quod intra munimenta urbis sex millia armatōrum trucidāti sunt. Triste deinde spectacŭlum victorĭbus ira praebuit regis. Duo millia, in quibus occidendis defecĕrat rabies, crucĭbus affixi per ingens litŏris spatium pependērunt.

Alexander in Egypt, 332 B. C.—He visits the Temple of Jupiter Hammon.

133. Aegyptii, olim Persārum opĭbus infensi, Alexandrum laeti recepērunt: nec sustinuēre adventum ejus Persae, defectiōne quoque perterrĭti. A Memphi, Nilo amne vectus rex in interiōra penĕtrat; compositisque rebus ita, ut nihil ex patrio Aegyptiōrum more mutāret, adīre Jovis Hammōnis oracŭlum statuit. Quatriduo per vastas solitudĭnes absumpto, tandem ad sedem consecrātam deo ventum est, undĭque ambientĭbus ramis contectam. Regem propius adeuntem maxĭmus natu e sacerdotĭbus FILIUM appellat, hoc nomen illi parentem Jovem reddĕre affirmans. Ille se vero et accipĕre ait et agnoscĕre, humānae sortis oblītus. Con-

sŭlit deinde, an totīus orbis imperium sibi destināret PATER. Aeque in adulatiōnem composĭtus, terrārum omnium rectōrem fore ostendit. Post haec instĭtit quaerĕre, an omnes parentis sui interfectōres poenas dedissent. Sacerdos PARENTEM ejus negat ullīus scelĕre posse violāri, PHILIPPI autem omnes luisse supplicia. Sacrificio deinde facto, dona et sacerdotĭbus et deo data, permissumque amīcis, ut ipsi quoque consulĕrent Jovem. Nihil amplius quaesivērunt, quam an auctor esset sibi divīnis honorĭbus colendi suum regem. Hoc quoque acceptum fore Jovi vates respondit. Vera et salūbri aestimatiōne fides oracŭli vana profecto ei viderī potuisset: sed fortūna, quos uni sibi credĕre coēgit, magna ex parte avĭdos gloriae magis quam capāces facit. Rex ex Hammōne rediens elēgit urbi locum, ubi nunc est Alexandrīa, appellatiōnem trahens ex nomĭne auctōris.

Darius makes his last proposals of Peace.

134. Jam Darīus pervenĕrat Arbēla vicum, nobĭlem sua clade factūrus. Hic, quum fides ei facta esset, regīnam suam quae captīva in Alexandri castris paulo ante decessĕrat, caste sanctēque habĭtam esse, victus continentia hostis, ad novas pacis conditiōnes ferendas decem legātos, cognatōrum princĭpes, misit. Neque jam imperio Alexandri finem destĭnat Halym amnem, qui Lydiam termĭnat: quicquid inter Hellespontum et Euphrātem est, in dotem filiae offert. Quum Parmenio ingrāta regi oratiōne suasisset, ut opīmum regnum conditiōne occupāret, non bello: "Et ego," inquit, "pecuniam quam gloriam mallem, si Parmenio essem." Dimissi legāti nuntiant, adesse certāmen.

Darius conquered near Arbēla, 331 B. C.

135. Alexander, non alias magis terrĭtus, sacrificio rite perpetrāto, relĭquum noctis acquietūrus in tabernacŭlum rediit. Sed nec somnum capĕre nec quiētum pati potĕrat : tandem gravātum anĭmi anxietāte corpus altior somnus oppressit. Jamque luce orta, quum duces ad accipienda imperia convenissent, Parmenio, regem saepius nomĭne compellātum, quum voce non posset, tactu excitāvit. Raro admŏdum, admonĭtu magis amicōrum quam metu discrimĭnis adeundi, thorāce uti solēbat : tunc quoque munimento corpŏris sumpto processit ad milĭtes. Haud alias tam alăcrem vidĕrant regem, et vultu ejus interrĭto spem victoriae augurabantur. Raro in ullo proelio tantum sanguĭnis fusum est. Tandem Darīi aurīga, qui ante ipsum sedens equos regēbat, hasta transfixus est; nec aut Persae aut Macedŏnes dubitavēre, quin ipse rex esset occīsus. Cedĕre Persae, et laxāre ordĭnes ; jamque non pugna sed caedes erat, quum Darīus quoque currum suum in fugam vertit; victōri Alexandro Asiae imperium obtĭgit.

Disturbances in Greece.

136. Dum haec in Asia gerebantur, Graecia fere omnis, spe recuperandae libertātis, ad arma concurrĕrat, auctoritātem Lacedaemoniōrum secūta. Dux hujus belli Agis, rex Lacedaemoniōrum, fuit. Quem motum Antipăter, dux ab Alexandro in Macedonia relictus, in ipso ortu oppressit. Magna tamen utrimque caedes fuit. Agis rex, quum suos terga dantes vidēret, dimissis satellitĭbus ut Alexandro felicitāte, non virtūte inferior viderētur, tantam stragem hostium edĭdit, ut agmĭ-

na interdum fugāret. Ad postrēmum, etsi a multitudĭne victus, gloria tamen omnes vicit.

Alexander invades India.

137. Post haec Indiam petit, ut Oceăno finīret imperium. Cui gloriae ut etiam exercĭtus ornamenta convenīrent, phalĕras equōrum et arma milĭtum argento indūcit; exercitumque suum, ab argenteis clypeis, Argyraspĭdas appellāvit. Quum ad Nysam urbem venisset, oppidānis non repugnantĭbus, fiducia Libĕri patris, a quo condĭta urbs erat, parci jussit. Tunc ad sacrum montem duxit exercĭtum, vite hederāque non alĭter vestītum, quam si manu cultus exornatusque esset. Ubi ad montem accessit, exercĭtus, repentīno mentis impĕtu correptus, ululāre coepit, et Bacchantium more discurrit.

The limit of Alexander's Conquests.

138. Quum ad Hyphăsim venisset, ubi eum cum ducentis millĭbus equĭtum hostes opperiebantur, exercĭtus omnis laborĭbus fessus, lacrўmis eum precātur, finem tandem belli facĕret; aliquando patriae reditusque meminisset, militumque annos respicĕret. Ostendĕre alius canitiem, alius vulnĕra, alius aetāte consumptum corpus et cicatricĭbus obductum. Motus eōrum precĭbus, velŭti finem victoriis factūrus, castra solĭto magnificentiōra fiĕri jussit, quorum molitionĭbus et hostis terrerētur, et postĕris sui admiratio relinquerētur. Nullum opus laetius milĭtes fecērunt. Ităque caesis hostĭbus cum gratulatiōne in haec castra revertērunt.

Alexander returns to Babylon, 324 B. C.

139. Ab ultĭmis oris Oceăni Babyloniam reverĭtenti nuntiātur, non solum legatiōnes Carthaginiensium ceterarumque Afrĭcae civitātum, sed et Hispaniārum, Siciliae, Galliae, Sardiniae, nonnullas quoque ex Italia ejus adventum Babyloniae opperīri. Hac igĭtur ex causa Babyloniam festinanti quidam ex Magis praedixit, ne urbem introīret, tes̄tātus, hunc locum ei fatālem fore. Sed ab Anaxarcho philosŏpho compulsus, ut Magōrum praedicta contemnĕret, Babyloniam reversus, convivium solemnĭter instituit. Ibi quum totus in laetitiam effūsus esset, recedentem jam e convivio Medius Thessălus, instaurāta comissatiōne invītat. Accepto pocŭlo, inter bibendum velŭti telo confixus ingemuit, elatusque e convivio semianĭmis, tanto dolōre cruciātus est, ut ferrum in remedia poscĕret.

Death of Alexander, 323 B. C.

140. Quarta die Alexander indubitātam mortem sentiens, agnoscĕre se fatum domus majōrum suōrum, ait; namque plerosque Aeacidārum intra tricesĭmum annum defunctos. Tumultuantes deinde milĭtes, insidiis periisse regem suspicantes, ipse sedāvit, eosque omnes ad conspectum suum admīsit, osculandamque dextram porrexit. Quum lacrymārent omnes, ipse non sine lacrỹmis tantum, verum etiam sine ullo tristiōris mentis argumento fuit. Ad postrēmum corpus suum in Hammōnis templo condi jubet. Quum deficĕre eum amīci vidērent, quaerunt, quem imperii faciat herēdem; respondit, dignissĭmum. Hac voce omnes amīcos suos ad aemŭlam regni cupiditātem accendit. Sexta die

praeclūsa voce, exemptum digĭto annŭlum Perdiccae tradĭdit, quae res gliscentem amicōrum discordiam sedāvit. Nam etsi non voce nuncupātus heres, judicio tamen electus esse videbātur.

Remarks on the character of Alexander.

141. Decessit Alexander mensem unum tres et triginta annos natus, vir supra humānum modum vi anĭmi praedĭtus. Omĭna quaedam magnitudĭnem ejus in ipso ortu portendisse existimabantur. Quo die natus est, pater ejus nuntium duārum victoriārum accēpit; alterius belli Illyrĭci, alterius certamĭnis Olympiăci, in quod quadrīgas misĕrat. Puer acerrĭmis literārum studiis erudītus fuit. Exacta pueritia, per quinquennium Aristotĕle, philosŏpho praestantissĭmo, usus est magistro. Accepto tandem imperio tantam militĭbus suis fiduciam fecit, ut, illo praesente, nullīus hostis arma timērent. Ităque cum nullo hoste unquam congressus est, quem non vicĕrit; nullam urbem obsēdit, quam non expugnavĕrit. Victus denĭque est non virtūte hostīli, sed insidiis suōrum et fraude.

PERIOD V.—*Decline of Grecian Power.*
FROM THE DEATH OF ALEXANDER TO THE SUBJUGATION OF GREECE BY THE ROMANS, 146 B. C.

Aridaeus, the son of Philip, is proclaimed King.

142. Pedĭtes Aridaeum, Alexandri fratrem, regem appellant, satellitesque illi ex turba sua legunt, et nomĭne Philippi patris vocāri jubent. Magna hinc in

castris seditiōne orta, tandem ab equitĭbus quoque Arĭ daeus rex agnoscĭtur. His ita composĭtis, Macedoniae et Graeciae Antipăter praeponĭtur: regiae pecuniae custodia Cratĕro tradĭtur: castrōrum et exercĭtus cura Meleāgro et Perdiccae assignātur; jubeturque Aridaeus rex corpus Alexandri in Hammōnis templum deducĕre. Tunc Perdicca, lustratiōne castrōrum indicta, seditiōsos supplicio occulte tradi jubet. Reversus inde, provincias inter princĭpes divīsit.

Disputes between Alexander's Generals.

143. Post haec bellum inter Perdiccam et Antigŏnum orĭtur, quod, velut incendium, mox latius serpsit. Macedonia, in duas partes discurrentĭbus ducĭbus, in sua viscĕra armātur, ferrumque a barbăris in civīlem sanguĭnem vertit. In hoc bello Perdicca occīsus est: pluresque ejusdem partis duces periērunt. Et jam finītum certāmen inter successōres Alexandri Magni videbātur, quum repente inter ipsos victōres nata est discordia. Ptolemaeus et Cassander, Antipătri filius, inĭta cum Lysimăcho et Seleuco societāte, contra Antigŏnum bellum terra marīque enixe instruunt. Tenēbat Ptolemaeus Aegyptum cum Afrĭcae parte minōre et Cypro et Phoenīce. Cassandro parēbat Macedonia cum Graecia. Asiam et partes Orientis occupavĕrat Antigŏnus, cujus filius Demetrius, prima belli congressiōne, a Ptolemaeo apud Gamălam vincĭtur. In quo proelio major Ptolemaei moderatiōnis gloria, quam ipsīus victoriae fuit. Siquĭdem et amīcos Demetrii non solum cum suis rebus, verum etiam addĭtis insŭper munerĭbus, dimīsit; et ipsīus Demetrii privātum omne instrumentum ac familiam reddĭdit, dicens: non se propter praedam,

sed propter dignitātem inisse bellum, indignātum, quod Antigŏnus, devictis diversae factiōnis ducĭbus, solus commūnis victoriae praemia corripuisset.

The Generals assume the title of Kings.

144. Interea Ptolemaeus cum Demetrio navāli proelio iterāto congredĭtur, et, amissa classe, in Aegyptum refūgit. Hac victoria elātus Antigŏnus regem se cum Demetrio filio appellāri jubet. Ptolemaeus quoque, ne minōris apud suos auctoritātis esset, rex ab exercĭtu cognominātur. Quibus audītis, Cassander et Lysimăchus et ipsi regiam sibi majestātem vindicārunt.

War in Greece.

145. Omnes ferme Graeciae civitātes, ducĭbus Spartānis, ad spem libertātis erectae, in bellum prorumpunt; et, ne cum Antigŏno, sub cujus regno erant, bellum cepisse viderentur, socios ejus Aetōlos aggrediuntur,— causam belli praetendentes, quod sacrātum Apollĭni campum Cirrhaeum per vim occupassent. Conjuncto exercĭtu, Aetolorumque finĭbus devastātis, magnam cladem passi sunt. Deinde, Spartānis bellum reparantĭbus, auxilium multae gentes negavērunt, existimantes, dominatiōnem eos, non libertātem Graeciae quaerĕre.

Irruption of the Gauls into Greece, 279 B. C.

146. Galli, abundante multitudĭne, quum eos non capĕrent terrae, quae genuĕrant, trecenta millia homĭnum ad sedes novas quaerendas misērunt. Ex his portio in Italia consēdit, quae et Romam incendit; alia portio in Illyrĭcos sinus penetrāvit, et in Pannonia con-

sēdit, ubi per multos annos bella cum finitĭmis gessĕrunt. Hortante deinde successu, divīsis agminĭbus, alii Graeciam, alii Macedoniam petivēre. Tantusque terror Gallĭci nomĭnis fuit, ut etiam reges non lacessīti ultro pacem ingenti pecunia mercarentur.

147. Paulo post Brennus, quo duce portio Gallōrum in Graeciam se effudĕrat, cum centum et quinquaginta millĭbus pedĭtum et quindĕcim millĭbus equĭtum in Macedoniam irrumpit. Victo exercĭtu, totīus regiōnis agros depraedātur. Tum Delphos iter vertit ad Apollīnis templum spoliandum. Hoc templum posĭtum est in monte Parnasso, in rupe undĭque impendente, cujus praecipitiis, ut naturāli praesidio, defendĭtur. Multa ibi et opulenta regum populorumque visuntur munĕra, quaeque magnificentia sua et gratam homĭnum voluntātem, et Apollĭnis responsa manifestant.

The Gauls are repulsed.

148. Brennus quum in conspectu habēret templum, ad acuendos suōrum anĭmos, praedae ubertātem militĭbus ostendēbat, statuasque cum quadrīgis, quarum ingens copia procul visebātur, solĭdo auro fusas esse affirmābat. Qua asseveratiōne incitāti Galli, simul et mero saucii, sine respectu periculōrum in bellum ruēbant. Habēbat Brennus lecta ex omni exercĭtu pedĭtum sexaginta quinque milĭa; Delphōrum sociōrumque nonnĭsi quatuor millia milĭtum erant. Hi plus in Deo, quam in virĭbus spei ponęntes, cum contemptu hostium resistēbant, Gallosque scandentes e summo montis vertĭce, partim saxo, partim armis obruēbant. Inter haec templōrum antistĭtes, sparsis crinĭbus, cum insignĭbus et infŭlis, in primam pugnantium aciem procurrunt, eos

hortantes, ne cunctarentur diis antesignanis hostem caedĕre. Quibus vocĭbus incensi omnes certātim in proelium prosiliunt. Praesentiam Dei statim sensēre. Nam et terrae motu portio montis abrupta Gallōrum stravit exercĭtum, et tempestas insecūta grandĭne et frigōre saucios absumpsit. Dux ipse Brennus, quum dolōrem vulnĕrum ferre non posset, pugiōne vitam finīvit. Alter ex ducĭbus cum decem millĭbus sauciōrum citāto agmĭne Graecia excēdit. Sed nec fugientĭbus fortūna aequior fuit; nullus sine labōre et pericŭlo dies; assidui imbres et gelu, nix, fames, lassitūdo, et pervigiliae misĕras infelīcis belli reliquias obterēbant. Quo pacto evēnit, ut brevi ex tanto exercĭtu nemo superesset.

Pyrrhus, King of Epirus, invades Macedonia, 274 B. C.

149. Interea Pyrrhus ex Sicilia in Epīrum reversus fines Macedoniae invādit; cui Antigŏnus cum exercĭtu occurrit, victusque proelio in fugam vertĭtur. Atque ita Pyrrhus Macedoniam in deditiōnem accĭpit; Antigŏnus autem cum paucis equitĭbus Thessalonīcam se recēpit, ut inde cum conducta Gallōrum manu bellum reparāret. Rursus a Ptolemaeo, Pyrrhi filio, fundĭtus victus, cum septem comitĭbus fugiens salūtis latĕbras in solitudĭne quaerit.

A general change of Rulers.

150. Iisdem ferme temporĭbus prope universi orbis imperia novā regum successiōne mutāta sunt. Nam et in Macedonia Philippus, mortuo Antigŏno, regnum suscēpit; et in Asia, interfecto Seleuco, impūbes adhuc rex Antiŏchus constitūtus est. Aegyptum, patre ac matre interfectis, occupavĕrat Ptolemaeus, cui ex cri

mĭne facinŏris cognōmen Philopător fuit. Etiam Spar- tāni in locum Cleomĕnis suffecēre Lycurgum; et apud Carthaginienses aetāte immatūra dux Hannĭbal consti- tuĭtur, non penuria seniōrum, sed odio Romanōrum, quo eum a pueritia sciēbant imbūtum. In his regĭbus puĕris magna indŏles virtūtis enituit. Solus Ptolemae- us, sicut scelestus in occupando regno, ita et segnis in administrando fuit.

The Romans declare War against Philip, 200 B. C.: Battle of Cynoscephalae, 197 B. C.

151. Nec multo post tempŏre tota Graecia, fiducia Romanōrum ad spem pristĭnae libertātis erecta, bellum Philippo intŭlit; atque ita quum rex undĭque urgerē- tur, pacem petĕre compellĭtur. Repudiāta a Senātu pace, proelium commissum est apud Cynoscephălas in Thessalia inter Philippum et Flaminīnum, Romanō- rum ducem. Macedŏnas Romāna fortūna vicit. Frac- tus ităque bello Philippus, pace accepta, nomen quidem regium retinuit; sed, omnĭbus Graeciae urbĭbus extra termĭnos antīquae possessiōnis amissis, solam Macedo- niam retinuit.

Perseus plots successfully against his brother's life.

152. Intĕrim regis Macedŏnum domus intestīnis malis agitabātur. Nam quum Demetrius, Philippi fili- us, a patre Romam missus, ob insīgnem pudōrem mul- ta favōris documenta a senātu accepisset, patri invīsus esse coepit, indignanti, plus momenti apud senātum persōnam filii, quam auctoritātem patris habuisse. Igĭ- tur Perseus, major filiōrum regis, perspecta patris aegri- tudĭne, quōtĭdie absentem Demetrium apud eum crimi- nāri, et primo invīsum, mox etiam suspectum reddĕre;

nunc amicitiam Romanōrum, nunc proditiōnem ei patris objectāre. Ad postrēmum insidias sibi ab eo parātas confingit, ad cujus crimĭnis probatiōnem immittit indĭces, testesque subornat. Quibus rebus patrem impŭlit, ut supplicium de innocente sumĕret.

Death of Philip, 179 *B. C.*

153. Occīso Demetrio sublatōque aemŭlo, non negligentior tantum Perseus in patrem, verum etiam contumacior erat ; nec herēdem regni, sed regem se gerēbat. His rebus offensus Philippus impatientius in dies mortem Demetrii dolēbat, et, denĭque fraude cognĭta, non minus scelĕre Persei, quam innoxii Demetrii morte cruciabātur. Brevi post tempŏre, morbo ex aegritudĭne anĭmi contracto decessit, relicto magno belli apparātu adversus Romānos, quo postea Perseus usus est.

Perseus conquered.—Macedonia a Roman Province.

154. Jam Macedonĭcum bellum summa omnium virium contentiōne a Romānis geri coeptum est. Prima equĭtum congressio fuit, qua Perseus victor suspensam omnium exspectatiōnem in sui favōrem traxit ; misit tamen legātos ad consŭlem, qui pacem petĕrent, quam patri suo Romāni etiam victo dedissent, impensas belli lege victi susceptūrus. Sed consul Sulpicius non minus graves, quam victo, leges dixit. Dum haec aguntur, Romāni Aemilium Paulum consŭlem creant, eīque extra ordĭnem Macedonĭcum bellum decernunt ; qui quum ad exercĭtum venisset, non magnam moram pugnae fecit. Pridie, quam proelium consererētur, luna nocte defēcit ; quod ostentum Perseo cladem finemque Macedonĭci regni portendĕre vaticinabantur.

Quod vaticinium non fefellit. Perseus rex fuga cum decem millĭbus talentum Samothraciam defertur; quem Cnaeus Octavius ad persequendum missus a consŭle, cum duōbus filiis, Alexandro et Philippo, cepit, captumque ad consŭlem duxit. Macedonia Romanōrum ditiōni addĭta. Aetolōrum, nova semper bella in Graecia excitantium, princĭpes Romam missi; ibĭque, ne quid in patria novārent, diu detenti sunt. Tandem per multos annos legationĭbus civitatium senātu fatigāto, in suam quisque patriam remissus est.

The Romans seek occasion to quarrel with the Achaeans.

155. Macedonĭbus subactis, Aetolorumque virĭbus debilitātis, soli adhuc ex universa Graecia Achaei nimis potentes tunc tempŏris Romānis videbantur, non propter singulārum civitatium nimias opes, sed propter conspiratiōnem universārum. Namque Achaei, licet per civitātes divīsi, unum tamen imperium habent, singularumque urbium pericŭla mutuis virĭbus propulsant. Quaerentĭbus igĭtur Romānis causas belli, tempestīve fortūna querēlas Spartanōrum obtŭlit, quorum agros Achaei propter mutuum odium populabantur. Spartānis a senātu responsum est, legātos se ad inspiciendas res sociōrum in Graeciam missūros. Legātis clam mandātum est, ut corpus Achaeōrum dissolvĕrent. Hi ităque, omnium civitātum principĭbus Corinthum evocātis, decrētum senātus recĭtant, dicentes, expedīre omnĭbus, ut singŭlae civitātes sua jura et suas leges habeant. Quod ubi omnĭbus innotuit, velut in furōrem versi universum peregrīnum popŭlum trucīdant: legātos quoque ipsos Romanōrum violassent, nisi hi, audīto tumultu, trepĭdi fugissent.

The Achacans are conquered.—Corinth plundered by Mummius,
146 B. C.

156. Haec ubi Romae nuntiāta sunt, statim senātus Mummio consŭli bellum Achaĭcum decernit, qui, omnĭbus strenue provīsis, pugnandi copiam hostĭbus fecit. Sed apud Achaeos omnia neglecta et solūta fuērunt. Ităque praedam, non proelium agitantes, vehicŭla ad spolia hostium reportanda, secum duxērunt, et conjŭges liberosque suos ad spectacŭlum certamĭnis in montĭbus posuērunt. Sed proelio commisso ante ocŭlos suōrum caesi sunt. Conjŭges quoque et libĕri eōrum praeda hostium fuēre. Urbs Corinthus diruĭtur: popŭlus omnis sub corōna vendĭtur; ut hoc exemplo cetĕris civitatĭbus metus novārum rērum imponerētur.

EXERCISES IN SYNTAX.

INTRODUCTION.

157. In Latin, as in English, words are divided, according to their use, into various classes, called *Parts of Speech.*

158. Parts of speech, either singly or combined, form *Propositions*; e. g.,

Audis.	*Thou hearest.*
Puer ludit.	*The boy plays.*

159. Propositions, either singly or combined, form *Sentences*; e. g.,

Equus currit (*one prop.*).	*The horse runs.*
Puer ludit et equus currit (*two propositions*).	*The boy is playing and the horse is running.*

160. Sentences, in their various forms and combinations, of course, comprise the *Language.*

161. The object of all language is the expression of thought.

162. A sentence may express thought,

1) In the form of an *assertion*, either affirmative or negative. It is then called a *declarative* sentence; e. g.,

Puer legit.	*The boy is reading.*
Puer non legit.	*The boy is not reading.*

2) In the form of a *question*. It is then called an *interrogative* sentence; e. g.,

| Quis legit? | *Who is reading?* |

3) In the form of a *command, exhortation*, or *en-treaty*. It is then called an *imperative* sentence; e. g.,

| Lege. | *Read thou.* |
| Legat. | *Let him read.* |

163. In each of the above forms, sentences sometimes imply *passion* or *emotion* on the part of the speaker, and may then be called *exclamatory declarative* if of the declarative form, *exclamatory interrogative* if of the interrogative form, and *exclamatory imperative* if of the imperative form. The *emotion*, however, does not affect the structure of the sentence, though it often renders it elliptical.

164. A sentence may express,

1) A single thought; i. e., may make but one assertion, ask but one question, or give but one command. It may then be called a *simple* sentence; e. g.,

Balbus a nullo videbātur. | *Balbus was seen by no one.*

2) Two or more thoughts so related to each other that one or more of them are made dependent upon the others. It may then be called a *complex* sentence; e. g.,

| Quod ubi Caesar compĕrit, se in Galliam recēpit. | *When Caesar learned this, he retired into Gaul.* |

REM.—The two simple sentences, which compose the above *complex*, are, (1) *Caesar learned this*, and (2) *Caesar retired into Gaul.*

These are, however, so combined that the first does little more than specify the *time* of the action denoted by the second. *Caesar retired into Gaul* (when?) *when he learned this.*

3) Two or more independent thoughts. It may then be called a *compound* sentence; e. g.,

| Balbus a nullo videbātur, ipse autem omnia vidēbat. | *Balbus was seen by no one, but he himself saw every thing.* |

CHAPTER I.
SIMPLE SENTENCES.

Lesson I.
Principal Elements of Sentences; Subject and Predicate.—Declarative Sentences.
[1 & 2.]

165. Every sentence, however simple, consists of two distinct parts; viz.,
1) The *Subject*, or that of which it speaks, as *puer* in the sentence, *puer ludit.*
2) The *Predicate*, or that which is said of the subject, as *ludit* in the above sentence.

166. In Latin the subject is often omitted, because the form of the predicate shows what subject is meant; thus, the single word *rides*, thou art laughing, is in itself a complete proposition, because the ending *es* shows that the subject in English cannot be *I*, *he*, or *they*, but must be *thou*.

167. When a proposition is thus expressed by a single word, that word is always a verb, and the omitted subject, implied in the ending of the verb, is always a pronoun of the same number and person as the verb itself; as, Amat, *He loves.*

168. The *analysis* of a proposition, or sentence, consists in separating it into its elements or parts.

MODELS.
1. Proposition: Puer ludit, *The boy is playing.*

This is a *simple* sentence, because it expresses a *single* thought.

Puer is the subject, because it is that of which the proposition speaks. *Ludit* is the predicate, because it is that which is said of the subject *puer*.

2. Proposition: Rides, *Thou art laughing.*

This is a *simple* sentence.

Rides is the predicate, because it is that which is said of the omitted subject. The subject is a pronoun of the second person singular (*tu*, thou), implied in the ending *es* of the predicate.

169. VOCABULARY.

Citadel, *arx, arcis,* f.
City, *urbs, urbis,* f.
Come, *venio, venīre, vĕni, ventum.*
Destroy, *everto, evertĕre, ti, sum.*
Flee, *fugio, fugĕre, fūgi, fugĭtum; aufugio, fugĕre, fūgi.*
Found, *condo, dĕre, dĭdi, dĭtum.*

He, *ille, a, ud,* or, as subject, it may be implied in the ending of the verb.
I, *ego, mei,* &c., or, as subject, it may be omitted.
You, *tu, tui,* &c., or, as subject, it may be omitted.
Teach, *doceo, ēre, ui, tum.*
Trojan, *Trojānus, a, um.*

170. EXERCISES.

I. *Translate and analyze the following Latin, explaining the omitted subjects:*

1. Latīnus imperābat. 2. Imperāvit. 3. Troja eversa est. 4. Aenēas aufūgit. 5. Aufugiēbant. 6. Hic docuit. 7. Docuērunt. 8. Docuĭmus.

II 1. *Construct one or more Latin declarative sentences on each of the following subjects:*

Puer, puellae, patres, avis, aves.

2. *Construct three Latin declarative sentences, using the following predicates:*
   Discēbant, legēbat, currunt.

3. *Construct five or more Latin declarative sentences with subjects omitted, using as predicates some parts of the following verbs:*
   Ridēre, laudāre, docēre, currĕre, timēre.

MODELS.

1. Ridebātis.	*You were laughing.*
2. Laudabĭtur.	*He will be praised.*

III. *Translate into Latin.*

1. They have come. 2. A citadel will be founded. 3. Cities will be founded. 4. Cities have been founded. 5. We have been taught. 6. The cities had been destroyed. 7. The Trojans fled. 8. You will flee. 9. We were fleeing. 10. I shall come.

Lesson II.

Subordinate Elements; Modifiers.—Declarative Sentences.
[1 & 2.]

171. Both subject and predicate may have qualifying words and clauses connected with them, to limit or modify their meaning; e. g.,

1. Latīnus *rex* regnāvit. | *Latinus the king reigned.*

> Rem.—In this example, *rex* limits Latinus; i. e., it shows that the predicate *regnāvit* is not affirmed of every one who may have borne the name Latinus, but only of Latinus *the king*.

2. Milĭtes *fortĭter* pugnant. | *The soldiers fight bravely.*

> Rem. 1.—Here the predicate is modified by *fortiter*, showing how the soldiers fight.

SUBORDINATE ELEMENTS.

Rem. 2.—Qualifying words and clauses, whether belonging to the subject or predicate, may be called *modifiers*.

172. Any modifier, whether in the subject or predicate, may be itself modified; e. g.,

| Latīnus, *bonus* rex, regnā- vit. | *Latinus, the good king, reigned.* |

173. The subject (*expressed* or *implied*) and the predicate are essential to the structure of every sentence, and may, therefore, be called the *essential* or *principal elements* of sentences.

174. All modifiers are subordinate to the subject and predicate, and may, therefore, be called the *subordinate elements* of sentences.

175. VOCABULARY.

Aeneas, *Aenēas, ae.*	with accus., as *in matrimonium*).
Agriculture, *agricultūra, ae,* f.	
Anchises, *Anchīses, ae.*	King, *rex, regis.*
Call, *appello, āre, āvi, ātum.*	Latinus, *Latīnus, i.*
Daughter, *filia, ae.*	Marriage, *matrimonium, i,* n.
Early, ancient, *antīquus, a, um.*	Rome, *Roma, ae,* f.
First, *primus, a, um.*	Saturn, *Saturnus, i.*
Give, *do, dăre, dedi, dătum.*	Saturnia, *Saturnia, ae,* f.
Italian, *Itălus, a, um.*	Son, *filius, i.*
In, *in* (with abl.; sometimes	Time, *tempus, ŏris,* n.

176. EXERCISES.

I. *Translate the following sentences, and analyze them so far as to show their* subjects *and* predicates, *and the separate* modifiers *of each:*

1. Hic docuit. 2. Hic *primus* docuit. 3. Hic *Itălos* primus docuit. 4. Hic Itălos primus *agricultūram* docuit. 5. Troja eversa est. 6. *Sub rege* Troja eversa

est. 7. Sub *hoc* rege Troja eversa est. 8. Aenēas aufūgit. 9. Aenēas *filius* aufūgit. 10. Aenēas, *Anchīsae* filius, aufūgit. 11. *Hinc* Aenēas, Anchīsae filius, aufūgit. 12. Hinc Aenēas, Anchīsae filius, *cum Trojānis* aufūgit. 13. Hinc Aenēas, Achīsae filius, cum *multis* Trojānis aufūgit.

II. *First construct three or more Latin declarative sentences without modifiers; then add modifiers, either to the subject or predicate, or to both.*

MODELS.

Without modifiers.

1. Puer scribēbat.	*The boy was writing.*
2. Canis mordēbit.	*The dog will bite.*

With modifiers.

1. *Bonus* puer *epistŏlam* scribēbat.	*The good boy was writing a letter.*
2. *Pastōris* canis *puĕrum* mordēbit.	*The shepherd's dog will bite the boy.*

III. *Translate into Latin.*

1. Saturn taught *the Italians*. 2. Saturn was *the first* to teach (lit. *the first* taught) the Italians. 3. *In very early times* he taught the Italians *agriculture*. 4. They will call the citadel Saturnia. 5. The city was called Rome. 6. Latinus gave his daughter to Aeneas. 7. Latinus the king gave his daughter in marriage to Aeneas. 8. Latinus the king gave his daughter in marriage to Aeneas, the son of Anchises.

Lesson III.

Elements of Sentences, continued.—Interrogative and Imperative Sentences.

[3 & 4.]

177. Interrogative sentences are used in asking questions, and may be introduced,

    1) By an interrogative pronoun, adjective, or adverb; e. g.,

Quis venit?	*Who has come?*
Quot sunt?	*How many are there?*
Unde venis?	*Whence do you come?*

    2) By one of the interrogative particles, *ne, nonne, num;* e. g.,

Scribit*ne* Caius?	*Is Caius writing?*
Nonne scribit?	*Is he not writing?*
Num scribit?	*Is he writing?*

REM. 1.—If *ne* is used, it must follow some other word, and be joined to it, as in the first example.

REM. 2.—A question with *ne* asks for information (Ex. 1), with *nonne* expects the answer *yes* (Ex. 2), and with *num* expects the answer *no* (Ex. 3).

REM. 3.—*Ne, nonne,** and *num,* are not modifiers of the predicate, but mere particles showing the *interrogative* character of the sentence.

178. Imperative sentences are used in *commands, exhortations,* and *entreaties,* and take the verb either in

---

* *Nonne,* strictly speaking, is compounded of the modal adverb *non* and the particle *ne;* but we are now regarding it merely as an interrogative particle.

the *imperative* or in the *subjunctive* mood, and usually in the *present* tense; e. g.,

Perge in exsilium.	*Go into exile.*
Conservāte vos.	*Preserve yourselves.*
Veniat servus.	*Let the slave come.*
Veniāmus.	*Let us come.*

179. VOCABULARY.

Alba, *Alba, ae,* f.	Longa, *Longa, ae,* f.
Ascanius, *Ascanius, i.*	Reign, *regno, āre, āvi, ātum.*
He, *is, ea, id; ille, illa, illud;* or, when subject, it may be implied by the ending of the verb.	Silvius, *Silvius, i.*
	Succeed, *sequor, sequi, secūtus sum.*
	Who? *Quis, quae, quid?*

180. EXERCISES.

I. *Translate and analyze the following sentences, stating whether declarative, interrogative, or imperative:*

1. Ascanius regnum accēpit. 2. Quis regnum accēpit? 3. Purga urbem. 4. Cogitāte de vobis. 5. Quis Albae regnāvit? 6. Omnes Albae regnavērunt. 7. Conservāte fortūnas vestras. 8. Quis te salutāvit? Num Albae regnāvit? Nonne Albae regnavērunt?

II. *Change the declarative sentences constructed in the first and second Lessons, to the interrogative or imperative form.*

MODELS.

Declarative.	*Interrogative.*
Puer ludēbat.	Num puer ludēbat?
The boy was playing.	Was the boy playing?
Declarative.	*Imperative.*
Ridebātis.	Ridēte.
You were laughing.	Laugh ye.

III. *Translate into Latin.*

1. Ascanius founded a city. 2. Who founded the city? 3. Let us found cities. 4. Who founded Alba Longa? 5. Did Ascanius found it? 6. He did found it. 7. Who was reigning? 8. Latinus was reigning. 9. Let him reign. 10. He will reign. 11. Who succeeded Ascanius? 12. Silvius succeeded him.

Lesson IV.

Simple Subject.

[5 & 6.]

181. Every simple sentence must have for its subject either

  1) A noun; e. g., *Puer ludit,* or
  2) A pronoun; e. g., *Ille ludit.*

182. Rule.—*Case of Subject.*

The subject of a finite verb is put in the nominative. (See examples above.)

[F. B. 609; A. & S. § 209; Z. § 879.]*

183. In the arrangement of the Latin sentence, the subject is put,

---

* These references relate respectively to the First Latin Book, to the Latin Grammar of Andrews & Stoddard, and to that of Zumpt, American edition.

Note.—The author indulges the hope that all who may use this book will constantly bear in mind that the writing of Latin cannot, in any way, supersede the necessity of thorough grammatical drills. Both exercises are indispensable to high scholarship, and should go, hand in hand, throughout the entire course of classical instruction. For this reason the *Rules of Syntax,* as we have occasion to use them in our Exercises, are inserted in this work, with references to the corresponding rules in the First Latin Book, in Andrews & Stoddard's Latin Grammar, and in that of Zumpt.

1) When not emphatic, at or near the beginning; e. g.,

Superbus cognōmen meruit. | *Superbus merited his name.*

2) When emphatic, at or near the end; e. g.,

Commōvit bellum *rex*. | *The king excited a war.*

184. VOCABULARY.

Boy, *puer, ĕri.*
Girl, *puella, ae.*
Play, *ludo, ĕre, lusi, lusum.*
Praise, *laudo, āre, āvi, ātum.*
Pupil, *discipŭlus, i,* m.
Read, *lego, ĕre, legi, lectum.*

Shield, *clypeus* or *clipeus, i,* m
Spear, *hasta, ae,* f.
Strike, *percutio, ĕre, cussi, cussum.*
Walk, *ambŭlo, āre, āvi, ātum.*

185. EXERCISES.

I. *Translate and analyze.*

1. Roma condĭta est. 2. Urbs condĭta est. 3. Quis veniet? 4. Venient. 5. Troja eversa est. 6. Roma eversa est. 7. Urbes eversae sunt. 8. Aenēas aufūgit. 9. Trojāni aufugērunt. 10. Aufugĭmus. 11. Silvius regnāvit. 12. Quis regnābat? 13. Rex regnābat. 14. Hic regnāvit. 15. Ille regnābat.

II. 1. *Explain position of elements in the above sentences.* (See 183.)

2. *Construct six Latin sentences: two declarative, two interrogative, and two imperative; two with substantives as subjects, two with pronouns, and two with subjects omitted.*

III. *Translate into Latin.*

1. The pupil was praised. 2. The boys will be praised. 3. Have not the girls been praised? 4. They have been praised. 5. The shields were struck. 6

The spears will be struck. 7. Will you read? 8. We have been reading. 9. Who will come? 10. Will not the king come? 11. He will come. 12. Let us walk. 13. Let them play. 14. They have been playing. 15. Were not the boys playing? 16. They were playing.

Lesson V.
Complex Subject.—Modifier; Simple.
[7 & 8.]

186. The elements of a sentence may be either *simple* or *complex*:

1) Simple, when not modified by other words; e. g.,

Rex regnāvit. | *The king reigned.*

2) Complex, when thus modified; e. g.,

Bonus rex bene regnāvit. | *The good king reigned well.*

REM.—In the first example (*Rex regnāvit*), both subject and predicate are simple, while, in the second, they are both complex.

187. Modifiers are of two kinds; viz.,

1) Such as limit other words by *completing* their meaning. These may be called *objective* modifiers; e. g.,

Mater *filiam* amat. | *The mother loves her daughter.*
Amor *auri.* | *The love of gold.*

REM.—In the first example, *filiam* not only qualifies *amat*, but also completes its meaning by showing the *object* loved. In the second example, too, *auri* both qualifies and completes the meaning of *amor*, by showing the object of that love: *the love of* (what?) *gold.*

2) Such as restrict the meaning of other words

by specifying some *quality* or *attribute*. These may be called *attributive* modifiers; e. g.,

Bonus rex *bene* regnāvit. | *The good king reigned well.*

> REM. 1.—*Bonus* expresses the attribute of *rex* (*good* king), and *bene* of *regnāvit* (reigned *well*).
>
> REM. 2.—It will be observed that the adverb *bene* sustains the same relation to the verb *regnāvit* as the adjective *bonus* does to the noun *rex;* both are attributive, but, for distinction's sake, the latter may be called the *adjective attribute;* and the former, the *adverbial attribute.*

188. The subject of a sentence may be limited,

1) By an *objective* modifier; e. g.,

Amor *gloriae* nos impŭlit. | *The love of glory actuated us.*

> REM.—This modifier has been very properly called the *objective genitive;* though some grammarians regard it as merely attributive. It will be readily seen that *gloriae*, in the above example, expresses no *attribute* of *amor* (love); it says nothing of the *character* or *qualities* of that *love;* but simply specifies the *object* on which it is exercised.

2) By an *attributive* modifier; e. g.,

Bonus rex regnat. | *A good king reigns.*
Regis filius regnābit. | *The king's son will reign.*

> REM.—It will be observed from the above examples that the attribute of the subject is expressed sometimes by an adjective, and sometimes by a noun used with the force of an adjective.

189. RULE.—*Agreement of Adjectives.*

Adjectives and adjective pronouns (whether in the subject or the predicate) agree in *gender, number,* and *case* with the nouns which they qualify; e. g.,

Bonus rex. | *The good king.*
Bona regīna. | *The good queen.*

[F. B. 614; A. & S. § 205.]

190. RULE —*Limiting Nouns.*

A noun limiting the meaning of another noun denoting a different* person or thing, is put in the *genitive*, unless it denotes *character* or *quality*, in which case it is accompanied by an adjective, and is put either in the *genitive* or *ablative*; e. g.,

Regis filius.	*The king's son.*
Puer eximiae pulchritudĭnis, *or* Puer eximia pulchritudĭne.	*A boy of remarkable beauty.*

[F. B. 624; A. & S. § 211 and R. 6; Z. § 426.]

Rem.—Instead of the *genitive* of the limiting noun, we sometimes find the *dative*, or the *accusative* or *ablative* with a *preposition*; e. g., Troja in Asia eversa est, *Troy in Asia was destroyed.*— Transmissus ex Gallia in Britanniam, *The passage from Gaul into Britain.*

191. In the arrangement of the parts of the complex subject,

    1) The adjective precedes or follows its substantive, according as it is or is not emphatic; e. g.,

Bonus rex regnat.
Rex *bonus* regnat. } *A good king is reigning.*

    2) The *attributive* genitive generally precedes its substantive when the latter is not emphatic; e. g.,

Aenēae filius regnāvit. | *The son of Aeneas reigned.*

    3) The *objective* genitive generally follows its substantive; e. g.,

Amor *gloriae* nos impŭlit. | *The love of glory actuated us.*

192. In analyzing a sentence which contains modifi

---

* See 441.

ers, the pupil is expected to show both the influence of the several modifiers upon the thought, and their grammatical relation to the elements which they limit.

MODELS.

1. Regis filius regnābit. | *The king's son will reign.*

This is a *simple* sentence.

Filius is the subject, and *regnābit* the predicate.

The subject filius is modified by *regis*, showing *whose* son, viz. *the king's.* Regis is in the *genitive*, according to Rule, 190.

Regis filius is the complex subject.

2. Rex bonus regnat. | *A good king is reigning.*

This is a *simple* sentence.

Rex is the subject, and *regnat* is the predicate.

The subject rex is modified by the adjective *bonus*, showing the *character* of the king (a *good* king). *Bonus* agrees with the subject *rex*, according to Rule, 189.

Rex bonus is the complex subject.

193. VOCABULARY.

Alban, *Albānus, a, um.*
Bite, *mordeo, ēre, momordi, morsum.*
Brother, *frater, tris.*
Dog, *canis, is,* c.
Five, *quinque,* indec.
Good, *bonus, a, um.*

Kill, *occīdo, ĕre, cĭdi, cīsum.*
Queen, *regīna, ae.*
Romulus, *Romŭlus, i.*
Shepherd, *pastor, ōris,* m.
What? *qui, quae, quod?* (See F. B. 284.)

194. EXERCISES.

I. *Translate and analyze, parsing the complex subjects.*

1. Multi Trojāni aufugērunt. 2. Anchīsae filius aufūgit. 3. Numa regnāvit. 4. Bonus Numa regnābat

5. Remus occīsus est. 6. Hic vir occīsus est. 7. Troja in Asia eversa est. 8. Rex Albanōrum mortuus est.

II. 1. *Explain position of elements in the above sentences.* (See 183 and 191.)

2. *Construct three or more Latin sentences with complex subjects.*

III. *Translate into Latin.*

1. What king was reigning? 2. A good king was reigning. 3. Had not the king of the Albans been reigning? 4. Were the good shepherds killed? 5. Five shepherds had been killed. 6. The brother of Romulus was killed. 7. The shepherd's son will be praised. 8. The shepherd's dog will bite. 9. The good queen will be praised. 10. The daughter of the queen has been praised.

Lesson VI.

Complex Subject.—Modifier; Complex.
[9 & 10.]

195. Any modifier in the complex subject, whether objective or attributive, may itself become complex.

196. Any substantive may be modified in the various ways already specified for the subject. (See last Lesson.)

197. VOCABULARY.

American, *Americānus, a, um.*
Citizen, *civis, is,* c.
Himself, he himself, *ipse, a, um.*
Increase (trans.), *augeo, ēre, auxi, auctum.*
Neighboring, *finitĭmus, a, um.*
Number, *numĕrus, i,* m.
People, *popŭlus, i,* m.
Roman, *Romānus, a, um.*
State, *civĭtas, ātis,* f.
United, *foederātus, a, um.*

198. Exercises.

I. *Translate and analyze, parsing the several parts of the complex subjects.*

1. Filius boni regis veniēbat. 2. Pastor illīus regiōnis occīsus est. 3. Novae urbis cives occīsi sunt. 4. Festum Neptūni magni institūtum est. 5. Popŭli illīus virgĭnes raptae erant. 6. Numĕrus civium Romanōrum auctus est.

II. 1. *In the first three of the above sentences, substitute other complex attributives in place of those now used.*

MODEL.

Filius *pulchrae regīnae* veniēbat.

2. *Construct two or more Latin sentences with simple subjects; then make these subjects complex, by the addition of simple attributives; and finally put these attributives in the complex form.*

MODEL.

1. Dux occīsus est.	*The leader was killed.*
2. Dux *exercĭtus* occīsus est.	*The leader of the army was killed.*
3. Dux exercĭtus *Romāni* occīsus est.	*The leader of the Roman army was killed.*

III. *Translate into Latin.*

1. Has the number of states been increased? 2. The number of the United States has been increased. 3. Will not the number of American citizens be increased? 4. The number of Roman citizens had been increased. 5. The shepherd was killed. 6. Will not the good shepherds be killed? 7. The sons of the good shepherds had been killed. 8. The neighboring

people came. 9. Did the sons of the neighboring shepherds come? 10. The shepherds themselves came.

Lesson VII.
Simple Predicate.
[11—13.]

199. The predicate of a sentence consists of two parts, an *attribute* of the subject and a *copula*, by which that attribute is predicated or asserted of the subject.

200. The attribute and copula, which form the predicate, sometimes appear separately, as when the former is expressed by a noun or adjective, and the latter by the verb *esse*, and sometimes united in one word, in which case they must be expressed by a verb.*

201. The predicate of a simple sentence may, therefore, be,

1) A verb; e. g.,

| Puer ludit. | The boy is playing. |

2) The verb *esse* (or sometimes a passive verb) with an attributive† noun or adjective; e. g.,

| Cicero fuit consul. | Cicero was consul. |
| Terra est rotunda. | The earth is round. |

Rem.—In the first example, the predicate is not simply *fuit*, but *fuit consul;* for the assertion is not that Cicero *was* (i. e. *existed*), but *was consul;* so in the second example, the predicate is *est rotunda*, the assertion being that the earth *is round.*

---

* Even in the verb, the *attribute* and *copula* are sometimes represented by distinct words, as in the compound tenses; e. g., *Rex occīsus est.* Here *occīsus* is the attribute and *est* the copula.

† By an attributive noun is meant one which is used to qualify or describe another noun.

202. RULE.—*Finite Verbs.*

A finite verb must agree with its subject in number and person; e. g.,

Latīnus regnābat. | *Latinus was reigning.*

[F. B. 612; A. & S. § 209; Z. § 365.]

203. RULE.—*Predicate Nouns.*

An attributive noun in the predicate after *esse* and a few *passive* verbs, is put in the same case as the subject, when it denotes the same* person or thing; e. g.,

Latīnus fuit rex. | *Latinus was king.*

[F. B. 613; A. & S. § 210; Z. § 365.]

☞ For agreement of attributive adjective, see 189.

204. VOCABULARY.

Amulius, *Amulius, i.*
Be, *sum, esse, fui, futūrus.*
Brave, *fortis, e.*
Choose, elect, *lego, ĕre, legi, lectum.*
Father, *pater, tris.*

Hundred, *centum,* indec.
Make, *creo, āre, āvi, ātum.*
Senator, *senātor, ōris.*
Who (interrog.), *quis, quae, quid?* (See F. B. 284.)

205. EXERCISES.

I. *Translate and analyze, parsing and explaining predicates.*

1. Silvius Procas fuit rex. 2. Faustŭlus fuit pastor. 3. Quis est avus? 4. Quae fuit mater? 5. Urbs fuit nova. 6. Urbes sunt novae. 7. Annŭli sunt aurei. 8. Numa rex creātus est. 9. Senatōres appellāti sunt Patres. 10. Romāni bellicōsi fuērunt.

II. *Construct two Latin sentences with verbs as predi-*

---
* See 435.

cates; two with esse *and* nouns; *and two with* esse *and* adjectives.

III. *Translate into Latin.*

1. Who was king? 2. Latinus was king. 3. Let him· be king. 4. Were not the Romans brave? 5. The Romans were brave. 6. Let us be good. 7. We will be good. 8. Who was made king? 9. Amulius was made king. 10. Was not the city called Rome? 11. The city was called Rome. 12. A hundred senators had been chosen. 13. These senators were called fathers. 14. Who will be made senators? 15. You will be elected senators.

Lesson VIII.

Complex Predicate.—Direct Object; Simple.
[14 & 15.]

206. The predicate, like the subject, may be limited,
    I. By Objective Modifiers.
    II. By Attributive Modifiers.

207. The *objective* modifiers of the verb-predicate may be divided into three classes; viz.,
    1) Direct Objects.
    2) Indirect Objects.
    3) Remote Objects.

Rem.—These objects appear both singly and combined.

208. In the arrangement of the Latin sentence, the object, of whatever kind, generally precedes its verb; e. g.,

Rex *bellum* gerit.	*The king is waging war.*
Legĭbus paret.	*He obeys the laws.*

Rem.—Any word is rendered emphatic by being placed in an unusual position, especially if that position is near the beginning or end of the sentence or clause.

209. The *direct* object of the predicate may represent,

1) The person or thing on which the action of the verb is directly exerted; e. g.,

| Caius puellam laudat. | *Caius praises* (what?) *the girl.* |

2) The direct effect of the action, i. e. the object produced by it; e. g.,

| Caius epistŏlam scribit. | *Caius is writing* (what?) *a letter.* |

210. RULE.—*Direct Object.*

Any transitive verb may take an *accusative* as the direct object of its action. (See examples above.)

[F. B. 641; A. & S. § 229; Z. § 382.]

211. Any thought, which may be expressed by a transitive verb with a direct object, may also be expressed by the passive voice of the same verb, having for its subject the noun used as the direct object of the active; e. g.,

| (*Act.*) Balbum accūsant. | *They accuse Balbus.* |
| (*Pass.*) Balbus accusātur. | *Balbus is accused.* |

Rem.—The agent of the action with passive verbs, when expressed, is generally put in the *ablative* with *a* or *ab*, but as it then becomes an *attributive modifier*, showing *by whom* the action is performed, we shall have occasion to examine it in another place.

212. VOCABULARY.

Ancus, *Ancus, i.*
Declare, *indĭco, ĕre, dixi, dictum.*
Enlarge, *amplio, āre, āvi, ātum.*
Marcius, *Marcius, i.*
War, *bellum, i,* n.

213. EXERCISES.

I. *Translate and analyze, explaining position.*

1. Numa Pompilius leges dedit. 2. Hic vir sacra instituit. 3. Ancus Marcius suscēpit imperium. 4. Numae nepos suscēpit imperium. 5. Hic vir urbem ampliāvit. 6. Carcĕrem primus aedificāvit. 7. Romŭlus foedus icit. 8. Quis Albam diruit? 9. Tullus Hostilius Albam diruit. 10. Rex bellum indixit.

II. *Construct nine or more sentences with objective modifiers in the accusative—three declarative, three interrogative, and three imperative.*

III. *Translate into Latin.*

1. They have declared war. 2. Will he not declare war? 3. Who has declared war? 4. Will you declare war? 5. Who founded Rome? 6. Romulus founded Rome. 7. Who enlarged the city? 8. Ancus Marcius enlarged the city. 9. The city was enlarged. 10. Rome was enlarged. 11. Did not Ancus Marcius enlarge the city? 12. Was not Rome enlarged? 13. Who was the first to teach (lit. *who the first taught*) the Italians? 14. Saturn was the first to teach the Italians.

LESSON IX.

Complex Predicate.—Direct Object; Complex.
[16 & 17.]

214. The object, and, in fact, any noun, whether in the subject or predicate, may be modified in the various ways already specified for the subject. (See Lesson V.)

215. VOCABULARY.

Build, *aedifĭco, āre, āvi, ātum.*
Capitol, *Capitolium, i,* n.
Commence, *inchoo, āre, āvi, ātum.*
Festival, *festum, i,* n.
Friendship, intimacy, *familiarĭtas, ātis,* f.
Game, *lŭdus, i,* m.
Institute, *instituo, ĕre, ui, ūtum.*
Large, *magnus, a, um.*
Many, *multus, a, um.*

Neptune, *Neptūnus, i.*
No, *nullus, a, um.* (See F. B 113, R.)
Ostia, *Ostia, ae,* f.
Prison, *carcer, ĕris,* m.
Secure, *consĕquor, sĕqui, secūtus sum.*
Sewer, *cloāca, ae,* f.
This, *hic, haec, hoc.*
Wage, *gero, ĕre, gessi, gestum.*

216. EXERCISES.

I. *Translate and analyze.*

1. Regnum Lucius Tarquinius Priscus accēpit. 2. Saturnus primus Itălos docuit. 3. Aenēae filius regnum accēpit. 4. Silvius Procas filios relīquit. 5. Silvius Procas duos filios relīquit. 6. Rex Albanōrum duos filios relīquit. 7. Anci familiaritātem consecūtus est. 8. Regis familiaritātem consecūtus est. 9. Romŭlus centum senatōres legit.

II. 1. *Arrange the elements in the first of the above sentences in the usual order, and state the effect of placing* regnum *first.* (See 208, R.)

2. *Construct five or more Latin sentences containing modifiers, either in the subject or predicate, or in both.*

3. *Answer the following questions in Latin in the form of declarative sentences:*

1. Who founded Rome? 2. Who founded Alba Longa? 3. Who was the first to build a prison? 4. Who founded Ostia? 5. What king waged no war?

COMPLEX PREDICATE.—INDIRECT OBJECT.   99

6. What king waged many wars? 7. Who built the sewers? 8. Who commenced the Capitol?

MODEL.
Romŭlus Romam condĭdit.

III. *Translate into Latin.*

1. Who instituted the festival of Neptune? 2. Did not Romulus institute these games? 3. Romulus instituted the festival of Neptune. 4. He founded Rome. 5. Shall you found a large city? 6. We have founded a large city. 7. Who secured the friendship of Ancus? 8. Have you secured the friendship of the king? 9. Let us secure the friendship of the good king.

LESSON X.

Complex Predicate.—Indirect Object; Simple or Complex.
[18—20.]

217. The verb of the predicate may be modified by a noun denoting the person or thing *to* or *for which* any thing is, or is done. This modifier is called an *indirect object.*

218. RULE.—*Indirect Object.*
The indirect object is put in the dative, and is used,
   1) After *esse* in expressions denoting possession;
      e. g.,
   Puĕro est liber. | *The boy has a book.* (*Lit.* There is a book to the boy.)

   2) After the compounds of *esse*, except *posse*,
      e. g.,

Mihi profuit. | *It profited me.*

3) After the compounds of *bene, satis,* and *male*, e. g.,

Officio suo satisfēcit. | *He has discharged his duty. (Lit.* He has done enough for, &c.)

4) After the compounds of the prepositions *ad, ante, con, in, inter, ob, post, prae, sub,* and *super,* together with a few others; e. g.,

Veni ut mihi succurras. | *I have come that you may assist* (succor) *me.*

5) After verbs signifying *to command* or *obey, please* or *displease, favor* or *injure, serve* or *resist,* together with *to indulge, spare, pardon, envy, believe, persuade,* &c. ; e. g.,

Legĭbus paret. | *He obeys the laws* (is obedient to).

[F. B. 643 ; A. & S. § 223 and R. 2, and §§ 224, 225, 226 ; Z. §§ 406, 412, 415, 420.]

REM.—The indirect object is sometimes expressed by the accusative with a preposition, as *ad* or *in ;* e. g., Culpam in multitudĭnem contulērunt, *They charged the blame upon the multitude.*

219. VOCABULARY.

All, *omnis, e*
Believe, *credo, ĕre, dĭdi, dĭtum.*
Census, *censŭs, us,* m.
Country, native country, *patria, ae,* f.
Educate, *edŭco, āre, āvi, ātum.*
Kill, *interficio, ĕre, fēci, fectum.*
Law, *lex, legis,* f.

Obey, *obedio, īre, īvi, ītum.*
Order, institute, *ordĭno, āre, āvi, ātum.*
Priscus, *Priscus, i.*
Servius, *Servius, i.*
Succeed, *succēdo, ĕre, cessi, cessum.*
Tarquinius, *Tarquinius, i.*
Tullius, *Tullius, i.*

220. EXERCISES.

I. *Translate and analyze.*

1. Numae successit Tullus Hostilius. 2. Numa Pompilius civitāti profuit. 3. Tanăquil conjŭgi persuāsit. 4. Tarquinio Servius successĕrat. 5. Nemo tibi credet. 6. Priscus Tarquinius plura bella gessit. 7. Agros urbis territorio adjunxit. 8. Hic rex interfectus est. 9. Boni patriae legĭbus parēbunt.

II. *Construct six Latin sentences: three with direct, and three with indirect objects.*

III. *Translate into Latin.*

1. The citizens will obey the laws. 2. Will you not obey the laws? 3. Let us obey the laws of our country. 4. Who will obey him? 5. Who will believe him? 6. They will believe you. 7. Whom did Servius Tullius succeed? 8. Servius succeeded Tarquinius Priscus. 9. Tarquinius Priscus was killed. 10. Who killed him? 11. The sons of Ancus killed him. 12. Who educated Servius Tullius? 13. Who ordered a census of the Roman people? 14. Servius was the first to order a census of all the Roman citizens.

LESSON XI.

Complex Predicate.—Remote Object; Genitive.
[21 & 22.]

221. The verb of the predicate may be modified by a *genitive* appearing in the English translation as the object of an action, though in the Latin the distinction between the *direct object* and this genitive is clearly

marked. To indicate this distinction, we will call the latter a *remote* object; e. g.,

Miseremĭni sociōrum. | *Pity the allies.*

> REM.—The accusative as object denotes that on which the action is directly exerted, while the genitive denotes that *in regard to which* the action or feeling is exercised, and sometimes seems really to express its cause. This genitive might perhaps, therefore, be not improperly treated, in some instances at least, as an *adverbial attributive;* but, as we uniformly render it by the *object*, it seems to present a more simple classification of the facts of the language to regard it as a *remote object.*

222. RULE.—*Genitive of Remote Object.*

The genitive is used,

1) After verbs of pitying; e. g.,

Miserētur sociōrum. | *He pities the allies.*

2) After verbs of remembering and forgetting; e. g.,

Memĭni vivōrum. | *I remember the living.*

3) After *refert* and *intĕrest;* e. g.,

Interest omnium. | *It interests all,* or *It is the interest of all.*

[F. B. 642; A. & S. §§ 215, 216, 219; Z. §§ 439, 442, 449.]

> REM. 1.—Verbs of remembering and forgetting sometimes take the accusative; e. g., Memĭni Cinnam, *I remember Cinna.*
>
> REM. 2.—According to Key's Latin Grammar, verbs of memory take the accusative of the object actually remembered, or the genitive of that *about which* the memory is concerned.

223. VOCABULARY.

Add, *addo, dĕre, dĭdi, dĭtum.*
Ardea, *Ardea, ae,* f.
Besiege, *oppugno, āre, āvi, ātum.*
Collatinus, *Collatīnus, i.*

Friend, *amīcus, i,* m.
His, her, its, *suus, a, um,* referring to the subject.
Jupiter, *Jupĭter, Jovis.* (See A. & S. § 85.)

Lucretia, *Lucretia, ae.*
Other, *alius, a, ud.* (See F. B. 113, R.)
Our, *noster, tra, trum.*
Persuade, *persuadeo, ēre, suāsi, suāsum.*
Poor, *pauper, ĕris*, adj.

Pity, *misereor, ēri, miserĭtus* or *misertus sum.*
Remember, *reminiscor, ci.*
Remus, *Remus, i.*
Temple, *templum, i,* n.
Wife, *conjux, ŭgis.*

224. EXERCISES.

I. *Translate and analyze.*

1. Vivōrum memĭni. 2. Reminiscātur popŭli Rŏmāni. 3. Reminiscantur vetĕris incommŏdi popŭli Romāni. 4. Reminiscĕre vetĕris famae popŭli Romāni. 5. Tarquinius Superbus cognōmen meruit. 6. Templum Jovis aedificāvit. 7. Ardeam oppugnābat. 8. Oppugnābat urbem Latii. 9. Brutus popŭlo persuāsit. 10. Alii nonnulli popŭlo persuasērunt. 11. Miseremĭni sociōrum.

II. 1. *Construct two or more Latin sentences, limiting the verb predicate by a genitive.*

2. *Construct Latin sentences in answer to the following questions:*

1. What city did Romulus found? 2. What became of Remus? 3. How many senators did Romulus choose? 4. What did he call them? 5. What king added to these a hundred other senators? 6. Who built the temple of Jupiter?

III. *Translate into Latin.*

1. Pity the poor. 2. We pity the poor. 3. Does he not pity us? 4. I pity them. 5. They remember the king. 6. Let them remember their friends. 7. Let us remember our friends. 8. We will persuade

the king. 9. Did the king wage many wars? 10. Tarquin besieged Ardea. 11. The wife of Collatinus slew herself. 12. Lucretia slew herself. 13. Who was Lucretia? 14. She was the wife of Collatinus.

Lesson XII.

Complex Predicate.—Remote Object; Ablative.

[23 & 24.]

225. After a few verbs, the ablative is used as a remote object, though it could probably be easily explained, at least in most instances, as an *adverbial attributive;* e. g.,

| Lacte vescuntur. | *They live upon milk,* or *are nourished by means of milk.* |

REM.—The *ablative lacte* in this example may be explained as an *adverbial attributive* of *means.*

226. RULE.—*Ablative of Remote Object.*

The ablative is used,

1) After the deponent verbs *utor, fruor, fungor, potior, vescor,* and their compounds; e. g.,

| Lacte vescuntur. | *They live upon milk.* |

2) After verbs signifying *to abound* or *be destitute of;* e. g.,

| Nemo aliōrum ope carēre potest. | *No one can be (do) without the assistance of others.* |

[F. B. 644; A. & S. §§ 245, 25C, Rem. 1, (2); Z. §§ 460, 465.]

227. Vocabulary.

Aid, s., *auxilium, i*, n.
Aid, bear aid, *auxilium fero, ferre, tuli, latum.*
Appoint, *creo, āre, āvi, ātum.*
Book, *liber, bri,* m.
Brutus, *Brutus, i.*
Confer, *tribuo, ĕre, bui, būtum.*
Consul, *consul, ŭlis,* m.
Discharge, *fungor, gi, functus sum.*
Duty, *officium, i,* n.
Enjoy, *fruor, i, ĭtus* or *ctus sum.*

For a year, lasting a year, *annuus, a, um.*
Junius, *Junius, i.*
Life, *vita, ae,* f.
Make, *facio, ĕre, feci, factum;* be made, *fio, fĭĕri, factus sum.*
Matron, *matrōna, ae.*
Mourn, *lugeo, ēre, luxi, luctum.*
Power, *imperium, i,* n.
Publicola, *Publicŏla, ae,* m.
Two, *duo, ae, o.* (See F. B. 317.)
Use, *utor, i, usus sum.*
Valerius, *Valerius, i.*
Your, *vester, tra, trum.*

228. Exercises.

I. *Translate and analyze, parsing objects.*

1. Lacte vescuntur. 2. Barbări pellĭbus utuntur. 3. Utātur suis bonis. 4. Fruantur suis bonis. 5. Luce fruĭmur. 6. Officiis fungebātur. 7. Fuit consul Brutus. 8. Fuit consul acerrĭmus libertātis vindex. 9. Valerius Publicŏla consul factus est. 10. Commōvit bellum Tarquinius. 11. Consul occīsus est. 12. Tarquinii filius occīsus est. 13. Primus annus quinque consŭles habuit.

II. 1. *Change the moods of the verbs in the first five of the above sentences; the indicative to the subjunctive or imperative, and the subjunctive to the indicative or imperative; and then translate.*

MODEL.

Lacte vescantur. | *Let them live upon milk.*

2. *Construct two Latin sentences, limiting the predicate by an ablative.*

3. *Construct Latin sentences in answer to the following questions:*

1. How many consuls were appointed? 2. For how long a time was power conferred upon them? 3. What Roman king waged war against the Romans? 4. Who aided Tarquin?

MODEL.

Consŭles duo creāti sunt.

III. *Translate into Latin.*

1. He has discharged all his duties. 2. Let us discharge our duties. 3. Let them enjoy life. 4. Do you enjoy life? 5. He is using his book. 6. Let all use these books. 7. Will he use this book? 8. He will use your books. 9. Were not two consuls appointed? 10. Junius Brutus was consul. 11. Who was made consul? 12. Valerius Publicola was made consul. 13. Did not the Roman matrons mourn for the consul? 14. They did mourn for him.

LESSON XIII.

Complex Predicate.—Direct Object with Attributive Accusative.

[25—27.]

229. RULE.—*Direct Object with Attributive Accusative.*

Verbs of *making, choosing, electing, calling, showing,* and the like, are followed by two accusatives denoting the same person or thing; e. g.,

| Saturnus arcem Saturniam appellāvit. | *Saturn called the citadel Saturnia.* |

[A. & S. § 230; Z. § 394.]

REM.—One of these accusatives is the direct object: the other is not a modifier, but an essential part of the predicate, and may be called the *attributive* accusative: thus, *Saturniam* is an essential part of the predicate, for the assertion is not that Saturn *called* the citadel, but that he *called* it *Saturnia*. Sentences of this class should be analyzed according to the following

MODEL.

Saturnus arcem Saturniam appellāvit.
Saturn called the citadel Saturnia.

This is a *simple* sentence.

Saturnus is the subject, and *Saturniam appellāvit* is the predicate.

Saturniam appellāvit, the predicate, is modified by the *direct object, arcem*.

Arcem Saturniam appellāvit is the complex predicate.

REM.—The *attributive* accusative is sometimes a noun, and sometimes an adjective.

230. When verbs of this class assume the passive form, the direct object becomes the subject, and the *attributive* accusative becomes the nominative, and still continues a part of the predicate; e. g.,

| (*Act.*) Numam regem creavērunt. | *They appointed Numa king.* |
| (*Pass.*) Numa rex creātus est. | *Numa was appointed king.* |

231. VOCABULARY.

Bridge, *pons, pontis*, m.
Cocles, *Cocles, itis*.
Defend, *defendo, ĕre, di, sum*.
Horatius, *Horatius, i*.
Insolent, *insŏlens, tis*.
Not, *non*; with imper. or subj. *ne*; in questions, generally *nonne*.

Render, *reddo, ĕre, dĭdi, dĭtum*.
Scaevola, *Scaevŏla, ae*.
Secretary, *scriba, ae*, m.
Show (as to show one's self), *praesto, āre, stĭti*.
Soldier, *miles, itis*, c.
Yourself, *tu; tu ipse*.

232. EXERCISES.

I. *Translate and analyze.*

1. Saturnus arcem condĭdit. 2. Eam Saturniam appellāvit. 3. Aenēas urbem Lavinium appellāvit. 4. Ascanius urbem condĭdit. 5. Eam Albam Longam nuncupāvit. 6. Romŭlus centum senatōres legit. 7. Eos patres appellāvit. 8. Diuturnĭtas potestātis reges insolentes reddĭdit. 9. Reges insolentiōres reddĭti sunt.

II. 1. *Change the first six of the above sentences to the passive form, omitting the agent of the action.*

MODELS.

1. Arx condĭta est.
2. Ea Saturnia appellāta est.

2. *Change the sentences, thus reconstructed, to the interrogative form.*

MODEL.

Nonne arx condĭta est?

III. *Translate into Latin.*

1. We will call this soldier Horatius Cocles. 2. This soldier was called Horatius Cocles. 3. Did he not call the city Rome? 4. He called it Rome. 5. The city was called Rome. 6. Who defended the bridge? 7. Which bridge will you defend? 8. Whom did Scaevola kill? 9. Did he kill the king himself? 10. He killed the secretary of the king. 11. They elected him king. 12. He was elected king. 13. The people will elect them senators. 14. He has been elected senator. 15. Do not render the boy insolent. 16. Show yourself brave.

Lesson XIV.

Complex Predicate.—Combined Objects; two Accusatives.
[28—31.]

233. The objects already considered are not only used singly as modifiers of verbs, but are variously combined with each other. These combinations we will now notice in order.

234. A few verbs take two direct objects, the one of a person and the other of a thing.

235. RULE.—*Combined Objects; two Accusatives.*

Verbs of *asking, demanding, teaching,* and *concealing,* may take two accusatives, the one of a person and the other of a thing; e. g.,

| Caesar frumentum Aeduos flagitābat. | *Caesar demanded corn of the Aedui.* |

[F. B. 645; A. & S. § 231; Z. §§ 391, 393.]

236. When verbs, which in the active voice take two accusatives, become passive, the direct object of the person generally becomes the subject, and the accusative of the thing is retained.

237. RULE.—*Object after Passive Verbs.*

Verbs in the passive voice are followed by the same cases as in the active, except the direct object, which becomes the subject of the passive; e. g.,

| (*Act.*) Caesărem sententiam rogant. | *They ask Caesar his opinion.* |
| (*Pass.*) Caesar sententiam rogātur. | *Caesar is asked his opinion.* |

Rem.—This rule, it will be observed, applies to all verbs which take combined objects in any of their several forms.

[F. B. 658; A. & S. § 234; Z. § 382.]

238. VOCABULARY.

Army, *exercĭtus, us*, m.
Ask, *rogo, āre, āvi, ātum.*
Coriolanus, *Coriolānus, i.*
Leader, *dux, ducis,* c.
Letter, *litĕra, ae,* f. ; letters, learning, *litĕrae, ārum.*

Marcius, *Marcius, i.*
Opinion, *sententia, ae,* f.
Quintus, *Quintus, i.*
Virginia, *Virginia, ae.*
Virginius, *Virginius, i.*
Volscians, *Volsci, ōrum.*

239. EXERCISES.

I. *Translate and analyze.*

1. Hic Itălos agricultūram docuit. 2. Te sententiam rogābunt. 3. Balbum sententiam rogābant. 4. Te litĕras docuit. 5. Quintus Marcius Coriolānus dictus est. 6. Coriolānus dux exercĭtus factus est. 7. Decemvĭri creāti sunt. 8. Quis te litĕras docuit? 9. Quem litĕras docuisti? 10. Familia Fabiōrum sola hoc bellum suscēpit. 11. Fabius Maxĭmus Hannibălem debilitāvit.

II. 1. *Change the first four of the above sentences to the passive form.*

2. *Change the next three of the above sentences to the active form, using some of the pronouns as subjects.*

3. *Construct three Latin sentences with two direct objects.*

III. *Translate into Latin.*

1. Who taught the Italians? 2. Who taught the Italians agriculture? 3. Saturn taught them agriculture. 4. Will you teach them this? 5. I will teach you this. 6. We asked him his opinion. 7. He asked us our opinion. 8. We were asked our opinion. 9.

Who taught him letters? 10. The king's son taught him letters. 11. Who was called Coriolanus? 12. Was not Quintus Marcius called Coriolanus? 13. Whom did the Volscians elect leader of the army? 14. A Roman was made leader of the army. 15. Who slew Virginia? 16. Virginius killed his daughter.

Lesson XV.

Complex Predicate.—Combined Objects; Accusative and Dative.

[32 & 33.]

240: RULE.—*Combined Objects; Accusative and Dative.*

Any transitive verb may take the accusative of the *direct*, and the dative of the *indirect* object; e. g.,

| Balbus puĕro viam monstrat. | Balbus shows the way to the boy. |

[F. B. 648; A. & S. § 229 and R. 1; Z. § 405 (a).]

241. In the arrangement of objects, the *direct* seems to prefer the place after the *indirect*, but this order is often reversed; e. g.,

| Fratri optiōnem dedit. | He gave the choice to his brother. |

REM. 1.—For passive construction, see 237.

REM. 2.—For accusative and dative after verbs of *depriving*, see Lesson XVIII.

242. VOCABULARY.

Camillus, *Camillus, i.*
Conquer, *vinco, ĕre, vici, victum.*

Deliver, give up, *trado, ĕre, dĭdi, dĭtum.*
Enemy, *hostis, is,* c.

Falerii, *Falerii, ōrum.*
Gaul, a Gaul, *Gallus, i.*
Golden, *aureus, a, um.*
Mother, *mater, tris.*
My, *meus, a, um.*

Ring, *annŭlus, i,* m.
Take possession of, *occŭpo, āre, āvi, ātum.*
That, *ille, a, ud.*
Three, *tres, tria.*

243. EXERCISES.

I. *Translate and analyze, parsing objects.*

1. Camillus scelestum homĭnem puĕris tradĭdit. 2. Virgas iis dedit. 3. Falisci urbem Romānis* tradidērunt. 4. Tarquinius bellum intŭlit. 5. Amulius fratri optiōnem dedit. 6. Numitōri regnum restituērunt. 7. Camillus Volscōrum civitātem vicit. 8. Tres triumphos egit. 9. Furius Camillus urbem obsidēbat. 10. Camillus expulsus est.

II. 1. *Change the first five of the above sentences to the passive form, omitting the agent.*

2. *Construct two or more Latin sentences with both direct and indirect objects.*

3. *Change the sentences thus constructed to the passive form.*

III. *Translate into Latin.*

1. Will you give me a book? 2. We will give you three books. 3. Who gave you that book? 4. My brother gave it to me. 5. What did he give to his mother? 6. He gave her a gold ring. 7. What city was Camillus besieging? 8. Who was besieging Falerii? 9. Whom did Camillus deliver to the boys? 10. Who conquered the enemy? 11. Camillus conquered them. 12. Who had taken possession of the city? 13. The Gauls had taken possession of Rome.

Lesson XVI.

Complex Predicate.—Combined Objects; Accusative and two Datives.

[34—36.]

244. After a few verbs the *direct* object is found combined with *two indirect* objects.

> REM.—One of these indirect objects generally represents the *person to whom*, and the other the *thing* or *object for which* the action is performed.

245. RULE.—*Combined Objects; Accusative and two Datives.*

Transitive verbs of *giving*, *sending*, *imputing* (dare, mittĕre, vertĕre, &c.), sometimes take a *direct* object in the accusative, together with *two indirect* objects in the dative; e. g.,

| Regnum suum Romānis dono dedit. | He gave his kingdom to the Romans as a present (for a present). |

[F. B. 649; A. & S. § 227 and R. 1; Z. § 422.]

246. With the passive construction, the *direct* object, of course, becomes the subject, and the two indirect objects remain after the passive verb. (See Rule, 237.)

247. VOCABULARY.

Accept, *accipio, ĕre, cĕpi, ceptum.*
Balbus, *Balbus, i.*
Brave, *fortis, e.*
Certain, certain one, *quidam, quaedam, quoddam,* and subs. *quiddam.*
Challenge, s., *provocatio, ōnis,* f.
Challenge, v., *provŏco, āre, āvi, ātum.*
Crime, *crimen, ĭnis,* n.
Cursor, *Cursor, ōris.*
Descendants, posterity, *postĕri, ōrum,* m.

Dictator, *dictātor, ōris*, m.
Impute, *do, dare, dedi, datum; tribuo, ĕre, ui, ūtum.*
Manlius, *Manlius, i.*

Papirius, *Papirius, i.*
Present, s., *donum, i,* n.
Titus, *Titus, i.*
Torquati, *Torquāti, ōrum.*

248. EXERCISES.

I. *Translate and analyze, parsing objects.*

1. Romāni haec Camillo crimĭni dedērunt. 2. Hoc Camillo crimĭni datum est. 3. Decemvĭri civitāti leges scripsērunt. 4. Regnum suum Romānis dono dedit. 5. Librum mihi dono dedit. 6. Gallus quidam fortissĭmum Romanōrum provocāvit. 7. Gallus quidam eximia corporis magnitudĭne fortissĭmum Romanōrum provocāvit. 8. Postĕri ejus Torquāti appellāti sunt. 9. Gallus quidam provocāvit unum ex Romānis.

II. 1. *Change the third, fourth, fifth, and sixth of the above examples to the passive form.*

2. *Change the declarative sentences, thus formed, to interrogative or imperative sentences.*

III. *Translate into Latin.*

1. What will you give Balbus? 2. We will give him these books as a present. 3. They will impute this to us as a crime. 4. Did not the Romans impute this to Camillus as a crime? 5. A certain Gaul challenged the bravest of the Romans. 6. Who accepted this challenge? 7. Who were called Torquati? 8. The Romans called the descendants of T. Manlius, Torquati. 9. The Romans appointed Papirius Cursor dictator.

Lesson XVII.

Complex Predicate.—Combined Objects; Accusative and Genitive.

[37—39.]

249. Rule.—*Combined Objects; Accusative and Genitive.*

Verbs of *accusing, convicting, acquitting, warning,* and the like, take the accusative of the person, and the genitive of the crime, charge, &c.; e. g.,

| Caium proditiōnis accū- sant. | They accuse Caius of treachery. |

[F. B. 646; A. & S. §§ 217, 229; Z. § 446.]

Rem.—The genitive is perhaps best explained by making it depend upon the ablative *crimine* understood. See F. B. 214, note.

250. Rule.—*Combined Objects; Accusative and Genitive.*

The impersonal verbs of feeling, *miseret, poenitet, pudet, taedet,* and *piget,* take the accusative of the person and the genitive of the object which produces the feeling; e. g.,

| Taedet me vitae. | I am weary of life. (*Lit.* It wearies me of life.) |

[F. B. 647; A. & S. §§ 215, 229; Z. § 441.]

251. In the arrangement of objects, the *direct* generally precedes the *remote;* e. g.,

| Caium furti accūsant. | They accuse Caius of theft. |

252. Vocabulary.

Accuse, *accūso, āre, āvi, ātum.*
Advice, *consilium, i,* n.
Cavalry, *equĭtes, um;* sing., *eques, ĭtis,* m.
Condemn, *damno, āre, āvi, ātum.*
Fabius, *Fabius, i.*
Master, *magister, tri.*
Must, *expressed by periphrastic conjugation.* (See F. B. 425; A. & S. § 162, 15.)
Pontius, *Pontius, i.*
Put to death, kill, *occĭdo, ĕre, cĭdi, cīsum.*
Reject, *imprŏbo, āre, āvi, ātum.*
To death, *capĭtis;* to condemn to death, *capĭtis damnāre.*
Treachery, *proditio, ōnis,* f.

253. Exercises.

I. *Translate and analyze, explaining position and parsing objects.*

1. Caium proditiōnis accūsant. 2. Dictator Rulliānum capĭtis damnāvit. 3. Vos furti accusavērunt. 4. Magister equĭtum capĭtis damnātus est. 5. Caius proditiōnis accusātus est. 6. Proditiōnis accusāti estis. 7. Tui me misĕret. 8. Taedet me belli. 9. Pyrrhum auxilium poposcērunt. 10. Hi Epīri regem auxilium poposcērunt. 11. Tarentīnis bellum indictum est. 12. Nox proelio finem dedit.

II. 1. *In the first three of the above sentences, make the subject the direct object, and the direct object the subject; then put the sentences in the interrogative form, and translate.*

MODEL.

1. Caius illos proditiōnis accūsat.
2. Num Caius illos proditiōnis accūsat?
   Does Caius accuse them of treachery?

REM.—In number 1 of the Model, it will be observed, the *object Caium* is changed to the *subject Caius,* and the *subject illi* implied in the ending of the verb is changed to the *object illos.*

and, as the subject is now in the singular, the predicate *accūsant* becomes *accūsat*. In number 2, the same sentence is put in the interrogative form.

2. *Construct two Latin sentences, limiting the predicate by an accusative and a genitive.*

3. *Change the sentences, thus constructed, to the passive form, omitting the agent.*

MODEL.

(*Act.*) Caium proditiōnis accūsant.	*They accuse Caius of treachery.*
(*Pass.*) Caius proditiōnis accusātur.	*Caius is accused of treachery.*

III. *Translate into Latin.*

1. Who condemned Fabius to death? 2. Was he condemned to death? 3. He was condemned to death. 4. The dictator condemned the master of the cavalry to death. 5. Will he not accuse us of treachery? 6. We shall be accused of treachery. 7. I have been accused of treachery. 8. You have all been accused of treachery. 9. Were the Romans put to death? 10. Must they all be put to death? 11. Did Pontius reject his father's advice?

Lesson XVIII.

Complex Predicate.—Combined Objects; Accusative and Ablative.

[40—42.]

254. Rule.—*Combined Objects; Accusative and Ablative.*

Verbs signifying to *separate from, deprive of,* &c., take

the accusative of the direct object, and the ablative of that from which it is separated; e. g.,

Me luce privant. | *They deprive me of light.*

[F. B. 650; A. & S. § 229 and R. 1, and § 251; Z. § 460.]

Rem.—Sometimes, especially in poetry, verbs of *depriving*, &c. take the accusative and dative; e. g., Id mihi eripuisti atque abstulisti, *You have taken this from me and carried it away.*

255. VOCABULARY.

Ambassador, *legātus, i,* m.
Appear, *videor, ēri, visus sum.*
Cineas, *Cineas, ae.*
Decemvirs, *decemvīri, ōrum.*
Deprive, *privo, āre, āvi, ātum.*
Fabius, *Fabius, i.*
Fabricius, *Fabricius, i.*
Fourth, *quartus, a, um.*
Glory, *gloria, ae,* f.
Home, *domus, i* or *us,* f. (See A. & S. § 89.)
How, of what kind, *qualis, e.*

Kingdom, *regnum, i,* n.
No one, nobody, *nemo (ĭnis,* not in good use).
Part, *pars, tis,* f.
Promise, v., *promitto, ĕre, mīsi, missum.*
Pyrrhus, *Pyrrhus, i.*
Rullianus, *Rulliānus, i.*
Samnites, *Samnītes, ium.*
Send, *mitto, ĕre, misi, missum.*
Write, prepare, *scribo, ĕre, scripsi, scriptum.*

256. EXERCISES.

I. *Translate and analyze, parsing objects.*

1. Me luce privātis. 2. Num me luce privātis? 3. Puĕrum libro fraudavērunt. 4. Gloria mea privātus sum. 5. Puĕri libris fraudabantur. 6. Puĕri boni libris fraudāti erant. 7. Fabricium admirātus est. 8. Unum ex legātis admirātus est. 9. Pyrrhus vulnerātus erat. 10. Hostes caesi sunt. 11. Viginti millia hostium caesa sunt.

II. 1. *Change the first three of the above sentences to the passive form.*

COMPLEX PREDICATE.—COMBINED OBJECTS. 119

2. *Change the next three to the active form, supplying such subjects as you please.*

3. *Construct Latin sentences in answer to the following questions:*

1. Who prepared (*Decemviri*) (*wrote*) the laws for Rome? 2. Who was made dictator (*Papirius cursor*)? 3. Whom did this dictator (*Fabio Rulliano*) condemn to death? 4. Who conquered the Samnites?

III. *Translate into Latin.*

1. Who deprived you of your books? 2. I will give you this book. 3. Will you deprive yourself of it? 4. Will you deprive the Romans of their glory? 5. No one will deprive them of their glory. 6. Who will deprive us of our city? 7. They have been deprived of their homes. 8. What did Pyrrhus promise to Fabricius? 9. He promised him a fourth part of his kingdom. 10. Whom did Pyrrhus send as ambassador? 11. Cineas was sent as ambassador. 12. How does the city appear to you? 13. We have seen the country of kings.

Lesson XIX.

Complex Predicate.—Combined Objects ; two Datives.
[43 & 44.]

257. RULE.—*Combined Objects ; two Datives.*

Intransitive verbs signifying *to be, to come, to go,* and the like, often take two datives, one denoting the object *to which,* and the other the object *for which ;* e. g.,

Caesări auxilio venit.	*He has come to the assistance of Caesar.*

[F. B. 651 ; A. & S. § 227 ; Z. § 422.]

REM.—Verbs of this class cannot, of course, assume the passive form

258. VOCABULARY.

Carthaginian, *Carthaginiensis, e.*	Hamilcar, *Hamilcar, ăris.*
Elephant, *elephantus, i,* m.	Service, *usus, us,* m.
Great, *magnus, a, um.*	Xanthippus, *Xanthippus, i.*

259. EXERCISES.

I. *Translate and analyze, parsing objects.*

1. Una res erat usui. 2. Una res Romānis erat magno usui. 3. Hoc fuit mihi magno usui. 4. Haec fuērunt fratri magno usui. 5. Balbo auxilio venit. 6. Vobis auxilio venĭmus. 7. Romanōrum exercĭtus Hierōnem superavērunt. 8. Romanōrum exercĭtus regem Syracusārum superavērunt. 9. Duillius septem millia hostium cepit. 10. Carthaginienses pacem petiērunt.

II. 1. *Construct three or more Latin declarative sentences.*

2. *Change the sentences, thus constructed, to the interrogative form.*

III. *Translate into Latin.*

1. Pyrrhus conquered the Romans. 2. Pyrrhus used elephants. 3. The elephants were of great service to Pyrrhus. 4. Were not the elephants of great service to him? 5. Are not books of great service to us? 6. Who conquered Hamilcar? 7. Who conquered the leader of the Carthaginians? 8. The Romans conquered him. 9. Who conquered the Romans? 10. Who conquered the Roman army? 11. Xanthippus conquered the Roman army.

Lesson XX.

Complex Predicate.—Combined Objects; Dative and Ablative.
[45—47.]

260. RULE.—*Combined Objects; Dative and Ablative.*
Opus est and *usus est*, having the force of impersonal verbs signifying need, take the dative of the person, and the ablative of the object needed; e. g.,

Duce nobis opus est.	We need a leader. (*Lit.* There is to us the need of a leader.)

REM.—With *opus*, the thing needed is frequently made the subject, and then *opus est* is used personally; e. g., *Dux nobis opus est.*
[F. B. 652; A. & S. § 243; Z. § 464 and N. 2.]

261. VOCABULARY.

Aid, s., *auxilium, i*, n.
Ask for, seek, *peto, ĕre, īvi, ītum.*
Captive, *captīvus, a, um.*
Exchange, s., *permutatio, ōnis*, f.
Favor, v., *fuveo, ēre, favi, fautum.*

Fortune, *fortūna, ae*, f.
Grant, *tribuo, ĕre, bui, būtum.*
Need, v., *opus est, usus est.*
Obtain, *obtineo, ēre, tinui, tentum.*
Peace, *pax, pacis*, f.
Regulus, *Regŭlus, i.*

262. EXERCISES.

I. *Translate and analyze, parsing the objects.*

1. Legĭbus nobis opus est. 2. Urbe vobis opus est. 3. Libris nobis omnĭbus opus est. 4. Liber mihi opus est. 5. Usus exercĭtu fuit Romānis. 6. Fortūna Carthaginiensĭbus favit. 7. Regŭlus Romānis suasit. 8. Septuaginta tres Carthaginiensium naves captae sunt

9. Tredĕcim millia hostium occīsa sunt. 10. Carthaginiensĭbus pax tribūta est. 11. Poeni omnem Hispaniam Romānis permisērunt.

II. *Construct five Latin sentences with combined objects in any of the forms above specified.*

III. *Translate into Latin.*

1. We need you. 2. Do you need us? 3. Who needs this book? 4. My brother needs it. 5. We all need aid. 6. Does not your father need aid? 7. The Romans needed Regulus. 8. The Carthaginians needed him. 9. Let fortune favor us. 10. Did the Carthaginians obtain an exchange of captives? 11. Who asked for peace? 12. The Carthaginians asked for peace. 13. Did the Romans grant them peace? 14. The Romans did grant peace to them. 15. Peace was granted to them.

Lesson XXI.

Complex Predicate.—Adverbial Attribute; Adverbs.
[48—51.]

263. The verb of the predicate, as already stated (Lesson VIII.), may be limited or modified by attributives. These are,

    I. Adverbs.
    II. Adverbial Expressions.

264. Adverbs, as attributive modifiers of the predicate, may denote

    1) The *place* of the action or event; e. g.,

Ibi scribam regis interfēcit.	*There* he killed the secretary of the king

ADVERBIAL ATTRIBUTE.—ADVERBS.

2) Its *time;* e. g.,

Tum se tribūnus obtŭlit.	*Then the tribune presented himself.*

3) Its *manner, means,* &c.; e. g.,

Plura bella *felicĭter* gessit.	*He waged many wars successfully.*

4) Its *cause;* e. g.,

Quamobrem regem interfēcit.	*Wherefore he killed the king.*

265. There is also a class of adverbs which do not express the attribute of the predicate, but show the *manner* or *mode* of the assertion. These are accordingly called *modal* adverbs, and strictly modify the *copula* (see 199). They denote either *certainty* or *uncertainty*, and are either *affirmative* or *negative;* e. g.,

Non veniet.	*He will not come.*
Fortasse veniet.	*Perhaps he will come.*
Certe veniet.	*He will certainly come.*

> REM. 1.—Adverbs of *manner, means,* &c., are the most numerous and present far the greatest variety, including *quality, degree, quantity,* &c.
> REM. 2.—*Cause* is generally denoted by adverbial expressions; accordingly but few adverbs of this class occur.
> REM. 3.—*Nonne* is compounded of *ne* and the adverb *non*, and may in future be thus treated in analyzing.

266. RULE.—*Adverbs.*

Adverbs modify *verbs, adjectives,* and *other adverbs*, e. g.,

Haud difficĭlis.	*Not difficult.*
Miles fortĭter pugnat.	*The soldier fights bravely.*

[F. B. 629; A. & S. § 277; Z. § 262.]

267. The *attributive* modifiers of the predicate, whether in the form of adverbs or adverbial expressions, generally stand immediately before the verb, between that and the object, if an object is used; e. g.,

Bellum *feliciter* gessit. | *He waged war successfully.*

> **Rem. 1.**—Interrogative adverbs are placed at the beginning of the sentence or clause; e. g., Quamdiu furor tuus nos eludet ! *How long shall your recklessness elude us ?*
>
> **Rem. 2.**—Emphasis often causes the *adverbial attributive* (187, R. 2) to stand at or near the beginning or end. (See examples, 264.)

268. VOCABULARY.

Afterwards, *postea*.
Assistance, *auxilium, i,* n.
Auxiliaries, *auxilia,* pl. of *auxilium*.
Be made, *fio, fĭĕri, factus sum,* pass. of *facio*.
Captive, *captīvus, i,* m.
Ever, at any time, *unquam*.
Fight, *pugno, āre, āvi, ātum*.
How long? *quamdiu?*
Island, *insŭla, ae,* f.
Macedonia, *Macedonia, ae,* f.
Not, *non ;* with imperat. or subj. *ne*.

Never, *nunquam*.
Occupy, *occŭpo, āre, āvi, ātum*.
Promise, *polliceor, ēri, pollicĭtus sum*.
Ransom, *redĭmo, ĕre, redēmi, redemptum*.
Senate, *senātus, us,* m.
Sicily, *Sicilia, ae,* f.
Slave, *servus, i,* m.
Then, *tunc*.
When? *quando?*
Where? *ubi?*
Why? *cur?*

269. EXERCISES.

I. *Translate and analyze, parsing and explaining* adverbs.

1. Hoc nunquam factum est. 2. Hoc semper factum erat. 3. Hi cives non sunt necessarii. 4. Hos omnes ille postea interfēcit. 5. Interea frater Hannibălis vincĭtur. 6. Res prospĕre gesta est. 7. Multae Italiae

civitātes Romānis paruĕrant. 8. Interea Hasdrŭbal perdit triginta quinque millia homĭnum. 9. Philippus Hannibăli auxilia pollicētur. 10. Rex Macedoniae Hannibăli auxilia pollicētur.

II. 1. *Specify all the adverbs in your reading lesson, showing the force of each.*

2. *Put the first five of the above sentences in the interrogative form, omitting the adverbs and substituting in their stead interrogative adverbs of time or place.*

MODELS.
1. Quando hoc factum est?
2. Ubi hoc factum est?

3. *Ask three questions in Latin, using interrogative adverbs, and then give appropriate answers to them.*

MODELS.

1. *Quando* patrem tuum vidēbis?	*When will you see your father?*
2. Patrem meum *cras* vidēbo.	*I shall see my father to-morrow.*

III. *Translate into Latin.*

1. Were slaves ever made soldiers? 2. They have never been made soldiers. 3. We will not fight. 4. The Roman senate did not ransom the captives. 5. Why did they not ransom them? 6. Were not the captives put to death? 7. They were afterwards put to death. 8. Who promised aid to Hannibal? 9. The king of Macedonia promised him auxiliaries. 10. I shall not promise him assistance. 11. Why will you not promise him assistance? 12. Who occupied Sicily at that time (*then*)? 13. The Carthaginians occupied it.

Lesson XXII.

Complex Predicate.—Adverbial Expressions of Manner, Means, &c.

[52—56.]

270. The attribute of the verb-predicate may be expressed by the oblique cases of nouns or adjectives, with or without prepositions. These oblique cases, with or without prepositions, may be called adverbial expressions, and may be referred to the following classes, viz.:

1) Adverbial expressions of *manner, means,* &c.
2) Adverbial expressions of *time.*
3) Adverbial expressions of *place.*
4) Miscellaneous adverbial expressions.

271. Rule.—*Manner, Means, &c.*

The *manner* or *cause* of an action, and the *means* or *instrument* employed, are expressed by the ablative; e. g.,

Domĭnum gladio occīdit.	*He killed his master with a sword.*

> Rem.—*Manner* is often expressed by the ablative with *cum*, especially if accompanied by an adjective; as, Cum ingenti pompa, *With great pomp.*
>
> [F. B. 666; A. & S. § 247; Z. §§ 452, 455.]

272. Rule.—*Price, Degree of Estimation, &c.*

Price, degree of estimation, &c., when expressed by nouns, are usually put in the ablative, and, when expressed by adjectives, usually in the genitive; e. g.,

ADVERBIAL EXPRESSIONS OF MANNER. 127

Avārus patriam auro vendet.	*The avaricious man will sell his country for gold.*
Avārus pecuniam magni aestĭmat.	*The avaricious man values money highly.*

[F. B. 667; A. & S. §§ 214, 252; Z. §§ 444, 456.]

REM. 1.—The genitive of a few nouns, and the ablative of a few adjectives, occur in expressions of price and value.

REM. 2.—To adverbial expressions of means must be referred the ablative of the agent after passive verbs.

273. RULE.—*Agent of Passive Verbs.*

The agent of the action after passive verbs is put,

   1) In the ablative with *a* or *ab*; e. g.,

Puer a Caio docētur.	*The boy is taught by Caius.*

   2) Except after the second periphrastic conjugation which requires the agent in the dative; e. g.,

Mihi scribendum est.	*I must write.*

[F. B. 659; A. & S. §§ 248, 225, III; Z. § 451.]

REM. 1.—The dative of the agent after the second periphrastic conjugation may be explained as an *indirect* object; thus, *Mihi scribendum est,* I must write, means *there is writing* for me *to do*.

REM. 2.—The *accusative* with *per* is sometimes used as agent; e. g., Per Anci filios occīsus est, *He was put to death by the sons of Ancus.*

274. VOCABULARY.

Arms, *arma, orum,* n. pl.
By (with voluntary agent), *a, ab, abs;* in other cases, indicated by abl.
Carthage, *Carthāgo, ĭnis,* f.
Cornelius, *Cornelius, i,* m.
Force, *vis, vis,* f. (pl. *vires*).
Hannibal, *Hannĭbal, ălis,* m.
How, *qui, quomŏdo.*

In vain, *frustra.*
Italy, *Italia, ae,* f.
Let, indicated by *subj. of the following verb.* (See F. B. 230, 231.)
Liberate, *libĕro, āre, āvi, ātum.*
New (as in "New Carthage"), *Novus, a, um.*
Once, *semel.*

P., *P.* for *Publius.*
Scipio, *Scipio, ōnis,* m.
Take, *capio, ĕre, cepi, captum.*

Thus, *sic.*
Try, *tento, āre, āvi, ātum.*

275. EXERCISES.

I. *Translate and analyze, parsing and explaining* adverbial *expressions.*

1. Duo Scipiōnes ab Hasdrubăle interfecti erant. 2. Quondam Publius Cornelius Scipio patrem singulāri virtūte servāvit. 3. Caius amīci sui labōrem parvi aestĭmat. 4. Plurĭmae civitātes ab Hannibăle tenebantur. 5. Hasdrŭbal strenue pugnāvit. 6. Ibi Scipio pugnat. 7. Scipio ingenti gloria triumphāvit. 8. Scipio Africānus appellātus est. 9. Sic finem accēpit secundum Punĭcum bellum.

II. 1. *Limit the predicates in the first five of the above examples by attributives of* time *or* place; *interrogative or not, at the pleasure of the pupil.*

2. *Explain all the adverbs in your reading lesson; also all the adverbial expressions of* manner, means, *&c.*

3. *Construct two or more Latin sentences, limiting the predicate of each, by some attribute of* time *or* place, *and then add that of* manner, means, *&c.*

MODELS.

1. *Tum* domum emit.
2. Tum domum *auro* emit.

He then bought the house.
He then bought the house with gold.

III. *Translate into Latin.*

1. Who took New Carthage? 2. P. Cornelius Scipio took it. 3. How did he take it? 4. He took it by force of arms. 5. Was not he made consul? 6

When was he made consul? 7. By whom was he made consul? 8. He was made consul by the Roman people. 9. The Roman people made Scipio consul then. 10. Thus P. Scipio liberated Italy. 11. Peace will be tried in vain. 12. Let us now try peace. 13. We will try peace once.

Lesson XXIII.

Complex Predicate.—Adverbial Expressions of Time.
[57—59.]

276. RULE.—*Time.*

Time *when* is expressed by the ablative without a preposition; e. g.,

Hiĕme ursus dormit. | *The bear sleeps in winter.*
[F. B. 669, A. & S. § 253; Z. § 475.]

REM.—The accusative with a preposition is frequently used to denote time, when it is spoken of with reference to the time of another event; e. g., Post Aenĕae mortem Ascanius regnum accĕpit, *After the death of Aeneas, Ascanius received the royal power.*

277. RULE.—*Length of Time.*

Length of time is generally expressed by the accusative; e. g.,

Caius annum unum vixit. | *Caius lived one year.*
[F. B. 670; A. & S. § 236; Z. § 395.]

REM.—The ablative is sometimes used to denote length of time; e. g., Regnāvit annis sexaginta, *He reigned sixty years.*

278. VOCABULARY.

Against, *indicated by the dative.*
Antiochus, *Antiŏchus, i,* m.
Battle, *proelium, i,* n.; *pugna, ae,* f.

Day, *dies, ēi,* m. & f. *in sing.;* m. *in pl.*
Die, *morior, mori* or *morīri, mortuus sum.*
Fifteen, *quindĕcim.*

Fortieth, *quadragesǐmus, a, um.*
Forty, *quadraginta,* indecl.
Great, *magnus, a, um; ingens, tis.*
Greece, *Graecia, ae,* f.
Here, *hic.*
How, *quam;* how many, *quot* or *quam multi;* how old, *quot annos* with *natus;* as, *Quot annos natus est?*
Numa, *Numa, ae,* m.
Old, *natus, a, um;* two years old, *duo annos natus.*
Reign, *regnum, i,* n.; *imperium, i,* n.

Remain, *maneo, ēre, mansi, mansum; remaneo, ēre,* &c.
Rout, *fundo, ēre, fudi, fusum.*
See, *video, ēre, vidi, visum.*
Seven, *septem.*
Seventh, *septǐmus, a, um.*
State, *civǐtas, ātis,* f.
Ten, *decem.*
Third, *tertius, a, um.*
Thirtieth, *tricesǐmus, a, um.*
Three, *tres, tria.*
To-morrow, *cras; crastǐno die.*
Two hundred, *ducenti, ae, a.*
Year, *annus, i,* m.
Yesterday, *heri; hesterno die.*

279. EXERCISES.

I. *Translate and analyze, explaining adverbial attributives.*

1. Post hoc proelium pax facta est. 2. Secundo anno iterum Tarquinius bellum Romānis intǔlit. 3. Sexto decimo anno post reges exactos popǔlus seditiōnem fecit. 4. Tum rex Antiǒchus pacem petit. 5. P. Licinius victus est. 6. Publius Licinius gravi proelio victus est. 7. Eōdem fere tempǒre dux Romanōrum gravi proelio a rege victus est. 8. Ancus Marcius vicesǐmo quarto anno imperii morbo obiit.

II. 1. *Substitute adverbs for the adverbial expressions in the first three of the above sentences.*

MODEL.

Postea pax facta est.

2. *Construct Latin sentences containing the following adverbial modifiers:*

Unum annum, biennium, hesterno die.

ADVERBIAL EXPRESSIONS OF PLACE. 131

3. *What adverbs are equivalent to the following expressions?*
Hoc tempŏre, illo tempŏre, longum tempus, hesterno die, crastĭno die.

4. *Construct Latin sentences in answer to the following questions:*
1. When did Saturn found a citadel? 2. When did Numa die? 3. How long did Romulus reign? 4. How many years did the seven kings reign?

III. *Translate into Latin.*

1. When will you read this book? 2. I will read it to-morrow. 3. When did you see your father? 4. I saw him yesterday. 5. How long will you remain here? 6. We shall remain here ten days. 7. How old are you? 8. I am fifteen years old. 9. Do not wage war against the states of Greece. 10. We have never waged war against Greece. 11. Who was routed in a great battle? 12. Who was routed by Cornelius Scipio Asiatĭcus? 13. Was not Antiochus routed in a great battle by Cornelius Scipio Asiatĭcus? 14. He was routed by the consul.

LESSON XXIV.

Complex Predicate.—Adverbial Expressions of Place.
[60—62.]

280. RULE.—*Place* IN WHICH; *Towns.*

The name of a town where any thing is, or is done, if of the first or second declension and singular number, is put in the genitive, otherwise in the ablative; e. g.,

Caius Cortōnae vixit.	*Caius lived at Cortona.*
Caius Tibŭre vixit.	*Caius lived at Tibur.*

[F. B. 672; A. & S. § 221; Z. § 398.]

REM.—The town *near which* is expressed by the accusative with *ad* or *apud;* e. g., Ad Pydnam, *Near Pydna.*

281. RULE.—*Place* IN WHICH; *not Towns.*

The name of a place where any thing is, or is done, when not a town, is generally put in the ablative with a preposition; e. g.,

Ursus in antro dormit.	*The bear sleeps in a cave.*

[F. B. 673; A. & S. § 254, R. 3; Z. § 489.]

282. RULE.—*Place* TO or FROM WHICH.

After verbs of motion;

    1) The place *to which* the motion is directed, if a town or small island, is expressed by the accusative without a preposition, otherwise by the accusative with one; e. g.,

Romam venīre.	*To come to Rome.*
In Italiam venīre.	*To come into Italy.*

    2) The place *from which* the motion proceeds, if a town or small island, is expressed by the ablative without a preposition, otherwise by the ablative with one; e. g.,

Roma venīre.	*To come from Rome.*
Ab Italia venīre.	*To come from Italy.*

[F. B. 674; A. & S. §§ 237, 255; Z. §§ 398, 404, 489.]

283. RULE.—*Domus, Rus, &c.*

Domus and *rus,* together with the genitives *belli, humi,* and *militiae,* are used like names of towns; e. g.,

ADVERBIAL EXPRESSIONS OF PLACE. 133

Caius rure rediit.	*Caius returned from the country.*
Balbus et domi et militiae mecum fuit.	*Balbus was with me both at home and on service.*

[F. B. 675; A. & S. § 221, R. 3, § 237, R. 4, and § 255, R. 1; Z. § 400.]

284. VOCABULARY.

Africa, *Afrĭca, ae,* f.
At, *before names of towns,* indicated by *gen.* or *abl.* (See 280.)
At home, *domi,* gen. of *domus.*
Athens, *Athēnae, ārum,* pl. f.
Boston, *Bostonia, ae,* f.
Hither, *huc.*
Home, *domus, us* or *i,* f.
In, *in* (with abl.).
Into, *in* (with acc.).

Providence, *Providentia, ae,* f.
Reside, *habĭto, āre, āvi, ātum.*
Rome, *Roma, ae,* f.
Serve in war, *milĭto, āre, āvi, ātum.*
There, *ibi.*
Thither, *illuc.*
To, *ad* (with acc.); *before names of towns,* indicated by *accus.*
Whither? *quo, quonam?*

285. EXERCISES.

I. *Translate and analyze, explaining adverbial attributives.*

1. Paullus Romam rediit. 2. Paullus cum ingenti pompa Romam rediit. 3. Paullus cum ingenti pompa Romam rediit in nave Persei. 4. Consŭles in Afrĭcam trajecērunt. 5. Multa ibi praeclāre gesta sunt per illustrem Scipiōnis Africāni nepōtem. 6. Ingens ibi praeda facta est. 7. Biennium Carthagĭne manēbunt 8. Misērunt legātos Carthagĭnem. 9. Caius rus ex urbe rediit. 10. Intĕrim in Macedonia quidam Pseudophilippus arma movit. 11. Intĕrim in Macedonia quidam Pseudophilippus Juvencium gravi proelio vicit.

II. 1. *In the above sentences, for the adverbial expressions of place, substitute adverbs meaning* here *or* there *after verbs of rest, and adverbs meaning* hither *or* thither *after verbs of motion.*

MODEL.

Paullus illuc rediit. | *Paullus returned thither* (to that place).

2. *In the fifth and six sentences, instead of* ibi *put the place denoted by it; also mark the form of the agent in the fifth* (per ... nepōtem), *and give the common construction.*

III. *Translate into Latin.*

1. Where did Scipio serve in war? 2. He served in Africa. 3. Whither are you going? 4. I am going home. 5. Are you going to Italy? 6. I shall go to Rome. 7. We shall go to Athens. 8. Where is your father? 9. He is at home—in the city—in Providence—in Boston. 10. Whom did the Romans appoint consul? 11. They appointed Scipio consul. 12. Scipio was appointed consul. 13. They sent Cornelius Scipio into Africa. 14. The consul was sent to Carthage. 15. He resides at Rome—at Athens—at Carthage.

Lesson XXV.

Complex Predicate.—Oblique Cases with Prepositions as Adverbial Expressions.

[63—65.]

286. Oblique cases with prepositions express a great variety of adverbial relations, as *time, place, manner, cause,* &c.

287. Rule.—*Prepositions with Accusative.*

The following twenty-six prepositions govern the accusative; viz., Ad, adversus, ante, apud, circa *or* circum, cis *or* citra, contra, erga, extra, infra, inter, intra, juxta, ob, penes, per, pone, post, praeter, prope, propter, secundum, supra, trans, ultra, versus (*rare*); e. g.,

Ad fugam.	*To flight.*
Intra muros.	*Within the walls.*

[F. B. 679; A. & S. § 235; Z. § 404.]

288. Rule.—*Prepositions with Ablative.*

The following eleven prepositions govern the ablative; viz., A (ab *or* abs), absque, coram, cum, de, e *or* ex, palam, prae, pro, sine, tenus; e. g.,

Ex urbe.	*From the city.*
Sine dubio.	*Without doubt.*

[F. B. 680; A. & S. § 241; Z. § 489.]

289. Rule.—*Prepositions with Accusative or Ablative.*

The five prepositions, *clam, in, sub, subter,* and *super*, take sometimes the accusative and sometimes the ablative; e. g.,

In exsilium.	*Into exile.*
In templo.	*In the temple.*

Rem. 1.—*In* and *sub* govern the accusative in answer to *whither* (i. e. after verbs of motion), and the ablative in answer to *where* (i. e. after verbs of rest). *Subter* generally takes the accusative. *Super* takes the accusative after verbs of motion, and also when it signifies upon, and the ablative when it signifies *on* or *of* (as of a subject spoken or written about).

Rem. 2.—Prepositions in composition often govern the same case as when they stand alone.

[F. B. 681 and R. 1 & 2; A. & S. § 235, 2, 3, & 4; Z. §§ 320, 404, 489.

290. VOCABULARY.

Ask, seek, *peto, ěre, petīvi* or *petii, petītum.*
Country (as opposed to city), *rus, ruris,* n.
Finally, *postrēmo, denĭque.*
From, *a, ab, de, e* or *ex,* &c.; *before names of towns,* indicated by the *abl.*
Go, *eo, īre, īvi, ĭtum;* go away or from, *abeo, abīre, abii, abĭtum.*
Jugurtha, *Jugurtha, ae,* m.

Metellus, *Metellus, i,* m.
Murderer, *interfector, ōris,* m.
My, *meus, a, um* (masc. voc. sing. *mi*).
Order, command, *jussu* (used only in abl. sing.).
Through, *per.*
Walk, v., *ambŭlo, āre, āvi, ātum.*
Whole, *totus, a, um* (gen. totīus, see F. B. 113, R).
Winter, *hiems, hiěmis,* f.
Viriathus, *Viriāthus, i,* m.

291. EXERCISES.

I. *Translate and analyze, parsing and explaining all attributive expressions.*

1. Viriāthus in Lusitania bellum excitāvit. 2. Viriāthus in Lusitania bellum contra Romānos excitāvit. 3. Post urbem condĭtam Viriāthus bellum excitāvit. 4. Anno sexcentesĭmo decĭmo post urbem condĭtam Viriāthus in Lusitania bellum contra Romānos excitāvit. 5. Tum P. Scipio Africānus in Hispaniam missus est. 6. Ante currum triumphantis Marii Jugurtha cum duōbus filiis ductus est.

II. 1. *Change the first four of the above sentences to the passive form, and the last two to the active.*

2. *Construct Latin declarative sentences, using the following adverbial expressions:*

In urbe, in horto, in agris, sub hoc rege, in monte Albāno, ultra ripam.

3. *Change the sentences, thus constructed, to the interrogative or imperative form.*

III. *Translate into Latin.*

1. Let us walk through the city. 2. They have gone from the city into the country. 3. My father will remain in the city the whole winter. 4. Who killed Viriathus? 5. The soldiers killed him. 6. The murderers of Viriathus asked a reward from the Roman consul. 7. By whom was Jugurtha conquered? 8. He was finally conquered in many battles by Q. Caecilius Metellus. 9. He was put to death by the order of Marius.

Lesson XXVI.

Complex Substantive-Predicate.—Modifier; Objective or Attributive.

[66—68.]

292. The substantive-predicate may be limited in the various ways already specified for the subject and for nouns generally (see Lessons V. and IX.); e. g.,

Aenēas fuit Anchīsae filius.	*Aeneas was the son of Anchises.*
Numa fuit bonus rex.	*Numa was a good king.*

293. The copula (*esse* or some passive verb) which belongs to the predicate, may also be modified by a modal adverb (see Lesson XXI.); e. g.,

Tarquinius non fuit bonus rex.	*Tarquin was not a good king.*

Rem.—Here the modal adverb *non* limits *fuit*.

294. Vocabulary.

Acca, *Acca, ae,* f.
Asia, *Asia, ae,* f.
Faustulus, *Faustŭlus, i,* m.
Hasdrubal, *Hasdrŭbal, ălis,* m.
Invade, *invādo, ĕre, invāsi, invāsum.*

Kind, *benīgnus, a, um.*
Laurentia, *Laurentia, ae,* f.
Man, *homo, homĭnis; vir, viri,* m.
Mithridates, *Mithridātes, is,* m.
Pontus, *Pontus, i,* m.

295. Exercises.

I. *Translate and analyze, parsing predicates.*

1. Silvius Procas fuit rex. 2. Silvius Procas fuit rex Albanōrum. 3. Hannĭbal fuit dux. 4. Hannĭbal fuit Carthaginiensium dux. 5. Latīnus fuit bonus rex. 6. Picentes popŭlo Romāno obediĕrant. 7. Picentes multos annos popŭlo Romāno obediĕrant. 8. Sulla adhuc cum legionĭbus suis in Italia morabātur. 9. Sulla cum exercĭtu Romam venit. 10. Tum in Asiam profectus est. 11. Sulla in Asia Mithridātem vicit. 12. Universus relĭquus senātus in Graeciam venit.

II. 1. *Construct two or more Latin sentences with substantive-predicates.*

MODEL.
Carthāgo fuit urbs.

2. *Add an attribute to each of these predicates.*

MODEL.
Carthāgo fuit magna urbs.

3. *Construct Latin sentences in answer to the following questions:*

1. Whose son was Aeneas? 2. Whose son was Ascanius? 3. Who was the father of Hannibal? 4. Who was the wife of Faustulus?

III. *Translate into Latin.*

1. Who was king of Pontus? 2. Was not Mithridates king of Pontus? 3. He was king of Pontus. 4. Hannibal was the brother of Hasdrubal. 5. Is this boy your brother? 6. He is not my brother. 7. Aeneas was the father of Ascanius. 8. Your father is a good man. 9. Balbus is a kind father. 10. Mithridates asked peace of (*from*) the Romans. 11. Who invaded Asia? 12. Mithridates invaded it.

Lesson XXVII.

Complex Adjective-Predicate.—Modifier ; Objective or Attributive.

[69 & 70.]

296. The adjective-predicate may be limited,

I. By Objective Modifiers.
II. By Attributive Modifiers.

297. The objective or completing modifier of the adjective-predicate may be expressed,

1) By the Genitive.
2) By the Dative.

298. Rule.—*Genitive after Adjectives.*

Many adjectives signifying *desire, knowledge, skill, participation, recollection, fulness,* and the like, together with their *contraries,* take the genitive ; e. g.,

Cupĭdus laudis est. | *He is desirous of praise.*

299. Rule.—*Dative after Adjectives.*

Many adjectives are followed by the dative of the

object to which the quality is directed, or for which it exists; e. g.,

Pax mihi gratissĭma erat. | Peace was very acceptable to me.

[F. B. 631, 632; A. & S. §§ 213, 222; Z. §§ 409, 436.]

300. The attributive or limiting modifier of the adjective-predicate may be expressed,
    1) By the Adverb.
    2) By the Ablative Case.

☞ For the use of adverbs, see Rule, 266.

301. RULE.—*Ablative after Adjectives.*
The ablative is used,
    1) After the adjectives *dignus, indignus, contentus, praedĭtus, fretus,* and *liber;* e. g.,

Virtus parvo contenta est. | *Virtue is content with little.*

    2) After any adjective, to denote *cause, manner,* or *means;* e. g.,

Aeger avaritiā fuit. | *He was diseased by avarice.*

[F. B. 633, 634; A. & S. §§ 244, 247; Z. §§ 452, 467.]

302. Adjectives in any situation, whether as predicate or attribute, are modified according to the above Rules.

REM.—In a few instances it will be found difficult to distinguish the object from the attribute; in most cases, however, the distinction is sufficiently obvious.

303. The modifiers of the adjective generally precede it, though the *objective* modifier not unfrequently follows it; e. g.,

Haud difficĭlis. | *Not difficult.*
Cupĭdus laudis. | *Desirous of praise.*

COMPLEX ADJECTIVE-PREDICATE.   141

Rem. 1.—The *attributive* modifier sometimes follows.
Rem. 2.—For the effect of emphasis on position, see 208, R.

304. VOCABULARY.

Already, *jam*.
Apulia, *Apulia, ae*, f.
Capua, *Capua, ae*, f.
Crassus, *Crassus, i*, m.
Desirous, *cupĭdus, a, um; avĭdus, a, um*.
Destroy, *diruo, ĕre, dirui, dirŭtum*.
Escape, *effugio, ĕre, effūgi, effugĭtum*.
Gladiator, *gladiātor, ōris*, m.
Gladiatorial, *gladiatorius, a, um*.

L., *L.* for *Lucius*.
M., *M.* for *Marcus*.
Much, *multus, a, um*, or *multum with gen*.
Praise, s., *laus, laudis*, f.
Proconsul, *proconsul, ŭlis*, m.
School, *ludus, i*, m.
Sufficiently, *satis*.
Unworthy, *indignus, a, um*.
Useful, *utĭlis, e*.
Wealthy, *dives, ĭtis*.
Worthy, *dignus, a, um*.

305. EXERCISES.

I. *Translate and analyze.*

1. Balbus est dives. 2. Balbus est satis dives. 3. Haec loca sunt frumentaria. 4. Haec loca sunt maxĭme frumentaria. 5. Virtus parvo contenta est. 6. Servus laude dignus est. 7. Puĕri laudis cupĭdi sunt. 8. Pax nobis gratissĭma est. 9. Nicomēdes testamento popŭlum Romānum fecit herēdem. 10. Adversus Mithridātem ambo consŭles missi sunt. 11. Anno urbis sexcentesĭmo septuagesĭmo octāvo novum in Italia bellum commōtum est.

II. 1. *Change the first five of the above sentences to the interrogative form.*

2. *Construct two or more Latin sentences with* adjective-predicates.

3. *Add attributives to these predicates.*

4. *Construct Latin sentences in answer to the following questions:*

1. How many wars did the Romans wage against Carthage? 2. Was Carthage destroyed? 3. If so, by whom? 4. Who waged war against Jugurtha? 5. By whom was he conquered?

III. *Translate into Latin.*

1. Are you already sufficiently wealthy? 2. We are not sufficiently wealthy. 3. Is he worthy of praise? 4. He is unworthy of much praise. 5. Many are desirous of praise. 6. These books will be useful to you. 7. Where was this gladiatorial school? 8. The school was at Capua. 9. How many gladiators escaped from it? 10. Who conquered them? 11. Where did he conquer them? 12. The proconsul conquered them in Apulia. 13. Who was this proconsul? 14. M. L. Crassus was proconsul.

Lesson XXVIII.

Complex Adjective-Predicate.—Modifier; Complex.

[71 & 72.]

306. The modifiers of the predicate, whether objective or attributive, may be themselves modified, and may thus become complex; e. g.,

Servus multa laude dignus est.	*The slave is worthy of much praise.*

REM. 1.—Here *laude*, which limits *dignus*, is itself limited by *multa*. *Multa laude* is, therefore, the *complex* modifier.

REM. 2.—We have seen (300) that the attribute may be either an *adverb* or a *noun*. When an *adverb*, it may be limited by ano-

COMPLEX ADJECTIVE-PREDICATE.

ther adverb; when a *noun*, by an *adjective or by an attributive noun*.

307. VOCABULARY.

Armenia, *Armenia, ae,* f.
Beautiful, *pulcher, chra, chrum.*
Cneus, *Cneus, i,* m.
Content, *contentus, a, um.*
End, *finis, is,* m. & f.
Honor, *honor, ōris,* m.
Lucullus, *Lucullus, i,* m.
Minor (as "Armenia Minor"), *Minor, ōris.*

Parent, *parens, entis,* m. & f.
Pompey, *Pompeius, i,* m.
Put to, *impōno, ĕre, imposui, impositum;* to put an end to, *finem imponĕre.*
That, *ille, a, ud.*
Their, *suus, a, um* (referring to subject of prop.). [*or orum.*
Tigranocerta, *Tigranocerta, ae,*

308. EXERCISES.

I. *Translate and analyze.*

1. Puer his libris indignus est. 2. Balbus domo sua contentus est. 3. Libri nobis omnĭbus utĭles sunt. 4. Caius magno ingenio praedĭtus est. 5. Intĕrim L. Lucullus bellum Mithridatĭcum persecūtus est. 6. Lucullus ipsum regem apud illam civitātem fugāvit. 7. Per illa tempŏra piratae omnia maria infestābant. 8. Hunc vitae finem habuit Mithridātes. 9. Contra Romānos bellum habuit annis quadraginta.

II. 1. *Change all the complex attributives in the above sentences to simple ones.*

MODEL.

Puer libris indignus est.

2. *In the first four sentences, substitute other complex attributives for those now used.*

MODEL.

| Puer patre suo indignus est. | The boy is unworthy of his father. |

3. Construct two or more Latin sentences, limiting the subjects by simple, *and the predicates by* complex *modifiers.*

MODEL.

Boni pueri parentĭbus suis benigni sunt.	*Good boys are kind to their parents.*

III. *Translate into Latin.*

1. They are not kind to their parents. 2. Are not these boys unworthy of their parents? 3. They are unworthy of them. 4. Let them be content with those beautiful books. 5. Let us be worthy of these honors. 6. What city of Armenia was taken by Lucullus? 7. Tigranocerta was taken by him. 8. Did Lucullus put an end to the war? 9. He did not put an end to the Mithridatic war. 10. By whom was Mithridates conquered? 11. He was conquered by Cneus Pompey. 12. Where was this battle? 13. This battle was fought in Armenia Minor.

Lesson XXIX.

Elements of Sentences; Recapitulation.
[73—75.]

309. We have seen that the elements of the simple sentence are,

    I. *Principal Elements;* viz.,
        1) Subject.
        2) Predicate.
    II. *Subordinate Elements;* viz.,
        1) Objective Modifiers.
        2) Attributive Modifiers.

310. We have also seen that these elements may stand either without limiting words, in which case they are called *simple*, or with them, in which case they are called *complex*.

311. All subordinate elements stand as the modifiers of *substantives* (including pronouns), *adjectives, verbs,* and *adverbs*.

I. Modifiers of Substantives.

312. The *objective* modifiers of substantives must be expressed either by substantives or by adjectives used substantively; e. g.,

Amor gloriae.	*The love of glory.*

313. The *attributive* modifiers of substantives may be expressed (1) by adjectives and (2) by substantives; e. g.,

Lingua Latīna.	*The Latin language.*
Ferrum Graecōrum.	*The sword of the Greeks.*

II. Modifiers of Adjectives.

314. The *objective* modifiers of adjectives must be expressed by substantives or by adjectives used substantively; e. g.,

Cupĭdus laudis.	*Desirous of praise.*

315. The *attributive* modifiers of adjectives may be expressed (1) by adverbs and (2) by substantives; e. g.,

Haud difficĭlis.	*Not difficult.*
Aeger avaritiā.	*Diseased by avarice.*

III. Modifiers of Verbs.

316. The *objective* modifiers of verbs must be expressed by substantives or by adjectives used substantively,

and are of three kinds; viz., (1) *direct* objects, (2) *indirect* objects, and (3) *remote* objects; e. g.,

Caius puellam laudat.	*Caius praises the girl.*
Legĭbus paret.	*He obeys the laws.*
Memĭni vivōrum.	*I remember the living.*

317. The *attributive* modifiers of verbs may be expressed (1) by adverbs and (2) by adverbial expressions consisting of oblique cases either with or without prepositions; e. g.,

Miles fortĭter pugnat.	*The soldier fights bravely.*
Hiĕme ursus dormit.	*The bear sleeps in winter.*

IV. Modifiers of Adverbs.

318. The *objective* modifiers of adverbs, like those of other words, must be expressed by substantives or by adjectives used substantively; e. g.,

Congruenter natūrae.	*Agreeably to nature.*

319. The *attributive* modifiers of adverbs are generally expressed by other adverbs; e. g.,

Satis bene scripsit.	*He has written sufficiently well.*

320. Prepositions and conjunctions are properly connectives, and neither modify nor are modified, though they are used (the former *always* and the latter *often*) as elements in objective or attributive expressions.

321. Interjections are expressions of emotion, or mere marks of address, and have no grammatical influence upon the rest of the sentence.

322. The name of the person to whom a sentence is addressed is often introduced into it, but forms no part of the sentence itself.

323. Rule.—*Vocative.*

The name of the person or thing addressed is put in the vocative; e. g.,

Quid est, Catilīna? | *Why is this, Catiline?*

[F. B. 617; A. & S. § 240; Z. § 492.]

ORDER OF ELEMENTS IN THE LATIN SENTENCE.

324. The Latin admits of great variety in the arrangement of the different parts of the sentence, thus affording peculiar facilities both for securing proper emphasis and for imparting to its periods that harmonious flow which characterizes the Latin classics. There are, however, certain general principles, by which we may be guided in determining the best position for the various elements in any sentence, whether with or without emphasis.

I. Position of Principal Elements.

325. The subject generally occupies the first place in the sentence, and the predicate the last; e. g.,

Tarquinius Superbus cognōmen morĭbus meruit. | *Tarquin the Proud merited his surname by his character.*

326. The subject may be rendered *emphatic* by being placed at or near the end, and the predicate by being placed at or near the beginning; e. g.,

Commōvit bellum rex Tarquinius. | *King Tarquin excited a war.*

Rem.—If the predicate consists of a copula and a noun, adjective or participle, the copula sometimes precedes and sometimes follows the attribute.

II. Position of Subordinate Elements.

327. All subordinate elements appear as the modifiers of *substantives, adjectives, verbs,* or *adverbs,* and, in regard to position, may be treated in four divisions.

1. *Position of the Modifiers of Substantives.*

328. The adjective precedes or follows its substantive according as it *is* or *is not* emphatic; e. g.,

Primus annus *quinque* consŭles habuit.	*The first year had five consuls.*

329. The *attributive* genitive usually precedes its substantive when the latter is not emphatic, and the *objective* genitive follows; e. g.,

Aenēae filius regnum accēpit.	*The son of Aeneas received the kingdom.*
Amor gloriae nos impŭlit.	*The love of glory actuated us.*

330. When a substantive is limited by both an adjective and an attributive genitive, the order is *adjective—genitive—substantive;* e. g.,

Auream regis corōnam vidit.	*He saw the king's golden crown.*

2. *Position of the Modifiers of Adjectives.*

331. The modifiers of the adjective generally precede it, though the objective modifier not unfrequently follows it; e. g.,

Satis dives.	*Sufficiently wealthy.*
Avĭdus laudis.	*Desirous of praise.*

3. *Position of the Modifiers of Verbs.*

I. Objects.

332. The object generally precedes the verb; e. g.,

Caius filiam laudat.	*Caius is praising his daughter.*

333. When two or more objects are used with the verb, the *direct* object seems to prefer the place after the *indirect*, but before the *remote;* e. g.,

Fratri optiōnem dedit.	*He gave the choice to his brother.*
Caium furti accūsant.	*They accuse Caius of theft.*

II. Adverbial Attributives.

334. The adverbial attributive generally stands between the object and verb; e. g.,

Tarquinius Superbus cognōmen morĭbus meruit.	*Tarquin the Proud merited his surname by his character.*

REM. 1.—The adverbial attribute, particularly that of *time* and *place*, not unfrequently stands at the beginning of the sentence; e. g., Hinc Aenĕas aufŭgit, *Aeneas fled from this place.*

REM. 2.—When the adverbial attribute is expressed by a preposition and an oblique case, the preposition (except *tenus* and *versus*) precedes the substantive, and if the latter has an attribute, the preposition often stands between the attribute and substantive; e. g., Hanc ob causam nonnulli in exitium regis conjurārunt, *For this reason some conspired for the destruction of the king.*

4. *Position of the Modifiers of Adverbs.*

335. The *attributive* modifier generally precedes the adverb, and the *objective* sometimes precedes and sometimes follows it; e. g.,

Satis bene.	*Sufficiently well.*
Congruenter natūrae.	*Agreeably to nature.*

REM.—Words are generally rendered emphatic by being placed in an *unusual* position, especially if that position is near the beginning or end of the sentence or clause.

336. VOCABULARY.

Catiline, *Catilīna, ae,* m.
Capital, *caput, capĭtis,* n.
Character, *ingenium, i,* n.
Depraved, *pravus, a, um.*
Family, *genus, genĕris,* n.
German, *Germānus, a, um;* the Germans, *Germāni, ōrum,* m. pl.
Himself *or* him (oblique case referring to subject), *sui, sibi,* &c.
Jerusalem, *Hierosolўma, ōrum,* n. pl., and *Hierosolўma, ae,* f.

John, *Johannes, is,* m.
Judea, *Judaea, ae,* f.
Noble, *nobĭlis, e.*
Surrender, *dedo, ĕre, dedĭdi, dedĭtum.*
Tigranes, *Tigrānes, is,* m.
Very, *indicated by superl. of adj.*
With, *cum;* with pers. pron. and generally with relatives, it is appended to its case, as *mecum, tecum, secum,* &c.

337. EXERCISES.

I. *Translate and analyze.*

1. Tigrāni deinde Pompeius bellum intŭlit. 2. Ille diadēma suum in ejus manĭbus collocāvit. 3. Parte regni eum multāvit. 4. Armeniam Minōrem Galatiae regi donāvit. 5. Hierosolўmam tertio mense cepit. 6. His gestis finem antiquissĭmo bello imposuit. 7. Ab Antonio Catilīna ipse proelio victus est.

II. 1. *Change the first five of the above sentences to the passive form, and make the rest interrogative.*

MODEL.

Tigrāni deinde a Pompeio bellum illātum est.

2. *Construct two or more Latin sentences illustrative of complex elements.*

III. *Translate into Latin.*

1. Who surrendered himself to Pompey? 2. John, to whom did Tigranes surrender? 3. He surrendered to Pompey. 4. Father, will you go to Judea with

me? 5. I will go with you to the capital of Judea. 6. What city is the capital of Judea? 7. Jerusalem is the capital of Judea. 8. Catiline was a man of a noble family. 9. Was not Catiline a man of a very depraved character? 10. Caesar waged war against the Germans. 11. The Germans were conquered by Caesar in many battles.

CHAPTER II.

COMPLEX SENTENCES.

§ 1.—*Complex Sentences; Unabridged.*

LESSON XXX.

Sentence as Subject.
[76—78.]

338. ENTIRE sentences are often used as elements in the formation of other sentences.

339. Sentences thus formed are called *complex*. (See 164.)

340. A sentence thus used as an *element* may be introduced,

    1) Without any changes of form or structure, as in *direct* quotation; e. g.,

(Simple Sentence.)
Caius est beātus. | *Caius is happy.*

(Complex—Direct Quotation.)
Dicunt, " *Caius est beātus.*" | *They say,* "Caius is happy."

    2) With certain changes to adapt it to the subordinate rank which it is to occupy in its new position, as in *indirect* quotation; e. g.,

Dicunt Caium esse beātum. | *They say* that Caius is happy.

SENTENCE AS SUBJECT. 153

REM.—It will be observed that the subordinate sentence in the above example, in the Latin, takes its subject and its predicate-adjective in the accusative, and its copula in the infinitive, but in the English assumes the connective *that*, and remains in other respects unchanged. Sometimes in Latin also the rank of the subordinate sentence is indicated by merely assuming a connective, and sometimes by both assuming a connective and changing its own form; e. g., Iter faciēbam, *quum* Balbum vidēbam, *I was making a journey, when I saw Balbus*.—Quae *quum* ita *sint*, egredĕre ex urbe, *Since these things are so, go forth from the city*. Here it must be observed that, in the first example, the sentence, "*Balbum vidēbam*," is united without change to the principal sentence by the connective *quum*, and thus is rendered subordinate to it as in the English; while in the second, the sentence, "*Quae ita sunt*" (these things are so), not only assumes the connective *quum*, but also changes its copula *sunt* to *sint*, thus becoming "*Quae quum ita sint*."

341. A complex sentence may take an entire sentence in place of any one of its elements; i. e.,

    1) As Subject.
    2) As Predicate.
    3) As Object.
    4) As Attribute.

Sentence as Subject.

342. Any sentence, whether declarative, interrogative, or imperative, may be used in direct quotation as subject; e. g.,

"*Terra est rotunda*," est sententia.	"The earth is round," *is a sentence.*
"*Quid casūrum est?*" est quaestio.	"What will happen?" *is the question.*
"*Nemo in urbe sepelītor*," erat lex.	"Let no one be buried in the city," was the law.

343. Any sentence, whether declarative, interroga-

7*

tive, or imperative, may be introduced as the subject of another sentence without being directly quoted; it then undergoes certain changes to adapt it to the place it is to hold in the new sentence.

I. *Changes in Declarative Sentences as Subject.*

344. Declarative sentences used as subject, except *in* direct quotation (see 340, 1) change their own subjects to the accusative, their predicates to the infinitive, and any predicate-adjectives or nouns to the accusative; e. g.,

Terra est rotunda.	*The earth is round.*
Terram esse rotundam certum est.	*That the earth is round, is certain.*

REM.—Here the decl. sentence, *Terra est rotunda,* is used as subject; accordingly its own subject (*terra*) is changed to the accus. (*terram*), and its predicate (*est rotunda*) to the infinitive (*esse*) and the accusative (*rotundam*).

345. RULE.—*Infinitive as Subject.*

The infinitive mood, either alone or with other words connected with it, may be used as the subject of a verb.

[F. B. 608; A. & S. § 269; Z. § 597.]

346. RULE.—*Subject of Infinitive.*

The subject of the infinitive is put in the accusative (as *terram* in the above example).

[F. B. 655; A. & S. § 239; Z. § 599.]

347. With a few verbs we find *quod* with the *indicative* as the real subject; e. g.,

Accessit etiam quod pars equitātus se trans Rhenum recepĕrat.	*An additional reason was that a part of the cavalry had crossed the Rhine.*

348. Instead of an infinitive sentence as subject, we

find *ut* with the *subjunctive* with *restat, sequĭtur, relĭquum est, primum est, proxĭmum est*, and the like ; e. g.,

Sequĭtur, ut haec enunciatio falsa sit.	*It follows that this statement is false.*
Restat ut omnia doceam.	*It remains that I should teach all things.*
Mos est homĭnum, ut nolint eundem plurĭbus excellĕre.	*It is a custom of men, that they are unwilling that the same one should excel in many things.*

Rem. 1.—In each of these examples, the clause beginning with *ut* is plainly the *real* subject, and the preceding part, as *sequĭtur, restat, mos est*, &c., the predicate. Thus, in the first example, we may ask, *what follows (sequĭtur)*: plainly *that this statement is false* (ut haec enunciatio falsa sit).

Rem. 2.—After *non dubium est* and the like, we sometimes find *quin* with the subjunctive; e. g., Non dubium est quin turpe sit, *There is no doubt but that it is disgraceful.* Here the clause, *quin turpe sit*, seems at first to be the subject, but if we observe closely the force of *quin* as compounded of *qui* (the old abl. of qui), by which, and *ne*, not, the sentence may be explained thus, *non est dubium*, there is no doubt, *quin turpe sit*, by which (i. e. in accordance with which) this is not disgraceful. Thus explained it assumes the nature of a relative clause.

II. *Changes in Interrogative Sentences as Subject.*

349. Interrogative sentences used as subject, except in direct quotation, change their predicates to the subjunctive mood; e. g.,

Quid casūrum est?	*What will happen?*
Quid casūrum sit incertum est.	*It is uncertain what will happen.*

III. *Changes in Imperative Sentences as Subject.*

350. Imperative sentences used as subject, except in

direct quotation, change their predicates to the *subjunctive* mood (if not already in that mood) with *ut* or *ne*; e. g.,

In urbe mane.	*Remain in the city.*
Ut in urbe maneas, praescribētur.	*That you remain in the city will be enjoined.*

351. The general rule for the position of subject and predicate is the same in *complex* as in *simple* sentences (325, 326), with this qualification, that the subject-sentence usually follows the predicates mentioned in articles 347, 348, and a few others.

352. VOCABULARY.

Caius, *Caius, i*, m.	It is well known, is an admitted fact, *constat*.
Certain, sure, *certus, a, um*.	Near, *apud*.
Dictator, *dictātor, ōris*, m.	Pharsalia, *Pharsalia, ae*, f.
It is ordered, the order is given, *praescribĭtur*.	Pharsalus, *Pharsālus, i*, f.
It is usual, *solet*.	Uncertain, *incertus, a, um*.

353. EXERCISES.

I. *Translate and analyze.*

1. Constat solem cuncta luce sua illustrāre. 2. Certum est solem urbem sua luce illustrāre. 3. Certum est Caium leges violavisse. 4. Quid Caium fecisse incertum est. 5. Pueros oportet diligentes esse. 6. Praescriptum erat, ut Caius in urbe manēret. 7. Circa eādem tempŏra M. L. Crassus contra Parthos missus est. 8. Reliquiae exercĭtus per quaestōrem servātae sunt. 9. Propter hanc injuriam ab Arimīno infesto exercĭtu Romam contendit.

II. 1. *Restore the* subordinate *sentences, used as subject in the above exercises, to the rank of* independent *sentences.*
MODELS.
1. Sol cuncta luce sua illustrat.
6. Caius in urbe maneat.

2. *Construct two or more Latin sentences with subordinate clauses as* subjects.

3. *Construct Latin sentences in answer to the following questions:*
1. Who was Mithridates? 2. Who was Tigranes? 3. Who conquered Mithridates? 4. Who conquered Tigranes? 5. What Roman made himself dictator? 6. Is it certain that Caesar made himself dictator? 7. Where was Pompey conquered?

III. *Translate into Latin.*

1. Caius is worthy of much praise. 2. It is well known that Caius is worthy of much praise. 3. Who conquered the king? 4. It is uncertain who conquered the king. 5. Caesar conquered Pompey near Pharsalia. 6. It is well known that Caesar conquered Pompey near Pharsalia. 7. Let the boys remain in the city. 8. The order has been given that the boys shall remain in the city.

Lesson XXXI.

Sentence as Predicate.
[79 & 80.]

354. Any sentence, whether declarative, interrogative, or imperative, may be used in direct quotation as predicate; e. g.,

Sententia fuit, "*Terra est rotunda.*"	The sentence was, 'The earth is round."
Quaestio est, "*Quid casūrum est?*"	The question is, "What will happen?"
Lex fuit, "*Nemo in urbe sepelītor.*"	The law was, "Let no one be buried in the city."

355. Any sentence may be used as the predicate of another sentence without being directly quoted; it then undergoes certain changes to adapt it to the place which it is to hold in the new sentence.

I. *Changes in Declarative Sentences as Predicate.*

356. Declarative sentences used as predicate, except, of course, direct quotation, generally change the subject to the accusative, the verb-predicate to the infinitive, and any predicate noun or adjective to the accusative. This change, it will be observed, is the same as that of Subject-Sentences; e. g.,

Exĭtus fuit oratiōnis, sibi nullam cum his amicitiam esse.	*The conclusion of the oration was, that he had no friendship with them.*

357. Sometimes the predicate-sentence takes *ut* or *ne* with the *subjunctive;* e. g.,

Consilium fuit, *ut* regem occidĕret.	*The design was to kill the king.*

REM.—This is usually the case when the idea of *purpose* is at all prominent in the sentence.

358. Sometimes the predicate-sentence takes *quŏd* with the *indicative;* e. g.,

Justissĭma causa fuit, *quŏd* Germāni *timuērunt.*	*The truest reason was that the Germans feared.*

II. *Changes in Interrogative Sentences as Predicate.*

359. Interrogative sentences used as predicate, except in direct quotation, take their own predicates in the subjunctive mood; e. g.,

Quaestio erat, *num* terra rotunda *esset*.	*The question was, whether the earth is round.*

III. *Changes in Imperative Sentences as Predicate.*

360. Imperative sentences used as predicate, except in direct quotation, change their own predicates to the subjunctive mood (*if not already in that mood*) with *ut* or *ne*; e. g.,

Praescriptum fuit, *ut* in urbe *manēret*.	*The order was that he should remain in the city.*

361. VOCABULARY.

Assassinator, *percussor, ōris*, m.
Design, *consilium, i*, n.
Favor, v., *faveo, ēre, favi, fautum*.
Question, *quaestio, ōnis*, f.
Report, *fama, ae*, f.
Return, v., *redeo, īre, redii, reditum*.
Violate, break, *violo, āre, āvi, ātum*.

Whether (in dependent questions), *ne, num, nonne*; *num* is more common than in direct questions, and here does not necessarily expect the answer *no*. (See 177, R. 2.)
Your (in reference to one person), *tuus, a, um*; (in reference to more than one) *vester, tra, trum*.

362. EXERCISES.

I. *Translate and analyze.*

1. Fama est, Caium urbem condidisse. 2. Fama fuit, Caesărem ad Alexandrīam venisse. 3. Oratio fuit, Caesărem regnum Cleopātrae dedisse. 4. Haec fuit oratio, Romānos Germānis bellum inferre. 5. Haec

erat oratio, Germānos popŭlo Romāno bellum intulisse. 6. Consilium fuit, ut Caesărem occidĕret. 7. Quaestio fuit, num Caesar occīsus esset. 8. Lex pacis fuit, ut Antiŏchus sumptum omnem belli Romānis restituĕret. 9. Lex pacis fuit, ut rex naves universas tradĕret.

II. 1. *Change the* subordinate predicate-clauses *in the above exercises to distinct* independent sentences.

MODEL.

Cajus urbem condĭdit.

2. *Construct two or more Latin sentences with* subordinate clauses *as* predicates.

III. *Translate into Latin.*

1. The report is, that your father is in the city. 2. The report was, that Caesar had returned to the city. 8. The report is, that he returned to Rome. 4. The report is, that the citizens are violating the laws. 5. The design was to kill (*that he should kill*) his father. 6. The question is, whether he will kill his father. 7. The question is, whether the senate favored the assassinators of Caesar.

Lesson XXXII.

Sentence as Modifier of Subject or other Noun.

[81 & 82.]

363. A sentence may be used as modifier of the subject of another sentence, or of some other noun in that sentence; e. g.,

| Ad cetĕras utilitātes haec quoque opportunĭtas adjungĭtur, *ut habeat exercĭtum.* | *To the other qualifications this advantage also is added,* that he has an army. |

Poētae, *qui res Romānas scribunt*, solent praeterīre nostras calamitātes.	*The poets,* who write Roman history, *are accustomed to pass over our misfortunes.*
Audīvit famam, *Caium regem occidisse.*	*He heard a report,* that Caius had killed the king.

Rem. 1.—The subordinate clause, in each of the first two of the above examples, modifies the subject, that in the first showing *what* poets, viz., *those who write Roman history*, and that in the second *what* advantage, viz., *that he has an army*. The subordinate clause in the third example modifies the object, and shows *what* report, viz., *that Caius had killed the king*.

Rem. 2.—The last example may be regarded as a form abridged from the relative clause, the relative and copula being omitted. Filled out, it might stand thus: *Audivit famam (quae fuit), Caium regem occidisse.* Abridged Complex Sentences will be noticed in another place. (See Lesson XLIII.)

364. The same general principles apply to the changes of sentences in these cases as in subject and predicate clauses, with the exception of relative sentences, which are very numerous.

365. Most declarative sentences, introduced to express the attribute of a substantive, are changed to relative clauses, and introduced by relative pronouns which always denote the same persons or things as the nouns which they limit; e. g.,

Aenēas fuit Anchīsae filius.	*Aeneas was the son of Anchises.*
Aenēas urbem condĭdit.	*Aeneas founded the city.*
Aenēas, *qui urbem condĭdit*, fuit Anchīsae filius.	*Aeneas,* who founded the city, *was the son of Anchises.*

| Aenēas, *qui fuit Anchīsae filius,* urbem condĭdit. | Aeneas, who was the son of Anchises, *founded the city.* |

> Rem.—It will be observed that the first and second of the above examples are simple sentences; that in the third, the second is made subordinate to the first by representing the subject *Aeneas* by the relative *qui;* and that in the fourth, the first is made subordinate to the second in the same way.

366. Rule.—*Relative Pronoun.*

The relative pronoun agrees with its antecedent in *gender* and *number*. (See examples above.)

[F. B. 625; A. & S. § 206.]

367. The predicate of a relative clause is sometimes in the *indicative* mood, and sometimes in the *subjunctive*. It may be observed, however, that the subjunctive is used,

1) To express *purpose, result,* or *reason;* e. g.,

| Legātos misērunt qui dicĕrent. | *They sent ambassadors to say* (*lit.* who might say). |
| Neque enim tu is es qui nescias. | *Nor indeed are you such an one as not to know* (who may not know). |

2) To define or explain an indefinite antecedent, either affirmative or negative; e. g.,

| Sunt qui putent. | *There are (some) who think.* |
| Nemo est qui haud intellĭgat. | *There is no one who does not understand.* |

> Rem. 1.—After negative expressions, we sometimes find *quin* with the *subjunctive* instead of the relative clause; e. g., Nemo est quin intellĭgat, &c., *There is no one who does not understand,* &c.
>
> Rem. 2.—It should be observed that the relative clause not only serves as attributive to the subject, but sometimes also expresses

the relation of *purpose, result, reason,* &c. to the predicate, as in the above examples.

368. The common position for the relative clause in Latin is directly after the antecedent, though one or two words are not unfrequently allowed to intervene. (See examples, 365, 367.)

> REM.—The same principle also applies to the position of any subordinate sentence used as modifier of a substantive or pronoun.

369. Instead of antecedent and relative, we sometimes find correlatives, as they are called, such as *tot—quot; talis—qualis; tantus—quantus,* &c.; e. g.,

Quanta vi civitātes libertātem expĕtunt, tantā regna reges defendunt.	*With whatever violence states seek liberty, with so great, kings defend their kingdoms.*

370. A relative adverb is sometimes used in place of the relative pronoun; e. g.,

Germāni Rhenum transiērunt non longe a mari, quo (= in quod) Rhenus influit.	*The Germans crossed the Rhine not far from the sea into which the Rhine flows.*

371. VOCABULARY.

Condition, terms, *conditio, ōnis,* f.
Hold as one's own, obtain, *obtineo, ĕre, obtinui, obtentum.*
In, *in* (with abl.).
Mountain, mount, *mons, tis,* m.
On, *in* (with abl.).
Part, portion, *pars, tis,* f.
Pyrrhus, *Pyrrhus, i,* m.
Second, *secundus, a, um.*

Send, *mitto, ĕre, misi, missum.*
Take, occupy, *occŭpo, āre, āvi, ātum.*
That (followed by a rel. clause explaining it), *is, ea, id.*
Undertake, *suscipio, ĕre, suscēpi, susceptum.*
With, *sometimes indicated by abl.*

372. EXERCISES.

I. *Translate and analyze.*

1. Caesar Octaviānus contra eos pugnāvit. 2. Caesar Octaviānus postea Augustus est appellātus. 3. Caesar Octaviānus, qui postea Augustus est appellātus, contra eos pugnāvit. 4. Caesar Octaviānus, qui contra eos pugnāvit, postea Augustus est appellātus. 5. Ingens fuit Romae timor, ne itĕrum Galli urbem occupārent. 6. Ei successit Marius, qui bello termĭnum posuit. 7. Ei successit Marius, qui ipsum Jugurtham cepit. 8. Sulla, qui in Italia morabātur, adversarios interfēcit. 9. Decemvĭri creāti sunt, qui civitāti leges scribĕrent.

II. 1. *In the sixth, seventh, and eighth of the above sentences, change the relative clauses to independent sentences.*

MODEL.

Marius bello termĭnum posuit.

2. *In the same sentences, change the places of the two parts, converting the relative clauses into principal sentences with the other parts subordinate to them.*

MODEL.

Marius, qui ei successit, bello termĭnum posuit.

III. *Translate into Latin.*

1. Ascanius was the son of Aeneas. 2. Ascanius founded a city on mount Albanus. 3. Ascanius, who was the son of Aeneas, founded a city on mount Albanus. 4. Ascanius, who founded a city on mount Albanus, was the son of Aeneas. 5. In the second battle, Brutus, who had undertaken the war, was killed. 6. Pyrrhus sent an ambassador to ask (*seek*) peace. 7. The ambassador asked peace with the condition that

Pyrrhus should (364) hold a portion of Italy. 8. The condition was that Pyrrhus should hold that part of Italy which he had taken by his arms.

Lesson XXXIII.

Accusative with Infinitive, or Sentence with Quòd *as Object.*
[83—85.]

373. A sentence, whether declarative, interrogative, or imperative, may be used, in direct quotation, as the object of the predicate of a new sentence. It is then introduced without change; e. g.,

Dixit, " *Caius est beātus.*"	*He said,* " Caius is happy."
Dixit, " *Quis est beātus ?*"	*He said,* " Who is happy ?"
Dixit, " *Sit beātus.*"	*He said,* " May he be happy."

374. Declarative sentences, when used as object of predicate, after verbs of *declaring, perceiving,* and the like (*verba declarandi* et *sentiendi*), except in direct quotation, change their *subjects* to the *accusative,* and their *predicates* to the *infinitive;* e. g.,

Dicit *Caium esse beātum.* | *He says* that Caius is happy.

375. After a few verbs, particularly those of *adding, omitting, passing over,* and the like, declarative sentences used as *object* are often introduced by *quòd;* e. g.,

Praetereo, *quod Sassia eam sibi domum delēgit.*	*I pass over* (*the fact*), that Sassia chose this house for herself.

376. In the arrangement of the different parts of complex sentences,

1) The general principle is, that the subordinate clauses dependent upon the predicate should be inserted between the different portions of the leading sentence; e. g.,

Romŭlus, *ut civium numĕrum augēret*, asȳlum patefēcit.	*Romulus*, that he might increase the number of citizens, *opened an asylum.*

2) It must be observed, however, that the subordinate clauses sometimes precede and sometimes follow the leading sentence, instead of being inserted within it; e. g.,

Haec dum nostri collīgunt, rex ipse effūgit.	While our men collect these, *the king himself escapes.*

377. Vocabulary.

Caligula, *Caligŭla, ae,* m.
Eye, *ocŭlus, i,* m.
Happy, *beātus, a, um.*
Livia, *Livia, ae,* f.
Mother, *mater, matris,* f.
Nero, *Nero, ōnis,* m.
Palace, *palatium, i,* n.

Say, *dico, ĕre, dixi, dictum.*
Think, *puto, āre, āvi, ātum.*
Third, *tertius, a, um.*
Turn, turn to, *converto, ĕre, converti, conversum.*
Upon, towards, *in* (with accus.).

378. Exercises.

II. *Translate and analyze, explaining* objects.

1. Tanăquil dixit regem grave vulnus accepisse. 2. Romŭlum a senatorĭbus interfectum esse existimavērunt. 3. Q. M. Scaevŏla ait, trecentos alios juvĕnes in eum conjurâsse. 4. Cupio me esse clementem. 5 Tenet fama, venēnum Claudio ab conjŭge datum. 6

Video in me omnium vestrum ocŭlos esse conversos.
7. Principia ejus imperii moderāta sunt Germanĭci Caesăris metu.

II. 1. *In each of the above sentences, develop the object* (if there is one) *into an independent sentence.*

MODEL.

Rex grave vulnus accēpit.

2. *Change the* indirect *to* direct *quotation.*

MODEL.

Tanăquil dixit, "*Rex grave vulnus accēpit.*"

3. *Construct Latin sentences, using the following* objects *in* indirect quotation :

1. Nero fuit gener Augusti. 2. Nepōtes suos fame necāvit. 3. Claudius Britanniam subēgit. 4. Claudius annos imperāvit quatuordĕcim.

III. *Translate into Latin, using both* direct *and* indirect quotation.

1. Who was the mother of T. Nero? 2. They say that Livia was the mother of Nero. 3. How long did Caligula reign? 4. They say that he reigned three years. 5. Where was Caligula killed? 6. The report is that he was killed in his palace in the third year of his reign. 7. They said that all eyes were turned upon them (*se*, vid. 336). 8. Were not all eyes turned upon you? 9. We saw that all eyes were turned upon us. 10. Do you think that Nero was happy? 11. We do not think that he was happy.

Lesson XXXIV.

Dependent Question as Object.

[86—91.]

379. An interrogative sentence may be used as the object of the predicate; and then, except in direct quotation, it takes its verb in the subjunctive; e. g.,

Quid dixit?	*What did he say?*
Nescio *quid dixĕrit.*	*I do not know* what he said.

Rem.—The tense of the subjunctive to be used in any case may be determined by the following

380. Rule.—*Subjunctive Tenses in Dependent Sentences.*

1) When dependent upon a *present* tense (*pres., perf. def.*, or *fut.*), the subjunctive is put in the *present* tense to denote an incomplete action, and in the *perfect* to denote a completed action.

2) When dependent upon a *past* tense (*imperf., perf. indef.*, or *pluperf.*), it is put in the *imperfect* to denote incomplete action, and in the *pluperfect* to denote completed action; e. g.,

Nescio quid dicat.	*I know not what he says.*
Nescio quid dixĕrit.	*I know not what he said.*
Nescīvi quid dicĕret.	*I knew not what he said.*
Nescīvi quid dixisset.	*I knew not what he had said.*

Rem.—The present tense is sometimes used in narration for the perfect indef., and may then be followed by the imperfect or pluperfect subjunctive.

DEPENDENT QUESTION AS OBJECT.

381. VOCABULARY.

Cremona, *Cremōna, ae,* f.
Die, *morior, mori* or *morīri, mortuus sum; demorior,* &c.
Famous, *clarus, a, um.*
Galba, *Galba, ae,* m.
Know, *scio, īre, scivi, scitum;* not to know, *nescio, īre, nescīvi, nescītum.*
Misenum, *Misēnum, i,* n.
Near, *ad, apud.*
Otho, *Otho, ōnis,* m.
Palestine, *Palaestīna, ae,* f.

Vespasian, *Vespasiānus, i,* m.
Vitellius, *Vitellius, i,* m.
Voluptuousness, pleasures, *deliciae, ārum,* f. pl.
Wear out, overcome, *conficio, ĕre, confēci, confectum.*
Whether (in dependent questions), *num, ne, nonne; num* is more common than in direct questions, and does not here necessarily expect the answer *no.* (See 177, R. 2.)

382. EXERCISES.

I. *Translate and analyze.*

1. Unde sol ignem habet? 2. Nescio unde sol ignem habeat. 3. Quid dicit? 4. Nescīmus quid dicat. 5. Quis scivit quid dixisset? 6. Quid futūrum sit, nescīmus. 7. Quid vere nobis prosit, non semper intelligĭmus. 8. Interrogāvit num terra rotunda esset. 9. Nero magnam urbis partem per ludum incendit. 10. Culpam in Christiānos transtŭlit. 11. Otho a Vitellio, qui a Germanĭcis legionĭbus imperium accepĕrat, ad Cremōnam levi proelio victus est.

II. 1. *Change the declarative sentences in the above exercises to the interrogative form.*

MODEL.

Num nescio unde sol ignem habeat?

2. *Construct complex Latin sentences, using the ninth and tenth of the above exercises as objects.*

3. *Construct Latin sentences in answer to the following questions:*

1. Who was the mother of Nero? 2. What became of her? 3. What became of Nero? 4. Who was conquered by Vitellius? 5. Where was he conquered? 6. Who succeeded Vitellius?

III. *Translate into Latin.*

1. Where is your father? 2. I do not know where he is. 3. They say he is in the city. 4. Will he go to Rome? 5. We do not know whether he will go to Rome. 6. My brother says that he has gone to Rome. 7. Who succeeded Nero? 8. Do you know who succeeded him? 9. We know that Galba succeeded him. 10. Which was the most famous city of Palestine? 11. Who does not know which was the most famous city of Palestine? 12. All say that Jerusalem was the most noble city of Palestine.

Lesson XXXV.

Sentence with ut *or* ne *as Object.—Indirect Object.*
[92—94.]

383. An imperative sentence used as object, except in direct quotation, is generally introduced by *ut* or *ne*, and takes its verb in the subjunctive; e. g.,

| Clypeos hastis percutĭte. | *Strike your shields with your spears.* |
| Milĭtĭbus imperāvit, ut clypeos hastis percutĕrent. | *He commanded the soldiers to strike their shields with their spears.* |

Rem.—As an exception to the above principle, it must be observed that *jubeo* usually takes the accusative with the infinitive as the object-clause; e. g., *Eos suum adventum exspectāre jussit*, *He ordered them to await his arrival.*

384. After verbs signifying to *ask, advise, seek,* and the like, the object-sentence usually takes the subjunctive with *ut* or *ne;* e. g.,

Fac *ut sciam.*	*Cause* me to know.
Illa petiit, *ut sibi annŭlos aureos darent.*	*She asked* that they would give her gold rings.

REM.—In these examples the clauses beginning with *ut* are the objects of the transitive verbs *fac* and *petiit.*

Final Sentences; Indirect Object.

385. Final sentences, or such as express *purpose*, are introduced by *ut, ne, quo, quomĭnus,* and *quin,* and take the verb in the subjunctive. These correspond to the indirect object in the simple sentence.

386. Clauses expressing an affirmative purpose are introduced by *ut,* unless a comparative occurs in the sentence, in which case *quo* is used; e. g.,

Venit *ut portas claudat.*	*He has come* to shut the gates.
Medĭco aliquid dandum est, *quo sit studiosior.*	*Something ought to be given to the physician* that he may be more attentive.

387. Clauses expressing a negative purpose are generally introduced by *ne;* e. g.,

Romŭlus, *ne vana urbis magnitūdo esset,* asȳlum apĕrit.	*Romulus,* that the large city might not be empty, *opened an asylum.*

388. Quomĭnus (*quo* and *minus*) is used after verbs of *hindering;* e. g.,

Quid obstat, *quomĭnus Caius sit beātus?*	What prevents Caius from being happy? (Lit. *by which* [in order that] *he may be less happy.*)

389. **Quin** (*quî* and *ne*), *how not, why not, by which not*, &c. is used after some verbs of *doubting* and *hindering* in negative sentences or questions implying a negative, and after *facĕre non possum, fĭĕri non potest*, &c. ; e. g.,

Non dubĭtant, *quin dii illud exaudiant.*	They do not doubt (but) that the gods hear this.
Facĕre non possum, *quin ad te mittam litĕras.*	I cannot but send letters to you.

> REM. 1.—The clause in the first example appears to be the *direct object* of *dubĭtant*; it is such, however, only in appearance, and may be explained thus: *They entertain no doubt* (by which, in accordance with which, &c.), to the effect that, *the gods do not hear.*

> REM. 2.—Relative clauses are sometimes used to express *purpose* (see Lesson XXXII.), e. g., Legātos misĕrunt qui dicĕrent, *They sent ambassadors to say.*

390. VOCABULARY.

Burning, *incendium, i,* n.
Cause (*with infin.* or *that*), *efficio*, followed by *ut* or *ne* with *subj.* ; *efficio, ĕre, effĕci, effectum.*
Citadel, *arx, arcis,* f.
Do, make, *facio, ĕre, feci, factum.*
Friend, *amīcus, i,* m.
In order (*with infin.* or *that*), *ut* (*with subj.*).

Inquire, *interrŏgo, āre, āvi, ātum.*
Lose, waste, *perdo, ĕre, perdĭdi, perdĭtum.*
Represent, *repraesento, āre, āvi, ātum.*
Set on fire, set fire to, *incendo, ĕre, incendi, incensum.*
Tell, say, *dico, ĕre, dixi, dictum.*
Titus, *Titus, i,* m.
Troy, *Troja, ae,* f.

391. Exercises.

I. *Translate and analyze.*

1. Tarpeiam rogābant, ut viam in arcem monstrāret.
2. Virgĭni permisērunt, ut munus sibi poscĕret.
3. Illa petiit, ut sibi armillas aureas darent.
4. Hannĭbal Romānis obtŭlit, ut captīvos redimĕrent.
5. Octaviānus extorsit, ut sibi consulātus darētur.
6. Nero magnam urbis partem per ludum incendit, ut Trojae repraesentāret incendium.
7. Romŭlus, ut civium numĕrum augēret, asȳlum patefēcit.
8. Regŭlus Romānis suasit, ne pacem cum Carthaginiensĭbus facĕrent.
9. Omnes occidendi sunt, ut Romanōrum vires frangantur.
10. Quid obstat, quomĭnus beāti simus.
11. Sapiens nunquam dubitābit, quin immortālis sit anĭmus.
12. Domitiānus se deum primus appellāri jussit.
13. Titus fuit vir omnium virtūtum genĕre mirabĭlis.
14. Negāvit quemquam oportēre tristem a princĭpe discedĕre.

II. 1. *In the first five of the above exercises, change the* object-clauses *to* independent sentences, *presenting them successively in the declarative, interrogative, and imperative forms.*

MODEL.

Tarpeia viam in arcem monstrāvit.
Nonne Tarpeia viam in arcem monstrāvit?
Tarpeia viam in arcem monstret.

2. *Substitute* dicunt *for the predicate in the first five of the above sentences, adapting the* object-clause *to this change.*

MODEL.

Dicunt Tarpeiam viam in arcem monstravisse.

3. *Construct three Latin sentences with* object-clauses—

one with the accusative and infinitive; *one with a* dependent question; *and one with* ut and the subjunctive.

III. *Translate into Latin.*

1. He caused them to go (lit. *effected that they should go*) into the citadel. 2. They ask us to go into the citadel. 3. They have inquired who has gone into the city. 4. They say that you all are going into the city. 5. The report is, that the king set fire to Rome. 6. Father will ask us our opinion. 7. He will ask us what we have done. 8. We were asked what we had done. 9. They will set fire to the city in order to represent the burning of Troy. 10. He praises you in order that he may be praised by you. 11. You praised them in order that you might be praised by them. 12. Who succeeded Vespasian? 13. The report is, that Titus succeeded him. 14. Titus said, "Friends, I have lost a day." 15. Titus told (*said to*) his friends that he had lost a day.

Lesson XXXVI.

Adverbial Attributive-Sentences.—Place.
[95—97.]

392. Sentences may be used to express some attribute of the action or event denoted by the predicate; and may then be called *adverbial attributive-sentences.*

393. Sentences used as adverbial attributives of place are introduced by some adverb of place, as *ubi* where, *unde* whence, &c. Generally this adverb has a correlative in the principal clause, as *inde—unde; ibi—ubi*, &c.; e. g.,

ADVERBIAL ATTRIBUTIVE-SENTENCES.—PLACE.

Ubi tyrannus est, ibi nulla est respublĭca.	*Where a tyrant is, there is no republic.*

REM. 1.—The learner will observe that the assertion is, that *there is no republic* (where?) *where there is a tyrant.* The clause beginning with *ubi* is therefore in effect an *adverb of place*.

REM. 2.—For position of subordinate clause, see 376.

394. Instead of a correlative adverb in the principal sentence, we often find an adverbial expression of place; e. g.,

Latobrĭgos in fines suos, unde erant profecti, reverti jussit.	*He ordered the Latobrigi to return to their territories, whence they had come.*

REM.—The subordinate clause in this sentence subserves a twofold purpose. With respect to *fines*, it sustains the relation of relative clause (see 370), and thus has the force of an *adjective attributive;* but with respect to the action expressed by the principal sentence, it denotes the *adverbial attribute* of place. In like manner, as already mentioned (367, R. 2), the relative clause not only serves as *attributive* to some noun, but sometimes also expresses the relation of *purpose, result, reason,* &c. to the predicate.

395. VOCABULARY.

Amphictyon, *Amphictyon, ŏnis,* m.
Athens, *Athēnae, ārum,* f. pl.
Atthis, *Atthis, ĭdis,* f.
Cecrops, *Cecrops, ŏpis,* m.
Country, region, *regio, ōnis,* f.
Cranaus, *Cranăus, i,* m.
Fifty, *quinquaginta,* indecl.
Force of arms, *arma, ōrum,* n. pl.
Grandfather, *avus, i,* m.

Live, dwell, *habĭto, āre, āvi, ā-tum.*
Name, *nomen, nomĭnis,* n.
Now, *nunc.*
Stay, abide, remain, *maneo, ēre, mansi, mansum.*
Thessalus, *Thessălus, i,* m.
Thessaly, *Thessalia, ae,* f.
Where, *ubi,* generally with the correlative *ibi* in the principal clause.

396. Exercises.

I. *Translate and analyze.*

1. Ubi nulla est respublĭca? 2. Ubi tyrannus est, ibi nulla est respublĭca. 3. Te redĭgam eōdem, unde ortus es. 4. Ubi tyrannus est, ibi dicendum est plane nullam esse rempublĭcam. 5. Incolēbant eos locos, ubi hodie est haec urbs. 6. Hic, ubi opus est, non verentur. 7. Ubi nihil opus est, ibi verentur. 8. Romŭlus cum hoste pugnam conseruit in eo loco, ubi nunc forum Romānum est. 9. Amphictyon regnāvit, qui primus Minervae urbem sacrāvit. 10. Hujus temporĭbus aquārum illuvies majōrem partem populōrum Graeciae absumpsit.

II. *Construct Latin sentences, using the following clauses as* adverbial attributives of place:

1. Ubi opus est. 2. Ubi nihil opus est. 3. Ubi haec urbs est. 4. Ubi es. 5. Unde venistis.

III. *Translate into Latin.*

1. Where is your brother? 2. He is staying where his grandfather has lived fifty years. 3. Shall you go to the city where he is? 4. I shall remain where I now am. 5. Where (there) are good laws, the citizens are happy. 6. Where did Amphictyon reign? 7. He reigned where Athens now is. 8. Who gave the name to Athens? 9. Atthis gave it a name. 10. Who was Atthis? 11. She was the daughter of Cranaus who succeeded Cecrops. 12. What country (*region*) did Thessalus take by force of arms? 13. The country which he took was called from his name Thessaly.

Lesson XXXVII.

Adverbial Attributive-Sentences.—Time.
[98—100.]

397. Sentences used to denote the adverbial attribute of time are generally introduced by adverbs of time, as *quum,* when; *dum,* until, &c.; e. g.,

Haec *dum* nostri collĭgunt, rex ipse e manĭbus effŭgit.	*While our soldiers are collecting these things, the king himself escapes from their hands.*

Rem.—It will be observed that the assertion in this sentence is contained in the part (*rex ipse, &c.*) *the king himself escapes from their hands,* and that the rest of it merely states the *time* of this action; viz., *while our soldiers are collecting these things.*

398. Sometimes the adverb which introduces the temporal clause has a correlative in the principal clause; e. g.,

Fructus omnis praestantiae *tum* maxĭme capĭtur, *quum* in proxĭmum quemque confertur.	*The fruit of all excellence is especially enjoyed,* (then) *when it is bestowed upon each nearest relative.*
Tum, quum ex urbe Catilīnam ejiciēbam, relĭquam conjuratōrum manum simul exitūram putābam.	*Then, when I banished Catiline from the city, I thought that the remaining band of conspirators would at once depart.*

399. Sometimes in place of the correlative adverb in the principal clause, we find an adverbial expression of time; e. g.,

Ligarius *eo tempŏre* paruit, | *Ligarius obeyed the senate*
quum parēre senatui ne- | *at that time when it was*
cesse erat. | *necessary.*

400. Temporal clauses may represent the action of the principal verb as taking place,

    1) At the time of some other action; e. g.,

Dum senātus bellum con- | *While the senate was prepar-*
tra Caesărem parābat, | *ing war against Caesar,*
hic dictatōrem se fecit. | *he made himself dictator.*

    2) Before some other action; e. g.,

Priusquam lucet, adsunt. | *They are present before it is light.*

    3) After some other action; e. g.,

Scipio, tertio anno *post-* | *Scipio, in the third year af-*
quam Romāni in Afrĭ- | *ter the Romans had pass-*
cam trajecĕrant, consul | *ed into Africa, was made*
est creātus. | *consul.*

    Rem.—For position of subordinate clause, see 876.

Use of Moods in Temporal Clauses.

401. Subordinate clauses used to express time generally have their predicates in the indicative mood; especially when they denote time merely. A few cases, however, require attention.

402. Subordinate sentences introduced by *quum* take,

    1) The indicative when they mark merely the *time* of an action or event *without* any accessory notion of *cause;* e. g.,

ADVERBIAL ATTRIBUTIVE-SENTENCES.—TIME.

Is qui non propulsat injuriam a suis, *quum potest*, injuste facit.	*He who does not ward off an injury from his friends, when he can, does wrong.*

2) The subjunctive imperfect or pluperfect in historical narration, as the one event is here regarded in some sense as the *cause* or *occasion* of the other; e. g.,

Zenōnem, *quum Athēnis essent*, audiēbant.	*They heard Zeno when they were in Athens.*

> REM.—The clause, *Quum Athēnis essent*, indicates not only the *time*, but also the *occasion* of the action expressed by the principal clause, as their being in Athens was really the occasion of their hearing Zeno.

403. Subordinate sentences introduced by *antĕquam* and *priusquam* take,

    1) The indicative mood when they denote mere *priority of time*; e. g.,

Priusquam lucet, adsunt.	*They are present before it is light.*

    2) The subjunctive when they indicate a dependence of one event upon another; e. g.,

Tempestas minātur antĕquam surgat.	*The tempest threatens before it rises.*

404. The two parts of which *antĕquam* and *priusquam* are compounded, are often separated, so that *ante* or *prius* appears in the principal clause, and *quam* in the subordinate part; e. g.,

Ante triennium, *quam* Carthāgo delerētur, Cato mortem obiit.	*Cato died three years before Carthage was destroyed.*

Rem. 1.—The learner must observe that *triennium* does not depend upon *ante* (which is the adverb, and not the preposition), but is in the accusative to denote *duration of time*, in accordance with Rule, 277.

Rem. 2.—*Postquam* is generally followed by the indicative, and, like *antequam* and *priusquam*, often has its parts separated.

Rem. 3.—*Duration of time* before or after any event may be expressed either by the accusative or ablative.

405. Subordinate sentences introduced by *dum, donec,* and *quoad*, take,

> 1) The indicative, (a) when these connectives signify *while*, or *as long as*, and (b) when they signify *till* or *until*, if the action or event spoken of is to be contemplated as a matter of fact; e. g.,

Dum senātus bellum contra Caesărem parābat, hic dictatōrem se fecit.	*While the senate was preparing war against Caesar, he made himself dictator.*
Epaminondas ferrum in corpŏre retinuit, *quoad* renuntiātum est vicisse Boeotios.	*Epaminondas retained the sword in his body, until it was announced that the Boeotians had conquered.*

> 2) The subjunctive, when they signify *until*, if the action or event spoken of is to be contemplated not as a *fact*, but as a merely conceived result for whose accomplishment an opportunity is presented; e. g.,

Differant, dum defervescat ira.	*Let them delay until their anger may cool.*

Rem.—Here the *object* of the delay is to allow anger time to cool.

406. Vocabulary.

After (*conj.*), *postquam.*
Before (*conj.*), *antĕquam, priusquam.*
Festival, *festum, i,* n.
Game, contest, *certāmen, ĭnis,* n.; Olympic games, *Olympia, ōrum,* n. pl.
Government, kingdom, *regnum, i,* n.
His (not referring to the subject), *ejus, illīus.*
Institute, *instituo, ĕre, institui, institūtum.*
Lacedaemonian, *Lacedaemonius, a, um;* the Lacedaemonians, *Lacedaemonii, ōrum,* m. pl.
Lycurgus, *Lycurgus, i,* m.
Neptune, *Neptūnus, i,* m.
Numitor, *Numĭtor, ōris,* m.
Observe, *servo, āre, āvi, ātum; observo, āre, āvi, ātum.*
Olympic games, *Olympia, ōrum,* n. pl.
Remus, *Remus, i,* m.
Restore, *restituo, ĕre, restitui, restitūtum.*
Seventy, *septuaginta,* indecl.
Sparta, *Sparta, ae,* f.
While, *dum.*

407. Exercises.

I. *Translate and analyze.*

1. Quum Romāni saepe hostes vicissent, apud Cremĕra castra posuērunt. 2. Quum Dracōnis leges crudeliōres essent, legĭtur Solon, qui civitātem novis legĭbus condĕret. 3. Quum Priscus Tarquinius occīsus esset, Tanăquil de superiōre parte domus popŭlum allocūtus est. 4. Is eos ludos instituit ante annos quam Roma conderētur septuaginta. 5. Hoc sacrum instituit Atreus, quum patri funĕbres ludos facĕret. 6. Quamdiu Sparta Lycurgi disciplīnae dilĭgens fuit, excelsissĭme floruit. 7. Dum Sulla in Asia Mithridātem vincit, Marius bellum in Italia reparāvit. 8. Quamdiu motus remănet in nobis, tamdiu vita remănet.

II. 1. *Convert the* subordinate *clauses in the above examples into* independent *sentences.*

MODEL.

Romāni saepe hostes vicērunt.

2. *Construct four Latin sentences with* temporal clauses—*two requiring the* indicative, *and two the* subjunctive.

III. *Translate into Latin.*

1. When was Rome founded? 2. He says that he does not know when it was founded. 3. It was founded seventy years after the Olympic games were instituted. 4. When was Remus killed? 5. He was killed while Rome was building (*pass.*). 6. He was killed before the festival of Neptune was instituted. 7. He was killed after the government had been restored to Numitor. 8. While Lycurgus remained at Sparta, the Lacedaemonians observed his laws. 9. The Lacedaemonians observed the laws of Lycurgus many years after he was dead (*had died*).

Lesson XXXVIII.

Adverbial Attributive-Sentences.—Cause.
[101—103.]

408. Sentences used to assign a cause or reason for the action or event denoted by the principal verb, are called *causal clauses*. They are usually introduced either by a pure causal conjunction, as *quod, quia,* or by *quum, quoniam,* or *quando,* which have reference both to *cause* and *time;* e. g.,

| Quoniam supplicatio decrēta est, celebrāte illos dies. | *Since a thanksgiving has been decreed, celebrate those days.* |

ADVERBIAL ATTRIBUTIVE-SENTENCES.—CAUSE.

Use of Moods in Causal Clauses.

409. Causal clauses take the subjunctive mood, when introduced by *quum*, and the indicative, when introduced by other conjunctions, unless the cause or reason is assigned as the opinion of some other person than the narrator; e. g.

Quae *quum* ita *sint*, Catilīna, perge.	*Since these things are so, Catiline, go on.*
Tardissĭme Lentŭlus venit, *quod* proxĭma nocte vigilavĕrat.	*Lentulus came last, because he had watched the last night.*
Praetōres, *quod* eōrum opĕra fidēli *usus essem*, laudantur.	*The praetors are praised, because I had employed their faithful assistance.*

REM.—It will be observed that the subjunctive is used in the first example after *quum*, the indicative in the second after *quod* to denote that the reason is assigned by the narrator as his own, and the subjunctive in the third example after *quod* to denote that the reason is given on the authority, not of the narrator, but of those who bestowed the praise. The meaning is, *the* praetors *were praised* (by the senate), *because I had employed their faithful assistance;* i. e., this reason was assigned by the senate.

410. VOCABULARY.

Armed, *armātus, a, um.*
Any one, *alĭquis, alĭqua, alĭquid;* any, *ullus, a, um* (see F. B. 118, R.).
Asia, *Asia, ae,* f.
Because, *quod, quia.*
Break down, *rumpo, ĕre, rupi, ruptum; interrumpo, ĕre, interrŭpi, interruptum.*

Bridge, *pons, pontis,* m.
Danube, *Danubius, i,* m.; *Ister, tri,* m.
Darius, *Darĭus, i,* m.
Datis, *Datis, is,* m.
Engage battle, *conflīgo, ĕre, conflixi, conflictum.*
Engagement, battle, *pugna, ae,* f.

Forces, *copiae, ārum,* f. pl.
Have, *habeo, ēre, habui, habĭtum.*
Hundred, *centum,* indecl.; seven hundred, *septingenti, ae, a.*
No one, *nemo* (*ĭnis,* not in good use).
Number, *numĕrus, i,* m.
Opportunity, power, *potestas, ātis,* f.
Over, *sometimes denoted by the genitive;* as, *pons* Istri, the bridge *over* the Danube.
Persian, *Perses, ae,* m.

Place, *locus, i,* m. (pl. *loci* or *loca*).
Relying upon, *fretus, a, um;* rely, *fretus sum.*
Scythians, *Scythae, ārum,* m. pl.
Seven hundred, *septingenti, ae, a.*
Ship, *navis, is,* f.
Terrify greatly, *perterreo, ēre, perterrui, perterrĭtum.*
Thousand, *mille,* indecl.; *millia, millium,* n. pl.
Unfavorable, *non aequus, a, um.*

411. EXERCISES.

I. *Translate and analyze.*

1. Cecrŏpem biformem (229) tradidēre, quia primus marem femīnae matrimonio junxit. 2. Vos, quoniam nox est, veneramĭni Jovem. 3. Darīus hostis fuit Atheniensĭbus, quod eōrum auxilio Iōnes Sardes expugnassent. 4. Quoniam de genĕre belli dixi, nunc de magnitudĭne pauca dicam. 5. Quum hostes ei pugnae potestātem non facĕrent, trepĭdus refūgit. 6. Quum ex Eurōpa in Asiam rediisset, classem quingentārum navium comparāvit. 7. Pythia respondit, ut moenĭbus ligneis se munīrent.

II. 1. *Convert the* causal *clauses in the above exercises into* independent interrogative *sentences.*

MODEL.

Nonne Cecrops primus marem femĭnae matrimonio junxit?

2. *Construct Latin complex sentences with the following* causal *clauses:*

1. Quoniam jam dies est. 2. Quod hostes pugnavērunt. 3. Quia Deiotărus auxilium contra Mithridātem tulĕrat. 4. Quod capĭtis damnātus est. 5. Quae quum ita sint.

III. *Translate into Latin.*

1. Did the Scythians give Darius an opportunity of coming to an engagement (lit. *the opportunity of a battle*)? 2. Why did they not do so (*it*)? 3. They did not give him an opportunity of coming to an engagement, because he had seven hundred thousand armed men. 4. Did any one break down the bridge over the Danube? 5. No one broke it down, because Darius had fled into Asïa. 6. Why did Datis engage battle in an unfavorable place? 7. He engaged battle, because he relied upon the number of his forces. 8. The Persians sought their ships, because they were terrified.

Lesson XXXIX.

Adverbial Attributive-Sentences.—Cause; Condition *and* Concession.

[104—107.]

412. Every conditional sentence consists of two parts—the *condition* and the *consequence;* e. g.,

Si quid habeat, dabit.	*If he has any thing, he will give it.*

Rem.—Here *si quid habeat* is the condition, and *dabit* the consequence.

413. Conditional sentences are of four kinds:

1) Those which assume the condition as a *fact*, i. e., as *already true*; e. g.,

Si quid habet, dat.	*If he has any thing, he gives it, or is giving it.*

Rem.—Here it is assumed that the condition is already realized.

2) Those which represent the condition as a *present uncertainty*, i. e., as one which may or may not be realized at the present moment; e. g.,

Si quid habeat, dabit.	*If he has any thing, he will give it.*

Rem.—Here the condition (*if he has any thing*) relates to the present time, and is represented as one which may or may not be true. It is not in itself dependent upon any contingencies, inasmuch as the fact, relating as it does to the present, is already determined, though we may not know what it is.

3) Those which represent the condition as a *mere possibility*, i. e., as one which has not yet been realized, but may or may not be so at some future time; e. g.,

Si quid habeat, det.	*If he should have any thing,*
Si quid habēret, daret.	*he would give it.*

Rem.—Here the condition is in itself dependent upon contingencies, as it relates to future time. It is to be determined by events which are yet to transpire.

4) Those which represent the condition as an *impossibility*, i. e., as one which has not been realized and never can be; e. g.,

Si quid habēret, daret.	*If he had any thing, he would give it.*
Si quid habuisset, dedisset.	*If he had had any thing, he would have given it.*

REM.—In both these examples, the condition relates to a definite time, and is represented as not then realized.

Use of Moods in Conditional Sentences.

414. In regard to the use of moods in conditional sentences, it may be observed,

> 1) That the *condition* is expressed in the first of the above forms by the *indicative*, in the second by the *subjunctive present* or *perfect*, in the third by the *subjunctive present, perfect* (or *imperfect*), and in the fourth by the *subjunctive imperfect* or *pluperfect.*
>
> 2) That the *consequence* is expressed in the first two of these forms by the *indicative* (or sometimes by the *imperative*), in the third by the *subjunctive present, perfect* (or *imperfect*), and in the fourth by the *subjunctive imperfect* or *pluperfect.*

REM. 1.—The conditional clause is sometimes omitted; e. g., Daret, *He would give* (if he had any thing, perhaps).

REM. 2.—The conditional clause of the 3d form is sometimes used in connection with the indicative; e. g., Spartāni pacem iis sunt pollicĭti, si naves tradĕrent, *The Spartans promised them peace, if they would give up their ships.*

415. Conditional sentences are sometimes introduced by *dum, modo,* or *dummŏdo,* provided, if only, &c. They then take the subjunctive; e. g.,

| Multi omnia recta neglĭgunt, dummŏdo potentiam consequantur. | *Many disregard all right, provided they can acquire power.* |

416. The condition is, of course, often expressed negatively; it is then introduced sometimes by *si* with *non,* sometimes by *nisi,* and sometimes by *ni;* e. g.,

Aequĭtas tollĭtur omnis, *si* habēre suum cuīque *non* licet.	*All equity is removed, if each one may not have his own.*
Parvi sunt foris arma, nisi est consilium domi.	*Arms are worth but little abroad, unless there is wisdom at home.*
An, ni ita se res habēret, Anaxagŏras patrimonia suą reliquisset?	*Would Anaxagoras then have left his patrimony, if this were not so?*

Concessive Sentences.

417. Intimately connected with conditional clauses, are those which express *concession*, which is merely a *conceded* condition or cause; e. g.,

Condition.

Medĭci, *si* intellĭgunt, nunquam aegris dicunt, eos esse moritūros.	*Physicians never tell the sick that they are going to die, if they know it.*

Concession.

Medĭci, *quamquam* intellĭgunt saepe, tamen nunquam aegris dicunt eos esse moritūros.	*Though physicians often know that the sick are going to die, yet they never tell them so.*

REM.—The conjunctions generally used to introduce a concession are *etsi, etiamsi, tametsi, quamquam, quamvis,* and *licet*.

Use of Moods in Concessive Clauses.

418. On the use of moods in concessive clauses, it may be remarked,

1) That *quamquam* is usually followed by the *indicative;* e. g.,

ADVERBIAL ATTRIBUTIVE-SENTENCES.—CAUSE.

Vestra tecta, *quamquam* jam pericŭlum *est depulsum*, tamen custodiis defendĭte.	*Although the danger is now removed, still guard your houses.*

2) That *etsi*, *etiamsi*, and *tametsi*, are generally followed by the *indicative*, unless the concession is presented as a mere supposition, in which case it, of course, requires the subjunctive; e. g.,

Caesar, *etsi* prope *exacta* jam aestas *erat*, tamen eo exercĭtum adduxit.	*Although the summer was nearly spent, still Caesar led his army thither.*
Sunt, qui quod sentiunt, *etiamsi* optĭmum *sit*, tamen non audent dicĕre.	*Some do not dare to say what they think, even if it be very excellent.*

REM.—The concession in the second example is a mere supposition.

3) That *quamvis* and *licet* are followed by the *subjunctive*; e. g.,

Illa *quamvis* ridicŭla *essent*, mihi tamen risum non movērunt.	*Although those things were ludicrous, yet they did not excite my laughter.*

419. VOCABULARY.

Although, though, *quamquam*.
Enemy, *hostis, is*, c.
Fleet, naval forces, *classiarii, ōrum*, m. pl.
Grecian, *Graecus, a, um;* the Greeks, *Graeci, ōrum*, m. pl.
If, *si*.
Leonidas, *Leonĭdas, ae*, m.
Persian, *Persĭcus, a, um*.
Plan, purpose, *consilium, i*, n.

Please, be pleasing to, *placeo, ēre, placui, placĭtum;* displease, be displeasing to, *displiceo, ēre, displicui, displicĭtum*.
Salamis, *Salămis, is*, f.; *Salamīna, ae*, f.
Take possession of, get possession of, *occŭpo, āre, āvi, ātum*.

Themistocles, *Themistŏcles, is,* m.	Wisdom, *consilium, i,* n.
There, *ibi.*	Withstand, sustain, *sustineo, ēre sustinui, sustentum.*
Thermopylae, *Thermopy̆lae, ā-rum,* f. pl.	Xerxes, *Xerxes, is,* m.

420. Exercises.

I. Translate and analyze.

1. Caesar peccāvit, si id fecit. 2. Peccabĭmus, si id faciāmus. 3. Peccārent, si id facĕrent. 4. Puĕri peccavissent, si id fecissent. 5. Spartāni pacem Atheniensĭbus sunt pollicĭti (414, R. 2), si longi muri brachia dejicĕrent. 6. Xerxes etsi male rem gessĕrat, tamen habēbat magnas copias. 7. Spartāni pacem Atheniensĭbus sunt pollicĭti, si naves tradĕrent. 8. Spartāni pacem Atheniensĭbus sunt pollicĭti, si respublĭca triginta rectōres accipĕret. 9. Datis etsi non aequum locum vidēbat suis, tamen conflixit.

II. 1. *Construct four Latin sentences illustrative of the four forms of conditional sentences.*

2. *Construct two or more Latin sentences with concessive clauses.*

III. *Translate into Latin.*

1. Who was Leonidas? 2. He was king of the Lacedaemonians. 3. He was sent to take possession of Thermopylae. 4. Will the Greeks withstand the force of the enemy, if they get possession of Thermopylae? 5. Leonidas did not withstand the force of the enemy, although he had taken possession of Thermopylae. 6. Would Themistocles have engaged the fleet of the Persians, if his plan had not been pleasing to the states of

Greece? 7. He did engage the Persian fleet, although his plan was not pleasing to many of the Grecian states. 8. Who was conquered at Salamis? 9. Xerxes was conquered there by the wisdom of Themistocles.

Lesson XL.

Adverbial Attributive-Sentences.—*Manner;* Consequence *and* Comparison.

[108—110.]

421. Attributive sentences of *manner* are of two kinds:

1) Such as indicate the manner or character of an action or event by giving its *results* or *consequences;* e. g.,

Lucullus ipsum regem ita vicit, ut robur milĭtum Armeniōrum delēret.	*Lucullus so vanquished the king himself as to destroy* (that he destroyed) *the strength of the Armenian soldiery.*

2) Such as indicate the manner or character of the action or event, or the degree of the quality denoted by the predicate, by means of *comparison.* This may be done in two ways; viz.,

(a) By a comparison of *equality*, generally expressed by the correlatives *ut—ita; tam—quam,* and the like; e. g.,

Nemo tam pauper vivit, quam natus est.	*No one lives as poor as he was born.*

(b) By a comparison of *inequality*, expressed by the comparative degree of an adjective or adverb; e. g.,

Eurōpa minor est quam Asia.	*Europe is smaller than Asia.*
Romāni fortius quam hostes pugnavērunt.	*The Romans fought more bravely than the enemy.*

REM. 1.—In a comparison of inequality, the connective *quam* is often omitted, and then the following noun is put in the ablative; e. g., Tullus Hostilius ferocior Romŭlo fuit, *Tullus Hostilius was more ferocious than Romulus.*

REM. 2.—As comparisons of inequality with *quam* are *elliptical;* and as without *quam* they undergo an important change of structure, we must defer the farther consideration and illustration of them to the section on Abridged Complex Sentences.

Use of Moods in Consecutive Clauses.

422. Clauses denoting consequence or result are introduced by *ut*, and take the verb in the subjunctive mood; e. g.,

Quis tam demens, *ut* sua voluntāte *moereat ?*	*Who is so mad as to be sad from choice ?*

REM. 1.—*Ut* in a consecutive clause generally corresponds to some correlative in the principal sentence, signifying *so, such, so great,* &c.; thus, in the above example, we find *tam* in the principal clause.

REM. 2.—If a result is to be expressed negatively, *non* must be used, unless the clause contains some adjective, pronoun, or adverb which may assume the negative form; e. g., Ita sunt multi imbecilli senes, ut *nullum* vitae munus exsĕqui possint, *Many old men are so feeble as to be unable to discharge any duty in life.*— Nemo adeo ferus est, ut *non* mitescĕre possit, *No one is so cruel as not to be able to become mild.*

REM. 3.—Relative clauses sometimes express *result;* e. g., Neque enim tu is es qui nescias, *Nor indeed are you such an one as not to know.*

ADVERBIAL ATTRIBUTIVE-SENTENCES.—MANNER.

423. Vocabulary.

Against, *contra* (with accus.).
Attica, *Attĭca, ae*, f.
Be envious, envy, *invideo, ēre, invīdi, invīsum*.
Conclude, make, *facio, ĕre, feci, factum*.
Country, territory, *fines, finium*, m. pl.
Fifty, *quinquaginta*, indecl.
Fleet, *classis, is*, f.
Forces, *vires, virium*, f., pl. of *vis*.
Greatness, *magnitūdo, ĭnis*, f.
Lay waste, devastate, *popŭlor, āri, populātus sum*.

Peloponnesian, *Peloponnesiăcus, a, um*.
So, to such an extent, *tam, ita*.
So great, such, *tantus, a, um*.
Spartan, *Spartānus, a, um;* the Spartans, *Spartāni, ōrum*, m. pl.
Syracusan, *Syracusānus, a, um;* the Syracusans, *Syracusāni, ōrum*, m. pl.
Syracuse, *Syracūsae, ārum*, f. pl.
Terror, *terror, ōris*, m.
Undertake, *suscipio, ĕre, suscēpi, susceptum*.

424. Exercises.

I. *Translate and analyze.*

1. Victōres rempublĭcam ita inter se divisērunt, ut Lepĭdus Afrĭcam accipĕret. 2. Piratae omnia maria infestābant ita, ut Romānis sola navigatio tuta non esset. 3. Titus fuit vir omnium virtūtum genĕre mirabĭlis adeo, ut amor humāni genĕris dicerētur. 4. Perĭcles agros reipublĭcae dono dedit. 5. Spartāni hostes ad proelium provocābant. 6. Senātus tantas ei gratias congessit, quantas nemĭni unquam egĕrat. 7. Viriāthus tantos ad bellum popŭlos concitāvit, ut vindex libertātis Hispaniae existimarētur.

II. 1. *Convert the* consecutive *clauses in the above exercises into* independent *sentences.*

MODEL.

Lepĭdus Afrĭcam accēpit.

2. *Select from the Latin text of our previous reading lessons five or more sentences with* consecutive *clauses.*

3. *Construct Latin sentences in answer to the following questions:*

1. Why did the Spartans undertake the Peloponnesian war against the Athenians? 2. What was the result of this war? 3. For how long a time was peace concluded? 4. Where did Themistocles engage the fleet of Xerxes? 5. What was the result? 6. Who was defeated in the battle of Salamis? 7. How was he defeated?

III. *Translate into Latin.*

1. The Athenians fought so bravely, that they defeated the enemy. 2. The enemy were so terrified, that they fled. 3. The Spartans were so envious of the greatness of Athens (*so envied greatness to Athens*), that they laid waste the country of Attica. 4. So great forces came to aid (*as aid to;* see 257) the Syracusans, that they were a terror to them. 5. Who sent these forces to Syracuse? 6. The Athenians sent a large fleet to that city.

Lesson XLI.

Complex and Compound Sentences as Elements of other Sentences.
[111—113.]

425. A sentence of any form, whether simple, complex, or compound (164), may be used as an element in the formation of complex sentences.

Rem.—We have thus far used only *simple* sentences as elements of the complex.

426. When a complex sentence is thus used, it must be observed,

1) That its principal clause assumes the same form as if it were a simple sentence.
2) That its subordinate clause, provided it is given either as the sentiment of some third person and not of the narrator himself, or as an essential part of the entire assertion, generally changes the indicative to the subjunctive, when the predicate of the principal clause is either in the subjunctive or infinitive; e. g.,

Ad haec Caesar respondit, se id quod in Nerviis fecisset, factūrum.	*To this Caesar replied, that he would do what he had done in the case of the Nervii.*

Rem. 1.—If the subordinate clause merely limits a particular term, without forming an essential part in the general thought of the proposition, the indicative must be used; e. g., Caesāri renuntiātur, Helvetiis esse in anĭmo iter in Santōnum fines facĕre, qui non longe a Tolosatium finĭbus absunt, *It is announced to Caesar, that it is the intention of the Helvetians to go to the territory of the Santonians, which is not far from the country of the Tolosatians.* Here the clause *qui non*, &c., is given merely to explain *fines*, and accordingly takes its verb in the indicative.

Rem. 2.—If the subordinate clause of the complex sentence is expressed by any other mood than the indicative before the sentence is thus made dependent, it remains unchanged; e. g., 1. Ubi jam *se ad eam rem parātos esse* arbitrāti sunt, oppĭda sua omnia incendunt, *When they thought that they were already prepared for this, they set fire to all their towns.* Here the adverbial attribute of time is expressed by a complex sentence which in its independent form requires its object-clause, *se ad eam rem parātos esse*, to take the infinitive; accordingly that mood is retained when the entire sentence becomes subordinate. 2. Caesar, etsi intelligēbat, *qua de causa ea dicerentur*, tamen Indutiomărum ad se venire jussit, *Caesar, although he knew why these things were spoken, still ordered Indutiomarus to come to him.* Here the subjunctive *dicerentur* is retained just as it would have been if this concessive clause were used as an independent sentence.

427. When a compound sentence (164) is used as an element in the formation of complex sentences, its several constituent parts, being independent of each other, assume the same form as if each one were used alone; e. g.,

Caesar certior fiēbat, omnes Belgas contra popŭlum Romānum conjurāre, et has esse causas.	*Caesar was informed, that all the Belgians were conspiring against the Roman people, and that these were the causes.*

Rem.—Here the compound sentence might stand thus: "*Omnes Belgae contra popŭlum Romānum conjuravērunt, et hae fuērunt causae.*" When, however, it is made subordinate, its two parts both change their verbs to the infinitive; just as either would have done, if the other had not been used at all.

428. VOCABULARY.

Adopt measures for or against, *consŭlo, ĕre, consului, consultum;* to adopt cruel measures, *crudelĭter consŭlo, ĕre,* &c.
Alcibiades, *Alcibiădes, is,* m.
Be occupied, be busy, *distringor, i, districtus.*
Commander, general, *dux, ducis,* m.

Cut off, *interclūdo, ĕre, interclūsi, interclūsum.*
Fortification, *munitio, ōnis,* f.
Four hundred, *quadringenti, ae, a.*
Historian, *historĭcus, i,* m.
Inhabitant, *incŏla, ae,* m. & f.
Inhabitant of Catina, *Catinensis, is,* or *Catiniensis, is,* m. & f.
People, *plebs, plebis,* f.

Recover, *recipio, ĕre, recēpi, receptum.*
Restore, *reddo, ĕre, reddĭdi, reddĭtum.*
Right, rights, *jus, juris,* n.
Supplies, *commeātus, us,* m.
Terms, condition, *conditio, ōnis,* f.
Unless, *nisi.*
When, *quum, tum—quum.*

429. EXERCISES.

I. *Translate and analyze.*

1. Legāti id fiĕri vetant. 2. Lacedaemonii legātos Athēnas misērunt, qui id fiĕri vetārent. 3. Themistŏcles muros Athenārum restituit, non sine pericŭlo suo, quum Lacedaemonii legātos Athēnas misissent, qui id fiĕri vetārent. 4. Id responsum quo valēret, quum intelligĕret nemo, Themistŏcles persuasit, consilium esse Apollĭnis, ut in naves se conferrent. \ 5. In epigrammăte erat haec sententia: suo ductu Barbăros apud Plataeas esse delētos, ejusque victoriae ergo Apollĭni donum dedisse. 6. Mittitur Gylippus, qui quum de belli jam inclināto statu audivisset, opportūna bello loca occŭpat.

II. *Construct two or more Latin sentences, each containing one or more* complex *sentences as elements.*

III. *Translate into Latin.*

1. The inhabitants of Catina asked aid of the Athenians. 2. Why did they ask aid? 3. Historians say that they asked aid, because the terms of peace were not observed by the Syracusans. 4. When they sent ambassadors to Athens to ask aid, the Athenians were occupied with the Peloponnesian war. 5. Do you know what the Athenian generals did in Sicily? 6. It is said that they built fortifications in order to cut off the inhabitants from supplies. 7. Who was ap-

pointed commander of the Athenian fleet, when the senate adopted cruel measures against the people? & Alcibiades was appointed commander, in order that he might recover the rights of the people from the four hundred, unless they should themselves restore them

§ 2.—*Complex Sentences; Abridged.*

Lesson XLII.

Principal Elements, Abridged.
[114—117.]

430. We have seen that sentences, used as elements of others, are sometimes introduced unchanged, as direct quotations, and sometimes undergo certain alterations to adapt them to their new situations; e. g.,

Direct Quotation.

| Dicit, "*Rex venit.*" | *He says,* "The king is coming." |

Indirect Quotation.

| Dicit *regem venīre.* | *He says* that the king is coming. |

431. In either of the above cases, the complex sentence appears in its full form; but sometimes a part of the subordinate clause is omitted, as when it can be easily supplied from the rest of the sentence; the complex sentence may then be said to be abridged.

432. Sentences are abridged in two ways:

    1) A portion of the subordinate clause is omitted, and the rest remains unchanged; e. g.,

PRINCIPAL ELEMENTS, ABRIDGED. 199

Cupio discĕre. | *I desire to learn.*
Eurōpa minor est quam | *Europe is smaller than Asia.*
Asia. |

> REM.—In the first example, the subject of the subordinate clause (*me*) is omitted, because it is the same person as the subject of the principal part (*ego*), and *discĕre* retains the same form as if the subject were expressed. So in the second example, the *predicate* of the subordinate clause is omitted, as it can be easily supplied from the principal part, while the subject and connective, *quam Asia*, remain unchanged.

2) A portion of the subordinate clause is omitted, and the rest is changed to adapt it to its new situation; e. g.,

Eurōpa minor est Asiā. | *Europe is smaller than Asia.*

> REM.—Here it will be observed that not only the predicate of the subordinate clause has disappeared (*as in case 1st*), but also the connective *quam*, and that the following noun *Asiā* loses its character as subject, and is put in the ablative.

Subordinate Clauses as Principal Elements, Abridged.

433. An infinitive sentence used as subject or predicate may have its own subject omitted, when it expresses a general truth, or when its subject may be easily supplied; e. g.,

Turpe est mentīri. | *To lie is base.*

> REM.—Here *mentīri* is subject, but its own subject is omitted, because, the truth being a general one, any subject we please may be supplied: thus, *that you, I, any one, should lie*, is base.

434. When the infinitive is used as the subject of a sentence, the predicate is sometimes expressed by the *copula* and a *genitive;* e. g.,

Regis est regnāre. | *It is the part of the king to reign.*

REM. 1.—Here it is obvious that *regnāre* is the subject, and *regis est* is the predicate.

REM. 2.—Combining articles 203 and 434, we have the following

435. RULE.—*Predicate Nouns.*

A noun in the predicate after the verb *esse* and a few passive verbs, is put,

    1) In the same case as the subject when it denotes the same person or thing; e. g.,

Cicĕro fuit consul. | *Cicero was consul.*

    2) In the genitive when it denotes a different person or thing; e. g.,

Regis est regnāre. | *It is the part of a king to reign.*

[F. B. 613; A. & S. §§ 210, 211, R. 8; Z. §§ 365, 448.]

436. The infinitive after passive verbs with personal subjects should be treated as a predicate nominative (see 229, 230), and, as the subject of the infinitive is omitted, being the same person or thing as that of the passive, any predicate noun, adjective, or participle after the infinitive is generally attracted into the nominative to agree with the subject of the passive verb; e. g.,

Rex beātus esse dicĭtur. | *The king is said to be happy.*
Coriolānus occīsus esse dicĭtur. | *Coriolanus is said to have been put to death.*

REM.—It will be observed that *beātus* in the first example and *occīsus* in the second would have been in the accusative to agree with the subjects of the infinitives if they had been expressed, but are here attracted into the nominative to agree with the subject of *dicĭtur*.

437. VOCABULARY.

Accept, *accipio, ĕre, accēpi, acceptum.*
Be wise, *sapio, ĕre, sapīvi* or *sapii.*
Besiege, *obsĭdeo, ēre, obsēdi, obsessum; obsidiōne circumdo, āre, dĕdi, dătum.*
Best, *optĭmus, a, um* (superl. of *bonus*).
Happily, *beāte.*
Live, *vivo, ĕre, vixi, victum.*

Lysander, *Lysander, dri,* m.
Promise, offer, *polliceor, ēri, pollicĭtus sum.*
Republic, *respublĭca, reipublĭcae,* f. (See A. & S. 91.)
Right, uprightly, *recte.*
Ruler, director, *rector, ōris,* m.
Thirty, *triginta,* indecl.
Thither, *eo, illo, illuc.*
Tyrant, *tyrannus, i,* m.

438. EXERCISES.

I. *Translate and analyze.*

1. Recte facĕre satis est. 2. Latīne loqui est in magna laude ponendum. 3. Bene sentīre non satis est. 4. Docto homĭni vivĕre est cogitāre. 5. Ne mihi noceant, vestrum est providēre. 6. Dum haec geruntur, a Lacedaemoniis Lysander classi praeficĭtur. 7. Atheniensium exercĭtum ad Aegos flumen oppressit. 8. Spartanōrum dux eo impĕtu totum bellum delēvit. 9. Triginta rectōres reipublĭcae constituuntur. 10. A principio tria millia satellĭtum sibi statuunt.

II. 1. *In the first four of the above sentences, insert subjects to the infinitives.*

MODEL.

Regem recte facĕre satis est.

2. *Construct three Latin sentences—one with infinitive as subject, one with infinitive as predicate, and one with infinitives both as subject and predicate.*

III. *Translate into Latin.*

1. It is always best to do right. 2. Is it certain that you have done right? 3. It is the part of a good citizen to observe the laws. 4. It is certain that good citizens will obey the laws. 5. To live happily is to do right. 6. To be wise is to be good. 7. With how many ships did Alcibiades go into Asia? 8. He went thither with one hundred ships. 9. It is said that he went thither to lay waste the country. 10. Athens was besieged by Lysander. 11. The Spartans promised peace to the Athenians, if the republic would accept thirty rulers. 12. This condition was accepted. 13. The thirty rulers whom the Spartans appointed were thirty tyrants.

Lesson XLIII.

Modifier of Subject or other Noun, Abridged.
[118 & 119.]

439. The relative clause, modifying the subject or any other noun, is sometimes abridged by dropping both the relative and the copula, and retaining only the attribute.

440. When a relative clause is thus abridged, the attribute may be expressed,

> 1) By a *participle* agreeing with the antecedent of the omitted relative. This occurs when the predicate of the relative clause would have been expressed by a *verb;* e. g.,

| Tullia aurīgam super patris corpus in via *jacens* carpentum agĕre jussit. | *Tullia ordered the charioteer to drive over her father's body, which lay* (lit. *lying*) *in the way.* |

2) By an *adjective* agreeing with the antecedent of the omitted relative. This occurs when the predicate would have been expressed by an *adjective* and the copula *esse;* e. g.,

| Habētis ducem *memŏrem vestri*. | *You have a leader* mindful (*who is mindful*) *of you.* |

3) By a *noun* in apposition with the antecedent of the omitted relative. This occurs when the predicate would have been expressed by a *noun* and the copula *esse;* e. g.,

| Aenēas, *Anchīsae filius*, mortuus est. | *Aeneas, the son of Anchises* (*who was the son*, &c.), *died.* |

Rem.—Combining the above with article 190, we have the following

441. RULE.—*Limiting Nouns.*

A noun limiting the meaning of another noun is put
1) In the same case as that noun, when it denotes the same person or thing; e. g.,

| Brutus consul. | *Brutus the consul.* |

2) In the genitive, when it denotes a different person or thing, unless it expresses *character* or *quality*, in which case it is accompanied by an adjective, and is put either in the *genitive* or *ablative;* e. g.,

| Regis filius. | *The king's son.* |

Puer eximiae pulchritudĭnis, *or* Puer eximia pulchritudĭne.	*A boy of remarkable beauty.*

[F. B. 624; A. & S. §§ 204, 211, R. 6; Z. §§ 370, 423, 426, 471.]

442. Instead of a sentence modifying a substantive, we often find either a gerund (with or without modifiers) or a gerundive (*fut. pass. participle*) in agreement with some other substantive; e. g.,

Omnis occasio *exercendi virtūtem* (or, *exercendae virtūtis*) arripiātur.	*Let every opportunity of practising virtue be seized.*

443. RULE.—*Gerund.*

The gerund is governed like a noun in the same case. (See above example.)

[F. B. 374; A. & S. § 275, III. R. 1, 2, 3, 4; Z. §§ 659, 664, 666, 667.]

444. RULE.—*Gerundive.*

Instead of a gerund governing its case, we may use the gerundive, *participle in dus*, agreeing with a noun. (See above example.)

[F. B. 382; A. & S. § 275, II.; Z. § 656.]

445. VOCABULARY.

Announce, *nuntio, āre, āvi, ātum.*
Appoint, commission, *praepōno, ĕre, praeposui, praeposĭtum.*
Artaxerxes, *Artaxerxes, is,* m.
Bequeathe, *lego, āre, āvi, ātum.*
Bind, *vincio, īre, vinxi, vinctum.*
Castle, *castellum, i,* n.
Chain, fetter, *compes, ĕdis,* f.
Cyrus, *Cyrus, i,* m.
Fortified, *munītus, a, um;* very strongly fortified, *munitissĭmus, a, um.*
Flee for refuge, *confugio, ĕre, confūgi, confugĭtum.*
Hold, *teneo, ēre, tenui, tentum.*
Phyle, *Phyle, es,* f.
Prepare, *paro, āre, āvi, ātum.*
Servitude, *servĭtus, ūtis,* f.
Summon, send for, *arcesso, ĕre, īvi, ītum.*
Thrasybulus, *Thrasybūlus, i,* m.

446. Exercises.

I. *Translate and analyze.*

1. Triginta tyranni, praepositi a Lacedaemoniis, servitūte tenuērunt Athēnas. 2. Quum triginta tyranni, praepositi a Lacedaemoniis, servitūte tenērent Athēnas, Thrasybūlus Phylen confūgit. 3. Neminem jacentem veste spoliāvit. 4. Obscūrum antea Macedŏnum nomen emersit. 5. Quibus rebus effectum est, ut obscūrum antea Macedŏnum nomen emergĕret. 6. In secundo proelio cecĭdit Critias, triginta tyrannōrum acerrĭmus. 7. Eōdem fere tempŏre Darius, rex Persārum, morĭtur. 8. Sapientia ars vivendi est.

II. 1. *Fill out the abridged clauses in the above sentences.*

MODEL.

Triginta tyranni, *qui* praepositi *sunt* a Lacedaemoniis, servitūte tenuērunt Athēnas.

2. *Construct two or more Latin sentences with modifiers of subjects abridged.*

III. *Translate into Latin.*

1. By whom was the city of Athens (*the city Athens*) held in servitude? 2. It is said that it was held in servitude by the thirty tyrants appointed by the Spartans. 3. Whither did Thrasybulus flee for refuge? 4. He fled for refuge to Phyle, a very strongly fortified castle in Attica. 5. Darius, the king of the Persians, bequeathed his kingdom to his son Artaxerxes. 6. When it was announced to Artaxerxes that his brother Cyrus was preparing war against him, he summoned him into his presence (*to himself*). 7. It is said that Cyrus, having been summoned into the presence of his brother, was bound in golden chains.

Recapitulation

LESSON XLIV.

Object of Predicate, Abridged.
[120 & 121.]

447. When the subject of an infinitive-sentence used as object is the same person or thing as that of the verb on which it depends, that subject is often omitted after verbs denoting *desire, intention, custom, ability, duty,* and the like, and also after various *passive verbs;* e. g.,

Cupio discĕre.	*I desire to learn.*
Assuefacti sunt muros defendĕre.	*They were accustomed to defend their walls.*

> REM.—It will be observed that, in the first example, the infinitive stands as *direct* object, and in the second, as *indirect* object. After verbs of *desiring, intending,* &c., the infinitive is used as *direct* object, while after verbs denoting *custom, ability, duty,* and the like, it stands only as *indirect* object.

448. When the subject of the infinitive mood is omitted in consequence of its denoting the same person or thing as that of the verb on which it depends, any predicate noun or adjective after the infinitive is attracted into the nominative to agree with the subject of the principal verb; e. g.,

Omnes volunt esse beāti. | *All wish to be happy.*

> REM.—It will be observed that *beāti*, which would be in the accusative if the subject of *esse* were expressed, is here attracted into the nominative to agree with the subject of the principal verb.

449. An infinitive-sentence used as object of a transitive verb may sometimes be abridged by making its subject the object of the principal verb, and converting

the infinitive into a participle agreeing with that object; e. g.,

Non audīvit Alexander dracōnem *loquentem*.	*Alexander did not hear the dragon* speak (lit. *speaking*).
Illud signum ita *collocandum* consŭles locavērunt.	*The consuls contracted to have this statue thus* placed.

450. Instead of a sentence modifying the substantive or adjective predicate, whether objective or attributive, we often find either a gerund, or a gerundive in agreement with some substantive; e. g.,

Epaminondas studiōsior *audiendi* fuit.	*Epaminondas was too fond of* hearing.

Rem.—The gerund *audiendi* depends upon *studiōsior*. See Rule, 443.

451. Instead of a subordinate clause denoting *purpose—indirect object*—a gerund, or a gerundive agreeing with some substantive, is often used, and is put sometimes in the dative, and sometimes in the accusative with a preposition; e. g.,

Aqua utĭlis est *bibendo*.	*Water is useful for* drinking.
Boum terga non *ad onĕra accipienda* figurāta sunt.	*The backs of oxen were not formed* for receiving burdens.

452. The supine in *um* is sometimes used after verbs of motion in place of a subordinate clause of *purpose*; e. g.,

Legāti ad Caesărem *gratulātum* convenērunt.	*Ambassadors came to Caesar to congratulate him.*

453. Rule.—*Supine in* um.

The supine in *um* follows verbs of motion to express the purpose or object of that motion. (See example above.)

[F. B. 676; A. & S. § 276, II; Z. § 668.]

454. Vocabulary.

Advice, *consilium, i,* n.
Belong to, be to, *sum, esse, fui, futūrus* (with dative).
Cadmea, *Cadmēa, ae,* f.
Choose, *delĭgo, ĕre, delēgi, delectum.*
Conon, *Conon, ōnis,* m.
Defeat, *vinco, ĕre, vici, victum.*
Depart, go, *proficiscor, ci, profectus sum.*
Desist, *discēdo, ĕre, discessi, discessum.*
Despair, desperation, *desperatio, ōnis,* f.
Drive, drive away, *pello, ĕre, pepŭli, pulsum.*
Engagement, battle, *proelium, i,* n.

Exile, banishment, *exsilium, i,* n.
Exile, a person banished, *exsul, ŭlis,* m. & f.
Land, field, *ager, agri,* m.
Naval, *navālis, e.*
Opening, beginning, *initium, i,* n.
Order, v., *jubeo, ēre, jussi, jussum.*
Otherwise, *alĭter.*
Pelopidas, *Pelopĭdas, ae,* m.
Pericles, *Perĭcles, is,* m. (See F. B. 174.)
Theban, *Thebānus, a, um.*
Untouched, uninjured, *intactus, a, um.*
Voluntary, *voluntarius, a, um.*

455. Exercises.

I. *Translate and analyze.*

1. Pausanias honorātum adversarium vidit. 2. Philippus regnāre cum amīcis volēbat. 3. Amāri pater maluit. 4. Hic metui maluit. 5. Alexander universum terrārum orbem vincĕre est aggressus. 6. Ille urbem obsidēre statuit. 7. Artaxerxes, rex Persārum, legātos in Graeciam mittit, per quos jubet omnes ab ar

mis discedĕre. 8. Liberandae patriae propria laus est Pelopīdae, qui, exsilio multātus, Athēnas se contulĕrat.

II. 1. *Construct two or more Latin sentences with objects abridged.*

2. *Construct Latin sentences in answer to the following questions:*

1. What state took the lead (*acted as leader*) against the Athenians in the Peloponnesian war? 2. What advice did Pericles give the Athenians in the opening of the war? 3. Why did he give his own lands to the republic? 4. In how many naval engagements did Alcibiades defeat the Spartans? 5. Why was Conon sent to take his place? 6. What became of Alcibiades? 7. What was the result of the Peloponnesian war? 8. Who were appointed over the Athenian republic?

III. *Translate into Latin.*

1. Who ordered the Greeks to desist from arms? 2. They were ordered by Artaxerxes, the king of the Persians, to desist from arms. 3. Did they not wish to do otherwise? 4. To whom belongs the praise of liberating the Cadmea from the Spartans? 5. This praise belongs to Pelopidas, the Theban exile, who, having chosen a day for liberating the state, drove the Spartans from the citadel.

Lesson XLV.

Attribute of Predicate, Abridged.—Comparison *and* Participles.

[122—125.]

456. Complex sentences involving comparisons of inequality (421, 2) take two different constructions; viz.,

>1) The connective *quam* may be used; and then the following noun is generally in the same case as the corresponding noun before *quam*; e. g.,

Eurōpa minor est quam Asia.	*Europe is smaller* than Asia.

> Rem.—When the same word belongs to both members of the comparison in Latin, it is generally expressed in the first and omitted in the second; in English, however, it is expressed in the first, and represented in the second by the pronoun *that* or *those;* e. g., Maris superficies major est quam terrae, *The surface of the sea is greater than* (that) *of the land.* Here the noun after quam (*terrae*) is in the same case as the corresponding noun *maris* before it.

>2) The connective *quam* may be omitted; and then the following noun is put in the ablative; e. g.,

Nihil est *clementiā* divinius.	*Nothing is more godlike* than clemency.

457. Rule.—*Comparison.*

The comparative degree is followed,

>1) *Without quam,* by the ablative.

2) *With quam*, generally by the case of the corresponding noun before it. (See examples above.)

[F. B. 636; A. & S. § 256; Z. § 483.]

458. An attributive sentence of *time, cause, manner, condition, concession,* &c., may be abridged,

1) When its subject is some person or thing mentioned in the principal clause, by dropping the *subject* and *copula*, and generally the *connective*, and retaining the attributive part of the predicate in the form of a *participle, adjective*, or *noun* (according to the form of predicate) in agreement with that noun in the principal clause; e. g.,

Caesar, *in Britanniam proficiscens*, Morĭnos relīquit.	*Caesar*, going (i. e. *when he went*) into Britain, *left the Morini*.
Quidam hanc patriam, *hinc nati*, urbem hostium esse judicavērunt.	*Some*, born here (*though born here*), *have judged this country to be a city of the enemies*.
Hic, *puer duodeviginti annōrum*, patrem servāvit.	*He*, (when) a boy of eighteen years, *preserved his father*.

Rem.—Whenever, in thus abridging a sentence, a participle would be required in the *perfect active* with an object, the perfect passive must be used in the *ablative absolute* (see 2 below) with that object, as the Latin has no perfect active; e. g., Hostes, *impĕtu facto*, nostros perturbavērunt, *The enemy*, having made an attack (lit. *an attack having been made*), *put our soldiers into disorder*.

2) When its subject is some person or thing not mentioned in the principal clause, by drop-

ping the connective and copula, and putting the subject in the ablative with the *participle, adjective,* or *noun* of the predicate in agreement with it. This construction is called the *ablative absolute;* e. g.,

Hostes, *nihil timentĭbus nostris,* celerĭter nostros perturbavērunt.	*The enemy,* while our soldiers feared nothing (lit. *our soldiers fearing nothing*), *quickly put them into disorder.*
Cicerōne consŭle, Catilīna ad delendam patriam conjurāvit.	In the consulship of Cicero (*when Cicero was consul*), *Catiline conspired for the destruction of his country.*

459. RULE.—*Agreement of Participles.*

Participles like adjectives (189) agree, in *gender, number,* and *case,* with the nouns to which they belong. (See examples above.)

[F. B. 614; A. & S. § 205.]

460. RULE.—*Ablative Absolute.*

A noun and a participle, a noun and an adjective, or two nouns, standing grammatically independent of the rest of the sentence, are put in the ablative absolute. (See above examples.)

[F. B. 678; A. & S. § 257, R. 7; Z. §§ 640, 644, 645.]

REM.—Participles are sometimes used to abridge independent clauses; e. g., Quos Tyrii contra jus gentium occisos praecipitavērunt in altum, *The Tyrians slew them contrary to the law of nations, and threw them into the sea.*

461. Vocabulary.

Add, join to, *adjungo, ĕre, adjunxi, adjunctum.*
All, the whole, *totus, a, um.* (See F. B. 113, R.)
As (before nouns), *often untranslated.*
Cavalry, *equĭtes, um,* m. pl. of *eques; equitātus, us,* m.
Distinguished, *praestans, tis.*
Epaminondas, *Epaminondas, ae,* m.
Hostage, *obses, ĭdis,* m. & f.
House, home, *domus, us* & *i,* f.
Instructed, learned, accomplished, *erudĭtus, a, um.*
Larissa, *Larissa, ae,* f.

Keep, have, *habeo, ēre, habui, habĭtum.*
Macedonia, *Macedonia, ae,* f.
Philip, *Philippus, i,* m.
Reside, *habĭto, āre, āvi, ātum.*
Strength, *robur, ŏris,* n.
Subjugate, impose the yoke of servitude, *servitūtis jugum impōno, ĕre, imposui, impositum.*
Thebes, *Thebae, ārum,* f. pl.
Thessalian, *Thessălus, a, um.*
Victorious, *expressed by* victor, *ōris, m. in apposition with the noun.*
Virtue, *virtus, ūtis,* f.

462. Exercises.

I. *Translate and analyze.*

1. Alexander, ad Persĭcum bellum proficiscens, patrimonium omne suum amīcis divīsit. 2. Philippus, in Scythiam profectus, numĕro praestantes Scythas dolc vicit. 3. Alexander virtūte patre major fuit. 4. Hic vitiis Philippo major fuit. 5. Motae quaedam civitātes Atheniensĭbus se jungunt. 6. Atheniensĭbus per insidias victis, Philippus incolŭmes sine pretio dimīsit. 7. Post haec, bello in Illyrios translāto, multa millia hostium caedit. 8. Philippus, obses triennio Thebis habĭtus in Epaminondae domo, Graeciae servitūtis jugum imposuit.

II. *Explain the force of the participles in the above sentences, showing to what kind of clause each is equivalent, i. e. whether temporal, causal, &c.*

· MODEL.

Ad Persicum bellum proficiscens, is an abridged *temporal* clause, showing when Alexander divided his patrimony, viz. *on going to the Persian war* = *when he went*, &c.

III. *Translate into Latin.*

1. How long did Philip reside at Thebes? 2. He was there three years. ˙3. He was kept as a hostage in the house of Epaminondas. 4. Having been kept as a hostage for three years at Thebes, he returned to Macedonia. 5. Having been kept as a hostage in the house of Epaminondas, he was instructed in all the virtues of this distinguished man. 6. On returning (458) to Macedonia, he subjugated all Greece. 7. Having taken Larissa in Thessaly, he added to his victorious army the strength of the Thessalian cavalry.

Lesson XLVI.

Attribute of Predicate, Abridged; Gerunds *and* Supines.
[126—129.]

463. The gerund, as already mentioned (450), sometimes expresses the attribute of a substantive or adjective predicate; e. g.,

Sapientia ars *vivendi* putanda est.	*Wisdom should be regarded as the art of living.*

REM.—The forms of the gerund are very properly regarded as the oblique cases of the infinitive, and accordingly are the abridged forms of subordinate clauses: thus, *ars vivendi*, in the first example, literally construed would stand, *the art of the to live* = the art of living.

ATTRIBUTE OF PREDICATE ABRIDGED. 215

464. Instead of a subordinate proposition modifying the verb predicate, the gerund with a preposition, or a gerundive and a substantive with a preposition, may be used to express adverbial relations; e. g.,

Inter ludendum cantābant.	*They were singing* while playing.
Brutus *in liberanda patria* est interfectus.	*Brutus was killed* in liberating his country.

465. The ablative of the gerund, or of the gerundive in agreement with a substantive, without a preposition often supplies the place of a subordinate clause of *cause, manner, means*, &c.; e. g.,

Mens *discendo* alĭtur.	*The mind is strengthened* by learning.
Loquendi elegantia augētur *legendis oratorĭbus*.	*Elegance of speech is cultivated* by reading orators.

☞ For Rules for the government of gerunds and gerundives, see 443, 444.

466. The supine in *u* may supply the place of an adverbial clause after certain adjectives, whether in the subject or predicate; e. g.,

Hoc optĭmum *factu* est. | *This is best* to be done.

467. RULE.—*Supine in* u.

The supine in *u* is used after adjectives signifying *good* or *bad, easy* or *difficult, agreeable* or *disagreeable*, &c. (See above example.)

[F. B. 635; A. & S. § 276, III; Z. § 670.]

☞ For the use of supine in *um*, see 452.

468. VOCABULARY.

Alexander, *Alexander, dri,* m.
Arrive, *advenio, ire, advēni, adventum.*
Deceive, *decipio, ĕre, decēpi, deceptum.*
Delight, rejoice, *gaudeo, ēre, gavīsus sum.*
Go, hasten, *contendo, ĕre, contendi, contentum.*
Hero, *heros, ōis,* m.
Learn, *disco, ĕre, didĭci.*
Macedonian, *Macedonĭcus, a, um; Macĕdo, ŏnis,* m.

Narrow passage, *angustiae, ārum,* f. pl.
Offer sacrifices, to sacrifice (in honor of parents, &c.), *parento, āre, āvi, ātum.*
Pausanias, *Pausanias, ae,* m.
See, witness, *specto, āre, āvi, ātum.*
Tomb, *tumŭlus, i,* m.
Whose, *cujus, a, um; cujus; quorum.*
Youth, young man, *adolcscens, entis,* m.

469. EXERCISES.

I. *Translate and analyze.*

1. Homĭnis mens discendo alĭtur. 2. Omnes multum tempŏris ludendo amittĭmus. 3. Philippus ad ludos spectandos contendit. 4. Atheniensium exercĭtus in terram praedātum exiĕrat. 5. Philippus, in Scythiam praedandi causa profectus, numĕro praestantes Scythas dolo vicit. 6. Parcendi victis filio anĭmus promptior. 7. Vincendi ratio utrīque diversa fuit. 8. Athenienses misērunt Delphos consultum, quidnam facĕrent de rebus suis.

II. *Construct two or more Latin sentences with gerunds, and two or more with supines.*

III. *Translate into Latin.*

1. They have learned much by reading. 2. All can learn much by reading good books. 3. Philip learned much by witnessing the virtues of Epaminondas the Theban. 4. Who killed Philip? 5. Pausanias, hav-

ing taken possession of (458, 1, R.) the narrow passage, killed him. 6. He was going to see the games, when this Macedonian youth killed him. 7. Who succeeded Philip? 8. Alexander succeeded his father Philip. 9. The father is said to have delighted in deceiving the enemy (lit. *in the enemy deceived*). 10. The son delighted in routing them. 11. At whose tomb did Alexander offer sacrifices on arriving in Asia? 12. He is said to have sacrificed at the tombs of the Trojan heroes.

10

CHAPTER III.

COMPOUND SENTENCES.

§ 1.—*Compound Sentences; Unabridged.*

Lesson XLVII.

Classes of Compound Sentences.

[130 & 131.]

470. A COMPOUND sentence is one which consists of two or more independent though related sentences.

Rem.—The sentences, thus united, may themselves be either simple, complex, or compound.

471. Compound sentences may be divided into three classes; viz.,

    1) *Copulative* sentences, in which two or more thoughts are presented in harmony with each other; e. g.,

Longas naves aestus complēbat; *et* onerarias tempestas afflictābat.	*The water filled the warships;* and *the storm tossed the ships of burden.*

    2) *Disjunctive* sentences, in which a choice between two or more thoughts is offered; e. g.,

Audendum est aliquid universis, *aut* omnia singŭlis patienda sunt.	*Something must be braved by all,* or *all things must be endured by each.*

CLASSES OF COMPOUND SENTENCES. 219

3) *Adversative* sentences, in which the thoughts stand opposed to each other; e. g.,

Difficĭle factu est, *sed* conā- bor.	*It is difficult to do*, but *I will try it.*

472. Copulative clauses may be connected by the conjunctions *et, atque, ac, que,* or *nec, neque.*

> REM. 1.—*Et* is the most common, and is used to connect thoughts (or words) of equal importance; *que,* which is an enclitic (i. e. *is always appended to some other word*), indicates a more intimate relationship, and is generally used when the second part represents something as belonging to the first or derived from it, &c.; *atque* is used when the second part is more important than the first; *ac,* which is abbreviated from *atque,* never stands before a vowel, and has generally the force of *et.* *Neque* and *nec* have the force of *et non.*
>
> REM. 2.—Associated with these conjunctions, we sometimes find *etiam, adeo, quoque,* &c., and sometimes these last only are used.

473. Sometimes a connective appears in both clauses; thus, we find the following correlative particles: *et—et; quum—tum; tum—tum =* both—and; *non solum—sed etiam =* not only—but also; *ut—ita; tamquam =* as—so; as well—as; both—and; *neque—neque; nec—nec =* neither—nor; e. g.,

Et longas naves aestus complēbat; *et* onerarias tempestas afflictābat.	Both *the water filled the war-ships,* and *the storm tossed the ships of burden.*

474. Sometimes a causal adverb or conjunction appears with the copulative, as *igĭtur, ideo, enim,* &c., and sometimes the copulative is omitted, leaving only the causal adverb as connective; the sentence, however, retains its co-ordinate character; e. g.,

Nihil laborās; *ideo* nihil habes.	*You do nothing,* and accordingly *have nothing.*

475. Disjunctive sentences usually employ some one or more of the following connectives: *aut, vel, sive, ve,* or the correlatives *aut—aut; vel—vel; sive—sive; seu —seu.* (See example, 471, 2.)

> REM.—When the second member is a stronger expression than the first, or is really the carrying out of the same idea, *vel* or *sive* is often accompanied by *etiam* or *potius;* e. g., Discessus fuit perturbātus, *sive potius* fuga turpissīma, *The departure was very disorderly,* or rather *the flight most disgraceful.*

476. Adversative sentences usually employ some one or more of the following connectives: *sed, autem, at, verum, vero, tamen* and its compounds *attămen* and *verumtămen,* and *atqui.* (See example, 471, 3.)

477. VOCABULARY.

And, *et, atque, ac, que* (enclitic). (See 472, R. 1.)
Around, *circa, circum.*
Become *or* be made unmanageable, *effĕror, āri, efferātus sum,* pass. of *effĕro.*
But, *sed, autem,* &c. (476).
Chariot, *currus, us,* m.
Fall (in battle), *cado, ĕre, cecĭdi, casum.*
Few, *pauci, ae, a.*
Fought, *commissus, a, um.*

High-minded, *magnanĭmus, a, um; magnifĭcus, a, um.*
Horse, *equus, i,* m.
Issus, *Issus, i,* f.
Pierce, *confodio, ĕre, confŏdi, confossum.*
Prudent, *prudens, tis.*
Slightly, lightly, *levĭter.*
Spear, *hasta, ae,* f.
Than, *quam,* or *indicated by ablative after comparatives.*
Wound, *vulnĕro, āre, āvi, ātum.*

478. EXERCISES.

I. *Translate and analyze.*

1. Philippo Alexander filius successit. 2. Prudentior ille consilio, hic anĭmo magnificentior. 3. Vini uterque nimis avĭdus; sed ebrietātis diversa ratio. 4. Perdicca occīsus est, pluresque duces periērunt. 5. De

exercĭtu Alexandri centum viginti equĭtes cecidērunt, et cognātis eōrum immunitātes a publĭcis munerĭbus dedit. 6. Quaedam civitātes Atheniensĭbus se jungunt; quasdam autem ad Philippum belli metus traxit. 7. Commisso proelio, Alexander non ducis magis quam milĭtis munia exsequebātur.

II. 1. *Explain the nature of the connection existing between the different members of the above compound sentences.*

2. *Construct three or more Latin sentences, illustrating the different kinds of co-ordination.*

III. *Translate into Latin.*

1. Philip was prudent, and Alexander was high-minded. 2. Philip was more prudent than his son Alexander, but the son was more high-minded than the father. 3. Alexander conquered the Persian king in a battle fought at Issus; and there the noblest leaders fell around the chariot of Darius. 4. Was not Darius himself wounded? 5. He was not wounded, but his horses, having been pierced with spears, became unmanageable. 6. Did many of the Macedonians perish at Issus? 7. A few of them perished, and the king himself is said to have been slightly wounded.

Lesson XLVIII.

Formation of Compound Sentences.

[132 & 133.]

479. Compound sentences may be formed by co-ordinating in some one or more of the ways just mentioned,

1) Two or more simple sentences; e. g.,

Gyges a nullo videbātur, ipse *autem* omnia vidēbat.	*Gyges was seen by no one,* but *he himself saw every thing.*

2) Two or more complex sentences; e. g.,

Hi sunt homĭnes ex iis coloniis, quas Sulla constituit; *sed tamen* hi sunt colōni, qui se in insperātis pecuniis insolentius jactārunt.	*These are men from those colonies which Sylla planted;* but yet *these are colonists who have become too insolent in their unexpected wealth.*

3) Two or more compound sentences; e. g.,

Graeciae Antipăter praeponĭtur; regiae pecuniae custodia Cratĕro tradĭtur; *sed* exercĭtus cura Perdiccae assignātur et Aridaeus rex agnoscĭtur.	*Antipater is appointed over Greece, and the guardianship of the royal treasury is intrusted to Craterus,* but *the care of the army is assigned to Perdicca, and Aridaeus is recognized as king.*

4) Simple, complex, and compound, in a single sentence, or either two of the three kinds, as simple and complex, simple and compound, or complex and compound; e. g.,

Nunquam ego a diis optābo ut haec audiātis, *sed* illa audiētis.	*I shall never desire of the gods that you may hear these things,* but *you will hear them.*

FORMATION OF COMPOUND SENTENCES. 223

480. VOCABULARY.

Ammon *or* Hammon, *Ammon or Hammon, ōnis*, m.
Approach, *adventus, us,* m.
Charles, *Carŏlus, i,* m.
Consult, *consŭlo, ĕre, consului, consultum.*
Contrary to, *contra.*
Design, designate, *designo, āre, āvi, ātum.*
Determine, *statuo, ĕre, statui, statūtum.*
Dutiful, *pius, a, um.*
Egypt, *Ægyptus, i,* f.
Egyptian, *Ægyptius, a, um;* the Egyptians, *Ægyptii, ōrum,* m. pl.
Empire, *imperium, i,* n.
Ever, always, *semper.*
Fear, *metuo, ĕre, metui, metūtum.*
Former—latter, *ille—hic.*
Gladly, *expressed by adj.* laetus, a, um, *in agreement with subject.*
Go, *eo, ire, ivi, itum*

God, *deus, i,* m. (See A. & S. § 53.)
John, *Johannes, is,* m.
Jupiter, *Jupĭter, Jovis,* m. (See A. & S. § 85.)
Latter, *hic, haec, hoc.*
Law *or* right of nations, *jus gentium.*
Lay siege to, besiege, *obsideo, ĕre, obsēdi, obsessum.*
Love, *amo, āre, āvi, ātum.*
Oracle, *oracŭlum, i,* n.
Receive, *recipio, ĕre, recēpi, receptum.*
Slay, kill, *occĭdo, ĕre, occĭdi, occīsum.*
Tyre, *Tyrus, i,* f.
Tyrian, *Tyrius, a, um;* the Tyrians, *Tyrii, ōrum,* m. pl.
Visit, go to, *adeo, īre, adii, adĭtum.*
Whether, *sometimes expressed by an.*
World, *orbis, is,* m.; *orbis terrae* or *terrārum.*

481. EXERCISES.

I. *Translate and analyze.*

1. Ægyptii Alexandrum laeti recepērunt, nec sustinuēre adventum ejus Persae. 2. Ægyptii, olim Persārum opĭbus infensi, Alexandrum laeti recepērunt; nec sustinuēre adventum ejus Persae, defectiōne perterrĭti. 3. Regnāre ille cum amīcis volēbat; hic in amīcos regna exercēbat. 4. Amāri pater voluit; hic

metui maluit. 5. Parcendi victis filio anĭmus promptior; ille nec sociis abstinēbat. 6. Motae quaedam civitātes Atheniensĭbus se jungunt; quasdam autem ad Philippum belli metus traxit.

II. 1. *Construct two simple sentences in Latin, and then unite them by some co-ordinate conjunction.*

2. *Construct a complex sentence, and unite it with the compound formed above.*

III. *Translate into Latin.*

1. The Egyptians received Alexander gladly, but the Persians were terrified at his approach. 2. Charles is feared, and John is loved; but the former is said to be a good father, and the latter has ever been a dutiful son. 3. Why did Alexander determine to lay siege to Tyre? 4. He determined to besiege the city, because the Tyrians, contrary to the law of nations, slew the ambassadors whom he had sent to them. 5. What oracle did he visit in Egypt? 6. He visited the oracle of Jupiter Ammon to consult whether the father of the gods designed the empire of the world for him.

§ 2.—*Compound Sentences; Abridged.*

Lesson XLIX.

Compound Elements.—Subjects, United.
[134—137.]

482. The several members of a compound sentence frequently differ from each other only in their *subjects*, and then these subjects are generally united, and the

other elements appear but once, though in such a form as to agree with the compound subject; e. g.,

Romāni bella multa gessērunt.	The Romans *waged many wars.*
Graeci bella multa gessērunt.	The Greeks *waged many wars.*
Romāni et Graeci bella multa gessērunt.	The Romans and Greeks *waged many wars.*

<small>REM.—Here it will be observed that the predicate and modifiers are the same in both the sentences united to form the compound, and accordingly they appear but once in that compound.</small>

Caesar bella multa gessit.	Caesar *waged many wars.*
Hannĭbal bella multa gessit.	Hannibal *waged many wars.*
Caesar et Hannĭbal bella multa *gessērunt.*	Caesar and Hannibal *waged many wars.*

<small>REM.—Here it will be observed that the predicate in the compound is changed to the plural to agree with the compound subject.</small>

483. RULE.—*Agreement.*

When the members of a compound subject are united by *copulatives* (except *nec, neque*), the predicate is generally put in the plural; but, when they are united by *disjunctives* or *adversatives*, it is generally in the singular, if the members themselves are of that number; e. g.,

Caesar *et* Hannĭbal bella multa *gessērunt.*	*Caesar* and *Hannibal waged many wars.*
Caesar *aut* Hannĭbal bella multa *gessit.*	*Caesar* or *Hannibal waged many wars.*

<small>[F. B. 612, R.; A. & S. § 209, R. 12; Z. § 365.]</small>

Rem. 1.—If the subjects are of different persons, the verb agrees with the first in preference to the second, and with the second in preference to the third; e. g., Si tu et Tullia valētis, ego et Cicĕro valēmus, *If you and Tullia are well, Cicero and I are well.*

Rem. 2.—If the subjects are of different genders, any predicate adjective or participle in the plural generally takes the gender of one of the subjects, preferring the *masculine* to the feminine and the *feminine* to the neuter; unless the subjects denote things without life, and then they are usually put in the neuter; e. g., Patĕr mihi et mater mortui sunt, *My father and mother are dead.*—Labor voluptasque inter se sunt juncta, *Labor and pleasure are united together.*

Rem. 3.—Sometimes the verb in the singular is used in agreement with one of the subjects connected by copulatives, and is understood with the rest, and sometimes the verb in the plural is used with subjects in the singular connected by disjunctives, especially when one of these subjects is in the first or second person; e. g., Omnes anĭmi cruciātus egestas ac mendicītas consequātur, *Let want and beggary follow all the agonies of mind.*—Si quid Socrătes aut Aristippus fecĕrint, &c., *If Socrates or Aristippus did any thing, &c.*

Rem. 4.—When different modifiers belong to the several subjects united, they must each be associated with their respective subjects; e. g., Fuērunt anno primo consŭles Brutus, acerrĭmus libertātis vindex, et Collatīnus, marītus Lucretiae, *Brutus, the most valiant defender of liberty, and Collatinus, the husband of Lucretia, were the consuls the first year.*

484. Vocabulary.

Arbela, *Arbēla, ōrum,* n. pl.
Both — and, *et — et ; quum — tum,* &c. (See 478.)
Bravely, *fortiter.*
Nearly, *fere.*
Or, *aut ;* in double questions, *an, ne,* sometimes *an* in the second clause, and *utrum, num,* or *ne,* in the first. (See F. B. 482.)
Reach, arrive at, *pervenio, ire, pervēni, perventum.*
Rush, rush together, *concurro, ĕre, concurri, concursum.*
Village, *vicus, i,* m.

COMPOUND SUBJECTS. 227

485. Exercises.

I. *Translate and analyze.*

1. Romŭlus et Remus pueritiam inter pastōres transēgērunt. 2. In exercĭtu Alexandri fuērunt pedĭtum triginta duo millia, equĭtum quatuor millia quingenti, naves centum octoginta duae. 3. De exercĭtu ejus novem pedĭtes, centum viginti equĭtes cecidērunt. 4. Inter captīvos castrōrum mater et uxor et filiae duae Darīi fuērunt. 5. Nec Persae nec Macedŏnes dubitavēre, quin ipse rex esset occīsus. 6. Puĕri virginesque templa complevĕrant.

II. *Give in full the sentences which have been united in the formation of the first four of the above compounds.*

MODEL.

Romŭlus pueritiam inter pastōres transēgit. (482.)
Remus pueritiam inter pastōres transēgit. (482.)

III. *Translate into Latin.*

1. Darius reached the village of Arbela. 2. The Persians reached the village of Arbela. 3. Darius and the Persians reached the village of Arbela. 4. The Lacedaemonians rushed to arms. 5. Did not all Greece rush to arms? 6. The Lacedaemonians and nearly all Greece rushed to arms. 7. Both Persians and Macedonians fought bravely. 8. Were the Lacedaemonians, or the Persians conquered at Arbela? 9. The Persians were conquered there.

Lesson L

Compound Elements.—Predicates, United.

[138—141.]

486. The several members of a compound sentence frequently differ only in their *predicates*, and then these predicates are united, while the other elements appear but once ; e. g.,

Scipio Carthagĭnem *cepit*.	*Scipio* took *Carthage*.
Scipio Carthagĭnem *diruit*.	*Scipio* destroyed *Carthage*.
Scipio Carthagĭnem *cepit ac diruit*.	*Scipio* took and destroyed *Carthage*.

REM.—When the modifiers of the several predicates are not the same, they must be associated with their respective predicates ; e. g., Is et in custodiam cives dedit et supplicationem mihi decrēvit, *He both delivered citizens into custody and decreed a thanksgiving to me.*

487. The copulative connective is often omitted both in the full and in the abridged form of the compound sentence ; e. g.,

Catilīna abiit.	*Catiline has gone.*
Catilīna evāsit.	*Catiline has escaped.*
Catilīna erūpit.	*Catiline has broken away.*
Catilīna abiit, evāsit, erūpit.	*Catiline has gone, has escaped, has broken away.*

488. If the predicate is expressed by a copula and attribute separately, the copula being the same in the several parts, we have only to unite the attributes ; e. g.,

Asia *opīma* est.	*Asia is* rich.
Asia *fertīlis* est.	*Asia is* fertile.
Asia *opīma* est *et fertīlis*.	*Asia is* rich and fertile.

489. If there are modal adverbs (265) or modifiers, connected with either part, they must generally be retained with that part; if the same modal adverb belongs to each member, it is generally repeated, either alone or in combination with the connective; e. g.,

Otii fructus est *non* contentio anĭmi.	*The fruit of ease is* not *the vigorous exercise of mind.*
Otii fructus est relaxatio anĭmi.	*The fruit of ease is the relaxation of mind.*
Otii fructus est *non* contentio anĭmi, *sed* relaxatio.	*The fruit of ease is* not *the vigorous exercise of mind,* but *the relaxation of it.*
Attĭcus mendacium *non* dicēbat.	*Attĭcus did* not *speak a falsehood.*
Attĭcus mendacium *non* pati potĕrat.	*Attĭcus was* not *able to endure a falsehood.*
Attĭcus mendacium *neque* (*et non*) dicēbat, *neque* (*et non*) pati potĕrat.	*Attĭcus* neither (*both not*) *spoke a falsehood* nor (*and not*) *was able to endure one.*

490. Vocabulary.

After, *post*.
Amphipolis, *Amphipŏlis, is,* f.
Appoint, institute, *instituo, ĕre, institui, institūtum*.
Babylon, *Babȳlon, ōnis,* f.
Beseech, pray, *precor, āri, precātus sum*.

Chaeronea, *Chaeronēa, ae,* f.
Death, *mors, mortis,* f.
Disregard, contemn, *contemno, ĕre, contempsi, contemptum*.
Enter, *introeo, īre, īvi* or *ii, ĭtum*.
Feast, *convivium, i,* n.

Hasten, *festīno, āre, āvi, ātum.*
Lead, *duco, ĕre, duxi, ductum.*
Magi, *Magi, ōrum,* m. pl.
Move, excite feeling, *moveo, ēre, movi, motum.*
One, certain one, *quidam, quaedam, quoddam.*
Prayers, *preces, um,* f. pl.
Prediction, *praedictum, i,* n.

Return, *reverto, ĕre, reverti, ro versum.*
Rise in importance, *emergo, ĕre, emersi, emersum.*
Show, *ostendo, ĕre, ostendi, ostensum* and *ostentum.*
Superior to, greater than, *major, us* (comp. of *magnus*).
Wound, *vulnus, ĕris,* n.

491. Exercises.

I. *Translate and analyze.*

1. Tumultuantes milĭtes Alexander ipse sedāvit, eosque omnes ad conspectum suum admīsit. 2. Darīus desĭlit et in equum, qui ad hoc ipsum sequebātur, imponĭtur. 3. Cetĕri dissipantur metu, et, qua cuĭque patēbat via, erumpunt. 4. Non solĭta sacra Philippus illa die fecit; non in convivio risit; non corōnas sumpsit; et ita vicit ut victōrem nemo sentīret. 5. Accepto pocŭlo, inter bibendum, velŭti telo confixus, ingemuit.

II. *Construct Latin sentences in answer to the following questions:*

1. What state rose in importance after the death of Epaminondas? 2. Why did Philip reside at Thebes? 3. Where did he first engage the Athenians? 4. Who fought at Chaeronea? 5. What were the particulars of the death of Philip? 6. Who succeeded him? 7. Was Alexander in any respect superior to his father? 8. What were the first acts of his reign? 9. What was the result of the battle of Issus? 10. What country did Alexander visit after taking Tyre?

III. *Translate into Latin.*

1. The soldiers showed Alexander their wounds,

and besought him to lead them home. 2. He was moved by their prayers, and hastened to Babylon. 3. One of the Magi besought him not to enter the city. 4. He disregarded the prediction of the Magi, returned to Babylon, and appointed a feast.

Lesson LI.

Compound Elements.—Modifiers of Subject, United.
[142—144.]

492. The several members of a compound sentence frequently differ only in the *modifiers* of their *subjects;* and then these modifiers may be united, and the other elements of the sentence appear but once; e. g.,

Venit Epicūrus, *homo minime malus.*	*Epicurus,* the least sinful of men, *came.*
Venit Epicūrus, *vir optĭmus.*	*Epicurus,* the best of the great, *came.*
Venit Epicūrus, *homo minime malus, vel potius vir optĭmus.*	*Epicurus,* the least sinful of men, or rather the best of the great, *came.*

☞ For the use of *potius* with *vel*, see 475, Rem.

493. VOCABULARY.

Antigonus, *Antigŏnus, i,* m.
Antipater, *Antipăter, tri,* m.
Aridaeus, *Aridaeus, i,* m.
Call, *voco, āre, āvi, ātum.*
Cassander, *Cassander, dri,* m.
Claim, *vindĭco, āre, āvi, ātum.*
Demetrius, *Demetrius, i,* m.

Direct, order, *jubeo, ēre, jussi, jussum.*
Gaul, *Gallia, ae,* f.
Glory, *gloria, ae,* f.
Majesty, dignity, rank, *majestas, ātis,* f.
Ptolemy, *Ptolemaeus, i,* m.

Regal, *regius, a, um.*
Sardinia, *Sardinia, ae,* f.
Self-control, *moderatio, ōnis,* f.

Victory, *victoria, ae,* f.
Wait for, await, *opperior, īrī, opperītus* and *oppertus.*

494. Exercises.

I. *Translate and analyze.*

1. Castrōrum et exercĭtus cura Perdiccae assignātur. 2. Septĭmo mense capta est urbs et vetustāte orīgĭnis et crebra fortunae varietāte insignis. 3. Legatiōnes Carthăginiensium ceterarumque Afrĭcae civitātum Alexandri adventum Babyloniae opperiebantur. 4. Macedoniae Antipăter praeponĭtur; jubeturque · Aridaeus corpus Alexandri in Hammōnis templum deducĕre. 5. Tunc Perdicca, lustratiōne castrōrum indicta, seditiōsos supplicio occulte tradi jubet.

II. 1. *Give in full the sentences united in the above compounds.*

MODEL.

Castrōrum cura Perdiccae assignātur.
Exercĭtus cura Perdiccae assignātur.

2. *Construct two or more Latin sentences differing only in the modifiers of the subject, and then unite them in the form of an abridged compound.*

III. *Translate into Latin.*

1. Aridaeus, who was king and the brother of Alexander, was directed to assume the name (*be called by the name*) of his father Philip. 2. The glory, both of self-control and of victory, belongs to Ptolemy. 3. Cassander, who was the son of Antipater and who had waged war against Antigonus, claimed for himself the royal majesty. 4. Philip, the son of Demetrius, and king of

COMPOUND OBJECTS.

Macedonia, sent ambassadors to Hannibal. 5. Ambassadors from Sicily, Gaul, and Sardinia, were awaiting the arrival of Alexander at Babylon.

LESSON LII.

Compound Elements.—Objects of Predicate, United.
[145—147.]

495. The several parts of a compound sentence sometimes differ only in the *objects* of their *predicates ;* and then these objects, may be united, and the other elements of the sentence appear but once ; e. g.,

Non *imperium* petĭmus.	*We do not seek* power.
Non *divitias* petĭmus.	*We do not seek* wealth.
Non *imperium,* neque (*et non*) *divitias* petĭmus.	*We do not seek* power or wealth.
Orābant Ubii, *ut Caesar sibi auxilium ferret.*	*The Ubii asked* that Caesar would bring aid to them.
Orābant Ubii, *ut Caesar exercĭtum Rhenum transportāret.*	*The Ubii asked* that Caesar would transport his army across the Rhine.
Orābant Ubii, *ut Caesar sibi auxilium ferret, vel exercĭtum Rhenum transportāret.*	*The Ubii asked* that Caesar would bring aid to them, or transport his army across the Rhine.

REM.—Observe that when the subordinate clauses are united in the last example, the subject *Caesar* disappears in the second part, because it has been used in the first.

496. Vocabulary.

Aim at, seek, *quaero, ĕre, quaesīvi* and *quaesii, quaesītum.*
Brennus, *Brennus, i,* m.
Infantry, foot-soldiers, *pedĭtes, um,* m. pl., from *pedes, ĭtis,* a foot-soldier.
Liberty, *libertas, ātis,* f.

Neither—nor, *nec—nec ; neque —neque.* (See 473.)
Power, domination, *dominatio, ōnis,* f.
Spartan, *Spartănus, a, um ;* the Spartans, *Spartāni, ōrum,* m. pl.

497. Exercises.

I. *Translate and analyze.*

1. Alexander, non juvĕnes robustos, sed veteranos elēgit. 2. Opulenta regum munĕra magnificentiā sua et gratam homĭnum voluntātem et Apollĭnis responsum manifestant. 3. Dona et sacerdotĭbus et deo data sunt. 4. Alexander omnes interfĭci, ignemque tectis injĭci jubet. 5. Jamque qui Darīum vehēbant equi jugum quatĕre et regem curru excutĕre coepĕrant. 6. Hic dies universae Graeciae et gloriam dominatiōnis et vetustissĭmam libertātem finīvit.

II. 1. *Give in full the sentences united in the formation of the above compounds.*

MODEL.

Alexander non juvĕnes robustos elēgit.
Alexander veteranos elēgit.

2. *Construct two or more simple sentences differing only in their* objects, *and then unite them in the form of an abridged compound.*

III. *Translate into Latin.*

1. The Spartans aimed at (*sought*) power. 2. They did not aim at the liberty of Greece. 3. They aimed at power, but not the liberty of Greece. 4 Did you

not see the king? 5. We saw both the king and his son. 6. You saw neither the king nor his son. 7. The Gauls sought Greece and Macedonia. 8. Brennus sent both infantry and cavalry into Macedonia.

Lesson LIII.

Compound Elements.—Attributives of Predicate, United.
[148—150.]

498. The several members of a compound sentence sometimes differ from each other only in the *attributives* of their *predicates;* and then these attributives may be united, and the other elements appear but once; e. g.,

Magnos homĭnes *virtūte* metīmur.	*We measure great men* by their worth.
Magnos homĭnes *non fortūna* metīmur.	*We do* not *measure great men* by their success.
Magnos homĭnes *virtūte* metīmur, *non fortūna*.	*We measure great men* by their worth, not by their success.

499. Vocabulary.

Booty, *praeda, ae*, f.
Either—or, *aut—aut; vel—vel*, &c. (See 475.)
Excite, *acuo, ĕre, acui, acūtum*.
Land, *terra, ae,* f.
Not only—but also, *non solum—sed etiam*.
Often, *saepe*.
Overwhelm, *obruo, ĕre, obrui, obrŭtum*.

Other, the rest, *relĭquus, a, um*.
Pannonia, *Pannonia, ae,* f.
Penetrate, *penĕtro, āre, āvi, ātum*.
Rock, piece of rock, *saxum, i,* n.
Sea, *mare, is*, n. (abl. *e* or *i*); by sea and land, *terra marique*.
Spirits, courage, *anĭmus, i,* m.
Statue, *statua, ae,* f.

500. Exercises.

I. *Translate and analyze.*

1. Dux Hannĭbal constituĭtur, non penuria seniōrum, sed odio Romanōrum. 2. Alexander et virtūte et vitiis patre major fuit. 3. Omnes ante eum reges continentia et clementia vicit. 4. Victus est non virtūte hostīli, sed insidiis suōrum et fraude. 5. Ptolemaeus et Cassander contra Antigŏnum bellum terra marīque instruunt. 6. Brennus quum in conspectu habēret templum, ad acuendos suōrum anĭmos praedae ubertātem militĭbus ostendēbat.

II. 1. *Give in full the sentences united in the formation of the above compounds.*

MODEL.

Dux Hannĭbal constituĭtur non penuria seniōrum.
Dux Hannĭbal constituĭtur odio Romanōrum.

2. *Construct one or more Latin sentences with compound adverbial attributives.*

III. *Translate into Latin.*

1. Brennus excited the spirits of his soldiers by the golden statues and other booty. 2. Did not Cassander wage war both by sea and land? 3. Wars have often been waged both by sea and land. 4. Did not the Gauls go into Italy? 5. They penetrated not only into Italy, but also into Pannonia. 6. The Greeks overwhelmed the Gauls with rocks and arms. 7. Will you go to Athens? 8. I will go either to Athens or to Rome. 9. Have you been at Rome and Athens? 10. I have been at Rome, but not at Athens.

Lesson LIV.
Elements Common to Different Members.
[151—153.]

501. The several members of a compound sentence sometimes differ from each other in two or more of their elements, and still have one or more in common. When this is the case, the parts which are common to the several members appear in one of them, but are usually omitted in the rest; e. g.,

Proxĭmo die Caesar e castris copias suas eduxit.	On the following day, Caesar led out his forces from the camp.
Proxĭmo die Ariovistus partem suārum copiārum praemīsit.	On the following day, Ariovistus sent forward a part of his forces.
Proxĭmo die Caesar e castris copias suas eduxit, et Ariovistus partem suārum copiārum praemīsit.	On the following day, Caesar led out his forces from the camp, and Ariovistus sent forward a part of his forces.

Rem.—It will be observed that here the common element *proxĭmo die* appears but once, and that all the other parts retain their positions in their respective members.

502. Vocabulary.

After (adv.), *post*.
Ancient, *antīquus, a, um*.
At one time, at a certain time, once, *quondam*.
Beyond, *extra*.
Compel, *compello, ĕre, compŭli, compulsum*.
Elder, greater (in age), *major, us*.
Even, *etiam, vel*.

Fight, engage (as battle), *com-mitto, ĕre, commīsi, commissum.*
Limit, *termĭnus, i,* m.
Lose, *amitto, ĕre, amīsi, amissum.*
Perseus, *Perseus, i,* m.
Possession, *possessio, ōnis,* f.

Receive, *accipio, ĕre, accēpi, acceptum.*
Reject, *repudio, āre, āvi, ātum.*
Short, *brevis, e.*
Sue for, seek, *peto, ĕre, petīvi* and *petii, petītum.*
Wage, *infĕro, inferre, intŭli, illātum.*

503. EXERCISES.

I. *Translate and analyze.*

1. Alexander aperte, Philippus artĭbus bella tractābat. 2. Verbis atque oratiōne hic, ille rebus moderatior. 3. Frugalitāti pater, luxuriae filius magis dedĭtus erat. 4. Occīso Demetrio sublatōque aemŭlo, non negligentior tantum Perseus in patrem, verum etiam contumacior; nec herēdem regni, sed regem se gerēbat. 5. His ita composĭtis, Macedoniae et Graeciae Antipăter praeponĭtur; regiae pecuniae custodia Cratĕro tradĭtur.

II. *Give in full the sentences united in the formation of the above compounds.*

MODEL.

Alexander aperte bella tractābat.
Philippus artĭbus bella tractābat.

III. *Translate into Latin.*

1. Did the Greeks ever wage war against Philip? 2. At one time, all Greece waged war against king Philip, and compelled him to sue for peace. 3. As this peace was rejected (*abl. abs.*) by the senate, a battle was fought, and Philip was conquered, and lost all the states of Greece beyond the limits of his ancient pos-

sessions. 4. Who was Perseus? 5. He was the elder of the sons of Philip, king of Macedonia. 6. A short time after, Demetrius was put to death, and Perseus received the government.

Lesson LV.
Classification of Sentences.—Recapitulation.
[154—156.]

504. Sentences may be divided, according to the form in which the thought is expressed, into three classes; viz.,

1) *Declarative Sentences*, which assume the form of an assertion.
2) *Interrogative Sentences*, which assume the form of a question.
3) *Imperative Sentences*, which assume the form of a command, exhortation, or entreaty.

505. In each of the above forms, sentences sometimes imply passion or emotion on the part of the speaker, and may then be called *exclamatory declarative* if of the declarative form, *exclamatory interrogative* if of the interrogative form, and *exclamatory imperative* if of the imperative form.

506. Again: sentences may be divided according to their structure into three classes; viz.,

1) *Simple Sentences*, which express but a single thought, i. e., make but one assertion, ask but one question, or give but one command.
2) *Complex Sentences*, which express two or more

thoughts, so related that one or more of them are made dependent upon the others.

3) *Compound Sentences*, which express two or more independent thoughts.

I. SIMPLE SENTENCES.

507. The elements of the simple sentence, as we have already seen, are of two kinds:

    I. *Principal Elements;* viz.,
        1) Subject.
        2) Predicate.
    II. *Subordinate Elements;* viz.,
        1) Objective Modifiers.
        2) Attributive Modifiers.

508. These elements appear in two different forms; viz.,

    1) *Simple*, i. e., without modifiers.
    2) *Complex*, i. e., with modifiers.

II. (*a*) COMPLEX SENTENCES.

509. A simple sentence may become complex by having one or more sentences substituted for one or more of its constituent elements.

510. A sentence thus used as an element in the formation of a complex sentence, may be itself either *simple, complex,* or *compound*.

511. The subordinate character of a sentence thus used may be denoted,

    1) By a subordinate connective without any change in the sentence itself.

    2) By a change of form without the use of a connective.

3) By a connective and a corresponding change of form.

(b) ABRIDGED COMPLEX SENTENCES.

512. Complex sentences are abridged in two ways:
1) A portion of the subordinate clause is omitted; and the rest remains unchanged.
2) A portion of the subordinate clause is omitted; and the rest is changed to adapt it to its new situation.

REM.—The first case, involving only the ellipsis of a part, requires but little attention, while the second, involving a change of structure, should be carefully studied.

1. *Change in the Form of the Subject.*

513. The subject of the subordinate clause, when changed by abridging the sentence, is put,
1) In the ablative with predicate omitted, as after comparatives without *quam*.
2) In the ablative absolute with the participle, adjective, or noun, which remains to represent the predicate.

2. *Change in the Form of the Predicate.*

514. (I) The verb-predicate of the subordinate clause, when changed by abridging the sentence, assumes the form
1) Of a *Participle*. This must agree with some noun in the principal clause, if the subject is omitted, otherwise it will be in the ablative absolute with that subject.
2) Of a *Gerund*.
3) Of a *Supine*.

515. (II) Both substantive and adjective predicates

in the subordinate clause, when changed by abridging the sentence, are put,

    1) When the subject is omitted, in agreement with some noun in the principal clause.

    2) When the subject is expressed, in the ablative absolute with that subject.

III. (a) COMPOUND SENTENCES.

516. Compound sentences may be formed by co-ordinating any two or more sentences.

> REM.—The sentences, thus co-ordinated, may be either simple, complex, or compound.

517. This co-ordination is of three distinct kinds; viz.,

    1) Copulative.
    2) Disjunctive.
    3) Adversative.

(b) ABRIDGED COMPOUND SENTENCES.

518. When the several members of a compound sentence have one or more parts in common, those parts, as we have seen in the last few lessons, generally appear but once in the sentence.

519. VOCABULARY.

Achaean, *Achaeus, a, um;* the Acheans, *Achaei, ōrum,* m. pl.
Aetolian, *Aetōlus, a, um;* the Aetolians, *Aetōli, ōrum,* m. pl.
Apollo, *Apollo, ĭnis,* m.
Arise, *orior, orīri, ortus sum* (inflected in most of its parts like verbs of 3d conj.).
As slaves, *sub corōna,* i. e. with crowns upon their heads.

Corinth, *Corinthus, i,* f.
Dagger, *pugio, ōnis,* m.
Delphi, *Delphi, ōrum,* m.
From, on account of, *propter.*
Happen, be effected, *fio, fĭĕri, factus sum;* how does it happen that, &c., *qui fit ut,* &c.
Individual, separate, *singŭli, ae, a,* distrib. pl.

Invade, *invādo, ĕre, invāsi, invāsum.*
Life, *vita, ae,* f.
Make an irruption, *irrumpo, ĕre, irrūpi, irruptum.*
Mummius, *Mummius, i,* m.
Perdiccas, *Perdiccas* or *Perdicea, ae,* m.
Plunder, *spolio, āre, āvi, ātum.*
Put an end to, *finio, īre, īvi, ītum.*

Sell, *vendo, ĕre, vendĭdi, vendĭtum.*
Strength, power, *opes, um,* m. pl.
Subdue, *subĭgo, ĕre, subēgi, subactum.*
Temple, *templum, i,* n.
Think of, *agĭto, āre, āvi, ātum.*
Union, *conspiratio, ōnis,* f.
Very powerful, *potentissĭmus, a, um* (superl. of *potens*).

520. EXERCISES.

I. *Translate and analyze.*

1. Perseus victor misit legātos ad consŭlem, qui pacem petĕrent. 2. Consul Sulpicius non minus graves, quam victo, leges dixit. 3. Dum haec aguntur, Romāni Aemilium Paulum consŭlem creant, eīque Macedonĭcum bellum decernunt. 4. Spartānis a senātu responsum est, legātos se ad inspiciendas res sociōrum in Graeciam missūros. 5. Apud Achaeos omnia neglecta et solūta fuĕrunt.

II. *Construct Latin sentences in answer to the following questions:*

1. Who was made king after the death of Alexander? 2. Who was appointed over Greece and Macedonia? 3. Between which of the generals did war arise? 4. What became of Perdiccas? 5. What people made an irruption into Greece a few years after? 6. Under whom did they invade Greece? 7. For what purpose did they march to Delphi? 8. What were the particulars of their defeat and flight? 9. What became of Brennus?

III. *Translate into Latin.*

1. By whom were the Macedonians subdued? 2. Both the Macedonians and Aetolians were subdued by the Romans. 3. The Achaeans were very powerful, not from (*on account of*) the strength of the individual states, but from the union of all. 4. They were conquered by Mummius, the Roman consul. 5. How did it happen that he conquered them? 6. They were defeated, because they were thinking of the booty, and not of the battle. 7. The Romans destroyed the city of Corinth, and sold all its citizens as slaves.

RULES FOR TRANSLATING.

521. TRANSLATION consists in transferring thought and feeling from one language to another. To do this correctly and elegantly, the pupil must both get a clear idea of the exact meaning of the passage before him, and must embody that meaning with its full force in the language into which he is rendering. Thus conducted, the exercise of translating from the ancient classics, those living embodiments of great thoughts and stirring sentiments, those finished models of taste and beauty, becomes, in the highest degree, interesting and instructive. To prepare the pupil for this work, and to form in him thus early the habit of translating into good idiomatic English, is the object of the following rules. They relate to a large class of important idioms found in the Latin, and indicate one or more ways of translating them without doing violence to our vernacular.

I. *Participles.*

522. The participle is much more extensively used in Latin than in English; hence the frequent necessity, in its translation, of deviating from the Latin construction. It must not, however, be supposed that this must always be done, or that it is desirable to attempt it. On the contrary, it often happens that the participle may be more elegantly translated literally than in any other way. The following rules, therefore, whether relating to participles or other subjects, are designed to apply only to those cases in which a literal translation would fail, in point of clearness, accuracy, or elegance, to do justice to the original.

523. Participles in the perfect and future passive may express the action of their verbs *substantively*; they should then be translated by corresponding verbal nouns; e. g.,

Ad Romam condĭtam.	*To the founding of Rome.* (*Lit.* To Rome founded.)
Ab urbe condĭta.	*From the founding of the city.*
Post reges exactos.	*After the banishment of the kings.*

524. Participles are sometimes used merely to limit or explain some noun or pronoun; they are then in most instances best translated by relative clauses; e. g.,

Romŭlus asȳlum patefēcit, ad quod multi ex civitatĭbus suis *pulsi* accurrērunt.	*Romulus opened an asylum to which many who had been banished from their own states, came.*
In proelio ibi *exorto* omnes perierunt.	*In a battle which was fought* (*lit.* arose) *there, all perished.*

525. Participles sometimes state the *time* of an action or event; they should then be translated by a *verb* or *participle* with *while, when*, or *after*, by a *noun* with *during* or *after;* or, if in the ablative absolute, by an active participle in agreement with the subject of the leading proposition; e. g.,

Urbem, omnĭbus *delētis* exercitĭbus, occupāvit.	*Having destroyed all their armies, he took the city.*

REM.—Sometimes participles, used as above, may be best translated by *on* with a *participial noun;* e. g., Qua re audīta, *On hearing this.*

526. Participles may state the *manner, cause,* or *reason* of an action or event; they should then be translated by *verbs* with *as, for, since,* &c., or by *substantives* (including participial nouns) with *by, from, through, in,* &c.; e. g.,

Aqua *refluens* eos in sicco reliquit.	*The water in or by subsiding left them on dry land.*
Porsěna auxilium ei ferente.	*As Porsena furnished him aid,* or *By the aid of Porsena.*

527. Participles may state the *condition* on which a given action or event depends; they may then be translated by *verbs* or *participles* with *if* or *when;* e. g.,

Accusatus damnabĭtur.	*If he is accused, he will be condemned.*

528. Participles are sometimes used to state a *concession* in connection with a given action or event; they may then be translated by *verbs* or *participles* with *though* or *although*; e. g.,

Is hanc urbem acerrĭme *defensam* cepit.	He took this city, though it was valiantly defended.

529. Participles in the future, whether active or passive, often express *purpose;* they may then be translated by the *infinitive* or by a *participial substantive* with *for the purpose of*, &c.; e. g.,

Ad oracŭlum Delphĭcum proficiscĭtur, *consultūrus*.	He goes to the Delphic oracle to consult.

530. Participles may add to a given action or event some *fact* or *circumstance* intimately connected with it; they may then be translated, if in the ablative absolute, by a *verb* agreeing with the *noun* used in the ablative absolute, otherwise by a *verb* agreeing with the *subject* of the proposition in which they stand, and connected with the verb of that proposition by *and;* e. g.,

Rex ei benigne *recepto* filiam dedit.	The king received him kindly, and gave him his daughter.
Medĭcus nocte venit *promittens*, se Pyrrhum occisūrum.	The physician came by night, and promised (*lit.* promising) that he would kill Pyrrhus.

531. Participles with *non* may often be best translated by *participial substantives* depending upon the preposition *without;* e. g.,

Non ridens.	*Without laughing.*

532. Two nouns, or a noun and adjective in the ablative absolute, as they have the participle of the verb *esse* implied though never expressed, may be used in the various ways already mentioned for the ablative absolute of participles, and should be translated accordingly: sometimes, too, a word denoting the *doer* of an action can be best rendered by the word which denotes the *thing done;* thus, instead of *guide, commander, consul, king*, &c., we shall have *guidance, command, consulship, reign*, &c., with a preposition; e. g.,

Duce Fabio consŭle.	Under the guidance (or command) of Fabius the consul.

533. The perfect participle of deponent verbs is best translated by the present participle,

    1) When it expresses *emotion* or *mental operation*, as the Romans speak of an emotion as past, and we as continuing; e. g.,

Hoc facinus rex *mirātus* juvĕnem dimīsit incolŭmem.	*The king admiring this act dismissed the youth unhurt.*

    2) When it relates to an action or event which must in strict accuracy precede that denoted by the following verb, and which would yet in English be represented as simultaneous with it; e. g.,

Popŭlus Romae seditiōnem fecit, *questus* quod tribūtis exhaurirētur.	*The people made a revolt at Rome, complaining that they were impoverished by tributes.*

II. *Principal Sentences.—Subjunctive Mood.*

534. The subjunctive may be used in principal sentences,

    1) To express a *wish, command,* or *entreaty;* it may then be translated by the *imperative,* by the *present potential,* or by some tense of that mood with a particle of *wishing;* e. g.,

Secernant se a bonis.	*Let them separate themselves from the good.*

    2) To express an affirmation *doubtfully* or *conditionally;* it may then be translated by the *potential* mood; e. g.,

Darent.	*They would give.*

III. *Relative Clauses.*

535. The relative clause often defines some indefinite antecedent, either affirmative or negative, and then its subjunctive should be translated by the indicative; e. g.,

Sunt qui dicant.	*There are some who say.*

    Rem.—The subjunctive in relative clauses introduced into propositions with the subjunctive, or the accusative with the infinitive, is also generally best translated by the indicative; e. g., Utrum regnum habēre vellet, an bona, quae pater reliquisset, *Whether he would prefer the kingdom or the property which his father had left.*

536. The relative clause with the subjunctive sometimes denotes *purpose* or *object ;* it should then be translated by the *infinitive*, or by *that he* with the *potential may* or *might ;* e. g.,

Decemvĭri creāti sunt qui civitāti leges scribĕrent.	*The decemvirs were appointed to prepare laws for the state.*

537. The relative clause with the subjunctive sometimes denotes *result ;* it should then be translated by *that he* with *will* or *would,* &c., or by the *infinitive* with *as ;* e. g.,

Nec tamen ego sum ille ferreus, qui non movear.	*Nor yet am I so iron-hearted as not to be moved.*

538. The relative clause with the subjunctive sometimes assigns a *reason* for some action or event; it should then be translated by a *subordinate clause* after *because,* or by a *participial substantive* with a *preposition ;* e. g.,

O fortunāte adolescens, qui tuae virtūtis praecōnem invenĕris.	*O fortunate youth in having found a herald for your bravery,* or *because you have,* &c.

539. The relative clause with the subjunctive after *dignus, indignus, aptus, idoneus,* and the like, stands in the place of object, and may be translated by the *infinitive* or by a *participial substantive* with a *preposition ;* e. g.,

Vidētur, qui impĕret, dignus esse.	*He seems to be worthy to command.*

540. The relative clause sometimes introduces a *condition* or *concession ;* and then the subjunctive should be translated by the *subjunctive* with *if, provided,* or *though ;* e. g.,

Nulla res vehementius rempublĭcam contĭnet, quam fides; *quae* esse nulla potest, &c.	*Nothing tends more to preserve the republic than credit, though this can be nothing,* &c.

IV. *Final Clauses with Particles.*

541. Final clauses with *ut* may be translated by the *infinitive* or by the *potential, may* or *might,* with *that ;* e. g.,

Romŭlus, ut civium numĕrum augēret, asÿlum patefēcit.	*Romulus, that he might increase the number of citizens, opened an asylum.*

11*

542. Final clauses with *ne* may be translated by the *infinitive* with *not*, or by the *potential, may, might*, with *that—not;* e. g.,

Ne vana urbs esset.	*That the city might not be empty.*

543. In final clauses after verbs of fearing, *ut* and *ne* seem to exchange meanings; *ut = that—not*, and *ne = that* or *lest;* moreover, the subjunctive present must generally be rendered by the future, *will*, and the imperfect by *would;* e. g.,

Verĭtus est ne rex bellāret.	*He feared that the king would wage war.*

544. Final clauses with *quo* may be rendered by the *potential, may* or *might*, with *that;* e. g.,

Medĭco aurum dabo quo sit studiosior.	*I will give the physician gold that he may be more attentive.*

545. Final clauses with *quomĭnus* (*quo* and *minus* = by which the less, so that the less) may generally be rendered by *participial substantives* with *from;* e. g.,

Regem impediit quomĭnus pugnāret.	*He prevented the king from fighting.*

546. Final clauses with *quin* may be rendered by *but, but that* with the *indicative; as not* with the *infinitive;* the *relative* with *not*, or by *participial substantives* with *from* or *without;* e. g.,

Non dubĭtant, quin dii illud audiant.	*They do not doubt (but) that the gods hear this.*

V. *Consecutive Clauses.*

547. Consecutive clauses with *ut* may generally be rendered by *that* with the *indicative*, or by *as* with the *infinitive;* e. g.,

Ita vicit, ut robur hostium delēret.	*He so conquered as to destroy the strength of the enemy.*

548. Consecutive clauses with *ut* after *in eo esse*, &c., may be rendered *on the point of*, with a *participial substantive;* e. g.,

In eo erant, ut pacem auro emĕrent.	*They were on the point of purchasing peace with gold.*

VI. *Temporal Clauses.*

549. *Quum* with the perfect or pluperfect subjunctive in temporal clauses, may often be translated by the *perfect participle* with *having;* e. g.,

In Capream quum secessisset, eam infāmem reddĭdit sua nequitia.	*Having removed to Caprea, he rendered it infamous by his profligacy.*

550. *Quum* with the imperfect or pluperfect subjunctive may sometimes be translated by the *present participle.* This use of the present instead of the past tense arises from the fact that the English often contemplates two events as simultaneous when one of them in strict accuracy must precede the other, while the Latin is strict to mark their precise order; e. g.,

Quum in Afrĭcam venissent, Poenos vicērunt.	*Going into Africa they conquered the Carthaginians.*

551. *Quum* with the pluperfect subjunctive in temporal clauses may sometimes be translated by the *imperfect* indicative. This use of the *imperfect* instead of the *pluperfect* is readily explained by reference to the principle mentioned above (see 550); e. g.,

Quum rediisset, respondit.	*When he returned, he replied.*

552. The subjunctive in temporal clauses should generally be rendered by the *indicative;* e. g.,

Quum tonāret, militĭbus imperāvit, &c.	*When it thundered, he commanded his soldiers, &c.*

553. The adverb which introduces the temporal clause sometimes has a correlative in the principal clause; this correlative, however, may generally be omitted in translating; thus, *tum—quum =* when. The adverbs, *antĕquam, priusquam,* and *postquam,* are sometimes separated into two parts, one standing in the principal clause and the other in the temporal; this separation, however, does not affect the translation; thus, *ante—quam* and *prius—quam =* before, and *post—quam =* after; e. g.,

Ante triennium, *quam* Carthāgo delerētur, Cato mortem obiit.	*Cato died three years before Carthage was destroyed.*

VII. Causal Clauses.

554. The subjunctive in causal clauses may often be best translated by the *indicative;* e. g.,

Quod albis equis triumphasset.	*Because he had triumphed with white horses.*

555. The imperfect and pluperfect subjunctive after *quod* may sometimes be translated by the *participial substantive* with *of* or *for;* e. g.,

Accusatus est quod praedam inique divisisset.	*He was accused of having unjustly divided the booty.*

VIII. Conditional Clauses.

556. In conditional clauses the subjunctive is often translated without the auxiliaries, *may, might, should, should have,* &c. This is especially the case when the condition is represented as impossible; e. g.,

Si quid habēret, daret.	*If he had any thing, he would give it.*

IX. Concessive Clauses.

557. The subjunctive in concessive clauses is generally best translated without the auxiliaries, *may, might,* &c.; e. g.,

Illa quamvis ridicula essent.	*Although these things were ludicrous.*

X. Intermediate Clauses.

558. The subjunctive in clauses introduced into propositions with the subjunctive, or the accusative with the infinitive, is generally best translated by the *indicative;* e. g.,

Utrum regnum habēre vellet, an bona quae pater reliquisset.	*Whether he would prefer the kingdom or the property which his father had left.*

XI. Dependent Questions.

559. The subjunctive in dependent questions may often be translated by the indicative, and the pluperfect tense by the imperfect; e. g.,

Quum comperissent, quae mater fuisset.	*When they had learned who their mother was.*

XII. Infinitive Mood.

560. The infinitive with the subject accusative must be translated by a *finite* verb with the *subject nominative* in a clause introduced by *that*; e. g.,

| Dixit se regem vidisse. | He said that he had seen the king. |

561. The infinitive is sometimes used in the place of a finite verb as the predicate of a sentence; it is then called the *historical infinitive*, and is translated by the *imperfect indicative*; e. g.,

| Iram pater dissimulāre. | The father concealed his anger. |

562. The infinitive may sometimes be rendered by the participial substantive with the preposition *of*, *with*, &c.; e. g.,

| Alcibiădes insimulātur mysteria Cerĕris violasse. | Alcibiades is accused of having violated the mysteries of Ceres. |

XIII. Miscellaneous.

563. *Certiōrem facĕre*, lit. to make more certain, should be translated *to inform*, and *certior fiĕri*, to be informed; e. g.,

| Caesar certior factus est. | Caesar was informed. |

564. *Inter se*, lit. between themselves, is best translated by *together*, after agree, compare, &c., but after *contrary*, &c., it = *to each other*; e. g.,

| Hi omnes inter se diffĕrunt. | All these differ from each other. |

565. *Licet* with the dative and infinitive, is best translated by rendering the dative as the subject of the potential forms *may* or *might*, with the English of the verb used in the infinitive; e. g.,

| Mihi ire licet. | I may go. |

REM.—The present infinitive after the past tenses of *licet* is often best translated by the auxiliary *have*. So also after the past tenses of *possum, oportet*, and *debeo*; e. g., Mihi ire licuit, *I might have gone.*—Ire potui, *I could have gone.*

566. *Medius, summus*, and the like, in agreement with substantives, are often best translated by *the middle* (*the midst*), *the top* followed by the substantive with *of*; e. g.,

Medius mons.	The middle of the mountain.
Summus mons.	The top of the mountain.
In media caede.	In the midst of the slaughter.

567. *Nec* or *neque* may often be translated by *and not*, sometimes by *not* only, especially in the phrase *neque vero;* e. g.,

Nec paucos agros urbi adjunxit.	*And he added not a few fields to the city.*

568. *Ne—quidem* with one or more words between the parts, should be translated by *not even;* or *even—not;* e. g.,

Ne nomen quidem.	*Not even the name.*

569. *Post* standing as an adverb between an adjective and its substantive in the ablative to denote *time*, may sometimes be translated by the preposition *after* governing the substantive, but should usually be rendered by *afterwards;* e. g.,

Paucis post annis.	*After a few years.*
	A few years afterwards.

570. *Quam ut* with the subjunctive, and *quam ut posset* with the infinitive, should be rendered by the *infinitive*, and the comparative before *quam* by the English positive with *too;* e. g.,

Leges erudeliōres erant, quam ut possent observāri.	*The laws were too cruel to be observed.*

571. *Qui* at the beginning of a sentence, or at the beginning of a distinct member of a sentence, is generally best translated by a demonstrative or personal pronoun; and if *quum* is used in the same connection with *qui*, it must be translated first; e. g.,

Quae quum ita sint.	*Since these things are so.*
Qui quum morbo exstinctus esset.	*When he was dead.*

572. *Quo factum est, ut, lit.* by which it was brought about that, *sic factum est, ut*, and similar expressions, may be rendered by, *the result of which was, that; the consequence of which was, that;* or by *consequently;* e. g.,

Quo factum est, ut plus, quam collēgae, Miltiādes valuĕrit.	*The result of which was that Miltiades had greater influence than his associates.*

573. Verbs which are used impersonally in the passive with the dative of the agent, because they have no direct object in the

active, are best translated by rendering the dative as the subject of the English passive; e. g.,

Vobis credĭtur.	*You are believed.*
Mihi credĭtur.	*I am believed.*

574. When two or more verbs stand together in the same compound tense, the copula *esse*, to be, is generally expressed with the last in Latin, and omitted with the rest; in the English translation, however, it should be expressed with the first and omitted with the others; e. g.,

Regŭlus captus et in vincŭla conjectus est.	*Regulus was taken and thrown into chains.*

NOTES.

 1. **Antiquissimis.** Very early: the superlative is often best translated by *very* instead of *most.* Give the regular endings of comparison. F. B. 306; A. & S. 124; Z. 104. —— **Temporibus.** 276; F. B. 669; A. & S. 253; Z. 475. —— **In Italiam.** What construction would have been used with the name of a town? 282; F. B. 674; A. & S. 237; Z. 398. —— **Janiculo.** A hill on the west side of the Tiber; not one of *the seven* hills of Rome, though included within the wall built by Aurelian in the third century. —— **Italos . . . . agriculturam.** 235; F. B. 645; A. & S. 231; Z. 391. —— **Primus.** *The first;* i. e. *he was the first to teach,* &c.

 2. **Illinc.** Hence, i. e. *from Troy.* —— **Quibus.** 218; F. B. 643; A. & S. 223, Rem. 2; Z. 412. —— **Pepercerat.** From *parco;* 2d root formed by *reduplication* and *change of vowel.* F. B. 222 and Rem. —— **Ei benigne recepto . . . . dedit.** Lit. *gave to him kindly received;* translate, *received him kindly and gave* (530). —— **Lavinium.** Town in Latium a few miles south of Rome.

 3. **Transtulit.** From *transfěro.* —— **Monte Albano.** *Mount Albanus,* about 16 miles southeast of Rome. —— **Ejus.** For whom does this pronoun stand? —— **Romam conditam.** (See 523.) —— **Albae.** 280; F. B. 672; A. & S. 221; Z. 398.

 4. **Horum regum.** *Of these kings,* i. e. *of those who reigned at Alba.* —— **Jove.** 457; F. B. 636; A. & S. 256; Z. 483. —— **Majorem.** Compare. F. B. 306, R. 3; A. & S. 125, 5; Z. 109. —— **Quum tonaret.** (552); F. B. 692, 2; A. & S. 263, 5, R. 2; Z. 578. —— **Ut . . . . percuterent.** (541); F. B. 692; A. & S. 262; Z. 531. —— **Dicebat.** What is the direct object of this verb? or, in other words, what did he say? Ans. *Hunc sonum multo,* &c. —— **Tonitru.** What case would be required if *quam* should be omitted? 457; F. B. 636, Obs.; A. & S. 256, R. 3; Z. 483. —— **Ictus, et**

2. .... **praecipitatus est.** (574.) —— **Albanum lacum.** *The Albar Lake*, 5 miles in circumference, west of Mount Albanus.

5. **Minor natu.** Lit. *smaller in respect to birth* or *age*; translate, *younger.* —— **Utrum regnum,** &c. This denotes the choice given to Numitor. —— **Vellet.** 349, 364; F. B. 692, 5; A. & S. 265; Z. 652. —— **Bona.** Lit. *good things* = *goods, property.* —— **Reliquisset.** (558); A. & S. 266; Z. 545.

6. **Ut** .... **possideret.** This final clause shows the object which Amulius had in view in killing the son of Numitor. (541;) F. B. 692; A. & S. 262; Z. 531. —— **Vestalem virginem.** The *Vestal Virgins* were the priestesses of the goddess Vesta: they ministered in her temple, and, by turns, watched the perpetual fire upon her altars night and day. They were bound by an oath of chastity, whose violation was punished by death. —— **Viro.** Indirect object after *nubĕre*, to marry = *to veil one's self for*, in allusion to the custom of the bride's wearing the veil at the marriage ceremony. —— **Hoc.** *This,* i. e. the fact spoken of in the preceding sentence. —— **Quum** .... **comperisset.** (552); 402; F. B. 692, 2; A. & S. 263, 5, R. 2; Z. 578.

7. **Quum** .... **positi.** (552.) —— **Refluens.** *By* or *in flowing back.* (526.) —— **Sicco.** Scil. *loco.* —— **Quod.** (571.) —— **Videns.** (525.) —— **Sustulit.** From *tollo.* —— **Nutriendos.** (529.)

8. **Sic.** *Thus,* i. e. as explained above. —— **Quum adolevissent** .... **comperissent.** See note at the close of 6. above. —— **Quis.** Subject of *fuisset* understood. —— **Fuisset.** (559); 379; F. B. 692, 5; A. & S. 265; Z. 552. —— **Aventino.** *One of the seven hills of Rome.* According to the best authority, Romulus founded his city not on the *Aventine* as here stated, but on the *Palatine,* which stands a little to the north of it. —— **Quum** .... **circumdaretur.** See note at the close of 6. above. —— **Moenibus.** Ablative of means. —— **Irridens.** *Deriding*: this participle may be thus rendered literally.

9. **Ut** .... **augeret.** This states the purpose or object for which Romulus opened an asylum. (541); 385; F. B. 692; A. & S. 262; Z. 531. —— **Asylum.** This was a place of refuge, where exiles and even criminals might obtain shelter and protection. —— **Pulsi.** (524.) —— **Civibus.** 218; F. B. 643, 2; A. & S. 224, R. 1; Z. 420, note. —— **Quum** .... **venissent.** (552); 402. —— **Inter ipsos ludos.** *In the midst of the very games.* —— **Spectantes.** (524.)

10. **Romae.** What is the usual construction for names of towns after verbs of motion? 282; F. B. 674; A. & S. 237; Z. 398. —— **Ut .... monstraret .... ut .... posceret.** (541.) See also note on the first line of 9. —— **Quod .... gererent.** (558); A. & S. 266; Z. 545. —— **Manibus.** Give gender. —— **Annulos .... armillas.** Rings and bracelets were often awarded to soldiers who had distinguished themselves in battle. —— **Perducti.** (525.)

11. **Tarpeium.** This was one of the seven hills of Rome: it was also called *Capitolīnus*. The Capitol was built upon it. —— **Forum Romanum.** This was an open space in the form of an irregular quadrangle between the Palatine and Capitoline Hills. In this were held the great public meetings of the Roman people —— **In media caede.** *In the midst of the slaughter.* (566.) —— **Raptae.** Sc. *muliĕres.* —— **Hinc .... hinc.** *On the one side .... on the other.* —— **Ut .... facerent.** See note on the first line of 9. —— **In urbem recepit.** Lit. *received into the city*: the meaning is, *he received them into full citizenship.*

12. **Cum .... tum.** *Not only .... but also.* —— **Debitam.** (524). —— **Raptarum.** (524.) —— **Lustraret.** *Reviewed*: lit. *purified*, as there were certain ceremonies appointed for the review of a Roman army. —— **Ortam.** From *orior.* (524.) —— **Oculis.** 218; F. B. 643, 4; A. & S. 224; Z. 415. —— **Hinc.** *Hence*, i. e. from the circumstance mentioned above. —— **Alii .... alii.** *Some .... others.* —— **Interfectum .... sublatum esse.** (560, 574.)

13. **Quo exacto.** (525, 571.) —— **Curibus.** 280; F. B. 672; A. & S. 254; Z. 398. —— **Natus.** (524.) —— **Ut .... molliret.** See note on the first line of 9. —— **Morbo decessit.** Lit. *he died of disease — he died a natural death.*

14. **Creatus.** (525.) —— **Horatiorum et Curiatiorum.** After the necessary preparations for hostilities had been made both by the Albans and the Romans, and the two armies were already drawn up face to face, it was agreed to decide the question of supremacy by a combat between the three brothers, the Horatii, on the part of the Romans, and the three Curiatii, also brothers, on the part of the Albans. The Curiatii were all slain; one of the Horatii survived; his victory therefore decided the question in favor of Rome. See *Schmitz's Hist. Rome.* —— **Perfidiam Metii Suffetii.** M. Suffetius, dictator of the Albans, having been summoned by the Romans to aid them against the Veientines, drew off his for-

4 ces at the very moment of battle, and awaited the issue of the engagement. For this perfidy he was put to death, and Alba was razed to the ground. See *Schmitz's Hist. Rome.* —— **Quum** .... **regnasset.** (552); 402; F. B. 692, 2; A. & S. 263, 5, R. 2; Z. 578. —— **Annis.** What is the common construction for duration of time? 277 and R.; F. B. 670; A. & S. 236; Z. 395, 396. —— **Ictus.** (525.) —— **Domo.** Give gender.

15. **Aequitate et religione.** 301; F. B. 633; A. & S. 250; Z. **5** 457. —— **Avo.** F. B. 632; A. & S. 222; Z. 409. —— **Nova el moenia circumdedit.** The same thought may be expressed thus: *novis eam moenĭbus circumdĕdit;* in which *eam* is the *direct object*, and *moenĭbus* the ablative of *means.* See P. C. 231. —— **Primus.** See note on 1. —— **Morbo obiit.** Compare *morbo decessit*, in 13.

16. **Advenienti.** Sc. *ei.* (525); 254, R.; A. & S. 224, R. 2. —— **Abstulit.** From *aufĕro.* —— **Auguriorum.** 298; F. B. 631; A. & S. 213; Z. 436.

17. **Pupillis.** 218, 4; F. B. 643, 4; A. & S. 224; Z. 415. —— **Minorum gentium.** Sc. *patres*, or *senatōres.* —— **Nec.** (567.) —— **Ademptos.** (524.) —— **Triumphans.** *Triumphing — in triumph.* The honor of entering Rome with an imposing triumphal procession was, in later times, often awarded to victorious generals. —— **Capitolium.** The Capitol was the citadel of Rome, and was erected on the Capitoline Hill. —— **Per Anci filios.** What is the usual construction for the agent after passive verbs? 273 and R. 2; F. B. 659; A. & S. 248; Z. 451.

18. **Genitus.** (524). —— **Conjugi.** 218, 5; F. B. 643, 5; A. & S. 228, R. 2; Z. 412. —— **Ut .... educaret.** (541); F. B. 692; A. & S. 262; Z. 531.

6 19. **Dicens.** What is the direct object? —— **Regem .... accepisse.** (560.) —— **Ut .... obediret.** See last note on 18. above. —— **Dum .... convaluisset.** (552); 405; A. & S. 263, 4; Z. 575. —— **Montes tres;** These were the *Quirinal, Viminal,* and *Esquiline* Hills. —— **Primus.** See note on 1. —— **Censum.** The *census* was taken every five years for the purpose of ascertaining the number of citizens, the amount of property, &c. —— **Capitum.** This need not be translated. —— **In agris.** In the country or territory about Rome.

20. **Cui.** 218; F. B. 643, 4; A. & S. 224; Z. 415. —— **Curiae.** Senate-house on the eastern side of the Forum. —— **Dejectus.**

(525.) —— **Quum .... fugeret.** (552.) —— **Domum.** 283; F. B. 6 675; A. & S. 237, R. 4; Z. 400. —— **Prima.** See note on 1. —— **Jacens.** (524.)

21. **Moribus.** Mark difference of signification between the singular and plural.

22. **In.** What cases does *in* govern, and with what significations? 289, R. 1; F. B. 681, R. 1; A. & S. 235, 2; Z. 404, 489. —— **Conjurarunt.** Contracted from what? —— **Ut .... clauderet.** (541.) —— **Ei.** *Against him*, indirect object. —— **Romae.** 280; 7 F. B. 672; A. & S. 221; Z. 398. —— **Regnatum est .. . reges.** Lit. *it was reigned*, &c.; translate, *the regal government was administered by seven kings.*

23. **Tarquinio expulso.** (525.) —— **Consules.** The consuls were joint presidents of the Roman Commonwealth with all the power and most of the ensigns of office which the kings had assumed. —— **Annuum.** *For one year.* —— **Ne .... redderentur.** (542); 385; F. B. 692, 1; A. & S. 262; Z. 532. —— **Diuturnitatem.** State the force of the termination *itas*, (1) when appended to adjectives, and (2) when appended to nouns. F. B. 519, 517. —— **Insolentiores.** *Too haughty:* the comparative is sometimes best rendered by *too* instead of *more*. —— **Expulsis regibus.** (525.) —— **Acerrimus.** Compare. —— **Sublata est.** From *tollo*. —— **Placuerat.** *It had been determined.* —— **Ex.** *Of.*

24. **Sese invicem.** *Each other.* —— **Qui quum.** *When he.* (571.)

25. **Porsena .... ferente.** (526.) —— **Pontem.** Give gender. 8 —— **Donec ... ruptus esset.** (552); 405; A. & S. 263, 4; Z. 575. —— **Tiberim.** Give the common ending of the accusative singular for masculine and feminine nouns of the third declension.

26. **Animi.** What other case might have been used? 190; F. B. 624; A. & S. 211, R. 6; Z. 471. —— **Castra.** Note difference of meaning between singular and plural. —— **Terreret.** *Endeavored to terrify.* —— **Allatis.** (523, 526.) —— **Miratus.** (533.) —— **Territus.** (526.) —— **Tusculum.** 282; F. B. 674; A. & S. 237; Z. 398.

27. **Post reges exactos.** (523.) —— **Exactos.** From *exĭgo*. —— **Questus.** (533.) —— **Quod .... exhauriretur.** (554); 409; A. & S. 266, 3. —— **Tributis, militia, senatu.** Explain derivation, with the force of the several endings. F. B. 524, 519, 517. —— **Patres.** *Senators.* —— **Turbati.** (526.) —— **Qui .... conciliaret.** (536); 367 —— **Qui .... defenderent.** (536.)

8   28. **Post exactos reges.** See 27, line 1. —— **Coriolanus dictus.**
9 See Lesson XIII. —— **Urbe expulsus.** 289, R. 2; F. B. 681, R. 2;
A. & S. 242. —— **Urbis.** *From the city.* —— **Nec.** (567.) —— **Ut
.... parceret.** (541.) —— **Quo facto.** Abl. of means, or cause:
for this act; for which or *whereupon.* —— **Exercitum, proditor.**
Explain derivation with the force of the several endings. F. B.
520, 521; A. & S. 102, 6, 7; Z. 236, 1, and 237.

29. **Quum .... gererent.** (552). —— **Duce .... consule.** (532.)
—— **Dolo.** 226; F. B. 644, 1; A. & S. 245; Z. 465. —— **Usi.** (526.)
—— **Exorto.** (524.) —— **Puerilem, cunctatione.** Explain derivation.

30. **Altero.** Lit. *another;* as a numeral, *second.* —— **Ab urbe
condita.** (523.) —— **Qui .... scriberent.** (536.) The *decemvirs*
were the authors of the Laws of the Twelve Tables, so called because they were engraved on twelve tables of brass. —— **Decemviris.** See 237, 254, R. —— **Civitati.** Explain derivation.

10   31. **Tribuni militares.** *Military tribunes;* they were also sometimes called *consular tribunes,* as they were appointed in place of
consuls. They were at first three in number; afterwards more.
—— **Deletis exercitibus.** (525.) —— **Triumphos.** See note on 17.

32. **Contra Veientanos.** This limits *bello.* See 190, Rem. ——
In qua. (571.) —— **Manibus .... illigatis.** *With his hands bound
behind his back.* —— **Reducendum.** (529.) —— **Quibus .... agerent.** (536.) —— **Scelestum, proditorem.** Explain derivation.

33. **Camillo .... datum est.** *It was imputed as a crime to Camillus,* that, &c. For the construction of *Camillo* and *crim'ni,*
see 237, 245; F. B. 649, 658; A. & S. 227; Z. 422. —— **Quod ....
triumphasset .... divisisset.** (554.) —— **Fame laborabat.** *Was
suffering from famine.* —— **In eo erant, ut .... emerent.** (548.)
—— **Auro.** 272; F. B. 667; A. & S. 252; Z. 456. —— **Nobilitate,
triumphasset, civitate, laborabat.** Explain derivation.

11   34. **Milliario.** The common construction for *place,* when not
expressed by the name of a town, is the ablative with a preposition. —— **Magnitudine.** 190; F. B. 624; A. & S. 211, R. 6; Z.
471. —— **Provocavit.** *Challenged.* —— **Torque.** 254; F. B. 650;
A. & S. 251; Z. 460. —— **Magnitudine, provocationem, spoliavit.**
Explain derivation.

35. **Novo .... exorto.** (525.) —— **Robore.** How may the nominative of this word be formed from the root, and how may the

root be found from the nominative? —— **Quum processisset.** (552.)
—— **Armatus.** *In arms.* —— **Ei.** Lit. *to him*, indirect object after *sedit*, best rendered by *his*. —— **Ita factum est, ut,** &c. Lit. *thus it was done that*, &c. Render as follows: *the result of which was, that the Gaul*, &c. (572.)

36. **Cum honore dictatoris.** *With the rank of dictator.* The dictator was appointed only in times of great danger, and was invested with almost unlimited power for a period of six months. —— **Qui quum.** (571.) —— **Magistro equitum.** This is the title of an officer always appointed in connection with the dictator or by him. —— **Ne .... committeret.** (542.) —— **Occasionem nactus.** *Taking advantage of a favorable opportunity.* —— **Nactus.** From *nanciscor*. —— **Confugit.** How is the second root formed from the first? F. B. 219.

37. **Annis.** 404, R. 3; A. & S. 236; Z. 476. —— **Post.** *Afterwards*, adverb. —— **Putaret.** 379; F. B. 692, 5; A. & S. 265; Z. 552. —— **Ut .... frangerentur .... ut .... obligarentur.** (541); 383; F. B. 692; A. & S. 262; Z. 531. —— **Sub jugum.** The yoke was thus used as the symbol of submission and servitude; it consisted of a spear supported horizontally by two others placed in an upright position.

38. **Devictis Samnitibus.** (525.) —— **Quia .... fecissent.** If this reason had been given on the authority of the narrator, the indicative would have been used. The subjunctive implies that this was the reason then alleged for waging the war. See 409. —— **Pyrrhum, auxilium.** 235; F. B. 645; A. & S. 231; Z. 393. —— **Poposcerunt.** How is the second root of this verb formed? F. B. 222. —— **Quaecunque .... agerentur.** 426; A. & S. 266, 1; Z. 547.

39. **Pugna commissa.** (525.) —— **Mille octingentos.** Could these words be transposed? A. & S. 120, 2; Z. 116. —— **Adversis vulneribus.** *With wounds in front:* it was a disgrace to receive a wound in the back. —— **Etiam mortuos.** *Even in death.*

40. **Perrexit.** From *pergo*. —— **Igne.** Give gender. —— **Exercitus.** Is this genitive *objective* or *attributive?* See 188. —— **Captivis redimendis.** (523.) With *gerund* we should have *captivos redimendo.* 464; F. B. 382. —— **Ex.** *Of.* —— **Ut .... promitteret.** (547.)

41. **Romanorum.** Is th's genitive *objective* or *attributive?* 188.

13 —— **Qui .... peteret.** (536); 367; F. B. 692, 6; A. & S. 264, 5; Z. 555. —— **Ut Pyrrhus .... obtineret.** This clause expresses the *condition* on which Cineas was to ask peace, and may accordingly be regarded as in apposition with *conditiōne*. See 363, R. 2, and 364. —— **Ex Italia.** What construction would be used, if the name of a *town* should be substituted here? —— **Quum redisset.** (551.) —— **Pyrrho.** Indirect object of *respondit;* the *direct* object is the clause, *se regum patriam vidisse.* See 374. —— **Qualis ... visa esset.** (559.)

42. **Altero.** *Second.* —— **Tarentum.** 282; F. B. 674; A. & S. 237; Z. 398. —— **Interjecto anno.** (525); 460; F. B. 678; A. & S. 257; Z. 640. —— **Nocte.** Abl. of time. —— **Promittens.** (530.) —— **Vinctum.** *Bound,* or *in chains.* —— "**Ille .... ab honestate .... potest.**" This entire sentence, as a direct quotation, is the
14 object of *dixisse.* See 373. —— **Fusus.** From *fundo.* —— **A Tarento.** What is the common construction? —— **Quum .... redisset.** (549.) —— **Apud Argos.** *Near Argos.* What would mean *at Argos?*

43. **C. Duillio .... consulibus.** (532); 460; A. & S. 257, R. 7; Z. 644. —— **Mari.** *Mare* has the ablative sing. in *e* or *i*, while most neuters in *e*, *al*, and *ar* have it in *i* only. See F. B. 127. —— **Mersit.** From *mergo.* —— **Romanis.** Objective modifier of *gratior.* —— **Duillio.** Indirect object after *concessum est.* —— **Concessum est.** What is the real subject of this verb? or, in other words, *What was granted to Duillius?* Ans. *Ut, quum a coena redīret, puĕri .... eum comitarentur.*

44. **Paucis interjectis.** (525); 460. —— **Translatum est.** From *transfĕro.* —— **Dux.** In apposition with Hamilcar. See
15 441. —— **Quum .... venissent.** (550.) —— **In fidem acceperunt.** *Received under their protection.* —— **Quam quum,** &c. (571.) —— **Captus et .... conjectus est.** (574.) —— **Interjectis, translatum est, recepit, amiserunt, acceperunt.** Explain composition. F. B. 513, 550, 551, 553; A. & S. 188, 189; Z. 260, 261.

45. **Carthaginiensibus.** 218, 5; F. B. 643, 5; A. & S. 223, R. 2; Z. 412. —— **Favit.** How is the second root of this verb formed? F. B. 219. How is this root regularly formed in the second conjugation? F. B. 192. —— **Quum .... victi essent.** (552.) —— **Ut .... proficisceretur, et .... obtineret.** Verbs of asking take two objects; these clauses may, accordingly, be regarded as one of

the objects of *rogavērunt*. —— **Inductus.** (525.) —— **Qua.** 276; **15**
F. B. 669; A. & S. 253; Z. 475. What is the antecedent of *qua?*
—— **Illos .... habere.** This infinitive-clause does not strictly depend upon *suasit*, but upon a verb or participle signifying *to say.*
The verb or participle on which sentences in oblique narration
depend is often omitted, when it can be easily supplied from the
context. See *Lat. Prose Comp.* 460, (c.). —— **Casibus.** Abl. of
means. —— **Fractos.** (526.) From *frango*. —— **Tanti non esse.**
This is the predicate. See F. B. 613; A. & S. 214; Z. 426. ——
Ut tot millia .... redderentur. This is the subject of *esse*.

46. **Punici.** Derived from *Poeni* = *Carthaginienses*. —— **Captae, ... demersae .... capta .... occisa sunt.** (574.) —— **Sicilia, Sardinia, Insulis.** These ablatives are governed by the preposition
de in the verb *decessērunt.* See F. B. 681, R. 2; A. & S. 242. ——
Citra Iberum. *On this side of the Ebro,* i. e. *on the side towards* **16**
Rome.

47. **Novem annos natum.** Lit. *having been born nine years;* render, *when he was nine years old.* (525); 277; F. B. 670; A. & S.
236; Z. 395. —— **Aris.** Indirect object after *admovērat*. —— **Ille
.... aetatis.** *He, when in his twentieth year.* —— **Oppugnare.**
Used as object of *aggressus est.* See 374, 447. —— **Denuntiaverunt.**
This verb, being transitive, may take both a direct and an indirect object: do both these objects appear in the present instance?
—— **Qui quum.** (571.) —— **Mandaretur.** What is the real subject
of this verb? —— **Reddita.** Sc. *sunt*. —— **Saguntinis .... victis.**
(525.) —— **Admoverat, perenne, oppugnare, indixerunt.** Explain
composition.

48. **Fratre .... relicto.** (525.) —— **Pyrenaeum, Alpes.** These
accusatives depend upon *trans* in the compound verb *transiit*.
F. B. 681, R. 2. —— **Traditur.** What is the subject of this verb?
—— **Se.** Why is *se* used here rather than *eos* or *illos?* A. & S.
208; Z. 125, note. —— **Primus.** See note on 1. —— **Interemptus
. . . . caesa sunt.** (574.)

49. **Intellectum erat.** What is the subject? —— **Hannibalem.** **17**
346; F. B. 655; A. & S. 239, 599. —— **Mora.** 271: F. B. 666;
A. & S. 247; Z. 452, 455. —— **Morae.** 298; F. B. 631; A. & S.
213; Z. 436. —— **Cannae appellatur.** This is the predicate of the
relative clause of which *qui* is the subject. The predicate noun
denoting the same person or thing as the subject, must agree with

17 that subject in *case*, though it may differ from it in gender or number, or in both, as in the present instance. —— **Victi .... interemptus est.** Here *sunt* is understood after *victi*. (574.) —— **Capti aut occisi.** Sc. *sunt*. —— **Quod.** This relative does not relate to any particular *word* as its antecedent, but to the leading proposition, or the fact mentioned in it; the relative is accordingly of the neuter gender, as clauses used substantively uniformly take that gender. See F. B. 44; A. & S. 206, 13.

50. .**Post eam pugnam.** 276, Rem. —— **Obtulit.** From *offĕro*. Here *obtŭlit* takes *Romānis* as its *indirect* object, while its *direct* object appears in the form of a clause, viz. *ut captīvos redimĕrent*. This is plainly the *offer* made to the Romans. 383, 384. —— **Responsum est.** The subject is the clause beginning with *eos*. —— **Armati.** (525, 528.) —— **Potuissent.** (535, R.); 426; A. & S. 266, .2; Z. 603. —— **Hos omnes.** Observe position at the beginning to mark emphasis. —— **Manibus.** Gender? —— **Detraxerat.** From *detrăho*. How is the second root formed? F. B. 208. —— **In Hispania .... Hasdrubal.** See 48, line 1. —— **Remanserat.** How is the second root of this verb formed? F. B. 225, 2. —— **Duobus Scipionibus.** *Cn. Cornelius Scipio* and *P. Cornelius Scipio*, the father of P. Cornelius Scipio Africānus who defeated Hannibal at Zama. See 56. —— **Transtulerunt, obtulit, detraxerat.** Explain composition.

51. **Qui legati.** (571.) —— **Qui .... impediret.** (536); 367, 1. —— **Quo minus .... trajiceret.** (545); 388; A. & S. 262, R. 9; Z. 531, 543. —— **Copias.** Observe difference of signification be-**18** tween the sing. and plur. —— **Penetrans.** (525.)

52. **Res prospere gesta est.** *A successful battle was fought.* In a military sense, *rem gerĕre* frequently has this meaning. —— **Magnam hujus insulae partem.** For arrangement of words, see 330. —— **Romam.** 282; F. B. 674; A. & S. 237; Z 398. —— **Inde.** *Thence*, i. e. Syracūsis, *from Syracuse*. —— **In Macedonia.** What construction would have been used if this had been the name of a town instead of that of a country? See 280. —— **Profectus.** (533, 2.) —— **In deditionem accepit.** Lit. *received into surrender;* the meaning is, *allowed the conditions of an honorable surrender*. —— **Ita.** Observe position. 334, R. 1. —— **Omni Sicilia recepta.** (525.)

53. **Duo Scipiones.** See *duōbus Scipionĭbus* (50), and note on

the same. —— **Hic, puer duodevigluti annorum.** *He, when a boy* **18**
eighteen years of age. See 458. —— **Post cladem Cannensem.** See
276, Rem. —— **Deserere.** Object of *cupientium.* —— **Cupientium.**
(524.) —— **Viginti .... juvenis.** *When a young man twenty-four
years of age.* —— **Die.** How governed? What is its gender? ——
Qua. Could *quo* be used here instead of *qua?* —— **Carthaginem
Novam.** *New Carthage,* a city in Spain founded soon after the first
Punic war by Hasdrubal, brother-in-law of Hannibal; its present
name is *Carthagena.*

54. **Ab eo inde tempore.** *From this time,* or *from this time
forth: inde* need not be translated. —— **In dies.** *Daily.* This
differs from *quotidie,* in denoting a daily increase or decrease;
here the *increase* of prosperity (*laetiōres*) requires *in dies.* See
Lat. Prose Comp. 69, t. —— **Evocatus.** What does this participle
express? i. e. does it serve to state any of the adverbial relations
of *time, cause, condition,* &c., and if so, which one? —— **Pugnans.**
Fighting, i. e. *while fighting.* —— **Plurimae.** Superlative of *multus:* observe comparison. F. B. 306; R. 3; A. & S. 125, 5; Z. 109.

55. **Consul creatus (est).** This is the predicate (229, 230); *con-* **19**
sul is the predicate-nominative. —— **Creatus, et .... missus est.**
(574.) —— **Romam.** 282; F. B. 674; A. & S. 237; Z. 398. ——
Qua re audita. *On hearing this.* (525, R. and 571.)

56. **Tentatam.** (524.) —— **Scipio victor recedit.** Lit. *withdrew
as victor;* render, *left the field as victor,* or simply, *was victorious.*
—— **Ingenti gloria triumphavit.** Compare *cum ingenti gloria....
regressus est,* 52. See 271 and Rem. —— **Africanus.** This title
was conferred upon Scipio in commemoration of his victories in
Africa. See also *nomen Asiatĭci,* 58, and *nomen Africāni juniōris,* 61. —— **Post——quam.** Compound word with parts separated. See 404, R. 2. —— **Coeperat.** What kind of verb? Give
parts in use. A. & S. 183, 2; Z. 221.

57. **Finito Punico bello.** (525); 458, 460. Which Punic war
is meant? See 43 and 47. —— **Macedonicum.** Sc. *bellum.* ——
Contra Philippum. Does this phrase modify the subject or the
predicate? See 190, R. —— **His legibus; ne .... inferret.** *On
these conditions; viz., that he should not wage war,* &c. The
clauses, *ne .... inferret, ut reddĕret,* &c., state the conditions or
terms on which peace was granted, and may therefore be regarded as in apposition with *legĭbus.* —— **Talenta.** The Attic talent

NOTES.

PAGE
19 was not a distinct coin, but a sum of money usually estimated at about $1080, though some authorities put it considerably lower.
20 —— **Obsidem.** See 229. —— **Finito, superatus, civitatibus, captivos.** Explain derivation.

58. **Se.** Could any other pronoun have been used here? See A. & S. 208; Z. 125, note. —— **Junxerat.** Explain formation of second root. F. B. 208. —— **Africanus.** See 56. —— **Victus.** Sc. *est.* —— **Ex Europa et Asia.** What is the construction for names of towns? —— **Intra Taurum.** *Within the limits of Taurus,* a mountain-range on the north and east of Syria. —— **Triumphavit.** See note on *triumphans,* 17. —— **Imitationem fratris.** See 56.

59. **Philippo .... mortuo ; copiis paratis.** (525). —— **Ejus.** To whom does this refer? —— **A rege.** F. B. 659; A. & S. 248. —— **Cui.** (571.) —— **Desertus.** (526.) —— **Cum ingenti pompa.** 271 and Rem. Compare *cum ingenti gloria,* 52, and *ingenti glo-*
21 *ria,* 56. —— **Inusitatae magnitudinis.** 190, 441; F. B. 624; A. & S. 211, R. 6; Z. 426, 471. —— **Remorum ordines.** *Banks of oars ;* these were arranged, one above another, so that the oars belonging to the highest *ordo* or *bank* were much longer than those belonging to the lowest. It was no uncommon thing for vessels to have four or five banks of oars, and some are said to have had thirty or forty. See *Smith's Dict. of G. and R. Antiquities.* —— **Latere.** This ablative is governed by a preposition understood. Explain the formation of the root from the nominative. F. B. 137 2, Rem.

60. **Tertium bellum.** See 43 and 47. —— **Altero.** *Second.* —— **Transactum erat.** From *transigo.* See 56. —— **Trajecerunt.** Sc. *se. Crossed over.* —— **Ibi.** *There,* i. e. *at Carthage.* —— **Per Scipionem.** What is the common construction for the *agent* of passive verbs? See 273 and R. 2. —— **Tribunus.** Military tribune, but not of the rank of the *military tribunes* described in 81; these last possessed consular power, and were sometimes called *consular tribunes.* The tribune here mentioned was an officer of the army, whose duty consisted in preserving order in the camp, in directing military exercises, and the like. The number of military tribunes to each legion was at first *four,* afterwards *six.* —— **Hujus.** Is this genitive *objective* or *attributive?* 188. —— **Committere.** Object of *vitabant* understood.

61. **Scipionis.** Which Scipio? —— **Postquam .... trajecerant.**

404, R. 2. —— Est creatus, et .... missus. What is the common place for copula? 326, R.; (574.) —— Defensam. (528.) Explain formation of 2d and 3d roots. F. B. 198, and 330, 2, c. —— Sua. *As their own.* —— Junioris. Why this epithet? See 56 How is this adjective compared? A. & S. 126, 4; Z. 113.

62. **Arma movit.** *Excited rebellion.* Explain formation of roots in *movit.* F. B. 219, 330. —— **Ex militibus ejus.** *Of his soldiers.* —— **Occisis.** (525.) —— **Civitati.** Logically this is in apposition with *Corintho* implied in *Corinthiis.* —— **Illatam.** (524.) From *infĕro*, *n* assimilated before *l* of the third root. See F. B. 550, 6. —— **Romae.** 280; F. B. 672; A. & S. 221; Z. 398. —— **Scipionis, Metelli, Mummii.** Supply *triumphus* with each of these genitives

63. **Post urbem conditam.** (523.) —— **Ut .... existimaretur.** (547); 422, R. 1; A. & S. 262, R. 1; Z. 531. (*a.*) —— **Quum .... peterent.** (552); 402, 2. —— **Responsum est.** What is logically the subject of this verb? in other words, what answer was given? —— **Placuisse.** What is the subject? —— **Pastor, interfector, imperator.** Explain derivation, and state the force of this ending.

64. **Exortum est.** From *exorior.* —— **Civitate.** See note on *civitati*, 62. —— **Victus.** Sc. *est.* —— **Jussit.** Could the plural have been used? 483; F. B. 612, R.; A. & S. 209, R. 12; Z. 365. Here *jussit* agrees with *senātus* and is understood after *popŭlus.* 483, R. 3. —— **Tradi.** This infinitive depends upon *jussit* in the line above. —— **Militem.** Lit. *soldier*, the individual used to represent the class; render, *soldiery.* —— **Partim—partim.** Lit. *partly—partly;* render, *either—or.* These words may, however, be often best rendered by *some—others*, followed by *of* with the objective case. Thus, *he captured some of the many cities of Spain and accepted others*, &c. —— **Infringi, corruptum, correxit.** Explain composition.

65. **P. Scipione .... consulibus.** (532.) —— **Quod .... intermisset.** (554); 409, Rem.; A. & S. 266, 3; Z. 549. —— **Corruptus.** *Bribed.* —— **Ei.** Observe position; it should stand at the beginning for a two-fold reason: 1st, it is somewhat emphatic; and 2d, the subject *Marius* should stand directly before the relative, as in this sentence. —— **Triumphantis.** (525.) See note on *triumphans*, 17. —— **Vinctus.** *In chains:* explain formation of second root. F. B. 208, and 225, 4. —— **Ductus est et .... strangulatus.** (574.)

23 66. **Ab urbe condita.** (523.) —— **Exarsit.** From *exardesco.*
24 —— **Annos.** 277; F. B. 670; A. & S. 236; Z. 395. —— **Cum illis.** *With them,* i. e. with the Roman people. —— **Perniciosum.** Explain derivation, giving the force of the ending *ōsus.* F. B. 530; A. & S. 128, L 4; Z. 252, 9. —— **Fusi fugatique.** Sc. *sunt.* —— **Cum—tum.** *Not only—but also.* F. B. 451. —— **Fudit.** Explain formation of second root. F. B. 219, 1, *b.* —— **Partis.** *Objective* or *attributive?* 188. —— **Id quod.** *Id* is in apposition with *jus,* or rather with the clause, *jus . . . . tribuērunt,* as that states what they had refused to do. —— **Jus civitatis.** *The right of citizenship.* —— **Bello finito.** (525.)

67. **Anno urbis conditae . . . . sexto.** *In the six hundred and sixty-sixth year from* or *after* (lit. *of*) *the founding of the city. Urbis condĭtae* = *post urbem condĭtam* (see 63, line 1), or *ab urbe condĭta* (see 66, line 1). —— **Romae.** What case would have been used if this had been a noun of the third declension? 280. —— **Mithridaticum.** Sc. *bellum.* —— **Causam . . . . dedit.** For position of words, see 335, Rem. —— **Adversus Mithridatem.** This modifies *bellum.* See 190, Rem. —— **Quum . . . . decretum esset.** (552); 402, 2; A. & S. 263, 5, R. 2; Z. 577, 578. —— **Marius . . . . conatus est.** For arrangement of elements, see 325, 332, 333. —— **Ei, honorem.** 254, Rem. —— **Cum—tum.** Usual meaning, *not only —but also;* both—and, &c.; render here, *either—or.* —— **Asia . . . . relicta.** (525.) —— **Finibus.** 301; F. B. 634; A. & S. 244; Z. 467. —— **Civile, morabatur.** Explain derivation.

68. **Unus ex.** *One of;* lit. *one from.* —— **Multos proscripserunt.** *Proscribed many.* In the civil wars, Sulla caused lists of the names of those persons whom he wished to have killed to be exposed to public inspection. Those whose names were on these lists were outlawed or proscribed, and any one might slay them and claim a reward; their property was confiscated, and their descendants were excluded from all offices of honor and trust. See *Smith's Dict. of G. and R. Antiquities;* also *Schmitz's Hist.*
25 *of Rome.* —— **Sanguine.** Gender? —— **Civium.** Rule for genitive plural? F. B. 141; A. & S. 83, 2; Z. 66. (*b.*) —— **Italicum, civile.** Sc. *bellum.* —— **Sociale dictum est.** This is the predicate of the relative clause. —— **Viros consulares.** *Men who had been consuls,* i. e. men of consular rank or dignity = *ex-consuls.* The consuls, it will be remembered, were two in number, were elect-

ed for one year, and had all the powers of king. See 23 and **25**
note on *consules*. —— **Praetorios.** *Those who had been praetors.*
When the office of praetor was first instituted, only one was appointed, who was to act as a kind of third consul with the leading part in the administration of justice; about a century later a second was added, called *praetor peregrinus*, to administer justice among foreigners and strangers resident at Rome. The number of praetors was increased from time to time, until at the beginning of the civil wars of Sulla and Marius, it was six; and in the dictatorship of Sulla it was raised to eight. See *Smith's Dict. of G. and R. Antiquities*, and *Schmitz's Hist. Rome*. —— **Aedilitios.** *Those who had been aediles.* The *aediles* (from *aedes*) were Roman magistrates who had charge of the public buildings, highways, &c., and acted as city police. They were at first two in number, afterwards more. See *Smith's Dict.* —— **Senatores.** The Roman senate (from *senex*) was regarded as a body of *elders* or *fathers* (patres). The number was at first 100 (see 12), then 200 (see 17), and finally 300, which continued to be the number until the time of the civil wars between Sulla and Marius. The number was then increased to 500 or 600 by the election of a large body of Roman knights. See *Smith's Dict.*

69. **L. Licinio Lucullo . . . . consulibus.** (532); 460; A. & S. 257, R. 7. —— **Populum . . . . heredem.** 229; A. & S. 230; Z. 394. —— **Habuere.** What other ending for the third plural of the perfect active? —— **Victus.** (525.) —— **Ut . . . . invaderet.** (541.) Why is *invadĕret* in the subjunctive and why in the imperfect? 380. —— **Ipse eum.** To whom do these pronouns refer? —— **Fame consumptum.** *After he had been reduced by famine.* See 525.

70. **Novum in Italia bellum.** Observe position of the phrase, **26** *in Italia.* Is this a modifier of the subject or of the predicate? —— **Gladiatores.** Gladiators were men who fought for the amusement of the Roman people. They consisted mostly of prisoners, slaves, and malefactors; they were trained in the skilful use of weapons at schools established for the purpose (*ludo gladiatorio*). —— **Capuae.** *At Capua.* —— **Hannibal.** Subject of *movit* understood. —— **Contraxerunt.** From *contrăho* : explain formation of second root. F. B. 208. —— **Proconsule.** The *proconsul*, as the name implies, was one who acted with the power of a consul.

26 Those who had been consuls (*viri consulāres*) were often allowed to assume the government of provinces, and to exercise in these provinces all the powers of a consul; they were then called *proconsuls.* —— **Italiae.** Is this genitive *objective* or *attributive?* 188.

71. **Superatum.** (530.) —— **Eidem.** 254, R.; A. & S. 224, R. 2. *Eidem,* of course, stands for *Mithridāti.* —— **Susceptus . . . . a Tigrane.** Mithridates, after he was defeated by Lucullus, fled to Armenia, and sought refuge in the dominions of Tigranes, his son-in-law. —— **Hujus.** This refers to Tigranes. —— **Tigranocerta.** This in the Armenian tongue means *the city of Tigranes;* it was built by Tigranes, and was the capital of Armenia. —— **Venientem.** (524.) —— **Vicit.** Form second root. F. B. 219, 1, b. —— **Ita . . . . ut . . . . deleret.** (547); 422, R. 1. —— **Deleret.** Form second root. F. B. 192 and foot-note. —— **Superatum, successor.** Explain derivation.

72. **Per illa tempora.** How does this expression differ from *illo tempŏre?* —— **Maria.** Give rule for ending of *nom. pl.* F. B. 127, Rem.; A. & S. 82, exc. 1 and 83; Z. 65. —— **Ut . . . . esset.** (547); 422, R. 1. —— **Orbe.** Supply preposition. Give gender of *orbe,* stating what it would have been if it had followed the common rule. See *Table of Gender,* F. B. 579; also A. & S. 62, and 63, 3; Z. 77. —— **Id bellum.** *This war,* i. e. *the management of it.* —— **Menses.** Give gender. —— **Contra regem.** This modifies *bellum.* 190, R. —— **Quo suscepto.** (525, 571.) —— **Tantum.** *Only.* —— **Neque.** (567.) —— **Hausit.** From *haurio.* —— **Hunc vitae finem.** For the order of these words, see 330, and for their position at the beginning of the sentence, see 335, Rem. —— **Industriae.** What other case might be used? 441; F. B. 624; A. & S. 211, R. 6. —— **Annis.** What case more common? 277 and Rem.; A. & S. 236; Z. 395.

73. **Ille se ei.** What nouns are represented by these pronouns? —— **Parte.** 254; A. & S. 251; Z. 460. —— **Pecunia.** *Sum of money.* —— **Quia . . tulerat; quod . . . . recepisset.** These are both causal clauses; why then does one take the indicative and the other the subjunctive? See 409. —— **Antiochiae.** 299; F. B. 632; A. & S. 222; Z. 409. —— **Libertate.** Ablative of means. —— **Caput.** Lit. *head;* render *capital.* —— **Triumphantis.** (525.) —— **Praelata.** Sc. *est.* —— **Infinitum.** Neuter adjective used substantively, *an immense amount.*

74. **M. T. Cicerone.... consulibus.** (532.) ——— **Generis, ingenii. 28**
What other case might be used? 441. ——— **Ad delendam patriam.**
(523.) ——— **Quidem.** *Indeed*, or *it is true*. ——— **Claris sed audacibus.**
440, 2. *Audacibus* is used in a bad sense. ——— **Urbe.** 289, R. 2;
F. B. 681, R. 2; A. & S. 242.

75. **Anno urbis conditae.** See note on first line, 67. ——— **Consul.** 201, 203. ——— **Vincendo.** Gerund; abl. of *means*. 465; F. B. 696, 2; A. & S. 275, III. R. 4; Z. 667. ——— **Annis.** See note on *annis*, 72. ——— **Omnem Galliam, quae,** &c. Not all Gaul, but that portion which is bounded as described. ——— **Ne nomen quidem.** *Not even the name.* (568.)

76. **Contra omina et auspicia.** It was deemed by the ancient Romans the height of folly to engage battle, or to undertake any important enterprise, when the auspices were unfavorable. ——— **Reliquiae exercitus.** *The remnant of the army.* ——— **Quaestorem.** There were two distinct classes of quaestors, the one having charge of the public money, and the other serving as prosecuting officers in certain criminal trials. See *Smith's Dict.*

77. **Victor.** *As victor.* ——— **Rediens.** F. B. 419: A. & S. 182. **29**
——— **Absens.** *In his absence*, or *even while absent.* ——— **Coepit.** Give parts in use. A. & S. 183, 2; Z. 221. ——— **Poscere.** Explain formation of second root. F. B. 222. ——— **Quem quum.... deferrent, contradictum est,** &c. *When some would confer this upon him,* &c., *opposition* (or *objection*) *was made,* &c. ——— **Dimissis exercitibus.... redire.** *Having dismissed his army, to return;* or *to dismiss his army and return.* (525, 530.) ——— **Dictatorem.** 229. See also note on *dictatoris*, 36, line 2.

78. **Inde.** *Thence,* i. e. from Rome. ——— **Hispanias.** *Spain.* The plural is often used, as the country was divided into two parts, viz. *citerior*, on this side of the Ebro, i. e. on the side toward Rome, and *ulterior*, beyond the Ebro. ——— **Nocte interveniente.** (525 or 526.) ——— **Nec.... superari.** This entire clause is the object of *dixit*. 374. ——— **Nec.** (567.) ——— **Vincere.** This is the object of *scire;* Caesar said that Pompey did not know (what?) *to conquer*, or *how to conquer*. ——— **Ingentibus.... commissis.** *With great forces engaged on both sides.* ——— **Pugnatum est.** *The battle was fought.* ——— **Fugatus.** (525.) ——— **Ut.... acciperet.** 385, 386; F. B. 692, 1; A. & S. 262; Z. 531. ——— **Tutor.... datus fuerat.** 229, 230. ——— **Quo conspecto.** *On see-*

12*

29 *ing this.* (525, 571.) —— **Fudisse.** Explain formation of second root. F. B. 219, 1, *b*. —— **Generi.** Pompey had married Julia, the daughter of Caesar; while she lived, she was, of course, a strong bond of union between the two, but she had died six years before the battle of Pharsalia.

30 79. **Qua de causa.** For order of words, see 334, R. 2. —— **Alexandria.** F. B. 644, 1; A. & S. 245; Z. 465. —— **Insolentius.** *Too insolently,* or *too haughtily.* The comparative is often best rendered by *too,* instead of *more.* —— **Conjuratum est.** *A conspiracy was formed.* —— **Illius Bruti.** See 23. —— **Regibus expulsis.** *After the banishment of the kings.* See 523, 525. —— **Confossus est.** From *confodio.*

80. **Percussoribus.** 218, 5; A. & S. 223, Rem. 2; Z. 412. —— **A Caesaris partibus stabat.** *Favored the party of Caesar* (stood by the party, &c.) —— **Hostis judicatus est.** 229, 230. —— **Caesari.** Dative after *fuerat.* 218, 1. —— **Magister equitum.** See note on *magistro equitum,* 36. —— **Vindicaturus.** (529.) —— **Extorsit.** From *extorqueo.* —— **Ut .... daretur.** This is the object of *extorsit;* Caesar extorted from them (what?) *that the consulship should be given,* &c. See 384. —— **Juveni.** See 440, 3, and

31 441. —— **Daretur.** For tense, see 380. —— **Proscripsit.** See note on *proscripserunt,* 68. —— **Per hos.** By whom?

81. **Profecti.** This is in the plural to agree with *Octaviānus et Antonius.* —— **Secundo.** Sc. *proelio.* —— **Victam interfecerunt.** Lit. *they slew* (them) *being conquered;* render, *they conquered and slew.* See 530. —— **Hispanias.** See note on this word in 78. —— **Gallias.** The plural is used because the Romans divided the country into two parts, viz. *Gallia ulterior* or *Transalpīna,* or *Gaul beyond the Alps;* and *Gallia citerior* or *Cisalpīna,* or *Gaul on this side of the Alps;* i. e. on the side toward Rome.

82. **Repudiata sorore.** (525.) Antony had married Octavia, the sister of Octavius. —— **Uxorem duxit.** *Married,* lit. *lead as wife,* in allusion to the custom of the bride's being conducted to her new home by her husband and friends. See note on *nubĕrc,* 6. —— **Qui locus.** The relative here has only the force of an adjective. —— **Quam.** This has the force of *postquam* (after). After designations of time, *quam* is not unfrequently thus used. —— **Ex eo inde tempore.** See note on 54, first line. —— **Ante.** Adverb, *before,* or *previously.*

83. **Idem.** Lit. *the same; idem* may sometimes be best rendered by *likewise, at the same time, at once.* Thus rendered the passage will stand, *Nero, being at once the step-son, the son-in-law, and the heir of Augustus.* —— **Totus.** Here best rendered by *wholly;* thus, *totus* . . . . *diversus* = wholly unlike. —— **Ingenio.** What other case might be used? —— **Fingendis virtutibus.** *In feigning virtues.* (523.) —— **Moderata.** Sc. *sunt.* —— **Petulantiae.** Indirect object after *obstitum* (*est*). —— **Petulantiae . . ·. . obstitum.** *His petulance was somewhat checked,* &c. The two negatives, *non* and *nihil,* are equivalent to an affirmative. —— **Per speciem amicitiae.** *Under the guise of friendship.* —— **Regni.** Genitive of the *crime* or *charge* after *suspectum.* —— **Affectati . . . . suspectum.** *Whom he suspected of aiming at the throne.* (523.) —— **Praefecti praetorii.** *The prefect* (or *commander*) *of the praetorian guards who protected the person of the emperor.* —— **Quum secessisset.** (549.)

84. **Germanico.** A. & S. 246; Z. 451. —— **Caligula.** This name is a diminutive from *caliga,* a kind of half-boot worn by the Roman soldiery: this surname was given to the emperor in allusion to the fact that from early youth he had been employed in military service. —— **Tiberio.** 457; F. B. 636; A. & S. 256; Z. 483. —— **Palatio.** *Palace;* Palatium, *the Palatine hill,* was the place where the Roman emperors and the most distinguished citizens had their residences; hence the term *palatium* came to be applied to any *royal mansion* or *palace.*

85. **Ad ludibrium reservatus.** When Caligula caused his own brother to be put to death, he spared Claudius (*ad ludibrium*) to make sport of him. —— **Gestas.** (524.) *Res gestae* is a common expression for *exploits, achievements,* &c. —— **Triumphantem.** (525.) —— **Caesar ipse.** *The emperor himself.* —— **Laevum . . . . latus.** Lit. *covered his left side;* render, *walked on his left.* —— **Illud.** Sc. *fecit.* —— **Tenet fama.** *The report is,* that, &c.; *tenet* takes the following clause as its object. —— **Datum.** Sc. *esse.*

86. **Avunculo.** F. B. 632; A. & S. 222; Z. 409. —— **Se similem.** See 229, Model, Rem. —— **Ad haec.** This has the force of *praeterea,* and may be rendered *moreover, in addition to these things,* &c. —— **Ausus.** From *audeo.* (526.)

87. **Caesar . . . . creatus.** *Having been made Caesar,* i. e. *emperor.*

34 88. **Eo.** F. B. 636; A. & S. 256; Z. 483.

89. **Jugulatus.** (530.)

90. **Obscure quidem natus.** *Of obscure birth indeed.* —— **Optimis comparandus.** *Worthy to be compared with the best.* *Optimis* is the indirect object. —— **Pecuniae.** A. & S. 213; Z. 436. —— **Ita ut . . . . anferret.** *Yet so as not to take it from any one unjustly.* —— **Eam nulli.** 254, R.; A. & S. 224, R. 2. —— **Auferrent.** Compounded of *ab* and *fero;* observe change in preposition. —— **Placidissimae lenitatis.** He was a man *of the most undisturbed lenity.* —— **Ut qui.** *As being one who;* it may be ren-

35 dered, *so much so, that.* —— **Accessit.** *Was added.* —— **Egerant.** *Had acted* or *lived.*

91. **Offensarum.** 298; A. & S. 213; Z. 436. —— **Dicta.** (524.) —— **Triumphavit.** See note on this word in 17.

92. **Generis.** Is this genitive *objective* or *attributive?* 188 —— **Qua antea.** *As before.* —— **Ut negaret.** (547.) —— **Quemquam . . . . discedere.** This clause is the object of *negaret.* —— **Nihil . . . . praestitisse.** This is the object of *recordātus fuisset.*

93. **Post—quam.** Compound word with its parts separated; render, *after.* —— **Biennium.** 277, and 404, R. 3; A. & S. 253,

36 R. 1; Z. 395. —— **Eo mortuo.** *At his death.* —— **Ei mortuo.** *To him, when dead.*

94. **Ipsius.** Domitian was the brother of Titus. —— **Patri.** This depends upon the adjective understood after *quam.* —— **Progressus.** (526.) —— **Ex senatu.** *Of the senate.* —— **Dominum se appellari.** 229. —— **Unam.** Sc. *expeditiōnem.* —— **De Dacis,** &c. *For his victories over the Dacians,* &c. —— **Solam lauream.** *The laurel branch only* (i. e. *merely*); victorious generals sometimes carried a laurel branch to the Capitol, instead of celebrating a triumph. —— **Vespillones.** These were the corpse-bearers who carried out the dead bodies of slaves and poor citizens at night.

37 95. **Athenas.** In apposition with *nomen.* —— **Aquarum illuvies.** *The flood.* —— **Sub quo.** *Under whom,* i. e. in whose time. —— **Triptolemo.** He is said to have been the inventor of the arts of agriculture, and is represented, by the aid of Ceres, to have distributed corn to the different parts of the earth. —— **Initiorum.** Lit. *beginnings;* render, *mysteries.* These were the mysteries of Ceres, generally celebrated with great secrecy, and sometimes at night; hence the expression in the text, *noctes initiōrum sacrātae*. —— **Cui quum.** (571.) —— **Quum** .... **successisset.** (552.) This is an adverbial attributive clause denoting *time*. See 397. —— **Astu.** *The city,* applied especially to Athens. —— **Quod appellatur.** Lit. *which it is called;* render, *as it is called.*

96. **Moenibus** .... **sepsisse.** Lit. *to have surrounded,* &c.; the meaning is, *that he induced them to live in towns and be governed by fixed laws.* —— **Generis. Sons-in-law.** These were the sons of Aegyptus, the brother of Danaus; they are said to have been murdered by their brides at the instigation of their father-in-law, who suspected them of aspiring to the throne. One of the daughters is generally represented as having disobeyed her father and spared her husband. —— **Deductis colonis,** &c. *Led colonists into the Peloponnesus, and gave the country its name.* (530.)

97. **Concussa est.** From *concutio.* —— **Pulsi.** (526.) —— **Athenas.** 282. —— **Acer belli.** *Valiant in war.* 298.

98. **Ea tempestate.** What other expression might have been used? —— **Generis regii.** Lycurgus was the brother of Polydectes king of Sparta. —— **Viris.** 299. —— **Cujus.** (571); 298. —— **Obsequia principum.** *Submission to rulers: princĭpum* is the *objective* genitive. See 188. —— **Justitiam imperiorum.** Lit. *justice of,* &c.; render, *just government* or *administration.* —— **Ut** .... **agerent.** Object-clause, indirect object. See 385. —— **Nubere.** See note on *viro,* 6. —— **Ut uxores,** &c. *That wives and not money might be chosen,* i. e. that wives might be selected for their good qualities, and not for their money. —— **Quoniam** .... **videbat.** Causal clause; why does it take the indicative? See 409. —— **Jurejurando.** From *jusjurandum,* a compound with both parts declined. See A. & S. 91. —— **Nihil de ejus legibus.** *None of his laws.* —— **Priusquam reverteretur.** A temporal clause. —— **Consulturum.** (529.) —— **Quid** .... **videretur.** An object-clause.

99. **Ad excitandam** .... **virtutem.** (523, 529.) —— **Auctore Iphito.** (532.) Iphitus *revived* the Olympic games, and from his time they were celebrated regularly. He was not, however, strictly the *founder* of them, as may be inferred from the next sentence in the text. —— **Ante—quam conderetur.** See 400. —— **Septuaginta.** Different dates are assigned for this event; some

PAGE
39 agreeing very nearly with the text and others making it half a century earlier. —— **Archontes.** The government of Athens, like that of Rome, was at first in the hands of kings, but was afterwards transferred to a new set of rulers called *archons*. These were at first appointed for life (*perpetui*); then for ten years (*in denos annos*), and finally for one year (*annui*), at which time their number was increased to *nine*.

100. **Crudeliores .... quam .... observari.** Lit. *more cruel* **40** *than that*, &c.; render, *too cruel to be observed.* —— **Munere.** 226; F. B. 644; A. & S. 245; Z. 465. —— **Agitatos.** (524.) —— **Parem iniret gratiam.** *That he secured equal favor*, i. e. became equally popular. —— **Dimicatum fuerat.** *A contest had been carried on.* This verb is here used impersonally. —— **Post .... acceptas.** *After sustaining many losses.* (523.) —— **Bellum reparandum.** (523.) —— **Insulae vindicandae.** *Of making good their claim to the island.* (523.) —— **Quod vetabatur.** *Which was forbidden*, referring to the renewal of the war. —— **Insula Atheniensium fieret.** *The island became the property of the Athenians.*

101. **Multis .... gestis.** (525.) —— **Pugnae .... facerent.** *Did not give him an opportunity of coming to an engagement.* —— **Ponte Istri.** *The bridge over the Ister*, i. e. the Danube; lit. *the bridge of the Ister.* —— **Quum rediisset.** Explain mood. 402. —— **Hortantibus amicis.** (526.) —— **Ut .... redigeret**, &c. This **41** clause is used as the *object* of *hortantibus*. See 384. —— **Causam interserens.** *Alleging as a reason;* here *causam* may be regarded as the *attributive accusative*, and the rest of the sentence as the direct object of *interserens*. See 229, 374. —— **Expugnassent, interfecissent.** The subjunctive here used in the *causal* clause after *quod* is explained by the fact that this reason was *assigned* by *Darius* and not by the historian. See 409.

102. **Abreptos.** (530.) —— **In Campum Marathona.** *Into the plain of Marathon.* —— **Atheniensibus auxilio.** 257; F. B. 651; A. & S. 227; Z. 422. —— **Quae.** (571.) —— **Quo factum est, ut.** *The result of which was, that.* (572.) —— **Primo quoque tempore.** *At the very first opportunity; quisque* with *primus* often has the force of *very, possible,* &c. —— **Sub montis radicibus.** *At the base of a mountain.* —— **Etsi .... videbat.** This clause expresses a concession. See 418. —— **Numero.** 301; F. B. 633; A. & S. 244; Z. 452. —— **Tanto plus.** *So much more.*

103. **In ipso apparatu.** *In the midst of his very preparations,* **42** *i. e.* while actually engaged in preparing for a second invasion. —— **Navium longarum.** *Ships of war,* called *longae* because they were built much longer than the ships of burden (*onerariarum*). —— **De adventu.** This is an attributive modifier of *fama,*—the report *of his approach.* See 190, Rem. —— **Peti.** *To be aimed at.* —— **Consultum.** Supine expressing purpose. See F. B. 676; A. & S. 276, II.; Z. 668, 2. —— **Respondit.** This verb has the clause, *ut . . . . munirent,* as object. See 383, 384. —— **Id . . . . valeret.** What this answer meant. —— **Ut . . . . conferrent.** This clause is the predicate after *esse,* as it states what the design was. —— **Salamina.** Accusative in *a* in imitation of the Greek. —— **Majoribus natu.** *Old or aged men, elders.* —— **Sacra procuranda.** (523, 529.)

104. **Dimicari.** This is the true subject of *placēbat.* —— **Qui . . . occuparent.** *To take possession of,* &c. (536.) See also 367. —— **Ducentae.** Sc. *naves.* —— **Ne . . . . circumiretur.** Final **43** clause; see 367, R. 2. —— **Quo factum est, ut.** (572.)

105. **Astu.** See note on this word in 95. —— **Themistocles unus restitit.** *Themistocles alone stood firm, objected.* —— **Universos.** *All together, united.* —— **Summae.** Dative depending upon *praeërat.* 218, 2. —— **De servis suis, quem,** &c. *One of his servants, whom,* &c. —— **Suis verbis.** *In his words,* i. e. *in his name, from him.* —— **Nuntiaret.** This verb has *ei* as its *indirect* object, and all the rest of the sentence after *verbis* as its *direct* object. See 240, 374. —— **Hoc eo valebat.** *The object of this was.* —— **Barbarus.** Xerxes. —— **Contra.** *On the contrary, on the other hand.*

106. **Hic etsi . . . . gesserat.** *Although he had fought an unsuc-* **44** *cessful battle.* This clause expresses *concession;* see 418. —— **Ut . . . . posset hostes.** See 422. —— **Ab eodem.** *By the same one,* i. e. Themistocles: *eodem,* it must be observed, does not belong to *gradu.* —— **Gradu.** *From his position.* —— **Ne . . . . perseveraret.** This is the object of *verens.* 384. —— **Id agi.** Lit. *that it was doing;* render, *was in contemplation.* —— **In Hellesponto.** *Over the Hellespont.* —— **Altera.** *Second.* —— **Post . . . . memoriam.** *Within the recollection of man.*

107. **Quam.** = *postquam.* —— **Duce Pausania.** (532.) —— **Quo proelio.** (571.) —— **Interfectus est.** *Destroyed, cut in pieces.* —— **Sua ducta . . . . dedisse.** This clause is in apposition with

NOTES.

44 *sententia.* —— **Victoriae.** This genitive depends upon *ergo*, which
45 may be regarded as a substantive in the ablative. —— **Quumque
.... uterentur.** This is a causal clause; explain mood; see 409.
—— **Id fieri.** Object of *vetarent.*

108. **Sociorum.** Objective genitive. —— **Fatigati.** (526.) ——
Ducibus Lacedaemoniis. (532.) —— **Invidentibus** (524.) —— **Quo.**
Ablative after *gravius.* F. B. 636; A. & S. 256; Z. 483. ——
Periclis. Pericles, a distinguished orator and statesman of Ath-
46 ens, directed the counsels of his state for many years. —— **Quod
intelligens.** (571.) —— **Agros reipublicae dono.** 245; F. B. 649;
A. & S. 227, R. 1; Z. 422. —— **Navali proelio dimicatum est.** Lit.
it was fought, &c.; render, *a naval battle was fought.* —— **Non
nisi.** *No more than, only.* —— **Ex sociorum persona.** *In the person of their allies :* these had never concurred in the peace.

109. **Exorto.** From *exorior.* (524.) —— **Iiii.** To whom does
this refer? —— **Duces.** Predicate nominative. —— **Ut .... essent.** (547.) See also 422. —— **Iis terrori, quibus auxilio.** 257.

110. **Alcibiades revocatus esset.** Alcibiades was accused of re-
vealing the mysteries of Ceres—a crime punishable by death.
—— **Secundo Marte pugnant.** Lit. *they fight, Mars being propitious ;* render, *they fight successfully.* —— **Urbi.** 237, 240. ——
47 Fracti. 526. —— **Quum .... audivisset.** (549, 550.) —— **Incli-
nato.** *Sinking, unfavorable :* the figure is taken from a building
just ready to fall. —— **Tertio.** Sc. *proelio.*

111. **Lacedaemone.** What construction would be required with
the name of a country? 282. —— **Quo cognito.** *On ascertaining
this.* —— **Amissi.** (524.) —— **Ex utraque parte.** *On each side.*
—— **Afflictae.** (528.) It will be observed that the participle
expressing *concession* here retains the connective *quamvis.* ——
Pudore male actae rei. *From shame at his want of success,* or
bad management. —— **Relictas.** (524.) —— **Partim—partim.** *Either—or; some—other;* the meaning is, *he either took or killed,*
or better, *he took some and killed others.*

48 112. **Alcibiades cum duce,** &c. Alcibiades was at this time in
exile, having fled for his life, when he was recalled from his
command in Sicily and learned that he was already under sentence of death. See 110, line 1, with note on the same. —— **Qui
quum.** *When this,* i. e. the senate. 571. —— **Crudeliter ...
consuleret.** *Adopted cruel measures against the people, acted cru-*

elly towards them. —— **Se . . . . redderent.** This entire clause is the object of *scripsit.* —— **Quum . . . . nequissent.** Explain mood and tense. 402, 380. —— **Intestino malo.** The senate, the four hundred. —— **Perrexit.** From *pergo.*

113. **Quam plurimas.** *Quam* before a superlative is intensive, and is often best rendered by *possible*, as *quam plurimas, the greatest possible number, as many as possible*, or sometimes *very many.*

114. **Darius.** This was *Darius the Second*, and of course not the one spoken of in 101, 102, 103. —— **Ut . . . . mitterent.** Consecutive clause; explain mood and tense. 422, 380. —— **In . . . . locum.** *To take the place of, to succeed.*

115. **Navibus.** 218, 2; F. B. 643; A. & S. 224, R. 1. —— **Proeliis adverso Marte pugnatis.** Lit. *battles fought, Mars being adverse;* render, *having lost battles*, or, *having fought unsuccessfully.* —— **Praedatum.** Supine. —— **Delevit.** *Destroyed — put an end to.* —— **Res . . . . inclinata est.** The power of the Athenians was utterly overthrown. See note on *inclináto,* 110.

116. **Neque.** *Not;* this is usually the best translation of *neque* when followed by *et.* —— **Novae.** Sc. *copiae*, stores, supplies. —— **Quae.** *This.* (571.) —— **Nomen Atheniensium.** *The Athenian name — the Athenian state or nation.* —— **Passuros.** What is the object? —— **Duobus oculis.** *The two eyes;* these were *Athens* and *Sparta.* —— **Longi muri brachia.** Reference is here made to the long walls which connected Athens with its ports. See 107, "*Phalerico portu,*" "*Piraeei portus.*"

117. **Dediti.** *Devoted to, devoted to the interests of.* —— **Quo factum est, ut,** &c. (572.)

118. **Praepositi a Lacedaemoniis.** This is an example of the abridged clause. See 440. —— **Quod.** This relative, it will be observed, does not agree with its antecedent, but with the predicate-nominative *castellum.* See *Lat. Prose Comp.* —— **Oppugnare.** Abridged object of *sunt adorti.* See 447. —— **Jacentem.** (524 or 525.) —— **Neminem . . . . spoliavit.** 254. —— **Quorum.** The common construction requires the ablative with verbs of *plenty* and *want;* the genitive is occasionally used.

119. **Quibus praefectus fuit.** See 114. —— **Ad se arcessitum . . . . vinxit.** *Summoned him into his presence and bound,* &c. See (530). —— **Interfecisset, nisi . . . . prohibuisset.** Explain mood

52 and tense. 414, 416. —— **Parare.** Observe that the subject of the infinitive is omitted, being the same as that of the principal verb *coepit.* See 447. —— **Imprudentius.** *Too imprudently.* —— **In auxilio,** &c. *In the service of.* —— **Per indomitas nationes revertuntur.** This remarkable achievement is known in history as the "Retreat of the Ten Thousand."

120. **Jubet .... discedere.** What mood is generally used after verbs of *ordering, commanding,* &c. ? —— **Pro hoste.** *As an enemy.* —— **Faceret.** Sc. *iter; was travelling through.* —— **Cadmeam.** This was the citadel of Thebes. —— **Quo .... resisterent.** Explain the use of *quo,* also mood and tense. 386, 380. —— **Laconum rebus studebant.** *Favored the interests of the Laconians.* —— **Neque eo magis.** Lit. *nor the more on this account,* i. e. still they did not restore, &c. —— **Liberandae patriae.** *Of liberating his country.* (523.) —— **Idem sentiebant.** *Entertained the same*

53 *opinions,* i. e. belonged to the same party. —— **Eum.** This belongs to *diem* above. —— **Vesperascente coelo.** *At the approach of evening.* —— **Pervenit.** Give the subject. —— **Usque eo.** *So utterly.* —— **Duce Pelopida.** *Under the guidance of Pelopidas.* (532.)

121. **Satis haberent.** Lit. *regarded it sufficient;* render, *were satisfied.* —— **Imperator.** *When commander,* or *when in command;* a noun in apposition being frequently the representative of a temporal clause which has been abridged, should sometimes be introduced in the translation by *when.* See 458. —— **Inquit.** Give object.

54 122. **Quod.** This agrees with the predicate-nominative *caput.* See note on *quod,* 118. —— **Ante eum natum.** *Before his birth.* (523.) —— **Effectum est.** Give subject. —— **Obses .... domo.** How may this abridged clause be filled out? See 440, 458.

123. **Robur Thessalorum equitum.** The Thessalian cavalry was regarded as the best in Greece.

55 124. **Olim destinato.** This may be regarded as a form abridged from the relative clause. See 440.

125. **Praedandi.** Gerund, governed by *causa;* see 443. —— **Virtute ..., praestantes.** Abridged clause; explain; 440. —— **Antea infestissimas.** Abridged clause; explain; 440. —— **Adversis vulneribus.** *With wounds in front:* it was a disgrace to receive a wound in the back. See same expression in 39. —— **Tuenda.** *To defend, to be defended.* (529.)

GRECIAN HISTORY. 283

126. **Quantum .... fuit.** Lit. *as much as was in him;* render, **56** *as far as was in his power.* —— **Ad formandum .... statum.** See 451. —— **Dubium erat.** This is the predicate affirmed of the following clause as subject.

127. **Ad ludos spectandos.** *To witness the games.* (529.) See also 451. —— **Attalo.** One of Philip's generals. —— **Honoratum ... adversarium.** See 449. —— **Poterat.** Sc. *exigĕre.*

128. **Vincendi.** 442. —— **Hic—ille.** When *hic* and *ille* are **57** thus used in reference to two persons or objects just mentioned, *hic* usually refers to the *latter* and *ille* to the former. —— **Gaudere.** This is an instance of what is called the *historical infinitive*, and should be rendered by the *imperfect indicative.* A. & S. 209, R. 5; Z. 599, N. Several other examples of the *historical infinitive* occur in this paragraph. —— **Amari.** This depends upon *malle.* —— **Parcendi.** 298, 443. —— **Victis.** Participle used substantively and governed by *parcendi.* 218. —— **Nec.** (567.)

129. **Proficiscens.** (525.) —— **Opes.** Object of *cogitabant* understood; construed literally the passage would read thus: *they thought of nothing if not the riches,* i. e. *if they did not think of the riches,* &c.; render, *they thought of nothing except the,* &c. —— **Invitae.** Best rendered by the adv. *unwillingly.* **58**

130. **In exercitu .... duae.** Observe that the *copulative connectives* between the several subjects are omitted. 487. —— **Electos.** See 449.

131. **Caeso rege.** Lit. *by the king slain;* render, *by slaying the king.* (523.) —— **Confossi, efferati.** (526.) —— **Ad hoc ipsum. 59** *For this very purpose.*

132. **Macedonum erat.** *Was the property of the Macedonians; erat* agrees with *Phoenīce,* and is understood after *Syria.* —— **Sibi .... impedimento.** 257; A. & S. 227; Z 422. —— **Occisos.** (530.) —— **Exceptis.** This agrees with the omitted antecedent **60** of *qui.* —— **His .... nuntiatis.** This ablative absolute is an abridged concessive clause. (528.) See also 458. —— **Opem a diis,** &c. *To seek aid from the gods,* i. e. by taking refuge in their temples. —— **Quantumque .... sit.** Subject of *potest.* —— **Trucidati sunt.** Observe that the *participle* does not agree in gender with the subject *millia,* but with *viri* or *homĭnes* implied in that subject.

133. **Aegyptii .... perterriti.** This is a compound sentence

60 consisting of two members, each of which is an abridged complex sentence. —— **Ventum est.** Impersonal verb. —— **Consecratam deo, undique.... contectam.** Abridged attributive clauses limiting *sedem.* See 440. —— **Maximus natu.** The eldest. ——

61 Destinaret. Explain mood and tense. 379, 380. —— **Aeque.... compositus.** Abridged clause; explain. —— **Colendi.** Gerund, depending upon *auctor.* 443.

134. **Principes.** In apposition with *legatos.* 440. —— **Neque.** (567.) —— **Neque.... Halym.** In the previous offers of Darius, this river was designated to be made the boundary of Alexander's dominions. —— **Inquit.** What is the direct object of this verb?

62 135. **Non alias.** *On no other occasion.* —— **Altior.** *Unusually deep.* —— **Nec aut Persae aut Macedones,** &c. Compound sentence abridged; subjects united; 482. —— **Cedere, laxare.** Historical infinitives; see note on *gaudēre,* 128.

136. **Recuperandae libertatis.** (523.) —— **Quem.** (571.) —— **Dux.... relictus.** Abridged relative clause. 440. —— **Dantes.** 449.

63 137. **Bacchantium more.** The votaries of Bacchus at their feasts indulged in various boisterous revels.

138. **Faceret.** Sc. *ut.* —— **Ostendere.** Historical infinitive; see note on *gaudēre,* 128. —— **Alius—alius.** *One—another.*

64 139. **Revertenti.** *To him on his return,* or *on his way home.* —— **Carthaginiensium.... Sardiniae,** &c. Compound attributive modifier of *legationes.* —— **Nonnullas.** Sc. *legationes.* —— **Totus.** Best rendered adverbially, *utterly, entirely.* —— **Inter bibendum.** *While drinking;* an abridged temporal clause. 461.

140. **Aeacidarum.** Alexander was, by his mother, a lineal descendant of Aeacus the grandfather of Achilles. —— **Dignissimum.** Adjective used substantively; object of *facĕre* understood. ——

65 Judicio. *By a tacit decision,* opposed to *voce.* —— **Electus esse.** 436.

141. **Quo die.** *The day in which;* the relative here must not be rendered according to 571. —— **Alterius—alterius.** *The one— the other;* sc. *victoriae.* —— **Quadrigas.** Chariots and horses were often sent to the Olympic games to contend for prizes. —— **Puer.** *When a boy.* —— **Tantam.... fiduciam fecit.** *He inspired his soldiers with such confidence*

142. **Appellant, legunt et jubent.** Compound sentence abridged by uniting predicates. 486. —— **His deducere.** This compound sentence should be carefully examined. It consists of four complex members, having the abridged subordinate clause, *his ita composĭtis,* common to each, with principal clauses as follows; viz., the first an abridged compound with objects (*Macedoniae et Graeciae*) united; the second simple; the third abridged compound with objects (*Meleagro et Perdiccae*) united, and also with modifiers of subject (*castrōrum et exercĭtus*) united; and the fourth complex. —— **Lustratione.** This was a review accompanied with expiatory sacrifices.

143. **In duas partes.** The disputes of Perdiccas and Antigonus resulted in the formation of two hostile parties. —— **Victoriae.** This depends upon *gloria* understood. —— **Familiam.** *Retinue of attendants* or *slaves.* —— **Dicens.** Explain direct object.

144. **Iterato,** adv. — *itĕrum. Again, a second time.* —— **Congreditur et .... refugit.** Compound predicate. —— **Cassander et Lysimachus.** Compound subject.

145. **Ducibus Spartanis.** *Under the guidance of the Spartans.* (532.) —— **Quod .... occupassent.** This is the alleged cause, and accordingly depends upon *praetendentes.*

146. **Hortante .... successu.** Lit. *success prompting them;* render, *encouraged* or *prompted by their success.* —— **Alii—alii.** *Some—others.* —— **Ut .... mercarentur.** Consecutive clause; see 421, 422. —— **Non lacessiti.** *Without being attacked.* (531.)

147. **Delphos.** 282. —— **Munera.** Observe the various modifiers of this subject. —— **Magnificentia sua.** *By their magnificence;* abl. of means. —— **Voluntatem et .... responsa.** Compound object.

148. **Statuas cum quadrigis.** These were the statues of those who had won prizes in the chariot races at the Pythian games. —— **Solido .... esse.** *That they were cast from solid gold.* —— **Spei.** This depends upon *plus.* —— **Diis antesignanis.** *With the gods as their champions* or *leaders.* —— **Nec.** *Not.* —— **Imbres .... et pervigiliae.** Compound subject.

149. **Salutis latebras.** *A place of safety.*

150. **Philopator.** This surname from its composition means *the lover of a father,* and was given to Ptolemy in irony, as he had murdered both his parents. —— **Aetate immatura.** 441. ——

PAGE
70 **Quo .... imbutum**: Allusion is here made to the oath of eternal enmity to the Romans which his father is said to have made him take when a boy.

151. **Nec.** *Not.* —— **Apud Cynoscephalas.** Compare 57. —— **Repudiata .... pace.** 458.

71 152. **Invisus.** See 448. —— **Criminari.** Sc. *coepit.* —— **Nunc —nunc.** *At one time—at another.*

153. **Occiso .... aemulo.** This abridged clause, it will be observed, is compound. —— **Nec.** (567.) —— **Contracto.** Attributive clause abridged. 440.

154. **Macedonicum bellum.** Compare account in 59. —— **Dedissent.** *They had given,* i. e. he said *they had given;* hence the *subjunctive.* 426. —— **Extra ordinem.** The ordinary method of
72 distributing the provinces was *by lot.* —— **Defecit.** *Was eclipsed.* —— **Talentum.** Genitive plural; see A. & S. 53. —— **Alexandro et Philippo.** Compound attributive modifier abridged.

155. **Tunc temporis.** *At that time;* it is equivalent to *illo tempŏris,* or *id tempŏris.* —— **Conspirationem universarum.** *The union of all.* —— **Responsum est.** *The reply was made.* —— **Ad inspiciendas res.** 451. —— **Ut .... dissolverent.** This clause may be treated as the subject of *mandātum est.*

73 156. **Pugnandi .... fecit.** *Offered the enemy battle.* —— **Urbs Corinthus diruitur.** Compare account in 62. —— **Sub corona venditur.** *Are sold as slaves:* some suppose that *sub corona* implies that a wreath was placed upon the head of the prisoner when offered for sale; and others that it merely refers to the ring (*corŏna*) of soldiers by whom he was guarded.

LATIN-ENGLISH VOCABULARY.

☞ For *proper names* the pupil is referred to the *Hist. and Geog. Index.*

A.

A. An abbreviation of *Aulus.*
A, ab, abs, prep. with abl. From, by.
Abdūco (ab, duco), *ĕre, duxi, ductum.* To lead away, take away, remove.
Abeo (ab, eo), *ire, ivi* or *ii, itum.* To go away, depart, withdraw from.
Abjicio (ab, jacio), *ĕre, jēci, jectum.* To throw away, throw, reject; prostrate, humble.
Aboleo, ĕre, ēvi, itum. To blot out, efface; ruin, destroy.
Abripio (ab, rapio), *ĕre, ripui, reptum.* To take away, carry off.
Abrumpo (ab, rumpo), *ĕre, rūpi, ruptum.* To break off *or* away, rend, sever.
Absens (part. of *absum*), *tis.* Absent.
Abstineo (abs, teneo), *ĕre, tinui, tentum.* To keep *or* hold back, abstain from.
Absum (ab, sum), *esse, fui, futūrus.* To be absent *or* away, to be distant from.
Absūmo (ab, sumo), *ĕre, sumpsi, sumptum.* To take from *or* away; destroy, consume.

Abundo (ab, undo), *āre, āvi, ātum.* To abound, superabound.
Ac (a shortened form of atque, used only before consonants). And.
Accēdo (ad, cedo), *ĕre, cessi, cessum.* To approach, accede to; be added to.
Accendo (ad, candeo), *ĕre, cendi, censum.* To set on fire, kindle; to excite, inflame.
Acceptus (accipio), *a, um.* Accepted; acceptable, pleasing.
Accipio (ad, capio), *ĕre, cēpi, ceptum.* To accept, receive.
Accurro (ad, curro), *ĕre, curri (cucurri* rare), *cursum.* To run to, hasten to.
Accūso (ad, causa), *āre, āvi, ātum.* To call to account, to accuse.
Acer, acris, acre. Sharp; powerful, severe, valiant; diligent, intense.
Acies, ēi, f. The order of battle, battle-array; line of soldiers; army in battle-array.
Acquiesco (*adquiesco* from *ad, quiesco*), *ĕre, ēvi, ētum.* To become quiet, to repose; to acquiesce in.
Acriter (acer). Vehemently, valiantly.

Acuo, ĕre, ui, ūtum. To sharpen, quicken; stimulate.
Ad, prep. with acc. To, towards; at, near.
Addo (ad, do), *ĕre, dĭdi, dĭtum.* To add, carry to, appoint to.
Addūco (ad, duco), *ĕre, duxi, ductum.* To lead to, conduct, bring, induce.
Adeo (ad, eo), adv. So, to such an extent.
Adeo (ad, eo), *ĭre, ĭvi* or *ii, ĭtum.* To go to, approach, visit; encounter.
Adhuc, adv. Thus far, as yet, even yet; still.
Adĭmo (ad, emo), *ĕre, ĕmi, emptum.* To take from, deprive of.
Adipiscor, ci, adeptus sum, dep. To obtain, get possession of.
Adjicio (ad, jacio), *ĕre, jēci, jectum.* To throw or cast to or against, add to.
Adjungo (ad, jungo), *ĕre, junxi, junctum.* To join to, unite with.
Administro (ad, ministro), *āre, āvi, ātum.* To administer, manage.
Admiratio (admīror), *ōnis,* f. Admiration, respect.
Admīror (ad, miror), *āri, admirātus sum,* dep. To admire, wonder at.
Admitto (ad, mitto), *ĕre, mīsi, missum.* To send to or forward, to admit, receive.
Admŏdum (ad, modus), adv. Very, exceedingly.
Admonĭtus, us, m. Warning, advice; instigation.
Admoveo (ad, moveo), *ĕre, mōvi, mōtum.* To move to, apply to, bring to.
Adolescens (adolesco), *entis,* adj. and subs., m. and f. Young, growing; a young man, a youth.
Adolescentŭlus (adolescens), *i,* m. A very young man, a youth.
Adolesco, ĕre, ēvi (*ui* rare), *ultum.* To grow, grow up, increase.

Adoptŏ, āre, āvi, ātum. To choose, adopt; take for a son, daughter, &c.
Adorior (ad, orior), *īri, ortus sum,* dep. To attack, attempt, strive; begin.
Adorno, āre, āvi, ātum. To adorn, furnish, equip.
Adsto, or *asto* (ad, sto), *āre, stĭti.* To stand near, stand by.
Adsum (ad, sum), *esse, fui, futūrus.* To be present or at hand, assist, stand by.
Adulatio, ōnis, f. Adulation, flattery.
Advectus (part. from *advĕho*), *a, um.* Brought, carried to.
Advĕho (ad, vcho), *ĕre, vexi, vectum.* To conduct, convey, import.
Advenio (ad, venio), *īre, veni, ventum.* To come to, arrive.
Adventus (advenio), *us,* m. Arrival, approach.
Adversariụs, a, um, adj. Opposite, opposing.
Adversarius, i, m. subst. Adversary, opponent, antagonist.
Adversus (adverto), *a, um.* Opposite, over against, adverse, hostile; fronting, in front.
Adversus, or *adversum* (adverto), adv. and prep. Against, towards, opposite to.
Aedes, or *aedis, is,* f. Temple *in the sing.; but in the plur.* dwelling, habitation, house.
Aedifĭco (aedes, facio), *āre, āvi, ātum.* To build.
Aedilitius, or *aedilicius* (aedes), *a, um.* Pertaining to the aediles: *aedilitius, i,* m., one who has been aedile. The aediles were Roman magistrates who had charge of the public buildings, highways, &c., and acted as city police.
Aegritūdo, ĭnis, f. Affliction, anguish; care, uneasiness.
Aemŭlus, a, um. Emulous; *often used substantively as* rival, competitor.

Aeneus, a, um. Brazen.
Aequaliter. Equally.
Aeque (aequus). Equally, similarly.
Acquiparo (aeque, paro), *are, avi, atum.* To equal, make equal.
Aequitas (aequus), *atis,* f. Equality, equity.
Aequus, a, um. Equal, similar; just, fair; favorable, propitious.
Aestas, atis, f. Summer.
Aestimatio (aestimo), *onis,* f. Estimation, worth.
Aestimo, are, avi, atum. To value, estimate: *parvi aestimare,* to think little of, esteem lightly.
Aetas, atis, f. Age, time of life.
Aeternitas, atis, f. Eternity, perpetuity.
Affectatus (part. from *affecto*), *a, um.* Desired, aimed at.
Affecto, are, avi, atum. To desire, aim at, strive after.
Affero (ad, fero), *ferre, attuli, allatum.* To bring, carry to, report.
Affigo, ere, fixi, fixum. To affix, fasten to.
Affirmo, are, avi, atum. To affirm, confirm, ratify.
Afflictus (part. from *affligo*), *a, um.* Afflicted, troubled, prostrated.
Affligo, ere, flixi, flictum. To afflict, trouble, overthrow.
Africus (sc. *ventus*), *i,* m. The south-west wind, i. e., the wind from Africa.
Ager, agri, m. Field, land, territory.
Aggredior, i, gressus sum. To approach, attack, attempt.
Agitatus (part. from *agito*), *a, um.* Agitated, troubled.
Agito, are, avi, atum. To harass, trouble, think of.
Agmen, inis, n. An army, *generally on the march,* band of soldiers, troop.
Agnosco, ere, novi, nitum. To recognize.

Ago, ere, egi, actum. To conduct, drive, do, act, execute: *annum vicesimum agere,* to be in his (or her) twentieth year.
Agricultura (ager, colo), *ae,* f. Agriculture.
Aio, ais, ait, &c. defect. (see A. & S. 183, 4). To say, affirm.
Ala, ae, f. Wing.
Alacer, cris, cre. Active, prompt; joyful.
Albus, a, um. White.
Alias. Otherwise, at another time; *non alias,* on no other occasion.
Alienus (alius), *a, um.* Belonging to another, foreign; unfavorable.
Aliquando. At some time, formerly, finally, now at last.
Aliquantum, adv. Somewhat, in some degree.
Aliquis (alius, quis), *qua, quod,* and *quid.* Some one, some.
Aliquot, indecl. pl. adj. Several, some.
Aliter (alius), adv. Otherwise.
Alius, a, ud (gen. alius, &c.; see F. B. 113. R.). Other, another; *alius—alius,* one—another; *alii —alii,* some—others.
Alloquor (ad, loquor), *i, quutus* or *cutus sum,* dep. To speak to, address.
Alo, ere, alui, alitum or *altum.* To support, keep, nourish, strengthen.
Alte (altus), adv. On high, high
Alter, era, erum (gen. alterius, &c.; F. B. 113. R.). One of two, the other; *alter—alter,* the one— the other; *alter* as numeral = *second.*
Altus, a, um. High, noble, great; deep, profound; *altum* substantively, the sea, the deep.
Amabilis (amo), *e.* Lovely, amiable.
Ambio, ire, ivi or *ii, itum.* To surround, encompass.

Ambo, ae, o. Both.
Amicitia (amīcus), *ae,* f. Friendship.
Amīcus, i, m. A friend.
Amīcus, a, um. Friendly, kind.
Amīta, ae, f. A father's sister, paternal aunt.
Amitto (a, mitto), *ĕre, mīsi, missum.* To send away, to lose.
Amnis, is, m. River.
Amo, āre, āvi, ātum. To love.
Amor (amo), *ōris,* m. Love, affection, desire.
Amphitheātrum, i, n. Amphitheatre, *in Rome* a circular or oval building used for public spectacles.
Amplio (amplus), *āre, āvi, ātum.* To enlarge.
Amplius (comp. of *ample*), adv. More, further.
Amplus, a, um. Ample, spacious, large.
An, interrog. particle. Or, whether.
Anceps, ancipĭtis. Twofold, double.
Angustia (angustus), *ae,* f., used mostly in pl. Narrow pass, difficulty.
Angustus, a, um. Narrow, confined.
Anĭma, ae, f. Breath, life.
Animadverto (anĭmus, adverto), *ĕre, ti, sum.* To notice, observe, perceive.
Anĭmus, i, m. Mind, soul, courage.
Annŭlus, or *anŭlus, i,* m. Ring.
Annus, i, m. Year.
Annuus (annus), *a, um.* Lasting a year, for a year, annual.
Ante, adv. and prep. Before *in respect to place or time,* formerly.
Antea. Formerly.
Antesignănus (ante, signum), *i,* m. Leader, commander.
Antiquĭtas (antĭquus), *ātis,* f. Antiquity.
Antīquus, a um. Ancient, early.
Antistes, ĭtis, m. and f. President; priest, priestess.
Anxiĕtas, ātis, f. Anxiety, solicitude.
Aperte. Openly, publicly.
Apparātus, us, m. Preparation, equipment.
Apparātus, a, um. Prepared, ready, equipped.
Appellatio (appello), *ōnis,* f. Name, title.
Appello, āre, āvi, ātum. To call, name.
Appello (ad, pello), *ĕre, pŭli, pulsum.* To drive to, bring to, induce.
Appropinquo, āre, āvi, ātum. To approach.
Apud, prep. with acc. At, near, among.
Aqua, ae, f. Water.
Aquĭla, ae, f. Eagle.
Ara, ae, f. Altar.
Arbĭtror, āri, ātus sum, dep. To think, judge.
Arcesso, ĕre, ivi, ītum. To call, invite; summon.
Archon, tis, m. The chief magistrate at Athens, archon.
Ardeo, ēre, arsi, arsum. To be on fire, burn.
Ardesco, ĕre, arsi. To take fire, kindle.
Argenteus (argentum), *a, um.* Made of silver.
Argentum, i, n. Silver.
Argumentum, i, n. Argument, sign, mark.
Argyraspis, ĭdis, adj. Armed with silver shields, *a title applied to a company of Macedonian soldiers who had silver shields.*
Arma, ōrum, n. pl. Arms, force of arms.
Armātus (armo), *a, um.* Armed.
Armilla, ae, f. Bracelet.
Armo (arma), *āre, āvi, ātum.* To arm.
Arrŏgans, tis. Proud, arrogant.
Ars, tis, f. Art, skill.

Arx, arcis, f. Citadel.
Aspis, ĭdis, f. Asp.
Asporto, āre, āvi, ātum. To bear or carry away.
Asseveratio, ōnis, f. Declaration, assertion.
Assiduus, a, um. Assiduous; frequent; continual, incessant.
Assigno, āre, āvi, ātum. Assign, bestow.
Asto, are, stĭti. To stand near or by.
Astu, n. indecl. A city, *generally applied to* Athens.
Asȳlum, i, n. Asylum, place of refuge.
At, conj. But, yet.
Atque, conj. And, and also, and besides; *atque—atque*, both—and.
Attingo, ĕre, tĭgi, tactum. To attain, touch.
Auctor (augeo), *ōris*, m. Author, founder; approver, adviser.
Auctorĭtas (auctor), *ātis*, f. Authority, influence.
Audax (audeo), *ācis.* Bold, audacious, desperate.
Audeo, ēre, ausus sum. To dare, attempt.
Audio, īre, īvi or *ii, ītum.* To hear, listen to.
Aufĕro (ab, fero), *ferre, abstŭli, ablātum.* To take away or from, remove.
Aufugio (ab, fugio), *ĕre, fūgi.* To flee from.
Augeo, ēre, auxi, auctum. To enlarge, increase.
Augurium, i, n. Augury, omen.
Augŭror, āri, ātus sum. To augur, predict.
Aurarius (aurum), *a, um.* Pertaining to gold; *auraria metalla*, gold mines.
Aureus (aurum), *a, um.* Made of gold, golden.
Aurīga, ae, m. and f. Charioteer, driver.
Auris, is, f. Ear.

Aurum, i, n. Gold.
Auspicium, i, n. Omen, auspices.
Aut. Or; *aut—aut*, either—or, partly—partly.
Autem. But, likewise, moreover
Auxilium (augeo), *i*, n. Aid, *plur.* auxiliaries.
Avaritia, ae, f. Avarice.
Averto (ab, verto), *erti, ersum.* To avert, turn from, remove.
Avĭdus, a, um. Desirous, eager.
Avis, is, f. Bird.
Avuncŭlus (avus), *i*, m. Maternal uncle, a mother's brother.
Avus, i, m. Grandfather.

B.

Bacchans, antis. Revelling.
Bacchantes, ium, pl. Votaries of Bacchus, the god of wine.
Barba, ae, f. Beard.
Barbărus, a, um. Foreign, barbarous, rude.
Barbărus, i, m. Foreigner, barbarian.
Beātus, a, um. Happy.
Bellicōsus (bellum), *a, um.* Warlike.
Bello (bellum), *āre, āvi, ātum.* To carry on war.
Bellum, i, n. War.
Bene, adv. Well.
Beneficium (bene, facio), *i*, n. Benefit, favor.
Benevolentia (bene, volo), *ae*, f. Kindness, benevolence.
Benigne, adv. Kindly.
Bibo, ĕre, bibi, bibĭtum. To drink.
Biennium (bis, annus), *i*, n. Period of two years, two years.
Bifoŗṃis (bis, forma), *e.* Having two forms, biformed.
Bis, adv. Twice.
Bolētus, i, m. Mushroom.
Bonum (bonus), *i*, n. Blessing, prosperity, any good; pl. *bona*, goods, property.
Bonus, a, um. Good, noble, brave

Brachium, i, n. Arm, fore-arm.
Brevis, e. Short; *brevi* (sc. tempŏre), shortly, in a short time.

C.

C. An abbreviation of Caius; *Cn.*, of Cneus.
Cado, ĕre, cecĭdi, casum. To fall, fall in battle.
Caduceātor, ōris, m. Herald or ambassador sent to treat for peace.
Caedes (caedo), *is,* f. Slaughter, bloodshed.
Caedo, ĕre, cecĭdi, caesum. To cut, kill, slay.
Calamĭtas, ātis, f. Loss, calamity, disaster.
Callĭde, adv. Shrewdly, skilfully.
Campus, i, m. A plain, field of battle.
Canities, ēi, f. Gray hairs, old age.
Capax (capio), *ācis.* Capacious, large, comprehensive, able.
Capesso (capio), *ĕre, ĭvi, ītum.* To take, seize; *fugam capessĕre,* to resort to flight, betake one's self to flight.
Capillus, i, m. Hair.
Capio, ĕre, cepi, captum. To take, hold.
Captivĭtas (captīvus), *ātis,* f. Captivity, bondage.
Captīvus (capio), *a, um.* Captive, enslaved; *substantiv ly,* a prisoner, a captive.
Captus (part. from *capio*), *a, um.* Captured, taken.
Caput, ĭtis, n. Head, capital; *capĭtis damnāre,* to condemn to death.
Carcer, ĕris, m. Prison.
Carpentum, i, n. Chariot, carriage.
Caste, adv. Virtuously, chastely.
Castellum (dimin. castrum), *i,* n. Castle, fortress.

Castra (pl. of castrum, *a castle*) *ōrum.* Camp.
Casus (cado), *us,* m. Fall, misfortune.
Causa, ae, f. Cause, purpose, business.
Causidĭcus (causa, dico), *i,* m. Pleader, advocate; speaker.
Cedo, ĕre, cessi, cessum. To give place to, yield to, withdraw, depart.
Celĕber, bris, bre. Renowned, celebrated.
Celĕbro (ce!ĕber), *āre, āvi, ātum.* To celebrate, solemnize.
Celerĭtas, ātis, f. Celerity, swiftness.
Celerĭter, adv. Swiftly, quickly.
Censeo, ĕre, ui, censum. To think, judge, decree.
Census, us, m. Census.
Centum, indecl. Hundred.
Centurio (centum), *ōnis,* m. Centurion.
Certāmen, ĭnis, n. Contest, game, engagement.
Certātim, adv. Earnestly, eagerly.
Certus, a, um. Sure, certain; *certiōrem facĕre,* to inform.
Cesso (cedo), *āre, āvi, ātum.* To cease, pause.
Cetĕrus, a, um, nom. sing. m. not used. The other, the rest.
Christiānus, a, um. Christian, often *used substantively.*
Cicātrix, īcis, f. Scar.
Circa, prep. with acc. About, around, among.
Circĭter, prep. with acc. About, near.
Circum = circa.
Circumdo (circum, do), *dăre, dĕdi, dătum.* To place round, surround, invest.
Circumeo (circum, eo), *īre, īvi* or *ii, ĭtum.* To go around, surround, encompass.
Circumspicio (circŭm, specio), *ĕre, exi, ectum.* To look round, look for, seek.

Circumvenio (circum, venio), *ire, veni, ventum.* To circumvent, deceive; surround.
Cito, āre, āvi, ātum. To excite, urge, hasten; *citāto equo*, at full gallop *or* speed.
Citra, adv. and prep. with acc. On this side.
Civīlis (civis), *e.* Civil, domestic.
Civilītas (civīlis), *ātis*, f. Civility, politeness.
Civis, is, m. and f. Citizen.
Civĭtas (civis), *ātis*, f. City, state, citizenship.
Clades, is, f. Loss, slaughter, destruction.
Clam, adv. and prep. with acc. or abl. Secretly, without the knowledge of.
Clarus, a, um. Splendid, renowned, clear.
Classiarius (classis), *i*, m. A marine, *pl.* naval forces.
Classis, is, f. A fleet.
Claudo, ĕre, si, sum. To close, shut.
Clemens, entis. Mild, gentle, clement.
Clementia (clemens), *ae*, f. Mildness, clemency.
Clipeus, or *clypeus, i,* m. Shield.
Cloāca, ae, f. Sewer, drain.
Coelum, i, n. The heavens, sky, weather.
Coena, ae, f. Principal meal of the Romans, supper, dinner.
Coeo (con, eo), *ire, ivi* or *ii, ĭtum.* To collect, assemble.
Coepi, isti, it, def. (See A. & S. 183, 2.) To begin.
Coerceo, ēre, ui, ĭtum. To check, confine, restrain.
Coercĭto (coerceo), *ōris*, m. Enforcer.
Cogĭto, āre, āvi, ātum. To think, ponder.
Cognatio, ōnis, f. Relationship, resemblance, relatives.
Cognātus, a, um. Related, *subs.* a relative.

Cognĭtus (part. from *cognosco*), *a, um.* Ascertained, known.
Cognōmen (con, nomen), *ĭnis*, n. Surname.
Cognomĭno (cognōmen), *āre, āvi, ātum.* To surname, call, name.
Cognosco, ĕre, nōvi, nĭtum. To ascertain, recognize.
Cogo, ĕre, coēgi, coactum. To collect, force, compel.
Cohibeo (con, habeo), *ēre, ui, ĭtum.* To hold, check, confine.
Cohors, rtis, f. Cohort, tenth part of a legion.
Collēga, ae, m. Colleague.
Collĭgo (con, lego), *ĕre, ēgi, ectum.* To collect, bring together.
Collŏco, āre, āvi, ātum. To place, set, erect.
Collŏquor (con, loquor), *qui, cūtus sum.* To converse, talk with.
Colo, ĕre, ui, cultum. To cultivate; honor, worship.
Colōnus (colo), *i,* m. Colonist.
Comes, ĭtis, m. and f. Companion.
Comissatio, ōnis, f. Revelling.
Comĭtor (comes), *āri, ātus sum.* To accompany.
Commeātus, us, m. Supplies.
Commĭgro (con, migro), *āre, āvi, ātum.* To migrate.
Committo (con, mitto), *ĕre, ĭsi, issum.* To bring together, unite, intrust, commit; *pugnam committĕre*, to engage battle.
Commŏror (con, moror), *āri, ātus sum.* To tarry, delay.
Commoveo (con, moveo), *ēre, ōvi, ōtum.* To move, excite.
Commūnis, e. Common.
Communĭter (commūnis), adv. In common, conjointly.
Commutatio, ōnis, f. Change.
Compăro (con, paro), *āre, āvi, ātum.* To prepare, compare.
Compello, āre, āvi, ātum. To address, call.
Compello (con, pello), *ĕre, ŭli, ulsum.* To force, compel, impel.

Compensatio, ōnis, f. Compensation, exchange, barter.
Comperio, ĭre, pĕri, pertum. To find, find out.
Compes (con, pes), *ĕdis,* f. Fetter, chain.
Compesco, ĕre, cui. To confine, check.
Complector, ti, exus sum. To embrace, encompass.
Compleo, ēre, ēvi, ētum. To fill, complete.
Compōno (con, pono), *ĕre, ŏsui, ositum.* To settle, adjust, adapt.
Comprehendo, ĕre, di, sum. To seize, arrest, comprehend.
Concēdo (con, cedo), *ĕre, essi, essum.* To concede, grant; *pass. impers.,* it is conceded.
Concĭdo (con, cado), *ĕre, ĭdi.* To fall, perish.
Concilio (concilium), *āre, āvi, ātum.* To unite, conciliate.
Concilium, i, n. Council, meeting.
Concio, ōnis, f. Public assembly.
Concĭto (con, cito), *āre, āvi, ātum.* To raise; excite, excite rebellion.
Concĭtor, ōris, m. Exciter, mover.
Concurro (con, curro), *ĕre, curri (cucurri), cursum.* To meet, assemble; engage, fight; rush to.
Concursus (concurro), *us,* m. Concourse, meeting, engagement.
Concutio (con, quatio), *ĕre, ussi, ussum.* To agitate, trouble.
Conditio (condo), *ōnis,* f. Condition, terms.
Condo (con, do), *ĕre, dĭdi, dĭtum.* To found; conceal, hide; place, bury.
Condūco (con, duco), *ĕre, xi, ctum.* To conduct, collect; hire, contract for.
Confĕro (con, fero), *ferre, tŭli, collātum.* To collect, confer, engage battle; *se conferre,* to betake one's self.
Confestim, adv. Immediately.

Conficio (con, facio), *ĕre, fēci, fectum.* To finish, accomplish, wear out.
Confīdo, ĕre, īsus sum. To trust, confide in.
Configo, ĕre, xi, xum. To transfix, fasten together.
Confingo (con, fingo), *ĕre, nxi, ictum.* To form, feign, pretend.
Confīsus (confīdo), *a, um,* part. Trusting, relying upon.
Confligo, ĕre, xi, ctum. To engage, fight.
Confodio, ĕre, fōdi, fossum. To pierce, wound.
Confugio (con, fugio), *ĕre, fūgi.* To flee for refuge.
Congĕro (con, gero), *ĕre, gessi, gestum.* To bring together, crowd, expend, bestow upon.
Congredior (con, gradior), *di, gressus sum,* dep. To encounter, fight.
Congrĕgo, āre, āvi, ātum. To collect, congregate.
Congressio (congredior), *ōnis,* f. Engagement, battle.
Conjicio (con, jacio), *ĕre, jēci, jectum.* To discharge, hurl, throw, drive.
Conjungo (con, jungo), *ĕre, nxi, nctum.* To join, conjoin.
Conjuratio (conjūro), *ōnis,* f. Conspiracy.
Conjurātus (Id.), *a, um.* Having conspired.
Conjūro (con, juro), *āre, āvi, ātum.* To conspire.
Conjux (conjungo), *ŭgis,* m. and f. Husband, wife.
Conor, āri, ātus sum, dep. To endeavor, attempt.
Conscendo (con, scando), *ĕre, di, sum.* To ascend, embark.
Conscius, a, um. Privy to; *subs.* accomplice, confidant.
Consĕcro (con, sacro), *āre āvi, ātum.* To consecrate.
Consector, āri, ātus sum, dep. To follow, pursue.

Consenesco, ĕre, senui. To grow old.
Consĕquor (con, sequor), *qui, cūtus sum.* To succeed, follow, pursue; secure.
Consĕro, ĕre, ui, tum. To join together; *manum* or *pugnam conserĕre,* to join battle.
Conservo (con, servo), *āre, āvi, ātum.* To preserve, watch over, rescue.
Consīdo, ĕre, sēdi, sessum. To encamp, settle.
Consilium, i, n. Counsel, advice, wisdom, design.
Consobrīnus, a, um. Cousin, *often subs.*
Conspectus (conspicio), *us, m.* Sight, presence.
Conspicio, ĕre, exi, ectum. To see, observe.
Conspiratio, ōnis, f. Union, conspiracy.
Constantia, ae, f. Constancy, firmness.
Constat, impers. It is known, is an admitted fact.
Constituo (con, statuo), *ĕre, ui, ūtum.* To constitute; build, erect; station, place; appoint.
Consto (con, sto), *āre, stĭti, stātum.* To stand together, halt.
Consuesco, ĕre, ēvi, ētum. To be accustomed.
Consuetūdo (consuesco), *ĭnis, f.* Custom, usage, habit.
Consul (consŭlo), *ŭlis, m.* Consul, Roman chief magistrate.
Consulāris, e. Consular; *subs.* one who has been consul, one of consular rank.
Consulātus (consul), *us, m.* Consulship.
Consŭlo, ĕre, ui, ultum. To consult, consider; *with dat.* to consult for one's good.
Consummo, āre, āvi, ātum. To finish, accomplish.
Consūmo (con, sumo), *ĕre, umpsi, umptum.* To consume, wear out, waste.

Contĕgo (con, tego), *ĕre, exi, ectum.* To cover.
Contemno, ĕre, mpsi, mptum. To contemn, despise, disregard.
Contemptus (contemno), *us, m.* Contempt, scorn, disregard.
Contendo, ĕre, di, tum. To contend, strive, attempt, labor; betake one's self, go.
Contentio (contendo), *ōnis, f.* Effort, contest, struggle.
Contentus, a, um. Content, contented.
Contĭnens (contineo), *tis.* Adjoining, continuous: *subs. f.* continent.
Continentia (contineo), *ae, f.* Forbearance, self-control.
Contineo (con, teneo), *ĕre, ui, tentum.* To hold, keep, check.
Contra, adv. and prep. with acc. Against, opposite to, contrary to; on the contrary.
Contradīco (contra, dico), *ĕre, dixi, dictum.* To contradict, object to.
Contrăho (con, traho), *ĕre, xi, ctum.* To collect, incur, contract.
Contrucīdo (con, trucido), *āre, āvi, ātum.* To slay, kill, mangle.
Contŭmax, ācis. Insolent, disobedient.
Convalesco, ĕre, lui. To gain strength, recover.
Conveniens (convenio), *tis.* Becoming, fit, proper.
Convenio (con, venio), *īre, vēni, ventum.* To convene, meet, agree, harmonize, befit.
Converto (con, verto), *ĕre, ti, sum.* To turn, change, alter, convert.
Convicium (con, vox), *i, n.* Reproof.
Convinco (con, vinco), *ĕre, īci, ictum.* To conquer, convict.
Convivium, i, n. Feast, banquet.
Convīvor, āri, ātus sum. To feast.
Copia, ae, f. Abundance; *pl.* forces, stores, supplies.
Cornu, us, n. Horn, wing of army.
Corōna, ae, f. Garland, crown.

Corpus, ŏris, n. Body, community.
Corrĭgo (con, rego), *ĕre, exi, ectum*. To reform, correct.
Corripio (con, rapio), *ĕre, ui, eptum*. To seize, lay hold of.
Corrumpo (con, rumpo), *ĕre, ûpi, uptum*. To corrupt, bribe, seduce.
Corvus, i, m. Raven.
Crastĭnus, a, um. Of to-morrow.
Creber, bra, brum. Frequent, numerous.
Credo, ĕre, ĭdi, ĭtum. To trust, believe.
Creo, āre, āvi, ātum. To appoint, elect, make.
Cresco, ĕre, ĕvi, ĕtum. To grow, increase.
Crimen, ĭnis, n. Crime, accusation.
Crimĭnor (crimen), *āri, ātus sum*. To accuse.
Crinis, is, m. Hair.
Crucio (crux), *āre, āvi, ātum*. To pain, afflict, torture.
Crudēlis, e. Cruel.
Crudelĭtas (crudēlis), *ātis*, f. Cruelty.
Crudelĭter (Id.), adv. Cruelly.
Crux, crucis, f. A cross.
Culpa, ae, f. Fault, blame.
Cultus, us, m. Culture, necessaries *as food, clothing, &c.*
Cum, prep. with abl. With
Cum, conj. = quum.
Cunctatio (cunctor), *ōnis*, f. Delay.
Cunctor, āri, ātus sum. To delay, hesitate.
Cunctus, a, um. All, all together, entire.
Cupĭde (cupĭdus), adv. Eagerly.
Cupidĭtas (Id.), *ātis*, f. Desire, wish.
Cupĭdus (cupio), *a, um*. Desirous, fond of.
Cupio, ĕre, ĭvi or *ii, ĭtum*. To desire.
Cura, ae, f. Care, management.
Curia, ae, f. Senate-house.

Curro, ĕre, cucurri, cursum. To run.
Currus (curro), *us*, m. Chariot.
Cursus (curro), *us*, m. Course.
Custodia, ae, f. Care, charge of.

D.

Damno (damnum), *āre, āvi, ātum*. To condemn; *capĭtis damnāre*, to condemn to death.
Damnum, i, n. Loss, damage.
De, prep. with abl. From, of, concerning.
Debeo, ēre, ui, ĭtum. To owe, ought.
Debilĭto, āre, āvi, ātum. To weaken, disable.
Decēdo (de, cedo), *ĕre, cessi, cessum*. To depart, withdraw, die.
Decem, indecl. Ten.
Decemplex, ĭcis. Tenfold.
Decemvir (decem, vir), *viri*, m. A decemvir.
Decerno, ĕre, crēvi, crētum. To decide; contend, fight; decree, intrust by decree.
Decĭmus (decem), *a, um*. Tenth.
Decipio (de, capio), *ĕre, cēpi, ceptum*. To deceive.
Decrētum (decerno), *i*, n. Decree.
Decus, ŏris, n. Ornament, honor.
Dedĕcus (de, decus), *ŏris*, n. Disgrace.
Dedicatio, ōnis, f. Dedication.
Deditio (dedo), *ōnis*, f. Surrender.
Dedo (de, do), *ĕre, dĭdi, dĭtum*. To surrender; devote one's self to, give one's self up to.
Deduco (de, duco), *ĕre, duxi, ductum*. To bring down, conduct; remove.
Defectio (deficio), *ōnis*, f. Failure, eclipse, defection.
Defendo, ĕre, di, sum. To defend, ward off.
Defĕro (de, fero), *ferre, tŭli, lātum*. To offer, exhibit, bestow, present; carry *or* bear away.

Deficio (de, facio), *ĕre, fēci, fectum.* To fail, spend itself; be eclipsed; desert, revolt.
Deformis (de, forma), *e.* Deformed, ugly.
Defungor (de, fungor), *gi, functus sum* To discharge, execute; die.
Dein or *deinde.* Then, afterwards.
Dejicio (de, jacio), *ĕre, jĕci, jectum.* To throw down, overthrow, slay.
Delectus (deligo), *a, um.* Chosen.
Deleo, ĕre, ēvi, ētum. To destroy, efface, put an end to.
Delibĕro, āre, āvi, ātum. To deliberate.
Deliciae, ārum, f. pl. Delights, pleasures.
Deligo (de, lego), *ĕre, ēgi, ectum.* To choose, select; love.
Delirium, i, n. Madness, dotage, instances of it.
Dementer, adv. Madly.
Dementia, ae, f. Madness, folly.
Demergo (de, mergo), *ĕre, si, sum.* To plunge in, bury in, sink.
Demigro (de, migro), *āre, āvi, ātum.* To remove, emigrate, migrate.
Demorior (de, morior), *mŏri, mortuus sum.* To die.
Demum, adv. At length, finally.
Deni, ae, a. Ten by ten, ten at a time.
Denĭque. Finally
Denūdo, āre, āvi, ātum. To make naked, strip.
Denuntiatio (denuntio), *ōnis,* f. Denunciation, warning.
Denuntio (de, nuntio), *āre, āvi, ātum.* To declare, denounce.
Denuo, adv. Again, afresh.
Depello (de, pello), *ĕre, ŭli, ulsum.* To drive away, expel.
Depōno (de, pono), *ĕre, posui, positum.* To lay down or aside, deposit, depose.
Depopŭlor, āri, ātus sum. To pillage, depopulate.
Deporto, āre, āvi, ātum. To carry off or away.

Depraedor, āri, ātus sum. To ravage, plunder.
Deprehendo, ĕre, di, sum. To seize catch, detect, surprise.
Depugno, āre, āvi, ātum. To fight.
Deripio (de, rapio), *ĕre, ipui, eptum.* To seize, tear away, snatch.
Descendo, ĕre, di, sum. To descend.
Descrībo (de, scribo), *ĕre, psi, ptum.* To describe; impose; cess; designate.
Desĕro, ĕre, ui, tum. To abandon, desert.
Desilio, ĕre, silui, sultum. To alight, dismount.
Desĭno, ĕre, sīvi or *sii, sĭtum.* To cease, desist.
Desperatio, ōnis, f. Despair, desperation.
Despĕro, āre, āvi, ātum. To despair.
Despicio, ĕre, exi, ctum. To despise, disregard.
Destĭno, āri, āvi, ātum. To destine, appoint, design.
Desum (de, sum), *esse, fui, futūrus.* To fail, be wanting.
Deterreo (de, terreo), *ĕre, ui, ĭtum.* To deter.
Detineo (de, teneo), *ēre, ui, entum.* To detain, hinder.
Detrăho (de, traho), *ĕre, axi, actum.* To draw or take away, detract.
Deus, i, m. God, deity. (See A. & S. 53.)
Devasto, āre. To devastate, pillage.
Devenio (de, venio), *ĭre, vēni, ventum.* To come down, arrive, reach.
Devinco (de, vinco), *ĕre, ĭci, ictum.* To conquer.
Dexter, tra, trum. Right, on the right hand.
Dextra, ae, f. The right hand.
Diadēma, ătis, n. Diadem.
Dico, ĕre, dixi, dictum. To say.
Dictātor (dico), *ōris,* m. Dictator, *an officer appointed by the Romans in times of great danger*

13*

Dies, ēi, m. and f. Day.
Difficĭle, adv. With difficulty.
Digĭtus, i, m. Finger.
Dignĭtas (dignus), *ātis,* f. Dignity, rank, office.
Dignor (dignus), *āri, ātus sum.* To deem worthy, deign.
Dignus, a, um. Worthy.
Dilatio, ōnis, f. Delay, delaying.
Dilĭgens (dilĭgo), *entis.* Fond of, mindful, observant, diligent.
Diligentia (dilĭgens), *ae,* f. Diligence.
Dilĭgo, ĕre, exi, ectum. To choose.
Dimĭco, āre, āvi, ātum. To encounter, fight.
Dimitto, ĕre, ĭsi, issum. To dismiss.
Diripio, ĕre, ui, eptum. To lay waste, pillage.
Diruo, ĕre, ui, ūtum. To destroy, demolish.
Discēdo, ĕre, essi, essum. To depart, retire from.
Disceptatio, ōnis, f. Debate, quarrel.
Disciplīna, ae, f. Discipline, instruction.
Disco, ĕre, didĭci. To learn.
Discordia, ae, f. Discord, strife.
Discrīmen, ĭnis, n. Danger, crisis.
Discurro, ĕre, curri, cursum. To run different ways, run about, separate.
Dispergo, ĕre, si, sum. To scatter, disperse.
Displiceo, ēre, ui, ĭtum. To displease.
Dissidium, i, n. Dissension.
Dissimŭlo, āre, āvi, ātum. To dissemble, conceal, omit.
Dissĭpo, āre, āvi, ātum. To dissipate, scatter.
Dissolvo, ĕre, olvi, olūtum. To destroy, abolish, dissolve.
Distribuo, ĕre, ui, ūtum. To distribute.
Districtus (distringo), *a, um.* Busy, occupied with.

Distringo, ĕre, nxi, ctum. To occupy, engage attention.
Ditio, ōnis, f. Rule, sway.
Diu, adv. Long, for a long time.
Diuturnĭtas (diuturnus), *ātis,* f. Long time.
Diuturnus (diu), *a, um.* Long, continual, lasting.
Diversus, a, um. Diverse, unlike, opposite.
Dives, ĭtis. Rich.
Divĭdo, ĕre, ĭsi, ĭsum. To divide, allot.
Divīnus, a, um. Divine.
Divitiae (dives), *ārum,* f. Riches, wealth.
Divus, a, um. Divine; *subs.* god, goddess.
Do, dăre, dedi, datum. To give, impute.
Doceo, ēre, ui, tum. To teach.
Doctus (doceo), *a, um.* Learned, skilled.
Documentum, i, n. Lesson, proof, specimen, mark.
Doleo, ēre, ui, ĭtum. To grieve.
Dolor (doleo), *ōris,* m. Pain, grief.
Dolus, i, m. Artifice, deceit.
Domestĭcus (domus), *a, um.* Domestic, private, personal.
Dominatio, ōnis, f. Rule, tyranny.
Domĭnus, i, m. Master, owner.
Domo, āre, ui, ĭtum. To subdue.
Domus, us or *i,* f. House; *domi,* at home.
Donec, conj. Until.
Dono (donum), *āre, āvi, ātum.* To give, present with.
Donum (do), *i,* n. Present, gift.
Dos, dotis, f. Gift, dowry.
Dubitatio (dubĭto), *ōnis,* f. Doubt, hesitation.
Dubĭto, āre, āvi, ātum. To doubt, hesitate.
Dubius, a, um. Doubtful; *neut. often subs.* doubt.
Ducenti, ae, a. Two hundred.
Duco, ĕre, duxi, ductum. To lead, conduct, *with uxōrem,* to marry.

Ductor (duco), *ōris,* m. Leader, general.
Ductus (duco), *us,* m. Guidance, command.
Dum, conj. While, until.
Duo, ae, o. Two, both.
Duodĕcim (duo, decem), indecl. Twelve.
Duodecĭmus (duodecim), *a, um.* Twelfth.
Duodeviginti, indecl. Eighteen.
Duplex, ĭcis. Double.
Durus, a, um. Hard, harsh, rude.
Dux (duco), *ŭcis,* m. and f. Leader, guide, general.

E.

E or *ex,* prep. with abl. From, out of.
Ebriĕtas, ātis, f. Drunkenness.
Edo, ĕre, edĭdi, edĭtum. To set forth, publish; do, perform; make.
Edūco, āre, āvi, ātum. To bring up, educate.
Edūco (e, duco), *ĕre, duxi, ductum.* To lead out or forth.
Effĕro, āre, āvi, ātum. To enrage, madden, render unmanageable.
Effĕro (ex, fero), *ferre, extŭli, elātum.* To bring forth, carry forth or out; elate.
Effĭcax (efficio), *ācis.* Effectual, efficacious.
Efficio (ex, facio), *ĕre, fēci, fectum.* To effect, occasion.
Effugio (ex, fugio), *ĕre, ūgi.* To flee, escape from.
Effundo (ex, fundo), *ĕre, ūdi, ūsum.* To pour out, pour; indulge in; squander, waste.
Effūsus (effundo), *a, um.* Extravagant, prodigal.
Ego, mei, &c. I.
Egregie (egregius), adv. Excellently, remarkably.
Egregius, a, um. Excellent.

Ejicio (e, jacio), *ĕre, jēci, jectum.* To throw or drive out, expel reject.
Elephantus, i, m. and f. Elephant.
Elīgo (e, lego), *ĕre, ēgi, ectum.* To choose, elect.
Emergo (e, mergo), *ĕre, si, sum.* To emerge, come to light, rise in importance.
Emineo, ēre, ui. To stand out, be prominent or conspicuous.
Emitto (e, mitto), *ĕre, ĭsi, issum.* To send forth or away; let go.
Emo, ĕre, emi, emptum. To buy.
Enim, conj. For.
Eniteo, ēre, ui. To shine forth; be distinguished.
Enixe, adv. Earnestly.
Eo, adv. Thither, therefore; *eo usque,* so far, to such an extent.
Eōdem, adv. To the same place.
Epigramma, ătis, n. Inscription.
Epŭlae, ārum, f. pl. Food, banquet, feast.
Epŭlor (epŭlae), *āri, ātus sum.* To feast.
Eques (equus), *ĭtis,* m. Horseman.
Equester (eques), *tris, tre.* Equestrian.
Equitātus, us, m. Cavalry.
Equus, i, m. Horse.
Ergo, adv. Therefore; *as subs.* abl. on account of, for, *with gen.*
Erĭgo (e, rego), *ĕre, exi, ectum.* To raise up, animate.
Eripio (e, rapio), *ĕre, ipui, eptum.* To snatch or take away.
Erudio, īre, īvi or *ii, ītum.* To instruct, refine.
Erudītus (erudio), *a, um.* Learned, instructed in.
Erumpo (e, rumpo), *ĕre, ūpi, uptum.* To break forth, rush forth.
Eruo, ĕre, ui, ūtum. To root out, destroy.
Et. And; *et—et,* both—and.
Etiam. Also, even.
Etsi (et, si). Although, though.
Evado, ĕre, āsi, āsum. To go out, escape; evade.

Evĕho (e, veho), *ĕre, exi, ectum.* To carry or lead forth.
Evenio (e, venio), *īre, vēni, ventum.* To come forth, happen; *evēnit, ut*, it chanced, that.
Everto (e, verto), *ĕre, ti, sum.* To pull down, overthrow.
Evŏco (e, voco), *āre, āvi, ātum.* To call forth, summon.
Evŏlo (e, volo), *āre, āvi, ātum.* To fly or flee away, hasten away.
Ex, prep. with abl. From. (See *e or ex*).
Exadversum or *exadversus*, adv. and prep. with acc. Opposite, against.
Exanĭmo, *āre, āvi, ātum.* To deprive of life or spirit; kill.
Exardesco, *ĕre, arsi.* To kindle, be inflamed; break out as war.
Excēdo (ex, cedo), *ĕre, cessi, cessum.* To retire, withdraw.
Excelse, adv. On high, aloft, highly.
Excidium, *ii*, n. Destruction, ruin.
Excipio (ex, capio), *ĕre, cēpi, ceptum.* To take out, except.
Excĭto, *āre, āvi, ātum.* To excite, arouse, awake.
Exclūdo (ex, claudo), *ĕre, si, sum.* To exclude, shut out, cut off.
Excogĭto (ex, cogĭto), *āre, āvi, ātum.* To devise, think out.
Excutio (ex, quatio), *ĕre, ussi, ussum.* To shake or throw off.
Exemplum, *i*, n. Example.
Exeo (ex, eo), *īre, īvi* or *ii, ītum.* To go from or forth.
Exerceo, *ĕre, cui, cĭtum.* To exercise, practise.
Exercĭtus (exerceo), *us*, m. Army.
Exhaurio (ex, haurio), *īre, hausi, haustum.* To exhaust, impoverish.
Exĭgo (ex, ago), *ĕre, ēgi, actum.* To drive out, expel; finish, end; demand.
Exiguus, *a, um.* Small.
Exilium, *i*, n. Banishment, exile.

Eximius, *a, um.* Excellent, choice remarkable.
Exĭmo (ex, emo), *ĕre, ēmi, emptum* To take away or from; exempt rescue.
Existĭmo, *āre, āvi, ātum.* To judge, think.
Exitium (exeo), *i*, n. End, death, destruction.
Exorior (ex, orior), *īri, ortus sum*, dep. partly of 3d conj. To arise; be derived from.
Exorno, *āre, āvi, ātum.* To adorn, furnish, equip.
Exōsus, *a, um.* Hating, hated, odious.
Expedio, *īre, īvi* or *ii, ītum* To release, extricate; *also* to be expedient.
Expeditio (expedio), *ōnis*, f. Expedition.
Expello (ex, pello), *ĕre, pŭli, pulsum.* To expel, drive away.
Expĕto (ex, peto), *ĕre, īvi* or *ii, ītum.* To seek, request.
Expleo, *ēre, ēvi, ētum.* To fill, make full; fulfil.
Explĭco, *āre, āvi, ātum.* To unfold; adjust; settle.
Explorātor, *ōris*, m. Explorer, spy.
Exporto, *āre, āvi, ātum.* To carry away.
Expugno (ex, pugno), *āre, āvi, ātum.* To take, conquer, storm.
Exscindo, *ĕre, ĭdi, issum.* To destroy.
Exsculpo, *ĕre, psi, ptum.* To erase.
Exsecrābĭlis c. Detestable.
Exsequiae, *ārum*, f. pl. Funeral.
Exsĕquor (ex, sequor), *qui, cūtus sum.* To prosecute, accomplish, finish; perform.
Exsilium, *i*, n. Banishment, exile.
Exspectatio (exspecto), *ōnis*, f. Expectation, high hope.
Expecto (ex, specto), *āre, āvi, ātum.* To await, expect.
Exstinguo, *ĕre, nxi, nctum.* To extinguish, destroy.

Exsto, āre, stĭti. To stand out, be conspicuous.
Exsul, ŭlis, m. and f. An exile.
Extemplo, adv. Immediately.
Extorqueo, ēre, orsi, ortum. To extort, obtain by force.
Extra, adv. and prep. with acc. Without, on the outside; beyond.
Extrăho (ex, traho), *ĕre, axi, actum.* To extract; rescue.

F.

Fabŭla, ae, f. Report, narrative.
Fabulōsus (fabŭla), *a, um.* Fabulous.
Facĭle (facĭlis), adv. Easily.
Facĭlis (facio), *e.* Easy.
Facilĭtas (facĭlis), *ātis,* f. Facility, affability.
Facĭnus, ŏris, n. Wickedness, crime; deed, act.
Facio, ĕre, feci, factum. To do, make.
Factio, ōnis, f. Faction, party.
Factum (facio), *i,* n. Deed, exploit.
Fallo, ĕre, fefelli, falsum. To deceive, foil.
Fama, ae, f. Fame, report.
Fames, is, f. Hunger, famine.
Familia, ae, f. Retinue of slaves, a family.
Familiarĭtas, ātis, f. Friendship, intimacy.
Famŭla, ae, f. Female slave.
Fatālis (fatum), *e.* Fated, fatal.
Fatīgo, āre, āvi, ātum. To oppress, trouble, weary, importune.
Fatum, i, n. Fate, destiny, oracle.
Faveo, ēre, favi, fautum. To favor.
Favor (faveo), *ōris,* m. Favor, kindness.
Felicĭtas, ātis, f. Felicity, success.
Felicĭter, adv. Happily, prosperously.
Femĭna, ae, f. Woman, female.
Femur, ŏris, n. Thigh.
Fĕra, as, f. Wild beast.

Fere, adv. Almost.
Ferme, adv. Almost.
Fero, ferre, tuli, latum. To bear, endure; raise, say, tell; propose *as law.*
Ferrum, i, n. Iron, sword.
Ferus, a, um. Wild, rude, cruel; *ferus* and *fera* (subs.), wild animal or beast.
Fessus, a, um. Wearied, exhausted.
Festīno, āre, āvi, ātum. To hasten.
Festus, a, um. Festal; *festum* (subs.), a festival, feast.
Fidēlis (fides), *e.* Faithful, trusty.
Fides, ĕi, f. Fidelity, allegiance; protection, confidence, assurance; *in fidem,* under protection.
Fiducia, ae, f. Trust, confidence.
Filia, ae, f., dat. and abl. pl. *filiabus.* Daughter.
Filius, i, m. Son.
Fingo, ĕre, finxi, fictum. To form, feign.
Finio, (finis), *īre, īvi, ītum.* To finish, put an end to.
Finis, is, m. and f. Limit, end; *pl.* territory.
Finitĭmus, a, um. Neighboring; *subs.* a neighbor.
Fio, fĭĕri, factus sum, pass. of *facio.* To be made; become, happen.
Firme, adv. Firmly, resolutely.
Flagitiōsus, a, um. Infamous, abandoned.
Flagro, āre, āvi, ātum. To burn, be carried on with zeal.
Flamma, ae, f. Flame.
Flecto, ĕre, xi, xum. To bend, turn.
Fletus, us, m. Weeping, tears.
Florens (floreo), *tis.* Blooming, excellent.
Floreo, ēre, ui. To bloom, flourish, prosper; excel.
Flumen, ĭnis, n. Stream, river.
Fluvius, i, m. River.
Foedus, ĕris, n. League, alliance.
Forem, es, &c. = *essem, es,* &c., might be; *fore* = *futūrum esse.*
Forma, ae, f. Form, shape.

Formo (forma), *āre, āvi, ātum.* To form, fashion.
Fors, tis, f. Chance; abl. *forte* as adv., by chance, perhaps.
Fortis, e. Brave, valiant.
Fortĭter (fortis). Bravely.
Fortitūdo (fortis), *ĭnis,* f. Fortitude, bravery.
Fortūna, ae, f. Fortune.
Forum, i, n. Market-place, forum.
Frango ĕre, fregi, fractum. To break.
Frater, tris, m. Brother.
Fraudo (fraus), *āre, āvi, ātum.* To defraud, cheat.
Fraus, dis, f. Fraud, deceit.
Frequenter, adv. Frequently, in great numbers.
Fretum, i, n. A strait, sound.
Fretus, a, um. Trusting, relying upon.
Frigus, ŏris, n. Coldness, cold.
Frugalĭtas, ātis, f. Frugality, integrity.
Frumentarius (frumentum), *a, um.* Producing corn, fruitful.
Frumentum, i, n. Corn, grain.
Fruor, i, ŭtus and *ctus sum.* To enjoy.
Frustra, adv. In vain.
Fuga, ae, f. Flight.
Fugio, ĕre, fugi, fugĭtum. To fly, flee.
Fugo, āre, āvi, ātum. To rout, put to flight.
Fulmen, ĭnis, n. Lightning, thunder-bolt.
Funāle, is, n. Torch.
Fundamentum, i, n. Foundation.
Fundĭtus, adv. Utterly, entirely.
Fundo, ĕre, fudi, fusum. To pour out, shed, rout; also to make, cast.
Fundus, i, m. Land, estate.
Funĕbris (funus), *e.* Funeral, funereal.
Funestus (funus), *a, um.* Deadly, destructive.
Fungor, gi, ctus sum, dep. To discharge, perform.
Funus, ĕris, n. Dead body, corpse.
Furcŭla, ae, f. Narrow defile.
Furor, ōris, m. Fury, madness.
Furtum, i, n. Theft.

G.

Gaudeo, ēre, gavīsus sum. To rejoice, take pleasure in.
Gelu, us, n. Cold, hail.
Gemĭnus, a, um. Twin, double.
Gener, ĕri, m. Son-in-law.
Gens, tis, f. Clan, race, tribe, nation.
Genus, ĕris, n. Race, people, kind.
Gero, ĕre, gessi, gestum. To bear, wear; carry on, perform; wage *as war.*
Gestio, īre, īvi or *ii, ītum.* To desire, long for.
Gesto (gero), *āre, āvi, ātum.* To bear, carry.
Gigno, ĕre, genui, genĭtum. To bring forth, beget, produce.
Gladiātor, ōris, m. Gladiator, a fighter at the public games.
Gladiatorius (gladiātor), *a, um.* Gladiatorial.
Gladius, i, m. Sword.
Glisco, ĕre. To grow, spread; rise.
Gloria, ae, f. Glory.
Gradus, us, m. Step, stair, position.
Grandis, e. Large, great.
Grando, ĭnis, f. Hail.
Gratia, ae, f. Favor, gratitude; *pl.* thanks.
Gratiis or *gratis,* adv. For nothing, without pay.
Gratulatio, ōnis, f. Gratulation, congratulation.
Gratus, a, um. Pleasing, acceptable; grateful.
Gravis, e. Heavy, severe.
Gravĭter (gravis), adv. Heavily, severely.
Gravo (gravis), *āre, āvi, ātum.* To burden, load.

H.

Habeo, ēre, ui, ĭtum. To have; regard; keep.
Habĭtus (habeo), *us,* m. Habit, dress, attire.
Hasta, ae, f. Spear.
Hastĭle, is, n. Spear.
Hastīlis (hasta), *e.* Belonging to a spear.
Haud, adv. Not.
Haurio, ĭre, si, stum. To drink, draw out, exhaust.
Hedĕra, ae, f. Ivy.
Heres, ēdis, m. and f. Heir, heiress.
Heros, ōis, m. Hero.
Hesternus, a, um. Of yesterday.
Hic, haec, hoc. This, he, she, it.
Hic, adv. Here, in this place.
Hiems, ĕmis, f. Storm, winter.
Hinc (hic), adv. Hence, on this side; *hinc—hinc,* on the one side—on the other side.
Hodie, adv. To-day.
Homo, ĭnis, m. and f. Human being, man.
Honestas, ātis, f. Honor, honesty.
Honor, ōris, m. Honor, rank, dignity.
Honorifĭce, adv. Honorably.
Honōro (honor), *āre, āvi, ātum.* To honor, reverence.
Hortor, āri, ātus sum. To exhort, incite.
Hortus, i, m. Garden.
Hostia, ae, f. Victim.
Hostīlis (hostis), *e.* Hostile.
Hostis, is, c. Enemy.
Humānus, a, um. Human.
Humo, āre, āvi, ātum. To bury.

I.

Ibi, adv. There, in that place.
Ico, ĕre, ici, ictum. To strike; make, ratify.
Idem, eădem, idem. The same; *sometimes best rendered by* also.
Idoneus, a, um. Suitable, fit.
Igĭtur, conj. Therefore, accordingly.
Ignāvus, a, um. Slothful, indolent.
Ignis, is, m. Fire.
Ignobilĭter, adv. Meanly, disgracefully.
Ignōro, āre, āvi, ātum. To be ignorant of, not know.
Ille, a, ud. That; he, she, it.
Illĭgo, āre, āvi, ātum. To bind.
Illustris, e. Illustrious, famous.
Illustro (illustris) *āre, āvi, ātum.* To enlighten, illumine, illustrate.
Illuvies, ēi, f. Flood.
Imber, bris, m. Rain, shower.
Imbuo, ĕre, ui, ūtum. To imbue, impress.
Imitatio, ōnis, f. Imitation.
Immānis, e. Inhuman, cruel.
Immatūrus, a, um. Young, immature.
Immĕmor, ŏris. Unmindful, forgetful.
Immitto (in, mitto), *ĕre, ĭsi, issum.* To send *or* let in; let go; bring forward.
Immortālis, e. Immortal.
Immunĭtas, ātis, f. Immunity, exemption.
Impatiens, tis. Impatient.
Impatienter (impatiens), adv. Impatiently.
Impedimentum (impedio), *i,* n. Impediment, obstacle; *pl.* baggage.
Impedio, īre, īvi or *ii, ītum.* To impede, embarrass; hinder, prevent.
Impello (in, pello), *ĕre, pŭli, pulsum.* To impel, induce.
Impendeo (in, pendeo), *ēre.* To impend, threaten, overhang.
Impensa, ae, f. Expense, cost.
Imperātor (impĕro), *ōris,* m. Commander, emperor.
Imperium (impĕro), *i,* n. Command, power, rule, sway, reign.
Impĕro, āre, āvi, ātum. To command, rule, govern.

Impĕtus, us, m. Attack, fury.
Impōno (in, pono), *ĕre, osui, osĭtum.* To place *or* put in *or* to; enjoin; impose.
Improbo, āre, āvi, ātum. To reject.
Imprudenter, adv. Imprudently.
Impūbes, ĕris. Youthful, young.
Impugno (in, pugno), *āre, āvi, ātum.* To assail, attack.
Impulsus (impello), *us,* m. Instigation.
In, prep. with acc. *or* abl. Into, to, for, against, *with acc.;* in, on, *with abl.*
Incendium (incendo), *i,* n. Fire, conflagration.
Incendo, ĕre, di, sum. To set on fire, inflame, excite.
Incertus (in, certus), *a, um.* Uncertain.
Incesso, ĕre, ĭvi or *i.* To attack.
Inchoo, āre, āvi, ātum. To begin, commence.
Incĭdo (in; cado), *ĕre, cĭdi, cāsum.* To fall into *or* upon, fall in with, happen.
Incīdo (in, caedo), *ĕre, cĭdi, cīsum.* To cut, destroy.
Incipio (in, capio), *ĕre, ēpi, eptum.* To begin, undertake.
Incitamentum (incĭto), *i,* n. Incentive, inducement.
Incitātus (incĭto), *a, um.* Running; *equo incitāto,* at full speed.
Incĭto, āre, āvi, ātum. To incite, hasten, spur on; inspire.
Inclīno, āre, āvi, ātum. To incline, bend; *pass.* to sink, go to ruin.
Incŏla (incŏlo), *ae,* c. Inhabitant.
Incŏlo (in, colo), *ĕre, colui, cultum.* To dwell, abide in, inhabit.
Incolŭmis, e. Safe, uninjured.
Incommŏdum, i, n. Misfortune, defeat.
Incredibĭlis, e. Incredible.
Incrementum, i, n. Growth, increase.
Inde, adv. Thence, from that place.
Indecōre, adv. Disgracefully.

Index (indĭco), *ĭcis,* m. and f. Informer, witness.
Indĭco (in, dico), *ĕre, dixi, dictum* To declare, publish, appoint.
Indigeo, ĕre, ui. To need; *part. indĭgens* subs. an indigent person.
Indignor (indignus), *āri ātus sum.* To disdain, scorn; be indignant.
Indignus (in, dignus), *a, um.* Unworthy, harsh, indecent.
Indōles, is, f. Nature, native quality, excellence.
Indomĭtus (in, domĭtus), *a, um.* Unsubdued, invincible.
Indubitātus, a, um. Undoubted, certain.
Induciae, or *indutiae, ārum,* f. pl. Truce.
Indūco (in, duco), *ĕre, duxi, ductum.* To induce, lead into, overlay, adorn with, gild.
Indurātus (indūro), *a, um.* Obdurate.
Indūro, āre, āvi, ātum. To harden.
Industria, ae, f. Industry.
Ineo (in, eo), *īre, ĭvi* or *ii, ĭtum.* To enter, go into; *gratiam inīre,* to obtain the favor of, conciliate.
Inermis (in, arma), *e.* Unarmed.
Infāmis, e. Infamous, notorious.
Infēlix (in, felix), *ĭcis.* Unhappy, unfortunate.
Infensus, a, um. Exasperated, enraged.
Inferior, us. Inferior.
Infĕro (in, fero), *ferre, tŭli, illātum.* To carry against, wage against.
Infesto (infestus), *āre, āvi, ātum.* To infest, trouble.
Infestus, a, um. Infested, troublesome, hostile.
Infinītus, a, um. Great, infinite.
Inflammo, āre, āvi, ātum. To inflame, arouse.
Informis (in, forma), *e.* Shapeless, deformed.
Infringo (in, frango), *ĕre, ēgi, actum.* To infringe, break.
Infŭla, ae, f. Fillet, head-dress, badge of office.

Ingĕmo, ĕre, ui. To groan, lament.
Ingenium, i, n. Character, genius.
Ingens, tis. Great, mighty.
Ingenuus, a, um. Freeborn, ingenuous.
Ingratia (ingrātus), *ae,* f. Ingratitude.
Ingratiis or *ingrātis,* adv. Against one's will.
Ingrātus (in, gratus), *a, um.* Disagreeable, offensive, ungrateful.
Ingredior (in, gradior), *di, gressus sum,* dep. To enter, encounter.
Inimicitia (inimīcus), *ae,* f. Enmity.
Inimīcus (in, amīcus), *a, um.* Hostile; *subs.* an enemy.
Inīque (inīquus), adv. Unjustly.
Inīquus (in, aequus), *a, um.* Unfavorable, unjust.
Initium (ineo), *i,* n. Beginning; *pl.* sacred mysteries.
Injicio (in, jacio), *ĕre, jēci, jectum.* To throw in; cause; inspire with.
Injuria, ae, f. Injury, wrong.
Injuste, adv. Unjústly.
Innŏcens, tis. Innocent.
Innotesco, ĕre, notui. To become known.
Innoxius, a, um. Harmless, innocent.
Inopinātus, a, um. Sudden, unexpected.
Inquam or *inquio,* defect. (See A. & S. 183, 5.) To say.
Inscitia, ae, f. Ignorance.
Insĕquor (in, sequor), *qui, cūtus sum.* To follow, pursue.
Insidiae, ārum, f. pl. Ambush, treachery.
Insigne, is, n. Mark, sign; *pl.* badges of office, insignia.
Insignis, e. Distinguished, noted.
Insistŏ, ĕre, stĭti, stĭtum. To persist; urge; entreat.
Insŏlens, tis. Unusual, insolent.
Insŏlenter (insŏlens). Insolently.
Inspicio, ĕre, exi, ectum. To consider, inspect.

Instauro, āre, āvi, ātum. To renew.
Instinctus, us, m. Instigation, impulse.
Instituo (in, statuo), *ĕre, ui, ūtum.* To institute, establish.
Instrumentum (instruo), *i,* n. Implements, movables, goods.
Instruo, ĕre, uxi, uctum. To prepare, build, furnish with, equip.
Insŭla, ae, f. Island.
Insŭper. Moreover.
Intactus, a, um. Unharmed.
Intellĭgo, ĕre, exi, ectum. To understand, perceive, know.
Inter, prep. with acc. Between, among, in the midst of.
Intercipio (inter, capio), *ĕre, cēpi, ceptum.* To catch; intercept, take from.
Interclūdo (inter, claudo), *ĕre, si, sum.* To prevent, cut off.
Interdum, adv. Sometimes.
Interea, adv. In the mean time.
Intereo (inter, eo), *ĕre, ĭvi* or *ii, ĭtum.* To perish.
Interfector (interficio), *ōris,* m. Murderer.
Interficio (inter, facio), *ĕre, fēci, fectum.* To kill.
Intĕrim, adv. In the mean time, meanwhile.
Interĭmo (inter, emŏ), *ĕre, ēmi, emptum.* To deprive of, to kill.
Interior, us. Interior, inland.
Interĭtus (intereo), *us,* m. Destruction.
Interjicio (inter, jacio), *ĕre, jēci, jectum.* To place between; *anno interjecto,* at the expiration of a year.
Internecio, ōnis, f. Slaughter.
Internuncius, or *internŭntius, i,* m. Messenger.
Interregnum (inter, regnum), *i,* n. An interreign, interregnum.
Interrĭtus (in, terrĭtus), *a, um.* Fearless, undismayed.
Interrŏgo (inter, rogo), *āre, āvi, ātum.* To ask, question.

Interrumpo (inter, rumpo), *ĕre, rūpi, ruptum.* To break down, interrupt.
Intersĕro, ĕre, ui, tum. To allege.
Intervenio (inter, venio), *ire, vēni, ventum.* To intervene, occur.
Intestīnus, a, um. Intestine, civil.
Intra, adv. and prep. with acc. Within.
Intro, āre, āvi, ātum. To enter.
Introeo, ire, ivi or *ii, itum.* To enter.
Intueor, ēri, itus sum. To look at, observe.
Inusitātus, a, um. Unusual, extraordinary.
Invādo, ĕre, si, sum. To invade, seize.
Invenio (in, venio), *ire, vēni, ventum.* To find, meet with.
Invicem, adv. By turns, one another.
Invictus (in, victus), *a, um.* Unconquered, invincible.
Invideo (in, video), *ēre, vīdi, vīsum.* To envy.
Invidia, ae, f. Envy.
Invīsus, a, um. Odious, hateful.
Invīto, āre, āvi, ātum. To invite, allure.
Invītus, a, um. Unwilling.
Ipse, a, um. Self, himself, herself, itself.
Ira, ae, f. Anger.
Iracundia, ae, f. Anger, hasty temper.
Irrideo (in, rideo), *ēre, si, sum.* To ridicule, laugh at.
Irrumpo (in, rumpo), *ĕre, rūpi, ruptum.* To rush into; make an incursion into.
Is, ea, id. He, she, it; that.
Ita, adv. Thus, so; to such an extent.
Ităque, conj. Therefore, and thus.
Item, adv. Likewise, also.
Iter, itinĕris, n. Way, march, route.
Iterato (itĕro), adv. Again, a second time.

Itĕro (itĕrum), *āre, āvi, ātum.* To repeat, renew.
Itĕrum, adv. Again, a second time.

J.

Jaceo, ēre, ui, itum. To lie.
Jacio, ĕre, jeci, jactum. To throw hurl; *also,* to lay, place, erect.
Jacŭlum (jacio), *i,* n. Dart, javelin.
Jam, adv. Now, already.
Jubeo, ēre, jussi, jussum. To order, direct.
Jucundus, a, um. Pleasing, delightful.
Judex (judĭco), *icis,* m. and f. Judge, arbiter.
Judicium (judex), *i,* n. Judgment, decision, trial.
Judĭco, āre, āvi, ātum. To judge.
Jugŭlo, āre, āvi, ātum. To kill, murder.
Jugum, i, n. Yoke.
Jungo, ĕre, nxi, nctum. To join, unite.
Junior (juvĕnis), *us.* Younger.
Juro, āre, āvi, ātum. To take oath, swear.
Jus, juris, n. Right, justice.
Jusjurandum jurisjurandi. (See A. & S. 91.) An oath.
Jussu (jubeo), abl. sing. used only in this case. Command, order.
Justitia (justus), *ae,* f. Justice.
Justus (jus), *a, um.* Just.
Juvĕnis, e. Young; *subs.* a youth, young man.

L.

L. An abbreviation of *Lucius.*
Labor, ōris, m. Labor.
Labōro (labor), *āre, āvi, ātum.* To labor, strive, take pains; toil; suffer.
Lac, lactis, n. Milk.
Lacesso, ĕre, ivi or *ii, itum.* To excite, assail, provoke.

Lacrĭma, or *lacrȳma*, *ae*, f. Tear.
Lacrĭmo, or *lacrȳmo* (lacrĭma), *āre, āvi, ātum*. To weep, shed tears.
Lacus, us, m. Lake.
Laete (laetus), adv. Gladly.
Laetitia (laetus), *ae*, f. Joy, gladness.
Laetus, a, um. Glad, joyous.
Laevus, a, um. Left, on the left hand.
Largior, īri, ītus sum. To bestow, lavish; bribe.
Lassitūdo, ĭnis, f. Fatigue, weariness.
Late, adv. Widely, far and wide.
Latĕbra, ae, f. Retreat, hiding-place, pretence.
Latīne (Latīnus), adv. In Latin.
Latro, ōnis, m. Mercenary, robber.
Latus, ĕris, n. Side.
Laudo (laus), *āre, āvi, ātum*. To praise.
Laureus, a, um. Of laurel, laurel; *laurea* (subs.), a laurel-tree or branch, laurel wreath.
Laus, laudis, f. Praise.
Laxo, āre, āvi, ātum. To relax, loosen.
Lectus (lego), *a, um*. Choice, excellent.
Legatio, ōnis, f. Legation, embassy.
Legātus, i, m. Ambassador, lieutenant.
Legio, ōnis, f. Legion.
Lego (lex), *āre, āvi, ātum*. To bequeathe as a legacy.
Lego, ĕre, legi, lectum. To choose, elect; read.
Lenĭtas, ātis, f. Lenity, mildness.
Lenĭter, adv. Gently, mildly.
Letālis, e. Deadly, mortal.
Levis, e. Light, easy.
Levĭter (levis), adv. Lightly, slightly.
Lex, legis, f. Law, condition, terms.
Liber, bri, m. Book.
Liber, ĕra, ĕrum. Free.

Liberalĭtas, ātis, f. Liberality, generosity.
Libĕri, ōrum, m. pl. Children.
Libĕro (liber), *āre, āvi, ātum*. To liberate, free.
Libertas (liber), *ātis*, f. Liberty, freedom.
Libertus, i, m. A freedman.
Libīdo, ĭnis, f. Desire, lust.
Licet, impers. It is lawful, is permitted.
Licet, conj. Although, though.
Ligneus, a, um. Wooden, of wood.
Litĕrae, ārum, f. pl. Letter, letters; literature.
Literarius (litĕrae), *a, um*. Literary.
Litus, ŏris, n. Shore, sea-shore.
Locuplēto, āre, āvi, ātum. To enrich, make rich.
Locus, i, m. pl. *loci*, or *loca*, n. Place.
Longe (longus), adv. Much, greatly, by far.
Longinquus, a, um. Remote, distant.
Longus, a, um. Long.
Loquor, qui, locūtus sum. To speak, converse.
Lorīca, ae, f. Coat of mail.
Luctus (lugeo), *us*, m. Grief, mourning.
Ludibrium, i, n. Sport, derision, laughing-stock.
Ludĭcra, crum, adj. nom. sing. m. not used. Sportive.
Ludĭcrum, i, n. Show, game.
Ludo, ĕre, lusi, lusum. To play, sport.
Ludus, i, m. Play, sport, school.
Lugeo, ēre, luxi. To grieve, mourn, weep for.
Luna, ae, f. Moon.
Luo, ĕre, lui, luĭtum or *lutum*. To pay; expiate, atone for.
Lupa, ae, f. A she-wolf.
Lustratio, ōnis, f. Expiatory sacrifice; review attended with sacrifices.
Lustro, āre, āvi, ātum. To purify, review.

Lux, lucis, f. Light, light of day.
Luxuria, ae, f. Luxury, excess.
Luxus, us, m. Luxury, luxuries, revelling.

M.

M. An abbreviation of *Marcus.*
Magis, adv. More.
Magister, tri, m. Master, leader; teacher.
Magistrātus, us, m. Magistracy, magistrate.
Magnifĭce (magnifĭcus), adv. Magnificently, splendidly.
Magnificenter, adv. = *magnifĭce.*
Magnificentia (magnifĭcus), *ae,* f. Magnificence, costliness.
Magnifĭcus, a, um; comp. *magnificentior,* superl. *magnificentissĭmus.* Splendid; stately; high-minded.
Magnitūdo (magnus), *ĭnis,* f. Greatness, size.
Magnus, a, um; comp. *major,* superl. *maxĭmus.* Great; *majōres,* forefathers, ancestors; *majōres* with *natu,* elders.
Magus, i, m. A wise man, particularly among the Persians.
Majestas, ātis, f. Majesty, dignity.
Major. (See *magnus.*)
Male (malus), adv. Badly, with ill success.
Malo, malle, malui, irregular. (See F. B. 410; A. & S. 178.) To prefer.
Malum, i, n. Misfortune, evil.
Malus, a, um; comp. *pejor,* superl. *pessĭmus.* Bad, wicked.
Mando, āre, āvi, ātum. To bid, enjoin, intrust.
Maneo, ēre, nsi, nsum. To remain.
Manifesto, āre, āvi, ātum. To show, manifest.
Manumitto, ĕre, īsi, issum. To emancipate, make free.
Manus, us, f. Hand, force.
Mare, is, n. Sea.
Marīnus (mare), *a, um.* Marine, of the sea, from or by the sea.
Marītus, i, m. Husband.
Mas, maris, m. Male, the male, man.
Mater, tris, f. Mother.
Materia, ae, f., or *materies, ēi,* f. Materials.
Matrimonium, i, n. Marriage.
Matrōna, ae, f. Matron.
Maxĭme, adv. Especially, in the highest degree.
Maxĭmus, a, um; superl. of *magnus.* Greatest. (See also H. & G. Index.)
Medĭcus, i, m. Physician.
Medius, a, um. Middle, midst of, middle of. (See F. B. 267.)
Melior (bonus), *us.* Better.
Membrum, i, n. Member, limb.
Memĭni, isti, defect. (See A. & S. 183.) To remember.
Memorabĭlis, e. Memorable.
Memoria, ae, f. Memory, recollection.
Memŏro, āre, āvi, ātum. To mention, relate.
Mens, tis, f. Mind, reason.
Mensis, is, m. Month.
Mentio, ōnis, f. Mention.
Mercātus, us, m. Public sale, fair; meeting.
Mercor, āri, ātus sum. To trade, buy.
Mereo, ēre, ui, ĭtum. To deserve, merit.
Mergo, ĕre, si, sum. To merge, sink, destroy.
Merĭtum, i, n. Reward, merit.
Merum, i, n. Wine, pure wine.
Merx, cis, f. Merchandise, goods.
Metallum, i, n. Metal, mine.
Metuo, ĕre, ui. To fear.
Metus, us, m. Fear, dread.
Meus, a, um, voc. sing. masc. *mi.* My, mine.
Migro, āre, āvi, ātum. To migrate, remove.
Miles, ĭtis, m. Soldier.
Militāris (miles), *e.* Military.

LATIN-ENGLISH VOCABULARY. 309

Militia (miles), *ae*, f. Warfare, military service.
Milito (miles), *āre*, *āvi*, *ātum*. To serve as a soldier, to serve.
Mille, subs. and adj. Thousand; *millia*, subs., a thousand, a thousand men.
Milliarius (or *um*, n.), *i*, m. Milestone, mile.
Minor (parvus), *us*. Smaller, less.
Minus, adv. Less.
Mirabilis (miror), *e*. Wonderful.
Miror, *āri*, *ātus sum*. To wonder, admire.
Miser, *ĕra*, *ĕrum*. Unfortunate, miserable.
Misereo, *ēre*, *ui*, *ĭtum*. To pity; *often impersonal*.
Misereor, *ēri*, *ertus* or *erĭtus sum*, dep. To pity.
Miseria (miser), *ae*, f. Misery, affliction.
Misericordia, *ae*, f. Compassion.
Mitto, *ĕre*, *misi*, *missum*. To send.
Moderāte (moderātus), adv. With moderation.
Moderatio, *ōnis*, f. Moderation, self-control.
Moderātus, *a*, *um*. Discreet, moderate.
Modius (or *um*, n.), *i*, m. Measure, *a little more than a peck*.
Modus, *i*, m. Manner, measure, limits.
Moenia, *ium*, n. pl. Walls of a city, city.
Moles, *is*, f. Mole, dam.
Molitio, *ōnis*, f. Undertaking, preparation.
Mollio, *īre*, *ĭvi* or *ii*, *ītum*. To soften.
Momentum, *i*, n. Weight, influence.
Monĭtus, *us*, m. Advice.
Mons, *tis*, m. Mountain, mount.
Monstro, *āre*, *āvi*, *ātum*. To show.
Mora, *ae*, f. Delay.
Morbus, *i*, m. Disease.
Morior, *ĭri* or *i*, *mortuus sum*, dep. To die.

Moror (mora), *āri*, *ātus sum*, dep. To delay, tarry.
Mors, *tis*, f. Death.
Mortĭfer (mors and fero), *ĕra*, *ĕrum*. Deadly, mortal.
Mos, *moris*, m. Custom, manner; *pl.* character, morals.
Motus, *us*, m. Motion; commotion, revolt.
Moveo, *ēre*, *movi*, *motum*. To move, excite.
Mox, adv. Presently, soon.
Mucro, *ōnis*, m. Point of sword, sword.
Muliĕbris (mulier), *e*. Belonging to women, womanly, woman's.
Mulier, *ĕris*, f. Woman.
Multitūdo (multus), *ĭnis*, f. Multitude.
Multo, *āre*, *āvi*, *ātum*. To punish, deprive of by way of punishment; to fine.
Multo, adv. By far, much.
Multus, *a*, *um*; comp. *plus*, n., superl. *plurĭmus*. Much, many.
Munia, *ium*, n. pl. Duties, functions of office.
Munimentum, *i*, n. Fortification, defence, covering.
Munio, *īre*, *ĭvi* or *ii*, *ītum*. To fortify, defend.
Munitio, *ōnis*, f. Fortification, rampart.
Munītus, *a*, *um*. Fortified.
Munus, *ĕris*, n. Reward, present service, office.
Murus, *i*, m. Wall.
Muto, *āri*, *āvi*, *ātum*. To change, alter.
Mutuus, *a*, *um*. Mutual.

N.

Nam, conj. For.
Namque, conj. For, but.
Nanciscor, *ci*, *nactus sum*, dep. To obtain, take advantage of.
Narro, *āre*, *āvi*, *ātum*. To relate, narrate.

Nascor, ci, natus sum. To be born, to arise.
Natio, ōnis, f. Nation, people.
Natu, defective, abl. sing. By birth, in age; *maxĭmus natu,* eldest.
Naturālis, e. Natural.
Navālis (navis), *e.* Naval.
Navigatio, ōnis, f. Navigation, sailing.
Navĭgo, āre, āvi, ātum. To sail upon, navigate.
Navis, is, f. Ship.
Ne, adv. and conj. used with imperative and subj. Not, that not, lest; *after verbs of fearing,* that, lest; *nequĭdem,* or *ne—quidem,* not even.
Ne, interrog. particle, 177, Rem. 1 and 2.
Nec or *neque,* adv. and conj. Neither, nor; and not, not; *nec—nec, neque—neque,* neither—nor.
Necessarius, a, um. Necessary.
Neco, āre, āvi, ātum. To slay, kill.
Neglĭgens, tis. Negligent, neglectful.
Neglĭgo, ĕre, exi, ectum. To neglect, disregard.
Nego, āre, āvi, ātum. To deny, refuse.
Negotium, i, n. Business, difficulty.
Nemo (ĭnis, gen. not in good use). No one, nobody.
Nepos, ōtis, m. Grandson.
Neque. (See *Nec.*)
Nequeo, īre, īvi or *ii, ītum,* irreg. like *eo.* (See A. & S. 182, R. 3.) To be unable, not to be able.
Nequĭdem. (See *Ne.*)
Nequis or *ne quis, qua, quod* or *quid.* That no one.
Nequitia, ae, f. Inactivity, remissness.
Nescio (ne *and* scio), *īre, īvi* or *ii, ītum.* To be ignorant, not to know.
Nĭhil; n. indecl. Nothing; adv. not, in nothing.

Nimis, adv. Exceedingly, too much.
Nimius, a, um. Excessive, too much, too great.
Nisi, conj. Unless, if not, except.
Nitor, ti, nisus or *nixus sum,* dep. To strive, attempt.
Nix, nivis, f. Snow.
Nobĭlis, e. Noble, famous.
Nobilĭtas (nobĭlis), *ātis,* f. Fame, nobleness; nobility, nobles.
Noceo, ēre, ui, ĭtum. To hurt, harm.
Noctū, abl. By night.
Nocturnus, a, um. Nocturnal, occurring at night.
Nolo, nolle, nolui, irreg. (See F. B. 410, and A. & S. 178.) To be unwilling.
Nomen, ĭnis, n. Name.
Non, adv. Not; *nonnĭsi,* only.
Nonagesĭmus, a, um. Ninetieth.
Nondum, adv. Not yet.
Nonne, interrog. particle. (See 177, R. 2.) Whether, *expecting answer* yes.
Nonnullus, a, um (declined like *nullus*). Some.
Nonus, a, um. Ninth.
Novem, indecl. Nine.
Noverca, ae, f. Stepmother.
Novo (novus), *āre, āvi, ātum.* To renew, change; revolutionize.
Novus, a, um. New; *novae res,* revolution.
Nox, noctis, f. Night.
Nubo, ĕre, psi, ptum. To veil one's self, to marry, *applied to the bride as she was covered with a veil.*
Nudus, a, um. Naked, uncovered.
Nullus, a, um. (See F. B. 113, R.) No one, no.
Num, interrog. particle. (See 177, R. 2, and 381.) Whether, *used both in direct and independent questions.*
Numĕrus, i, m. Number.
Nunc. Now.

Nuncŭpo, āre, āvi, ātum. To call, name.
Nunquam. Never.
Nuntio (or *cio*), *āre, āvi, ātum.* To announce, relate.
Nuntius, i, m. Message, news, messenger.
Nuptiae, ārum, f. pl. Marriage, nuptials.
Nutrio, īre, īvi or *ii, ītum.* To nourish, support.
Nympha, ae, f. Spouse, wife, nymph.

O.

Ob, prep. with acc. On account of, for.
Obdūco (ob, duco), *ĕre, duxi, ductum.* To draw over, overspread, cover.
Obedio, īre, īvi or *ii, ītum.* To obey, serve; be subject to.
Obeo (ob, eo), *īre, īvi* or *ii, ītum.* To meet; die.
Objecto, āre, āvi, ātum. To expose, set forth; endanger.
Objicio (ob, jacio), *ĕre, jēci, jectum.* To expose, offer, present.
Obītus, us, m. Death.
Oblīgo, āre, āvi, ātum. To oblige, put under obligation.
Obliviscor, ci, cōlītus sum, dep. To forget.
Obruo, ĕre, ui, ŭtum. To destroy, overwhelm.
Obscūre (obscūrus), adv. In obscurity, obscurely.
Obscūrus, a, um. Obscure, hidden; mean.
Obsequium, i, n. Submission, fealty.
Observo, āre, āvi, ātum. To observe, keep.
Obses, ĭdis, m. and f. Hostage.
Obsideo (ob, sedeo), *ĕre, ēdi, essum.* To besiege, invest.
Obsidio (obsideo), *ōnis,* f. Siege, blockade.

Obsto (ob, sto), *āre, stĭti, stătum.* To oppose, prevent.
Obtĕro, ĕre, trīvi, trītum. To crush, wear down.
Obtestor, āri, ātus sum, dep. To call to witness, implore, conjure.
Obtineo (ob, teneo), *ēre, inui, entum.* To obtain, hold, prevail.
Obtingo, ĕre, tīgi. To befall, happen to.
Obtrunco, āre, āvi, ātum. To slaughter.
Occasio, ōnis, f. Opportunity, occasion.
Occīdo (ob, caedo), *ĕre, cīdi, cīsum.* To kill.
Occulte (occultus), adv. In secret, secretly.
Occultus, a, um. Secret, hidden; reserved, dissembling.
Occŭpo, āre, āvi, ātum. To occupy, take possession of.
Occurro (ob, curro), *ĕre, curri* (cucurri), *cursum.* To meet, attack.
Oceănus, i, m. Ocean.
Octāvus (octo), *a, um.* Eighth.
Octingenti, ae, a. Eight hundred.
Octo, indecl. Eight.
Octoginta (octo), indecl. Eighty
Ocŭlus, i, m. Eye.
Odium, i, n. Hatred, enmity.
Offendo, ĕre, di, sum. To offend, injure.
Offensa, ae, f. Offence, harm.
Offensus (offendo), *a, um.* Offended, hostile.
Offĕro (ob, fero), *ferre, obtŭli, ŏblātum.* To offer, show; *se offerre,* to offer one's self as an antagonist, to oppose; expose one's self.
Officium, i, n. Office, duty.
Olim, adv. Formerly.
Omen, ĭnis, n. Omen, sign.
Omnīno (omnis), adv. Wholly; only, in all; at all.
Omnis, e. All, every.
Oneraria (onus), *ae,* f. Ship of burden.

Onustus (onus), *a, um.* Laden, full of.
Optĭmus, a, um. Rich, fertile.
Oportet, impers. It behooves, one ought.
Opperior, ĭri, oppertus or *opperītus sum.* To wait for, await.
Oppĕto, ĕre, īvi or *ii, ītum.* To encounter, seek.
Oppidānus (oppĭdum), *a, um.* Inhabitant of a town.
Oppĭdum, i, n. Town, city.
Opportunĭtas (opportūnus), *ātis,* f. Opportunity, fitness.
Opportūnus, a, um. Suitable, fit.
Opprĭmo, ĕre, essi, essum. To put down, defeat, overcome; suppress; oppress.
Oppugno (ob, pugno), *āre, āvi, ātum.* To attack, storm, take by storm.
Ops, opis, f., nom. sing. not used. Power, resources, force, aid.
Optĭmas (optĭmus), *ātis,* m. and f. A noble, one of the aristocracy.
Optĭmus (superl. bonus), *a, um.* Best, most excellent.
Optio, ōnis, f. Choice, option.
Opto, āre, āvi, ātum. To wish, desire; ask.
Opŭlens, tis, or *opulentus, a, um,* adj. Wealthy, rich.
Opus, ĕris, n. Work.
Opus, nom. and accus. Need.
Ora, ae, f. The shore, coast.
Oracŭlum, i, n. Response, oracle.
Oratio (oro), *ōnis,* f. Oration, speech, language.
Orātor (oro), *ōris,* m. Orator.
Orbis, is, m. Circle, world; *orbis terrārum,* the world.
Orbĭtas, ātis, f. Bereavement, orphanage.
Ordĭno (ordo), *āre, āvi, ātum.* To arrange, establish.
Ordo, ĭnis, m. Row, rank, order; bank *as of oars; extra ordĭnem,* out of the common course.
Oriens (part. orior), *tis.* Rising, east.

Orīgo, ĭnis, f. Origin, source.
Orior, ĭri, ortus sum, dep. mostly of 3d conj. (See A. & S. 177.) To rise, appear.
Ornamentum, i, n. Equipage, ornament.
Orno, āre, āvi, ātum. To adorn, equip.
Oro, āre, āvi, ātum. To ask, speak.
Ortus (orior), *us,* m. A rising; birth; beginning.
Os, ossis, n. Bone.
Oscŭlor, āri, ātus sum. To kiss.
Ostendo, ĕre, di, sum or *tum.* To show.
Ostentum, i, n. Prodigy.
Ostium, i, n. Mouth, door.

P.

P. An abbreviation of *Publius.*
Paco (pax), *āre, āvi, ātum.* To subdue.
Pactum, i, n. Bargain, contract; abl. *pacto,* way, manner.
Paene, adv. Almost.
Palam, adv. Openly.
Palatium, i, n. Palace.
Pango, ĕre, nxi, nctum, or *pepĭgi, pactum.* To contract, ratify.
Par, paris, adj. Equal, a match for.
Parātus (paro), *a, um.* Prepared, ready.
Parco, ĕre, peperci or *parsi, parcĭtum* or *parsum.* To spare.
Parens, tis, m. and f. Parent.
Parento (parens), *āre, āvi, ātum.* To sacrifice in honor of parents, or friends.
Pareo, ĕre, ui, ĭtum. To obey, be subject to.
Pario, ĕre, pepĕri, parĭtum or *partum.* To bear, bring forth, produce.
Paro, āre, āvi, ātum. To prepare, equip.
Pars, partis, f. Part, portion; party.

Parsimonia, ae, f. Frugality, parsimony.
Partim, adv. Partly, in part; *partim—partim,* some—others, either—or.
Parvus, a, um ; comp. *minor ;* superl. *minimus.* Small, little.
Passus, us, m. Pace ; *mille passus,* a mile.
Pastor (pasco), *ōris,* m. Shepherd.
Patefacio, ĕre, fēci, factum. To disclose.
Pateo, ēre, ui. To lie open, be exposed.
Pater, tris, m. Father.
Paternus (pater), *a, um.* Paternal.
Patior, ti, passus sum. To permit, keep, endure.
Patria, ae, f. Country, native country.
Patrimonium, i, n. Estate, patrimony.
Patrius (pater), *a, um.* Fatherly.
Patruēlis, is, m. and f. Cousin by the father's side.
Patruus, i, m. Uncle by the father's side.
Pauci, ae, a. Few.
Paulātim, By degrees, gradually.
Paulus, Little, small.
Pax, pācis, f. Peace.
Pecco, āre, āvi, ātum. To err, sin.
Pecunia, ae, f. Money, sum of money.
Pedes, ĭtis, m. Foot-soldier.
Pedester, tris, tre. Pedestrian, on foot, on land.
Pellicio, ĕre, lexi, lectum. To allure, cajole.
Pellis, is, f. Skin, hide.
Pello, ĕre, pepŭli, pulsum. To drive.
Pendeo, ēre, pependi. To hang, be suspended.
Penĕtro, āre, āvi, ātum. To penetrate.
Penĭtus, adv. Inwardly ; fully, entirely.
Penuria, ae, f. Poverty, want.

Per, prep. with acc. Through, by.
Percussor (percutio), *ōris,* m. Assassin, murderer.
Percutio, ĕre, ussi, ussum. To kill, slay, strike.
Perdĭtus, a, um. Lost, abandoned, desperate.
Perdo, ĕre, dĭdi, dĭtum. To destroy, waste, lose.
Perdūco (per, duco), *ĕre, duxi, ductum.* To conduct, bring to.
Peregrīnus, a, um. Foreign.
Perennis (per, annus), *e.* Continual, perpetual.
Pereo, īre, īvi or *ii, ĭtum.* To perish.
Perfĕro (per, fero), *ferre, tŭli, lātum.* To carry through ; bear; suffer.
Perfĭdia, ae, f. Perfidy.
Pergo, ĕre, rexi, rectum. To go on or to, persevere.
Periculōsus (periculum), *a, um.* Dangerous.
Periculum, i, n. Danger, peril.
Perītus, a, um. Skilled in, skilful.
Permitto (per, mitto), *ĕre, ĭsi, issum.* To send ; grant, permit ; *permittĭtur,* impers. it is permitted.
Permutatio, ōnis, f. Exchange, barter.
Perniciōsus (pernicies), *a, um.* Destructive, pernicious.
Perpaucus, a, um. Few, very few.
Perpĕtro, āre, āvi, ātum. To finish, achieve.
Perpetuo, adv. Constantly, ever.
Perpetuus, a, um. Perpetual, constant.
Persĕquor, qui, cūtus sum. To follow, carry on, prosecute.
Persevĕro, āre, āvi, ātum. To persevere, persist.
Persōna, ae, f. Part, character, person.
Perspicio, ĕre, exi, ectum. To perceive.
Perstringo, ĕre, inxi, ictum. To graze, wound slightly.

Persuadeo, ēre, si, sum. To persuade.
Perterreo, ēre, ui, ĭtum. To terrify greatly.
Pertineo, ēre, ui. To pertain to, tend.
Pervenio (per, venio), *īre, vēni, ventum.* To reach, come to.
Pervigilia, ae, f. A vigil, keeping awake.
Peto, ēre, īvi or *ii, ĭtum.* To seek, ask, aim at.
Petulantia, ae, f. Petulance, wantonness.
Phalĕrae, ārum, f. pl. Trappings, ornaments for horses.
Philosŏphus, i, m. Philosopher.
Pictus (pingo), *a, um.* Painted.
Pileus (or, *um, n.*), *i, m.* Hat.
Pingo, ĕre, pinxi, pictum. To paint, depict.
Pirāta, ae, m. Pirate.
Placeo, ēre, ui, ĭtum. To please, be pleasing to; be determined.
Placĭdus (placeo), *a, um.* Quiet, gentle.
Plane, adv. Plainly.
Plebs, bis, f. Common people.
Plerumque, adv. Commonly, frequently.
Plerusque, ăque, umque. Most, many.
Plurĭmus. (See *Multus.*)
Plus, adv. More.
Plus, uris, n. adj. (See *Multus.*) Much, *pl.* many.
Pocŭlum, i, n. Cup.
Poena, ae, f. Punishment.
Poēta, ae, m. Poet.
Polliceor, ēri, ĭtus sum. To promise.
Polluo, ĕre, ui, ūtum. To pollute, defile.
Pompa, ae, f. Pomp.
Pono, ĕre, posui, posĭtum. To place, build, pitch.
Pons, tis, m. Bridge.
Populatio, ōnis, f. Pillaging, booty; people, population.
Popŭlo (popŭlus), *āre, āvi, ātum.* To depopulate; *popŭlor,* dep *= popŭlo.*
Popŭlus, i, m. People.
Porrĭgo, ĕre, rexi, rectum. To extend, stretch.
Porta, ae, f. Gate.
Portendo, ĕre, di, tum. To portend.
Portio, ōnis, f. Portion, share.
Portus, us, m. Port, harbor.
Posco, ĕre, poposci. To demand, ask.
Possessio, ōnis, f. Possession.
Possideo, ēre, ēdi, essum. To possess.
Possum, posse, potui, irreg. (See F. B. 407, and A. & S. 154.) To be able.
Post, adv. and *prep.* with acc. Afterwards, after, since.
Postea, adv. Afterwards.
Posterĭtas, ātis, f. Posterity.
Postĕrus, a, um. Following, ensuing; *postĕri,* posterity, descendants; *postrēmo, ad postrēmum,* at last.
Postquam, or *post quam,* conj. After, after that.
Postrēmus (superl. ▓▓▓ *a, um.* The last.
Postridie, adv. O▓▓▓owing day.
Postŭlo, āre, āvi, ātum. To demand.
Potens (possum), *tis.* Able, powerful.
Potestas, ātis, f. Power.
Potior, īri, ītus sum. To obtain, get possession of.
Praebeo, ēre, ui, ĭtum. To show, furnish.
Praecēdo, ĕre, essi, essum. To precede.
Praeceptor, ōris, m. Preceptor, commander.
Praecipio, ĕre, cēpi, ceptum. To admonish, advise, order.
Praecipitium, i, n. Precipice.
Praecipĭto, āre, āvi, ātum. To throw down, precipitate.

Praecipue (praecipuus), adv. Especially.
Praecipuus, a, um. Remarkable, prominent, special.
Praeclāre, adv. Excellently, nobly.
Praeclūdo, (prae, claudo), *ĕre, si, sum.* To hinder, preclude, cut off.
Praeco, ōnis, m. Herald, crier.
Praeda, ae, f. Prey, booty.
Praedīco (prae, dico), *ĕre dixi, dictum.* To predict, forewarn.
Praedictum, i, n. Prediction, warning.
Praedītus, a, um. Endued with.
Praedor (praeda), *āri, ātus sum.* To plunder.
Praefāri, defective. (See *Fari*, A. & S. 183, 6.) To predict, prophesy; say.
Praefectus, i, m. Commander, prefect.
Praefĕro (prae, fero), *ferre, tŭli, lātum.* To prefer, choose; carry or bear before.
Praeficio (prae, facio), *ĕre, fēci, fectum.* To place over, put in command.
Praemium, i, n. Reward.
Praepōnō (prae, pono), *ĕre, posui, posĭtum.* To place over, intrust with.
Praescrībo (prae, scribo), *ĕre, psi, ptum.* To direct, prescribe.
Praesens, tis. Present.
Praesentia (praesens), *ae*, f. Presence.
Praesidium, i, n. Guard, garrison.
Praestans, tis. Excellent, eminent.
Praesto, āre, stĭti, ĭtum. To surpass, be superior to; furnish, do, pay; evince, show.
Praesum (prae, sum), *esse, fui, futūrus.* To preside over, command.
Praetendo, ĕre, di, tum. To pretend, allege.

Praeter, prep. with acc. Except, besides.
Praeterea, adv. Besides, moreover.
Praetereo (praeter, eo), *īre, īvi* or *ii, ĭtum.* To pass by, omit.
Praetorius, a, um. Praetorian, belonging to a praetor or general; *praetorius*, subs. one who has been praetor.
Pravus, a, um. Depraved, bad.
Precor, āri, ātus sum. To beseech, pray.
Premo, ĕre, essi, essum. To press, urge.
Pretium, i, n. Price, worth.
Preces, um, f. pl. dat. acc. and abl. sing. also occur. Prayers, entreaties.
Pridie, adv. On the day before.
Primo, primum (primus), adv. At first, first.
Primus (superl. prior), *a, um.* First.
Princeps, ĭpis, m. Prince, ruler; chief man.
Principātus, us, m. Sovereignty, imperial power.
Principium, i, n. Beginning.
Prior, us. Former, previous.
Pristĭnus, a, um. Ancient, pristine.
Prius, adv. Before; *priusquam* or *prius quam*, before that, before.
Privātus, a, um. Private, personal, *subs.* a private citizen.
Privignus, i, m. Step-son.
Privo, āre, āvi, ātum. To deprive of.
Pro, prep. with abl. Before, in front of; for, instead of, as; *pro hoste*, as an enemy.
Probatio, ōnis, f. Approbation, proof.
Probo, āre, āvi, ātum. To prove show; approve.
Procēdo, ĕre, essi, essum. To step forth, advance, proceed, come on.

Proconsul (pro, consul), *ŭlis*, m. Proconsul, one with the authority of consul.
Procul, adv. At a distance, far off.
Procūro, *āre*, *āvi*, *ātum*. To attend to, have the care of.
Procurro (pro, curro), *ĕre*, *curri* (cucurri), *cursum*. To run forth, project.
Prodigium, *i*, n. Prodigy, prophetic omen.
Proditio (prodo), *ōnis*, f. Treachery, treason.
Proditor (prodo), *ōris*, m. Traitor.
Prodo, *ĕre*, *dĭdi*, *dĭtum*. To disclose, betray.
Prodūco (pro, duco), *ĕre*, *duxi*, *ductum*. To lead forth, produce.
Proelium, *i*, n. Battle, conflict.
Profecto, adv. Indeed, truly.
Proficiscor, *ci*, *profectus sum*. To depart, set out, go.
Profĺgo, *āre*, *āvi*, *ātum*. To overthrow, ruin.
Profugio (pro, fugio), *ĕre*, *fūgi*, *ĭtum*. To flee, escape.
Progredior, *i*, *essus sum*. To proceed, advance.
Prohibeo, *ēre*, *ui*, *ĭtum*. To prohibit, prevent.
Promissus, *a*, *um*. Growing long, long.
Promitto (pro, mitto), *ĕre*, *ĭsi*, *isum*. To send forth, promise.
Promontorium, *i*, n. Promontory.
Promptus, *a*, *um*. Prompt, ready.
Propāgo, *āre*, *āvi*, *ātum*. To propagate; prolong.
Prope, adv. Near, nearly.
Propĕro, *āre*, *āvi*, *ātum*. To hasten.
Propius (comp. prope), adv. Nearer.
Propōno (pro, pono), *ĕre*, *posui*, *posĭtum*. To set forth, state, propose.
Proprius, *a*, *um*. Peculiar, proper, one's own.
Propter, prep. with acc. For, on account of.

Propterea, adv. Therefore, on that account.
Propulso, *āre*, *āvi*, *ātum*. To repel, ward off.
Prorumpo, *ĕre*, *rūpi*, *ruptum*. To rush or break forth.
Proscrībo (pro, scribo), *ĕre*, *psi*, *ptum*. To proscribe, outlaw.
Prosĕquor, *qui*, *cūtus sum*. To follow, attend; pursue, prosecute.
Prosilio, *ĭre*, *ĭvi*, *ii* or *ui*. To leap up, spring forth.
Prospĕre, adv. Happily, prosperously.
Prosterno, *ĕre*, *strāvi*, *strātum*. To prostrate, overthrow.
Prosum (pro, sum), *desse*, *fui*. To profit, avail.
Protĭnus, adv. Directly, immediately after.
Provideo (pro, video), *ēre*, *vīdi*, *vīsum*. To provide, be on one's guard.
Provincia, *ae*, f. Province.
Provocatio (provŏco), *ōnis*, f. Challenge.
Provŏco, *āre*, *āvi*, *ātum*. To challenge.
Proxĭmus, *a*, *um*. Nearest, next.
Prudens, *tis*. Prudent, wise.
Prudentia (prudens), *ae*, f. Prudence.
Pubes, *ĕris*. Grown up, adult.
Publĭce (publĭcus), adv. Publicly.
Publĭcus, *a*, *um*. Public.
Pudor, *ōris*, m. Regard, respect, modesty, awe, shame.
Puella, *ae*, f. Girl.
Puer, *ĕri*, m. Boy.
Puerīlis (puer), *e*. Boyish, youthful.
Pueritia (puer), *ae*, f. Boyhood.
Pugio, *ōnis*, m. Dagger, poniard.
Pugna, *ae*, f. Battle.
Pulcher, *chra*, *chrum*. Beautiful.
Punio, *īre*, *īvi*, *ītum*. To punish.
Pupillus, *i*, m. Pupil.
Purgo, *āre*, *āvi*, *ātum*. To purify, purge.
Puto, *āre*, *āvi*, *ātum*. To think, imagine.

Q.

Q. or **Qu.** An abbreviation of *Quintus*.
Quadragesĭmus, a, um. Fortieth.
Quadraginta, indecl. Forty.
Quadriennium, i, n. Space of four years.
Quadrīga, ae, f. Chariot, four-horse chariot.
Quadringentesĭmus, a, um. The four hundredth.
Quadringenti, ae, a. Four hundred.
Quaero, ĕre, sīvi, sītum. To seek, inquire, ask.
Quaestio (quaero), *ōnis,* f. Question.
Quaestor, ōris, m. Treasurer, quaestor.
Quaestorius (quaestor), *a, um.* Quaestorian; *quaestorius* (subs.), one who has been quaestor.
Qualis, e. What, what sort; *talis—qualis,* such—as.
Quam, adv. and conj. How; *quam multi,* how many; *with superl.* intensive, *quam maxĭmus,* as great as possible; than, after.
Quamdiu, adv. How long, as long as.
Quamquam, conjunc. Although, though.
Quamvis. However, however much, though.
Quando? adv. When?
Quantus, a, um. How great; *tantus—quantus,* so great as.
Quare. Wherefore, whereby.
Quartus, a, um. Fourth.
Quasi. As if.
Quatio, ĕre, —, quassum. To shake.
Quatriduum (quatuor, dies), *i,* n. Space of four days, four days.
Quatuor, indecl. Four.
Quatuordĕcim (quatuor, decem), indecl. Fourteen.
Que, appended to another word. And.
Querēla (queror), *ae,* f. Complaint.

Queror, i, questus sum, dep. To complain.
Qui, quae, quod, rel. and interrog. Who, which, what.
Quia, conj. Because.
Quicumque (or *cunque*), *quaecumque, quodcumque.* Whoever, whatever.
Quidam, quaedam, quoddam or *quiddam.* A certain one, certain.
Quidem. Indeed.
Quiētus, a, um. Quiet, at rest.
Quin. That not, but that.
Quindĕcim, indecl. Fifteen.
Quingenti, ae, a. Five hundred.
Quinquagesĭmus, a, um. Fiftieth.
Quinquaginta, indecl. Fifty.
Quinque, indecl. Five.
Quinquennium, i, n. Five years, space of five years.
Quintus, a, um. Fifth.
Quippe, conj. Indeed.
Quis, quae, quid? interrog. subs. Who, which, what!
Quisnam or *quinam, quaenam, quodnam* or *quidnam.* Who, which, what.
Quisquam, quaequam, quidquam or *quicquam.* Any, any one.
Quisque, quaeque, quodque or *quidque.* Every, every one, whoever, whatever; *with superl.* intensive, *primo quoque tempŏre,* on the very first opportunity.
Quisquis, quaequae, quidquid or *quicquid.* Whoever, whatever.
Quo. Where, whither, that, in order that.
Quoad. Till, until.
Quod, conj. That, because.
Quomĭnus (quo, minus). That not, from.
Quondam, adv. Formerly.
Quoniam, conj. Since.
Quoque. Also, likewise.
Quotidie. Daily, every day.
Quum or *cum.* When, since *quum*—tum, not only—but also, both—and; *rarely,* either—or.

R.

Rabies, ēi, f. Madness, rage.
Radix, īcis, f. Root, foot, base as of mountain.
Ramus, i, m. Branch.
Rapina, as, f. Rapine, plunder.
Rapio, ĕre, ui, tum. To rob, carry off.
Rapto (rapio), āre, āvi, ātum. To carry or drag, ravage, rob.
Raptor (rapio), ōris, m. Robber, plunderer.
Raro (rarus), adv. Rarely, seldom.
Rarus, a, um. Rare, uncommon.
Ratio, ōnis, f. Plan, method; kind.
Ratis, is, f. Raft.
Rebello, āre, āvi, ātum. To rebel.
Recēdo, ĕre, essi, essum. To withdraw, recede.
Recipio (re, capio), ĕre, cēpi, ceptum. To receive, recover, resume; *se recipĕre*, to betake one's self, withdraw.
Recĭto, āre, āvi, ātum. To repeat, recite.
Recognosco, ĕre nōvi, nĭtum. To recognize.
Recordor, āri, ātus sum, dep. To recollect.
Recte, adv. Rightly
Rector, ōris, m. Director, ruler.
Recupĕro, āre, āvi, ātum. To regain.
Reddo, ĕre, dĭdi, dĭtum. To restore, return; render; assign.
Redeo, īre, īvi or ii, ĭtum. To go back, return.
Redĭgo, ĕre, ēgi, actum. To force, reduce, compel.
Redĭmo, ĕre, ēmi, emptum. To ransom.
Redĭtus (redeo), us, m. Return, revenue.
Redūco, ĕre, xi, ctum. To lead back, reduce.
Refĕro, ferre, tŭli, lātum. To refer; requite; place among.

Reficio, ĕre, ēci, ectum. To repair, restore; recover.
Refluo, ĕre, xi, xum. To flow back.
Refugio, ĕre, ūgi, ugĭtum. To retreat.
Regīna, ae, f. Queen.
Regio, ōnis, f. Region, country.
Regius (rex), a, um. Royal.
Regno (regnum), āre, āvi, ātum. To reign, rule.
Regnum (rex), i, n. Kingdom, sovereignty.
Rego, ĕre, xi, ctum. To direct, manage.
Regredior, i, essus sum. To return.
Religio, ōnis, f. Religion, obligation.
Relinquo, ĕre, līqui, lictum. To leave, desert.
Reliquiae, ārum, f. pl. Remnant, those who escaped.
Relĭquus, a, um. The rest, remaining.
Remaneo, ēre, ansi, ansum. To remain.
Remedium, i, n. Remedy.
Reminiscor, ci, dep. To remember.
Remitto, ĕre, mīsi, missum. To send back.
Removeo, ēre, mōvi, mōtum. To take away, remove.
Remus, i, m. Oar.
Renŏvo, āre, āvi, ātum. To renew.
Renuntio, āre, āvi, ātum. To report.
Repăro, āre, āvi, ātum. To renew, repair.
Repello, ĕre, ŭli, ulsum. To repel, drive back.
Repente, adv. Suddenly.
Repentīnus, a, um. Unexpected, sudden.
Reperio, īre, pĕri, pertum. To find.
Repleo, ēre, ēvi, ētum. To fill, fill again.
Repōno, ĕre, osui, osĭtum. To replace, restore, lay up.
Reporto, āre, āvi, ātum. To gain, bear off.

Repraesento, āre, āvi, ātum. To represent.
Reprehendo, ĕre, di, sum. To blame, censure.
Repudio, āre, āvi, ātum. To reject, divorce.
Repugno, āre, āvi, ātum. To resist.
Res, rĕi, f. Thing; state; deed; battle.
Reservo, āre, āvi, ātum. To keep, reserve; spare, save.
Resisto, ĕre, stĭti, stĭtum. To oppose, resist.
Respectus, us, m. Respect, regard.
Respicio, ĕre, exi, ectum. To look back; regard, respect.
Respondeo, ēre, di, sum. To reply.
Responsum, i, n. Answer, response.
Respublĭca, reipublĭcae, f. comp. (See A. & S. 91.) Republic.
Restituo, ĕre, ui, ūtum. To restore.
Retardo, āre, āvi, ātum. To detain, retard, check.
Retineo, ēre, ui, tentum. To retain.
Reus, i, m. Criminal, defendant.
Reverentia, ae, f. Reverence.
Revereor, ēri, ĭtus sum. To fear, reverence.
Reverto, ĕre, ti, sum; revertor, dep. To come back, return.
Revŏco, āre, āvi, ātum. To recall.
Rex, regis, m. King.
Rideo, ēre, si, sum. To laugh.
Ripa, ae, f. Bank *as of a river.*
Rite, adv. Rightly, in due form.
Robur, ŏris, n. Strength.
Robustus (robur), *a, um.* Robust, strong.
Rogo, āre, āvi, ātum. To ask.
Rotundus, a, um. Round, spherical.
Ruīna, ae, f. Ruin, fall.
Rumpo, ĕre, rupi, ruptum. To break.
Ruo, ĕre, rui, ruĭtum or *rutum.* To run, rush forth.
Rupes, is, f. Rock, cliff.
Rursus (or *um*), adv. Back, again.
Rus, ruris, n. Country *as opposed to city*

S.

S. An abbreviation of *Sextius* or *Spurius; Sp.* for *Spurius.*
Sacer, sacra, sacrum. Sacred.
Sacerdos (sacer), *ōtis,* m. and f. Priest, priestess.
Sacrificium, i, n. Sacrifice.
Sacro (sacer), *āre, āvi, ātum.* To consecrate.
Sacrum, i, n. Sacred rite *or* institution; sacrifice.
Saepe, adv. Often.
Saevio, īre, īvi or *ii, ītum.* To rage, be cruel.
Salūber, bris, bre. Healthful, salubrious.
Salus, ūtis, f. Safety.
Salūto, āre, āvi, ātum. To salute.
Salvus, a, um. Safe, unhurt.
Sancte, adv. Chastely.
Sanguis, ĭnis, m. Blood.
Sapiens, tis. Wise; *subs.* a wise man.
Sapientia (sapiens), *ae,* f. Wisdom.
Satelles, ĭtis, m. and f. Lifeguard, attendant.
Satio, ōnis, f. Sowing.
Satis, adv. adj. subs. Enough, sufficiently; *satis habēre,* to be content.
Saucius, a, um. Wounded, intoxicated.
Saxum, i, n. Rock, stone.
Scando, ĕre, di, sum. To climb.
Scelestus (scelus), *a, um.* Wicked.
Scelus, ĕris, n. Crime, wickedness.
Scio, scīre, scivi, scitum. To know
Scriba (scribo), *ae,* m. Scribe clerk.
Scribo, ĕre, psi, ptum. To write, prepare.
Scutum, i, n. Shield.
Secēdo, ĕre, cessi, cessum. To retire, withdraw.
Secundus, a, um. Second, favorable.
Sed. But.
Sedĕcim, indecl. Sixteen.

Sedeo, ĕre, sedi, sessum. To sit, stay.
Sedes, is, f. Seat, abode, residence.
Seditio, ōnis, f. Quarrel, sedition.
Siditiōsus (seditio), *a, um.* Mutinous, seditious.
Sedo, āre, āvi, ātum. To allay, quiet.
Segnis, e. Slothful, inactive.
Segnĭter, adv. Slothfully.
Semel, adv. Once.
Semianĭmis, e. Half-dead.
Semper, adv. Always, ever.
Senātor (senex), *ōris,* m. Senator.
Senātus (senex), *us,* m. Senate.
Senex, senis, m. and f., comp. *senior.* An old man, an aged person.
Sententia, ae, f. Opinion, sentence.
Sentio, ĭre, si, sum. To perceive, think, judge.
Sepelio, ĭre, pelīvi or *ii, pultum.* To bury.
Sepio, ĭre, psi, ptum. To guard, shelter.
Septem, indecl. Seven.
Septĭmus, a, um. Seventh.
Septingentesĭmus, a, um. The seven hundredth.
Septingenti, ae, a. Seven hundred.
Septuagesĭmus, a, um. Seventieth.
Septuaginta, indecl. Seventy.
Sepultūra, ae, f. Burial.
Sequor, qui, cūtus sum. To follow, succeed.
Serpo, ĕre, psi, ptum. To spread, extend.
Servĭtus, ūtis, f. Servitude.
Servo, āre, āvi, ātum. To observe, keep; preserve.
Servus, i, m. Slave.
Seu. Whether; *seu—seu,* whether —or.
Severĭtas (sevērus), *ātis,* f. Severity.
Sevērus, a, um. Severe, strict.
Sex, indecl. Six.
Sexagesĭmus, a, um. Sixtieth.
Sexaginta, indecl. Sixty.
Sexcentesĭmus, a, um. Six hundredth.
Sexcenti, ae, a. Six hundred.
Sextus, a, um. Sixth.
Si, conj. If.
Sic, adv. Thus, so.
Siccus, a, um. Dry.
Sicut or *sicŭti.* Just as, so as, as if.
Sido, ĕre, sidi or *sedi.* To sit, to settle down.
Signifĭco, āre, āvi, ātum. To show, indicate, mean.
Signum, i, n. Mark, standard.
Simĭlis, e. Similar, like.
Simul, adv. At the same time.
Simŭlo, āre, āvi, ātum. To counterfeit, feign.
Sine, prep. with abl. Without.
Singulāris, e. Single, singular.
Singŭlus, a, um. Single, one by one.
Sinister, tra, trum. Left, on the left.
Sino, ĕre, sivi, situm. To permit; *situs,* put, placed.
Sinus, us, m. Bosom, bay.
Siquĭdem. If indeed, inasmuch as.
Socer, ĕri, m. Father-in-law.
Sociālis (socius), *e.* Social, friendly.
Sociĕtas (socius), *ātis,* f. League, alliance.
Socius, i, m. Ally, confederate.
Sol, solis, m. Sun.
Solemnĭter, adv. Solemnly, in due form.
Soleo, ēre, ĭtus sum. To be accustomed.
Solertia, ae, f. Sagacity, shrewdness.
Solĭdus, a, um. Solid.
Solitūdo (solus), *ĭnis,* f. Solitude.
Solĭtus (soleo), *a, um.* Usual.
Solum, adv. Only, alone.
Solus, a, um. (See F. B. 113, R.) Alone.
Solūtus (solvo), *a, um.* Unrestrained, dissolute.
Solvo, ĕre, vi, ūtum. To loose, unbind.
Somnus, i, m. Sleep.
Sonus, i, m. Sound.
Sordĭdus, a, um. Sordid, filthy.

Soror, ōris, f. Sister.
Sors, sortis, f. Lot.
Spargo, ĕre, si, sum. To scatter, let fall loose.
Spatium, i, n. Space.
Species, ēi, f. Appearance, guise.
Spectacŭlum, i, n. Spectacle, show.
Specto, āre, āvi, ātum. To view, witness.
Spes, ei, f. Hope.
Spolio (spolium), *āre, āvi, ātum.* To rob; spoil; despoil.
Spolium, i, n. Plunder, spoil, booty.
Statim, adv. At once, immediately.
Statua, ae, f. Statue.
Statuo, ĕre, ui, ūtum. To determine; appoint, place.
Status, us, m. State, condition.
Sterno, ĕre, stravi, stratum. To prostrate.
Sto, sare, steti, statum. To stand.
Strages, is, f. Slaughter, defeat.
Strangŭlo, āre, āvi, ātum. To strangle.
Strenue (strenuus), adv. Vigorously, carefully.
Strenuus, a, um. Active, valiant.
Studeo, ĕre, ui. To study, favor.
Studiōse, adv. Diligently, earnestly.
Studium, i, n. Zeal, study.
Suadeo, ēre, si, sum. To advise.
Sub, prep. with acc. or abl. Under, at the foot of.
Subdŏlus, a, um. Crafty, deceitful.
Subdūco (sub, duco), *ĕre, duxi, ductum.* To take away, withdraw.
Subĭgo (sub, ago), *ĕre, ēgi, actum.* To subdue.
Subĭto, adv. Suddenly.
Sublīmis, e. High, on high.
Suborno, āre, āvi, ātum. To bribe, suborn.
Subsidium, i, n. Aid, reinforcement.
Subsum (sub, sum), *esse, fui.* To be at hand or near; be under.
Subtrăho (sub, traho), *ĕre, axi, actum.* To take away, remove.

Subvenio (sub, venio), *īre, vēni, ventum.* To come to; to aid, relieve.
Suburbānus, a, um. Suburban; *suburbānum* (subs.), an estate near a city.
Succēdo (sub, cedo), *ĕre, essi, essum.* To succeed, come after.
Successio, ōnis, f. Succession.
Successor (succēdo), *ōris,* m. Successor.
Successus, us, m. Success.
Succumbo, ĕre, cubui, cubĭtum. To yield, submit to.
Sufficio (sub, facio), *ĕre, fēci, fectum.* To substitute; be sufficient, suffice.
Sui, sibi, &c. Himself, herself, itself, &c.
Sum, esse, fui, futūrus. To be.
Summa (summus), *ae,* f. Supreme power.
Summoveo (sub, moveo), *ĕre, mōvi, mōtum.* To remove, displace.
Summus. (See *Supĕrus.*)
Sumo, ĕre, mpsi, mptum. To take, inflict.
Sumptus, us, m. Expense, cost.
Super, prep. with acc. or abl. Over, above, upon; of, concerning.
Superbia, ae, f. Pride, haughtiness.
Superbus, a, um. Proud.
Supĕro (supĕrus), *āre, āvi, ātum.* To surpass; conquer; pass by.
Supersum (super, sum), *esse, fui.* To remain, be left, survive.
Supervenio (super, venio), *īre, vēni, ventum.* To come to, surprise.
Supĕrus, a, um; comp. *superior;* superl. *suprēmus* or *summus.* High, above; past, former.
Supplementum, i, n. Supplies, reinforcement.
Supplicium, i, n. Punishment.
Supra, prep. with acc. Above, upon.
Suscipio, ĕre, cēpi, ceptum. To bear, endure; receive; undertake.

Suspectus, a, um. Suspected.
Suspendo, ĕre, di, sum. To suspend, hang up.
Suspensus (suspendo), *a, um.* Uncertain, undecided; anxious.
Suspicio, ōnis, f. Suspicion.
Suspicio, ĕre, exi, ectum. To suspect.
Suspĭcor, āri, ātus sum. To suspect.
Sustineo, ēre, ui, tentum. To sustain, withstand; endure, endure the thought of.
Suus, a, um. His, her, its, their, &c.; *pl. often,* one's party, friends.

T.

T. An abbreviation of *Titus.*
Tabernacŭlum, i, n. Tent.
Tabŭla, ae, f. Tablet, table.
Tactus, us, m. Touch.
Taedet, impers. It disgusts, wearies.
Talentum, i, n. Talent, sum of money.
Talis, e. Such.
Tam. So.
Tamdiu. So long.
Tamen, conj. Yet, nevertheless.
Tandem, adv. At length.
Tanquam, adv. As, just as
Tantum. Only.
Tantus, a, um. Such, so great; *tanti esse,* to be worth the while.
Tectum (tego), *i,* n. House.
Tego, ĕre, texi, tectum. To cover.
Telum, i, n. Weapon.
Temĕre, adv. Rashly.
Tempestas (tempus), *ātis,* f. Time; tempest, storm.
Tempestīve, adv. Seasonably, just at the time, opportunely.
Templum, i, n. Temple.
Tempus, ŏris, n. Time.
Teneo, ēre, ui, tentum. To hold, keep, occupy.
Tento, āre, āvi, ātum. To try; attack.

Tergemĭnus, a, um. Threefold *tergemĭni,* three brothers born at a birth.
Tergum, i, n. Back.
Termĭno (termĭnus), *āre, āvi, ātum.* To limit, bound.
Termĭnus, i, m. Limit, boundary end.
Terra, ae, f. Earth, land.
Terreo, ēre, ui, ĭtum. To terrify.
Terrester (terra), *tris, tre.* Terrestrial, on land, land (*as adj.*).
Territorium, i, n. Territory.
Terror (terreo), *ōris,* m. Terror, alarm; fear of.
Tertius, a, um. Third.
Testamentum, i, n. Testament, will.
Testis, is, m. and f. Witness.
Testor (testis), *āri, ātus sum.* To affirm; call to witness.
Theātrum, i, n. Theatre.
Thorax, ācis, m. Breastplate.
Tibīcen, ĭnis, m. Fluter, piper.
Timeo, ēre, ui. To fear.
Timor, ōris, m. Fear.
Tollo, ĕre, sustŭli, sublātum. To raise, elate; take away; destroy; discard.
Tonĭtru, us, n. Thunder.
Tono, āre, ui. To thunder; *impers.* it thunders.
Torquis, is, m. and f. Collar.
Tot, indecl. So many.
Totidem, indecl. Just as many, the same number.
Totus, a, um. (See F. B. 113, R.). All, the whole, *sometimes best rendered by adv.* wholly, entirely.
Tracto, āre, āvi, ātum. To use, treat, manage.
Trado, ĕre, dĭdi, dĭtum. To deliver, give, consign to; *also* to relate, say; *traditur* (when impers.), it is said.
Traho, ĕre, xi, ctum. To draw; protract; derive.
Trajicio (trans, jacio), *ĕre, jēci, jectum.* To throw over; to cross conduct over.

Trano, āre, āvi, ātum. To swim over.

Trans, prep. with acc. Across, beyond.

Transeo (trans, eo), *ĭre, ĭvi* or *ii, ĭtum.* To go over.

Transfĕro (trans, fero), *ferre, tŭli, lātum.* To transport, transfer.

Transfīgo, ĕre, fīxi, fīxum. To transfix.

Transfŭga, ae, m. Deserter, fugitive.

Transgredior, i, gressus sum. To go or pass over.

Transĭgo (trans, ago), *ĕre, ēgi, actum.* To accomplish, finish.

Transilio, ĭre, ĭvi, ii, or *ui.* To leap or pass over.

Transĭtus, us, m. Passage.

Transmarīnus, a, um. Transmarine, over the sea.

Transno = trano.

Trecentesĭmus, a, um. The three hundredth.

Trecenti, ae, a. Three hundred.

Tredĕcim, indecl. Thirteen.

Trepĭdus, a, um. Alarmed, in terror.

Tres, tria. Three.

Tribūnus, i, m. Tribune.

Tribuo, ĕre, ui, ūtum To bestow, impute.

Tributarius, a, um. Tributary.

Tribūtum (tribuo), *i,* n. Tax, tribute.

Tricesĭmus, a, um. The thirtieth.

Tricies, adv. Thirty times.

Trigemĭnus = tergemĭnus.

Trigesĭmus = tricesĭmus.

Triginta, indecl. Thirty.

Triplex, ĭcis. Triple, threefold.

Tripudio, āre. To leap, dance.

Tripus, ŏdis, m. Tripod.

Trirēmis, is, f. Galley with three banks of oars.

Tristis, e. Sad.

Triumpho (triumphus), *āre, āvi, ātum.* To triumph, have a triumphal procession.

Triumphus, i, m. Triumph.

Tropaeum, i, n. Trophy, victory

Trucīdo (trux, caedo), *āre, āvi, ātum.* To slay, massacre.

Trux, trucis. Fierce, stern.

Tu, tui, &c. Thou, you.

Tueor, ēri, tuĭtus or *tutus sum.* To look upon; preserve, defend.

Tum. Then; *tum—tum,* not only —but also; both—and.

Tumultuo, āre, āvi, ātum. To make a noise or tumult.

Tumultus, us, m. Tumult, sedition.

Tumŭlus, i, m. Tomb, grave.

Tunc, adv. Then; *tunc tempŏris,* then.

Turba, ae, f. Crowd, throng, multitude.

Turbo (turba), *āre, āvi, ātum.* To disturb, throw into confusion.

Turpĭter, adv. Basely, disgracefully, in disgrace.

Turris, is, f. Tower.

Tutor, ōris, m. Tutor, guardian.

Tutus, a, um. Safe.

Tyrannis, ĭdis, f. Tyranny.

Tyrannus, i, m. Tyrant, monarch.

U.

Uber, ĕris, n. Udder, dug.

Ubertas, ātis, f. Richness, fertility.

Ubi, adv. Where, when, *sometimes interrog.*

Ubīque. Every where.

Ulciscor, ci, ultus sum, dep. To avenge, revenge.

Ullus, a, um. (See F. B. 113, R.) Any, any one.

Ulterior, us; superl. *ultĭmus.* Further, more remote; *superl.* last.

Ultio, ōnis, f. Revenge.

Ultra, adv. and prep. with acc. Beyond, more than.

Ultro, adv. Voluntarily, of one's own accord.

Ulŭlo, āre, āvi, ātum. To howl

Unde, adv. Whence, *also interrog* whence?

Undĕcim, indecl. Eleven.
Undenonagēsimus, a, um. The eighty-ninth.
Undequinquaginta, indecl. Forty-nine.
Undevicesĭmus, a, um. Nineteenth.
Undīque, adv. From all quarters or sides.
Unguentum, i, n. Ointment, perfume.
Unguis, is, m. Nail, claw, talon.
Universus, a, um. Whole, entire; all together.
Unquam, adv. At any time, ever.
Unus, a, um. (See F. B. 113, R.) One, alone.
Unusquisque, unaquaque, &c. (unus, quisque, both parts declined.) Each, each one.
Urbs, urbis, f. City.
Urgeo, ēre, ursi. To urge, drive; press upon.
Usque, adv. So far as; *usque ad,* even to; *usque eo,* to such an extent.
Usurpo, āre, āvi, ātum. To usurp, assume.
Usus, us, m. Use, service; need.
Ut or *uti*, conj. That, as; *after verbs of fearing,* that not.
Utcumque or *utcunque*, adv. However, somewhat.
Uterque, utrāque, utrumque, like *uter.* (See F. B. 113, R.) Both, each.
Utĭlis, e. Useful.
Utilĭtas, ātis, f. Utility, service.
Utor, i, usus sum. To use.
Utrimque or *utrinque*, adv. On both sides.
Utrum, in double questions. Whether.
Uxor, ōris, f. Wife.

V.

Vacuus, a, um. Vacant, empty.
Vadum, i, n. Ford, shallow water.
Vagītus, us, m. Crying.
Vagor, āri, ātus sum. To wander about.
Vagus, a, um. Wandering.
Valeo, ēre, ui, ĭtum. To have strength, avail.
Valĭdus, a, um. Strong, powerful.
Vanus, a, um. Empty, vain, false.
Variĕtas (varius), *ātis, f.* Variety, change.
Varius, a, um. Various.
Vasto (vastus), *āre, āvi, ātum.* To lay waste, devastate.
Vastus, a, um. Waste, desert, vast.
Vates, is, m. and *f.* Prophet, prophetess.
Vaticinium, i, n. Prediction.
Vaticĭnor (vates), *āri, ātus sum.* To prophesy, predict.
Vecors, dis. Mad, insane.
Vehicŭlum (veho), *i, n.* Carriage.
Veho, ĕre, xi, ctum. To carry, bear.
Vel, conj. Or, even; *vel—vel,* either—or.
Velut or velŭti, adv. As, like as, as if.
Vendo, ĕre, dĭdi, dĭtum. To sell; *sub corōna vendĕre,* to sell as slaves.
Venēnum, i, n. Poison.
Venĕror, āri, ātus sum. To venerate, worship.
Venio, īre, veni, ventum. To come.
Venter, tris, m. Belly, stomach.
Verbĕro, āre, āvi, ātum. To whip, scourge, beat.
Verbum, i, n. Word.
Vere (verus), adv. Truly.
Vereor, ēri, ĭtus sum. To fear.
Vero (verus), adv. and conj. Truly indeed; but.
Verso, āre, āvi, ātum, or *versor,* dep. To turn; busy one's self, be occupied with.
Versus, us, m. A verse.
Vertex (verto), *ĭcis, m.* Summit, top.
Verto, ĕre, ti, sum. To turn.
Verum, conj. But.
Verus, a, um. True, real.

Vesānus, a, um. Mad, frantic.
Vescor, ci. To enjoy, feed upon.
Vespĕra, ae, f. Evening.
Vesperasco (vespĕra), *ĕre, rāvi.* To become evening.
Vespillo, ōnis, m. A corpse-bearer.
Vester, tra, trum. Your.
Vestĭbŭlum, i, n. Vestibule, entrance.
Vestio (vestis), *īre, īvi, ītum.* To clothe.
Vestis, is, f. Garment.
Veterānus (vetus), *a, um.* Veteran.
Veto, āre, ui, ītum. To forbid.
Vetus, ĕris. Old, of long standing, ancient.
Vetustas (vetus), *ātis,* f. Antiquity, age.
Vetustus, a, um. Old, ancient.
Via, ae, f. Way.
Vicesĭmus, a, um. Twentieth.
Vicīnus, a, um. Neighboring.
Victor, ōris, m. Conqueror.
Victoria, ae, f. Victory.
Victus (vivo), *us,* m. Food, provisions.
Vicus, i, m. Village.
Video, ēre, di, sum. To see; *pass. videor, &c.,* to be seen; to seem.
Vigeo, ēre, ui. To flourish, thrive.
Viginti, indecl. Twenty.
Villa, ae, f. Country-seat, villa.
Vincio, īre, vinxi, vinctum. To bind.
Vinco, ĕre, vici, victum. To conquer.
Vincŭlum or *vinclum, i,* n. Fetter, chain.
Vindex, īcis, m. and f. Defender.

Vindĭco, āre, āvi, ātum. To claim; rescue, defend; punish, avenge.
Vinolentus (vinum), *a, um.* Full of wine, intoxicated with wine.
Vinum, i, n. Wine.
Viŏlo, āre, āvi, ātum. To violate, do violence to; profane, harm.
Vir, viri, m. Man, hero, husband.
Virga, ae, f. Rod, twig.
Virgo, ĭnis, f. Virgin, maiden.
Virtus (vir), *ūtis,* f. Manliness, bravery, virtue.
Vis, vis, pl. *vires.* Power, strength, force; forces; abundance.
Viscus, ĕris, n. Vitals, bowels.
Viso, ĕre, si, sum. To view, see, visit.
Vita, ae, f. Life.
Vitis, is, f. Vine.
Vitium, i, n. Fault, vice.
Vito, āre, āvi, ātum. To shun, avoid.
Vivo, ĕre, xi, ctum. To live.
Vivus, a, um. Living, alive.
Voco (vox), *āre, āvi, ātum.* To call, name.
Volo, velle, volui, irreg. (See F. B. 410.) To will, be willing.
Voluntarius, a, um. Voluntary.
Voluntas (volo), *ātis,* f. Wish, inclination; good will.
Vox, vocis, f. Voice, word.
Vulgus, i, n. Populace, common people.
Vulnĕro (vulnus), *āre, āvi, ātum.* To wound.
Vulnus, ĕris, n. Wound.
Vultus, us, m. Countenance.

ENGLISH-LATIN VOCABULARY.

A.

Acca. *Acca, ae, f.*
Accept. *Accipio, ĕre, cēpi, ceptum.*
Accompany. *Comĭtor, āri, ātus sum.*
Accuse. *Accūso, āre, āvi, ātum.*
Achaean. *Achaeus, a, um;* subs. *Achaeus, i, m.*
Act, do. *Ago, ĕre, ēgi, actum;* to act, behave, *se gero, ĕre, gessi, gestum.*
Add. *Adjungo, ĕre, junxi, junctum; addo, ĕre, dĭdi, dĭtum.*
Adopt measures, to deliberate. *Consŭlo, ĕre, ui, tum;* to adopt cruel measures, *crudelĭter consulĕre,* &c.
Advice. *Consilium, i, n.*
Advise. *Suadeo, ēre, suasi, suasum.*
Aeneas. *Aenĕas, ae, m.*
Aetolian. *Aetōlus, a, um;* subs. *Aetōlus, i, m.*
Africa. *Afrĭca, ae, f.*
After (*prep.*). *Post,* with acc.
After (*adv.*). *Post; postquam; postea;* a few years after, *paucis post annis.*
Afterwards. *Postea.*
Against. *Contra,* with acc.; also indicated by the *indirect object.*
Agriculture. *Agricultūra, ae, f.*
Agrippina. *Agrippīna, ae, f.*
Aid. *Auxilium, i, n.*
Aid, to bear aid. *Auxilium fero, ferre, tuli, latum.*
Aim at, seek. *Quaero, ĕre, sīvi or ii, ītum.*
Alba. *Alba, ae, f.*

Alban. *Albānus, a, um;* subs. *Albānus, i, m.*
Albanus. *Albānus, i, m.*
Alcibiades. *Alcibiădes, is, m.*
Alexander. *Alexander, dri, m.*
All, every. *Omnis, e.*
All, the whole. *Totus, a, um.* (See F. B. 113, R.)
Already. *Jam.*
Although. *Quamquam, etsi, etiamsi.*
Always. *Semper.*
Ambassador. *Legātus, i, m.*
American. *Americānus, a, um;* subs. *Americānus, i, m.*
Ammon or Hammon. *Ammon* or *Hammon, ōnis, m.*
Amphictyon. *Amphictyon, ŏnis,* m.
Amphipolis. *Amphipŏlis, is, f.*
Amulius. *Amulius, i, m.*
Anchises. *Anchīses, ae, m.*
Ancient. *Antīquus, a, um.*
Ancus. *Ancus, i, m.*
And. *Et, atque, ac, que* (enclitic).
Anger. *Ira, ae, f.*
Announce. *Nuntio, āre, āvi, ātum.*
Antigonus. *Antigŏnus, i, m.*
Antiochus. *Antiŏchus, i, m.*
Antipater. *Antipăter, tri, m.*
Any. *Ullus, a, um* (F. B. 113, R.); any one, *alĭquis, qua, quid.*
Apollo. *Apollo, ĭnis, m.*
Appear, seem. *Videor, ēri, visus sum.*
Appoint. *Creo, āre, āvi, ātum: instituo, ĕre, ui, ūtum.*
Appoint over, commission. *Praepōno, ĕre, posui, posĭtum.*

Approach, arrival. *Adventus, us,* m.
Apulia. *Apulia, ae,* f.
Arbela. *Arbēla, ōrum,* n.
Ardea. *Ardea, ae,* f.
Aridaeus. *Aridaeus, i,* m.
Arise. *Orior, ĭri, ortus sum.*
Arm, furnish with arms. *Armo, āre, āvi, ātum.*
Armed. *Armātus, a, um.*
Armenia. *Armenia, ae,* f.
Arms. *Arma, ōrum,* n. pl.
Army. *Exercĭtus, us,* m.
Around. *Circa, circum* with acc.
Arrival, approach. *Adventus, us,* m.
Arrive, arrive at *or* in. *Advenio, īre, vēni, ventum.*
Artaxerxes. *Artaxerxes, is,* m.
Artemisium. *Artemisium, i,* n.
As. *Ut ; as* is often omitted in rendering into Latin.
As slaves. *Sub corōna ;* to sell as slaves, *sub corōna vendĕre, dĭdi, dĭtum.*
Ascanius. *Ascanius, i,* m.
Asia. *Asia, ae,* f.
Asiaticus. *Asiatĭcus, i,* m. Surname of one of the Scipios.
Ask. *Rogo, āre, āvi, ātum ;* ask, ask for, seek, *peto, ĕre, īvi* or *ii, ītum.*
Assassinator, assassin. *Percussor, ōris,* m.
Assistance. *Auxilium, i,* n.
At. *In* with abl. ; *ad, apud* with acc. ; before names of towns indicated by *gen.* or *abl.* 280.
At a high price. *Magni ;* at a very high price, *maxĭmi ;* at a low price, *parvi.*
At home. *Domi.*
At one time, at a certain time. *Quondam.*
At that time, then. *Illo tempŏre, tunc.*
Athenian. *Atheniensis, e ;* subs. *Atheniensis, is.*
Athens. *Athēnae, ārum,* f. pl.
Atthis. *Atthis, ĭdis,* f.
Attica. *Attĭca, ae,* f.
Auxiliaries. *Auxilia, ōrum,* n. pl.

Await, wait for. *Opperior, īri, perītus* or *oppertus sum.*

B.

Babylon. *Babўlon, ōnis,* f. ; *Babylonia, ae,* f.
Bad, depraved. *Malus, a, um ; pravus, a, um.*
Balbus. *Balbus, i,* m.
Battle. *Pugna, ae,* f. ; *proelium, i,* n.
Battle-array. *Acies, ēi,* f.
Be. *Sum, esse, fui futūrus.*
Be able, can. *Possum, posse, potui.*
Be envious. *Invideo, ēre, vīdi, vīsum.*
Be made. *Fio, fĭĕri, factus sum.*
Be occupied. *Distringor, gi, ictus sum.*
Be willing. *Volo, velle, volui.*
Be wise. *Sapio, ĕre, īvi* or *ii ; sapiens esse.*
Beautiful. *Pulcher, chra, chrum ; formōsus, a, um.*
Because. *Quod ; quia.*
Become. *Fio, ĕri, factus sum.*
Become unmanageable. *Effĕror, āri, ātus sum.*
Before (*adv.*). *Antĕquam, priusquam.*
Believe. *Credo, ĕre, dĭdi, dĭtum.*
Belong, be to. *Sum, esse, fui, futūrus.*
Benefit. *Beneficium, i,* n.
Bequeathe. *Lego, āre, āvi, ātum.*
Beseech. *Precor, āri, ātus sum.*
Besiege. *Oppugno, āre, āvi, ātum · obsideo, ēre, sēdi, sessum.*
Best. *Optĭmus, a, um,* superl. of *bonus.*
Between. *Inter* with accus.
Beyond. *Extra,* with acc.
Bind. *Vincio, īre, nxi, nctum.*
Bird. *Avis, is,* f.
Bite. *Mordeo, ēre, momordi, morsum.*
Book. *Liber, bri,* m.
Booty. *Praeda, ae,* f.
Boston. *Bostonia, ae,* f.

Both—and. *Et—et; quum—tum.*
Boy. *Puer, ĕri,* m.
Brave. *Fortis, e.*
Bravely. *Fortĭter.*
Bravery, boldness. *Virtus, ūtis,* f.; *fortitūdo, ĭnis,* f.
Break, break down. *Rumpo, ĕre, rupi, ruptum.*
Brennus. *Brennus, i,* m.
Bridge. *Pons, tis,* m.
Brother. *Frater, tris,* m.
Brutus. *Brutus, i,* m.
Build. *Aedifĭco, āre, āvi, ātum.*
Burning, a fire, a conflagration. *Incendium, i,* n.
But. *Sed, at, autem.*
By. *A, ab, abs* with abl. (before voluntary agent); in other cases, indicated by *abl. alone.*

C.

Cadmea. *Cadmēa, ae,* f.
Caecilius. *Caecilius, i,* m.
Caesar. *Caesar, ăris,* m.
Caius. *Caius, i,* m.
Caligula. *Caligŭla, ae,* m.
Call, name. *Appello, āre, āvi, ātum; voco, āre, āvi, ātum.*
Camillus. *Camillus, i,* m.
Capital. *Caput, ĭtis,* n.
Capitol. *Capitolium, i,* n.
Captive. *Captīvus, a, um;* subs. *captīvus, i,* m.
Capua. *Capua, ae,* f.
Carthage. *Carthāgo, ĭnis,* f.
Carthaginian. *Carthaginiensis, e* subs. *Carthaginiensis, is.*
Cassander. *Cassander, dri,* m.
Castle. *Castellum, i,* n.
Cat. *Feles* or *felis, is,* f.
Catiline. *Catilīna, ae,* m.
Cause, to effect, make. *Efficio, ĕre, fēci, effectum.*
Cavalry. *Equĭtes, um,* m. pl.; *equitātus, us,* m.
Cecrops. *Cecrops, ŏpis,* m.
Censure (verb). *Vitupĕro, āre, āvi, ātum.*

Census. *Census, us,* m.
Certain. *Certus, a, um.*
Certain one, some one. *Quidam, quaedam, quoddam.*
Chaeronea. *Chaeronēa, ae,* f.
Chain, fetter. *Compes, ĕdis,* f.; *vincŭlum, i,* n.
Challenge (subs.). *Provocatio, ōnis,* f.
Challenge (verb). *Provŏco, āre, āvi, ātum.*
Change. *Muto, āre, āvi, ātum.*
Character, nature. *Ingenium, i,* n.
Chariot. *Currus, us,* m.
Charles. *Carŏlus, i,* m.
Check, put down. *Compesco, ĕre, ui.*
Choose. *Lego, ĕre, legi, lectum; delĭgo, ĕre, lēgi, lectum.*
Christian. *Christiānus, i,* m.
Cineas. *Cineas, ae,* m.
Citadel. *Arx, arcis,* f.
Citizen. *Civis, is,* m. and f.
City. *Urbs, urbis,* f.
Civil. *Civīlis, e.*
Claim. *Vindĭco, āre, āvi, ātum.*
Cloud. *Nubes, is,* f.
Cnaeus or Cneus. *Cnaeus* or *Cneus, i,* m.
Cocles. *Cocles, ĭtis,* m.
Cold, frost. *Frigus, ŏris,* n.; *gelu, us,* n.
Collatinus. *Collatīnus, i,* m.
Come. *Venio, īre, veni, ventum.*
Command (verb). *Impĕro, āre, āvi, ātum.*
Commander, leader. *Imperātor, ōris,* m.; *dux, ducis,* m.
Commence, enter upon. *Incipio, ĕre, cēpi, ceptum; inchŏo, āre, āvi, ātum.*
Compel. *Compello, ĕre, pŭli, pulsum.*
Conceal. *Occulto, āre, āvi, ātum.*
Conclude, finish, make. *Facio, ĕre, feci, factum;* to conclude peace, *pacem facĕre.*
Condemn. *Damno, āre, āvi, ātum;* to condemn to death, *capĭtis damnāre.*
Condition, terms. *Condĭtio, ōnis,* f.

Confer upon, commit to. *Tribuo, ĕre, ui, ūtum.*
Conon. *Conon, ōnis,* m.
Conquer. *Vinco, ĕre, vici, victum.*
Consul. *Consul, ŭlis,* m.
Consult. *Consŭlo, ĕre, ui, tum.*
Content, contented. *Contentus, a, um.*
Continual, incessant. *Assiduus, a, um.*
Contrary to, on the contrary. *Contra,* adv. and prep. with *acc.*
Corinth. *Corinthus, i,* f.
Corinthian. *Corinthius, a, um;* subs. *Corinthius, i,* m.
Coriolanus. *Coriolănus, i,* m.
Cornelius. *Cornelius, i,* m.
Country, region, territory. *Regio, ōnis,* f.; *fines, ium,* m.; native country, one's country, *patria, ae,* f.; country (as opposed to city), *rus, ruris,* n.
Cranaus. *Cranaus, i,* m.
Crassus. *Crassus, i,* m.
Cremona. *Cremōna, ae,* f.
Crime. *Crimen, ĭnis,* n.
Cursor. *Cursor, ōris,* m.
Cut off, hinder. *Interclūdo, ĕre, si, sum.*
Cyrus. *Cyrus, i,* m.

D.

Dagger. *Pugio, ōnis,* m.
Danger. *Pericŭlum, i,* n.
Danube. *Danubius* (the upper part), *i,* m.; *Ister* (the lower part), *tri,* m.
Darius. *Darīus, i,* m.
Datis. *Datis, is,* m.
Daughter. *Filia, ae,* f. (Dat. pl. *filiabus.*)
Day. *Dies, ēi,* m. and f.
Death. *Mors, mortis,* f.
Deceive. *Decipio, ĕre, cēpi, ceptum.*
Decemvir. *Decemvir, ĭri,* m.
Declare. *Indīco, ĕre, dixi, dictum;* to declare war, *bellum indicĕre.*
Defeat. *Vinco, ĕre, vici, victum.*

Defend. *Defendo, ĕre, di, sum.*
Defraud. *Fraudo, āre, āvi, ātum.*
Delight in, rejoice. *Gaudeo, ĕre, gavīsus sum.*
Deliver. *Trado, ĕre, dĭdi, dĭtum.*
Delphi. *Delphi, ōrum,* m.
Demetrius. *Demetrius, i,* m.
Depart. *Proficiscor, cī, profectus sum; abeo, ĭre, īvi* or *ii, ĭtum.*
Depraved. *Pravus, a, um.*
Deprive. *Privo, āre, āvi, ātum.*
Descendants, posterity. *Postĕri, ōrum,* m. pl.
Design, s. *Consilium, i,* n.
Design, designate. *Designo, āre, āvi, ātum.*
Desirous; desirous of. *Cupĭdus, a, um.*
Desist. *Discēdo, ĕre, cessi, cessum.*
Despair. *Desperatio, ōnis,* f.
Destroy. *Everto, ĕre, ti, sum; diruo, ĕre, ui, ŭtum; deleo, ēre, ēvi, ētum.*
Destruction. *Pernicies, ēi,* f.
Determine. *Statuo, ĕre, ui, ūtum.*
Dictator. *Dictātor, ōris,* m.
Die. *Morior, ĭri* or *i, mortuus sum.*
Difficult. *Difficĭlis, e.*
Direct, order. *Jubeo, ēre, jussi, jussum.*
Discharge. *Fungor, gi, functus sum.*
Discourse. *Sermo, ōnis,* m.
Disregard, despise. *Contemno, ĕre, psi, ptum.*
Distinguished. *Praestans, tis.*
Divine. *Divīnus, a, um.*
Do, make. *Facio, ĕre, feci, factum.*
Do wrong. *Pecco, āre, āvi, ātum.*
Dog. *Canis, is,* c.
Dove. *Columba, ae,* f.
Drive. *Pello, ĕre, pepŭli, pulsum*
During. *Inter* with acc.
Dutiful. *Pius, a, um.*
Duty. *Officium, i,* n.
Dwell. *Habĭto, āre, āvi, ātum.*

E.

Early, ancient. *Antīquus, a, um.*
Earth. *Terra, ae, f.*
Educate, bring up. *Edŭco, āre, āvi, ātum.*
Egypt. *Aegyptus, i, f.*
Egyptian. *Aegyptius, a, um;* subs. *Aegyptius, i, m.*
Eight. *Octo, indecl.*
Either. *Aut;* either—or, *aut—aut; vel—vel.* 475.
Elder. *Major, us,* comp. of *magnus; major natu.*
Elect, choose. *Creo, āre, āvi, ātum; lego, ĕre, legi, lectum; elĭgo, ĕre, lēgi, lectum.*
Elephant. *Elephantus, i, m.; elĕphas, antis, m.*
Embassy. *Legatio, ōnis, f.*
Eminent. *Insignis, e; praestans, tis.*
Empire. *Imperium, i, n.*
End. *Finis, is, m. and f.*
Enemy. *Hostis, is, m. and f.;* personal enemy or foe, *inimīcus, i, m.*
Engage battle, engage. *Confligo, ĕre, flixi, flictum.*
Engagement. *Proelium, i, n.; pugna, ae, f.*
Enjoy. *Fruor, frui, fructus sum.*
Enlarge. *Amplio, āre, āvi, ātum.*
Enter. *Introeo, īre, īvi* or *ii, ītum.*
Envy, be envious. *Invideo, ēre, vīdi, vīsum.*
Epaminondas. *Epaminondas, ae, m.*
Equity. *Aequĭtas, ātis, f.*
Escape. *Effugio, ĕre, fūgi.*
Even, equal. *Par, paris.*
Ever, at any time. *Unquam;* ever, always, *semper.*
Exchange (*subs.*). *Permutatio, ōnis, f.*
Excite, arouse, sharpen. *Acuo, ĕre, ui, ūtum.*
Exile, person banished. *Exsul, ŭlis, m.*
Exile, banishment. *Exsilium, i, n.*
Expense. *Sumptus, us, m.*
Eye. *Ocŭlus, i, m.*

F.

Fabius. *Fabius, i, m.;* pl. *Fabii.*
Fabricius. *Fabricius, i, m.*
Falerii. *Falerii, ōrum, m.*
Fall in battle, fall. *Cado, ĕre, cecĭdi, casum.*
Falsehood. *Mendacium, i, n.*
Family, descent. *Genus, ĕris, n.;* family, members of a family, *familia, ae, f.*
Famous. *Clarus, a, um; nobĭlis, e.*
Father. *Pater, tris, m.*
Father-in-law. *Socer, socĕri, m.*
Faustulus. *Faustŭlus, i, m.*
Favor (*verb*). *Faveo, ēre, favi, fautum.*
Fear (*trans. v.*). *Metuo, ĕre, ui, ūtum.*
Feast. *Convivium, i, n.; coena, ae, f.*
Festival. *Festum, i, n.*
Few. *Pauci, ae, a.*
Field. *Ager, agri, m.*
Fifteen. *Quindĕcim, indecl.*
Fifth. *Quintus, a, um.*
Fifty. *Quinquaginta, indecl.*
Fight. *Pugno, āre, āvi, ātum; committo, ĕre, mīsi, missum.*
Fill. *Compleo, ēre, ēvi, ētum.*
Finally. *Postrēmo;* ad postrēmum; *denĭque.*
Finish. *Finio, īre, īvi, ītum.*
First. *Primus, a, um.*
Fish. *Piscis, is, m.*
Five. *Quinque, indecl.*
Flatterer. *Adulātor, ōris, m.*
Flee. *Fugio, ĕre, fugi, fugĭtum;* to flee for refuge, *confugio, ĕre, fūgi, fugĭtum.*
Fleet. *Classis, is, f.; naves, ium, f. pl.*
For (*conj.*). *Enim, nam, namque.*
For (*prep.*). *Pro* with abl.; *also indicated by the dative.*
For a year, lasting a year. *Annuus, a, um.*
For ever. *Perpetuo.*

Force, force of arms. *Vis, vis,* f.; pl. *vires; arma, ōrum,* n. pl.
Forces. *Copiae, ārum,* f. pl.; *vires, ium,* f. pl.
Forget. *Obliviscor, ci, lītus sum.*
Former—latter. *Ille—hic.*
Fortieth. *Quadragesĭmus, a, um.*
Fortification. *Munitio, ōnis,* f.
Fortified. *Munītus, a, um;* very strongly fortified, *munitissĭmus, a, um.*
Fortune. *Fortūna, ae,* f.
Forty. *Quadraginta,* indecl.
Fought. *Commissus, a, um;* in a battle fought at Chaeronea, *in proelio ad Chaeronēam commisso.*
Found, to build. *Condo, ĕre, dĭdi, dĭtum.*
Four. *Quatuor,* indecl.
Four hundred. *Quadringenti, ae, a.*
Fourth. *Quartus, a, um.*
Fraud. *Fraus, dis,* f.
Friend. *Amīcus, i,* m.
Friendly. *Amīcus, a, um.*
Friendship, intimacy. *Familiāritas, ātis,* f.
From. *A, ab, de, e, ex* with abl.; *also indicated by abl. alone;* from, on account of, *propter* with acc.
Frost, cold. *Gelu, us,* n.; *frigus, ŏris,* n.

G.

Galba. *Galba, ae,* m.
Game. *Ludus, i,* m.; *certāmen, ĭnis,* n.
Gaul. *Gallia, ae,* f.
Gaul, a Gaul. *Gallus, i,* m.
General, leader. *Dux, ducis,* m. and f.
German. *Germānus, a, um;* subs. *Germānus, i,* m.
Get or take possession of. *Occŭpo, āre, āvi, ātum.*
Girl. *Puella, ae,* f.
Give. *Do, dăre, dedi, datum;* to give as a present, *dono dare.*

Gladiator. *Gladiātor, ōris,* m.
Gladiatorial. *Gladiatorius, a, um.*
Gladly. Expressed by adj. *laetus, a, um,* in agreement with the subject.
Glory. *Gloria, ae,* f.
Go. *Eo, īre, ivi, itum; contendo, ĕre, di, sum;* go, set out, *profi ciscor, ci, profectus sum.*
God, a god. *Deus, i,* m. (See A. & S. 53.)
Golden, of gold, gold. *Aureus, a, um.*
Good. *Bonus, a, um.*
Government, royal authority. *Regnum, i,* n.
Grand-daughter. *Neptis, is,* f.; *nepos, ōtis,* f.
Grand-father. *Avus, i,* m.
Grand-mother. *Avia, ae,* f.
Grand-son. *Nepos, ōtis,* m.
Grant, assign to. *Tribuo, ĕre, ui, ūtum.*
Great. *Magnus, a, um; ingens, tis.*
Greatness. *Magnitūdo, ĭnis,* f.
Grecian, Greek. *Graecus, a, um;* subs. *Graecus, i,* m.
Greece. *Grecia, ae,* f.

H.

Hamilcar. *Hamilcar, ăris,* m.
Hannibal. *Hannĭbal, ălis,* m.
Happen, come to pass. *Fio, fiĕri, factus sum.*
Happily. *Beāte.*
Happy. *Beātus, a, um.*
Hasdrubal. *Hasdrūbal, ălis,* m.
Hasten, make haste. *Festino, āre, āvi, ātum.*
Have. *Habeo, ĕre, ui, ĭtum.*
He, she, it. *Ille, a, ud; is, ea, id.*
He himself, himself. *Ipse, a, um.*
Here. *Hic.*
Hero. *Heros, ōis,* m.
High, lofty. *Altus, a, um.*
High-minded, magnanimous. *Magnanĭmus, a, um.*

Him, himself, herself, itself (oblique case referring to subject). *Sui, sibi,* &c.
His, her, its, &c. *Suus, a, um,* referring to the subject; *ejus* (gen. of *is*) not referring to subject.
Historian. *Historĭcus, i,* m.
Hither. *Huc.*
Hold. *Teneo, ēre, ui, tum;* obtineo, ēre, ui, tum.
Home. *Domus, us* or *i,* f.; at home, *domi.*
Honor. *Honor, ōris,* m.
Horatius. *Horatius, i,* m.
Horse. *Equus, i,* m.
Hostage. *Obses, ĭdis,* m. and f.
House. *Domus, us* or *i,* f.; *tectum, i,* n.
How. *Quam;* how many, *quam multi; quot.*
How, by what means? *quomŏdo, qui?* How does it happen? *qui fit?*
How, of what sort or nature. *Qualis, e.*
How long? *Quamdiu?*
How old. *Quot annos* with *natus;* How old is he? *Quot annos natus est?*
Hundred. *Centum,* indecl.
Hunger. *Fames, is,* f.

I.

I. *Ego, mei.*
If. *Si.*
Impute, give. *Do, dăre, dedi, datum;* to impute as a crime, *crimĭni dare.*
In. *In* with abl.
In the mean time. *Interim; interea.*
In order that, in order. *Ut, quo.*
In vain. *Frustra.*
Increase. *Augeo, ēre, xi, ctum.*
Individual, separate, one by one. *Singŭli, ae, a.*
Infantry. *Pedĭtes, um,* m.
Inhabitant. *Incŏla, ae,* m. and f.

Inhabitant *or* citizen of Catina. *Catinensis* or *Catiniensis, is,* m. and f.
Inquire. *Interrŏgo, āre, āvi, ātum.*
Insolent. *Insŏlens, tis.*
Institute. *Instituo, ĕre, ui, ūtum.*
Instructed, accomplished in. *Erudītus, a, um.*
Into. *In* with acc.
Invade. *Invādo, ĕre, si, sum.*
Invite. *Invīto, āre, āvi, ātum.*
Island. *Insŭla, ae,* f.
Issus. *Issus, i,* f.
It is better. *Praestat.*
It is characteristic of, duty of, part of, &c. *Est* with genitive. (See 434; also F. B. 187.)
It is ordered, the order is given. *Praescribĭtur.*
It is usual. *Solet.*
It is well known, is an admitted fact. *Constat.*
Italian. *Itălus, a, um;* subs. *Itălus, i,* m.
Italy. *Italia, ae,* f.

J.

Jerusalem. *Hierosolўma, ae,* f., or *ōrum,* n. pl.
John. *Johannes, is,* m.
Journey. *Iter, itinĕris,* n.
Judea. *Judaea, ae,* f.
Jugurtha. *Jugurtha, ae,* m.
Junius. *Junius, i,* m.
Jupiter. *Jupĭter, Jovis,* m.
Just. *Justus, a, um.*

K.

Keep, hold. *Habeo, ēre, ui, ĭtum.*
Kid. *Haedus, i,* m.
Kill. *Interfĭcio, ĕre, fēci, fectum; occīdo, ĕre, cīdi, cīsum.*
Kind. *Benignus, a, um.*
King. *Rex, regis,* m.
Kingdom. *Regnum, i,* n.
Know. *Scio, scīre, scivi, scitum;* not to know, *nescio, īre, īvi* or *ii, ītum.*

L.

L. *L.*, abbreviation of *Lucius; L. Crassus* for *Licinius Crassus.*
Lacedaemonian. *Lacedaemonius, a, um;* subs. *Lacedaemonius, i,* m.
Lamb. *Agnus, i,* m.
Land. *Terra, ae,* f.; *ager, agri,* m.
Large, great. *Magnus, a, um.*
Larissa. *Larissa, ae,* f.
Lasting *Sempiternus, a, um.*
Latinus. *Latīnus, i,* m.
Latter, this. *Hic, haec, hoc;* former—latter, *ille—hic.*
Laugh, laugh at. *Rideo, ēre, risi, risum.*
Laurentia. *Laurentia, ae,* f.
Law. *Lex, legis,* f.; law, right, *jus, juris,* n.; law of nations, *jus gentium.*
Lay siege to, besiege. *Obsideo, ēre, sēdi, sessum.*
Lay waste. *Popŭlor, āri, ātus sum.*
Lead. *Duco, ēre, duxi, ductum;* to lead back, *redūco, ēre, duxi, ductum;* to lead forth, *edūco, ēre, duxi, ductum.*
Leader. *Dux, ducis,* m. and f.
Learn. *Disco, ēre, dĭdĭci.*
Leonidas. *Leonĭdas, ae,* m.
Letter. *Litěrae, ārum,* f. pl.; *epistŏla, ae,* f.; letters, learning, *litěrae, ārum,* f. pl.
Liberate, set free. *Liběro, āre, āvi, ātum.*
Liberty. *Libertas, ātis,* f.
Life. *Vita, ae,* f.
Limit. *Termĭnus, i,* m.; *finis, is,* m. and f.
Literary. *Literarius, a, um.*
Live. *Vivo, ēre, vixi, victum;* to live, dwell, *habĭto, āre, āvi, ātum.*
Livia. *Livia, ae,* f.
Longa (in *Alba Longa*). *Longa, ae,* f.
Lose. *Amitto, ēre, mĭsi, missum;* to lose, waste, destroy, *perdo, ēre, dĭdi, dĭtum.*
Love (*subs.*). *Amor, ōris,* m.
Love (*verb*). *Amo, āre, āvi, ātum.*
Lucius. *Lucius, i,* m.
Lucretia. *Lucretia, ae,* f.
Lucullus. *Lucullus, i,* m.
Lycurgus. *Lycurgus, i,* m.
Lysander. *Lysander, dri,* m.

M.

M. *M.*, abbreviation of *Marcus.*
Macedonia. *Macedonia, ae,* f.
Macedonian. *Macedonĭcus, a, um;* subs. *Macĕdo, ŏnis,* m.
Magi, wise men. *Mugi, ōrum,* m. pl.
Majesty, dignity, rank. *Majestas, ātis,* f.
Make, form. *Facio, ēre, feci, factum;* to make, appoint, *creo, āre, āvi, ātum.*
Make an irruption. *Irrumpo, ēre, rūpi, ruptum.*
Man. *Homo, ĭnis,* m.; man, hero, husband, *vir, viri,* m.
Manlius. *Manlius, i,* m.
Many, much. *Multus, a, um;* many, several, very many, *plures, a.*
March, advance. *Incēdo, ēre, cessi, cessum; proficiscor ci, profectus sum.*
Marcius. *Marcius, i,* m.
Marius. *Marius, i,* m.
Marriage. *Matrimonium, i,* n.
Master. *Magister, tri,* m.; master as owner or proprietor, *domĭnus, i,* m.
Matron. *Matrōna, ae,* f.
Metellus. *Metellus, i,* m.
Minor (in proper names). *Minor, ōris,* m. and f.
Misenum. *Misēnum, i,* n.
Mithridates. *Mithridātes, is,* m.
Mithridatic. *Mithridatĭcus, a, um.*
Mother. *Mater, tris,* f.
Mountain, mount. *Mons, tis,* m.
Mourn, mourn for. *Lugeo, ēre, xi, ctum.*
Move (*trans.*). *Movĕo, ēre, movi, motum.*

Much. *Multus, a, um ;* much good, *multum boni ;* much time, *multum tempŏris.*
Mummius. *Mummius, i,* m.
Murderer. *Interfector, ōris,* m.
Must. Expressed by periphrastic conj. (F. B. 425; A. & S. 162, 15.)
My. *Meus, a, um,* voc. m. sing. *mi.*

N.

Name. *Nomen, ĭnis,* n.
Narrow pass or passage. *Angustiae, ārum,* f. pl.
Nation, race. *Gens, gentis,* f.
Naval. *Navālis, e.*
Near. *Apud, ad* with acc.
Nearly. *Fere.*
Need, there is need. *Opus est.*
Neighboring. *Finitĭmus, a, um.*
Neither. *Neque, nec ;* neither— nor, *neque—neque, nec—nec.*
Neptune. *Neptūnus, i,* m.
Nero. *Nero, ōnis,* m.
Nest. *Nidus, i,* m.
Never. *Nunquam.*
New. *Novus, a, um.*
Night. *Nox, noctis,* f.
No, adj. *Nullus, a, um.* (F. B. 113, R.) No one, nobody, *nemo, ĭnis,* gen. and abl. not in good use.
Noble. *Nobĭlis, e.*
Not. *Non ;* with imper. and subj. *ne ;* not only—but also, *non solum—sed etiam.*
Not to know, be ignorant of. *Nescio, īre, īvi* or *ii, ītum.*
Now. *Nunc.*
Numa. *Numa, ae,* m.
Number. *Numĕrus, i,* m.
Numitor. *Numĭtor, ōris,* m.

O.

Obey. *Obedio, īre, īvi* or *ii, ītum.*
Observe, keep as a law. *Observo, āve, āvi, ātum ; servo, āre, āvi, ātum.*

Obtain. *Obtineo, ēre, ui, tentum.*
Occupied with, busy with. *Districtus ;* to be occupied with, *distringor, gi, districtus sum.*
Occupy. *Occŭpo, āre, āvi, ātum.*
Offer sacrifices (*in honor of the dead*). *Parento, āre, āvi, ātum,*
Often. *Saepe.*
Olympic. *Olympius, a, um ;* Olympic games, *Olympia, ōrum,* n. pl
Old (*in expressions of age*). *Natus, a, um ;* two years old, *duo annos natus.*
On. *In* with abl.
On account of. *Propter* with accus.
Once. *Semel.*
One. *Unus a, um.* (F. B. 113, R.) Certain one, *quidam, auaedam, quoddam,* subs. *quiddam.*
Opening, beginning. *Initium, i,* n.
Opinion. *Sententia, ae,* f.
Opportunity, power. *Potestas, ātis,* f.
Or. *Aut, vel.*
Oracle. *Oracŭlum, i,* n.
Oration. *Oratio, ōnis,* f.
Orator. *Orātor, ōris,* m.
Order, to direct. *Jubeo, ēre, jussi, jussum ;* to order, arrange, institute, *ordĭno, āre, āvi, ātum.*
Order, by order. *Jussu,* used only in abl. sing.
Other. *Alius, a, ud.* (F. B. 113, R.) Some—others, *alii—alii.*
Otherwise. *Alĭter.*
Otho. *Otho, ōnis,* m.
Ostia. *Ostia, ae,* f.
Our. *Noster, tra, trum.*
Over. *Super, supra,* sometimes indicated *by gen.,* as, the bridge over the Ister, *pons Istri.*
Overwhelm. *Obruo, ĕre, ui, ŭtum.*

P.

P. *P.,* abbreviation of *Publius.*
Pain, grief. *Dolor, ōris,* m.
Palace. *Palatium, i,* n.

Palestine. *Palaestīna, ae,* f.
Pannonia. *Pannonia, ae,* f.
Papirius. *Papirius, i,* m.
Pardon. *Ignosco, ĕre, nŏvi, nōtum.*
Parent. *Parens, tis,* m. and f.
Part. *Pars, tis,* f.
Past. *Praeterĭtus, a, um;* the past, *praeterita, ōrum,* n. pl.
Pausanias. *Pausanias, ae,* m.
Peace. *Pax, pacis,* f.
Peacock. *Pavo, ōnis,* m.
Pelopidas. *Pelopĭdas, ae,* m.
Peloponnesian. *Peloponnesiăcus, a, um.*
Penetrate. *Penĕtro, āre, āvi, ātum.*
People. *Popŭlus, i,* m.; common people, plebeians, *plebs, plebis,* f.
Perdiccas. *Perdiccas* or *Perdicca, ae,* m.
Pericles. *Perĭcles, is,* m.
Perish. *Pereo, īre, īvi* or *ii, ĭtum.*
Perseus. *Perseus, i,* m.
Persian. *Persĭcus, a, um;* subs. *Persa* or *Perses, ae,* m.
Persuade. *Persuadeo, ēre, si, sum.*
Pharsalia. *Pharsalia, ae,* f.
Pharsalus. *Pharsălus, i,* f.
Philip. *Philippus, i,* m.
Phyle. *Phyle, es,* f.
Pierce. *Confodio, ĕre, fōdi, fossum.*
Pity (*verb*). *Misereor, ēri, miserĭtus* or *misertus sum.*
Place. *Locus, i,* m. (pl. *i,* m. and *a,* n.)
Plan. *Consilium, i,* n.
Play, sport. *Ludus, i,* m.
Play (*verb*). *Ludo, ere, si, sum.*
Please, be pleasing to. *Placeo, ēre, ui, ĭtum;* to displease, not to be pleasing to, *displiceo, ēre, displicui, displicĭtum.*
Plunder, rob. *Spolio, āre, āvi, ātum.*
Pompey. *Pompeius, i,* m.
Pompilius. *Pompilius, i,* m.
Poniard. *Pugio, ōnis,* m.
Pontius. *Pontius, i,* m.
Pontus. *Pontus, i,* m.
Poor, poor man. *Pauper, ĕris.*

Porsena. *Porsĕna, ae,* m.
Portion, part. *Part, tis,* f.
Possession. *Possessio, ōnis,* f.
Power, reign. *Imperium, i,* n.; unrestricted power, tyranny, *dominatio, ōnis,* f.
Powerful. *Potens, tis;* very powerful, most powerful, *potentissĭmus, a, um.*
Praise (*subs.*). *Laus, dis,* f.
Praise (*v.*). *Laudo, āre, āvi, ātum.*
Prayers. *Preces, um,* f. pl.
Prepare. *Paro, āre, āvi, ātum; praepăro, āre, āvi, ātum.*
Prediction. *Praedictum, i,* n.
Present. *Donum, i,* n.
Priest, priestess. *Sacerdos, ōtis,* m. and f.
Priscus. *Priscus, i,* m.
Prison. *Carcer, ĕris,* m.
Prize. *Aestĭmo, āre, āvi, ātum;* prize highly, *magni aestimāre.*
Proconsul. *Proconsul, ŭlis,* m.
Promise. *Promitto, ĕre, mīsi, missum;* to promise, offer, *polliceor, ēri, ĭtus sum.*
Provided, provided that. *Dum mŏdo.*
Providence. *Providentia, ae,* f.
Prudence. *Prudentia, ae,* f.
Prudent. *Prudens, tis.*
Ptolemy. *Ptolemaeus, i,* m.
Publicola. *Publicŏla, ae,* m.
Pupil. *Discipŭlus, i,* m.
Put, place. *Pono, ĕre, posui, posĭtum.*
Put an end to. *Finio, īre, īvi, ĭtum.*
Put to or upon. *Impōno, ĕre, posui, posĭtum.*
Put to death, kill. *Occīdo, ĕre, cīdi, cīsum.*
Pyrrhus. *Pyrrhus, i,* m.

Q.

Q. Q., abbreviation of *Quintus.*
Queen. *Regīna, ae,* f.
Question. *Quaestio, ōnis,* f.

Quickly. *Celerĭter.*
Quintus. *Quintus, i,* m.

R.

Ransom. *Redĭmo, ĕre, ēmi, emptum.*
Reach, arrive at. *Pervenio, īre, vēni, ventum.*
Read. *Lego, ĕre, legi, lectum.*
Rebellious, rebelling. *Rebellans, antis.*
Receive. *Accipio, ĕre, cēpi, ceptum; recipio, ĕre, cēpi, ceptum.*
Recover. *Recipio, ĕre, cēpi, ceptum.*
Regal, royal. *Regius, a, um.*
Regulus. *Regŭlus, i,* m.
Reign (*subs.*). *Regnum, i,* n.; *imperium, i,* n.
Reign (*v.*). *Regno, āre, āvi, ātum.*
Reject. *Imprŏbo, āre, āvi, ātum;* reject, divorce, *repudio, āre, āvi, ātum.*
Relying upon, trusting to. *Fretus, a, um;* to rely upon, *fretus esse.*
Remain. *Maneo, ēre, si, sum;* remaneo, *ēre,* &c.
Remember. *Rĕminiscor, ci.*
Remnant, part left. *Reliquiae, ārum,* f. pl.
Remus. *Remus, i,* m.
Render. *Reddo, ĕre, dĭdi, dĭtum.*
Render thanks, to thank. *Gratias agĕre, egi, actum.*
Report, rumor. *Fama, ae,* f.; *rumor, ōris,* m.
Report, communicate. *Nuntio, āre, āvi, ātum.*
Represent. *Repraesento, āre, āvi, ātum.*
Republic. *Respublĭca, reipublĭcae.* (See A. & S. 91.)
Reside, dwell. *Habĭto, āre, āvi, ātum.*
Response, answer. *Responsum, i,* n.
Restore. *Restituo, ĕre, ui, ūtum; reddo, ĕre, dĭdi, dĭtum.*
Return, come back. *Reverto, ĕre, ti, sum; redeo, īre, īvi or ii, ĭtum.*

Reward. *Praemium, i,* n.
Right (*subs.*). *Jus, juris,* n. rights, *jura.*
Right, rightly. *Recte.*
Ring. *Annŭlus, i,* m.
Rise, rise in importance, come into notice. *Emĕrgo, ĕre, si, sum.*
River. *Flumen, ĭnis,* n.; *fluvius, i,* m
Rock, piece of rock, stone. *Saxum, i,* n.
Roman. *Romānus, a, um;* subs. *Romānus, i,* m.
Rome. *Roma, ae,* f.
Romulus. *Romŭlus, i,* m.
Rout. *Fundo, ĕre, fudi, fusum.*
Royal. *Regius, a, um.*
Ruler. *Rector, ōris,* m.
Rullianus. *Rulliānus, i,* m.
Rush, rush together to or into. *Concurro, ĕre, curri, cursum.*

S.

Sacrifice, offer sacrifices (*in honor of the dead*). *Parento, āre, āvi, ātum.*
Salamis. *Salămis, is* or *ĭnis,* f.; *Salamīna, ae,* f.
Samnites. *Samnītes, ium,* m. pl.
Sardinia. *Sardinia, ae,* f.
Saturn. *Saturnus, i,* m.
Saturnia. *Saturnia, ae,* f.
Say. *Dico, ĕre, dixi, dictum.*
Scaevola. *Scaevŏla, ae,* m.
Scipio. *Scipio, ōnis,* m.
School. *Ludus, i,* m.
Scythian. *Scythes* (or *a*), *ae,* m.
Sea. *Mare, is,* abl. *e* or *i,* n.; by sea and land, *terra marique.*
Secretary. *Scriba, ae,* m.
Second. *Secundus, a, um;* sometimes *alter, a, um.* (F. B. 113, R.)
Secure, obtain. *Consĕquor, qui, cūtus sum.*
See. *Video, ēre, vidi, visum;* to see, witness, *specto, āre, āvi, ātum.*
Seek. *Peto, ĕre, īvi or ii, ĭtum.*
Self-control. *Moderatio, ōnis,* f.

Sell. *Vendo, ěre, dǐdi, dǐtum;* to sell as slaves, *sub corōna venděre.*
Senate. *Senātus, us,* m.
Senator. *Senātor, ōris,* m.
Send. *Mitto, ěre, misi, missum;* to send to take one's place, *in locum mittěre.*
Serve as soldier, serve in the field or in war, serve. *Milǐto, āre, āvi, ātum.*
Service, use. *Usus, us,* m.
Servitude. *Servǐtus, ūtis,* f.
Servius. *Servius, i,* m.
Set fire to, set on fire. *Incendo, ěre, di, sum.*
Seven. *Septem,* indecl.
Seven hundred. *Septingenti, ae, a.*
Seventh. *Septǐmus, a, um.*
Seventy. *Septuaginta,* indecl.
Severe. *Acer, acris, acre.*
Sewer, drain. *Cloāca, ae,* f.
Shepherd. *Pastor, ōris,* m.
Shield. *Clypeus* or *clipeus, i,* m.
Ship. *Navis, is,* f.
Short. *Brevis, e;* shortly, a short time, *brevi;* a short time after, *brevi postea.*
Show, exhibit. *Ostendo, ěre, di, sum; praesto, āre, stǐti, stǐtum* or *stātum; monstro, āre, āvi, ātum.*
Shun. *Vito, āre, āvi, ātum.*
Sicily. *Sicilia, ae,* f.
Silver. *Argentum, i,* n.
Silvius. *Silvius, i,* n.
Since. *Quum* with subj.
Six. *Sex,* indecl.
Sixth. *Sextus, a, um.*
Slave. *Servus, i,* m.
Slay. *Occǐdo, ěre, cǐdi, cīsum.*
Sleep. *Somnus, i,* m.
Slightly, lightly. *Levǐter.*
Snow. *Nix, nivis,* f.
So. *Tam, sic, adeo;* so—as, just —as; *ut—ita, tam—quam.*
So great, such. *Tantus, a, um.*
Soldier. *Miles, ǐtis,* m. and f.
Son. *Filius, i* (abl. sing. *fili*), m.
Son-in-law. *Gener, ěri,* m.

Sparta. *Sparta, ae,* f.
Spartan. *Spartānus, a, um;* subs. *Spartānus, i,* m.
Spear. *Hasta, ae,* f.
Spirit, courage. *Anǐmus, i,* m.
Sport. *Ludus, i,* m.
Spring. *Ver, veris,* n.
State. *Civǐtas, ātis,* f.
Star. *Stella, ae,* f.
Statue. *Statua, ae,* f.
Stay, remain. *Maneo, ēre, si, sum.*
Storm. *Imber, bris,* m.
Strength. *Vis, vis* (pl. *vires*), f.; *robur, ōris,* n.; *opes, um,* f. pl.
Strike, strike through. *Percutio, ěre, cussi, cussum.*
Study. *Studeo, ēre, ui.*
Subdue. *Subǐgo, ěre, ēgi, actum.*
Subjugate. *Subǐgo, ěre, ēgi, actum;* to subjugate, impose the yoke of servitude, *servitūtis jugum impōno, ěre, imposui, posǐtum.*
Succeed. *Succēdo, ěre, cessi, cessum; sequor, qui, cūtus sum.*
Sue for, seek. *Peto, ěre, ǐvi* or *ii, ǐtum.*
Sufficiently. *Satis.*
Summon. *Arcesso, ěre, ǐvi* or *ii, ǐtum.*
Superbus (surname of one of the Tarquins.) *Superbus, i,* m.
Superior. *Superior, us;* superior, greater, *major, us.*
Supper. *Coena, ae,* f.
Supplies, provisions. *Commeātus, us,* m.
Surpass. *Supěro, āre, āvi, ātum.*
Surrender, give up. *Dedo, ěre, dǐdi, dǐtum.*
Surround. *Circumdo, āre, dědi, dātum; cingo, ěre, cinxi, cinctum.*
Syracusan. *Syracusānus, a, um;* subs. *Syracusānus, i,* m.
Syracuse. *Syracūsae, ārum,* f. pl.
Sword. *Gladius, i,* m.

T.

T   T., abbreviation for *Titus;* T. Nero for *Tiberius Nero.*
Take. *Capio, ĕre, cepi, captum.*
Take, take possession of. *Occŭpo, āre, āvi, ātum.*
Tarquinius. *Tarquinius, i,* m.
Teach. *Doceo, ēre, ui, tum.*
Tell. *Dico, ĕre, dixi, dictum.*
Temple. *Templum, i,* n.
Ten. *Decem,* indecl.
Tenth. *Decĭmus, a, um.*
Terms, condition. *Conditio, ōnis,* f.
Terrify. *Terreo, ēre, ui, ĭtum ;* to terrify greatly, *perterreo, ēre, ui, ĭtum.*
Terror. *Terror, ōris,* m.
Than. *Quam.*
Thanks. *Gratiae, ārum,* f. pl. ; to give *or* render thanks, *gratias agĕre, egi, actum.*
Thanksgiving. *Supplicatio, ōnis,* f.
That. *Ille, a, ud;* (followed by a relative clause explaining it) *is, ea, id.*
That (*conj.*). *Ut ;* with comparatives *quo.*
That not. *Ne, quomĭnus, quin.*
Theban. *Thebānus, a, um ;* subs. *Thebānus, i,* m.
Thebes. *Thebae, ārum,* f. pl.
Theft. *Furtum, i,* n.
Their (*referring to the subject*). *Suus, a, um ;* their (*not referring to the subject*), *expressed by genitive of the demonstratives, as illōrum, eōrum,* &c.
Themistocles. *Themistŏcles, is,* m.
Then. *Tunc, illo tempŏre.*
There. *Ibi, illic.*
Therefore. *Ergo, igĭtur.*
Thermopylae. *Thermopўlae, ārum,* f. pl.
Thessalian. *Thessălus, a, um ;* subs. *Thessălus, i,* m.
Thessalus. *Thessălus, i,* m.
Thessaly. *Thessalia, ae,* f.
Thing. *Res, rĕi,* f.

Think. *Puto, āre, āvi, ātum ;* to think earnestly about, weigh in mind, *agĭto, āre, āvi, ātum.*
Third. *Tertius, a, um.*
Thirst. *Sitis, is,* f.
Thirtieth. *Tricesĭmus, a, um.*
Thirty. *Triginta,* indecl.
This. *Hic, haec, hoc.*
Thither. *Eo, illo, illuc.*
Thou, you. *Tu, tui,* &c.
Though, although. *Etiamsi, etsi, quamquam.*
Thousand. *Mille ;* a thousand men, *mille,* oftener *millia.*
Thrasybulus. *Thrasybŭlus, i,* m.
Three. *Tres, tria.*
Through. *Per* with accus.
Thus. *Sic, ita.*
Tigranes. *Tigrānes, is,* m.
Tigranocerta. *Tigranocerta, ōrum.*
Time. *Tempus, ŏris,* n.
Titus. *Titus, i,* m.
To. *Ad, in* with acc. ; before names of towns indicated by *the accusative without a preposition.*
To-day. *Hodie, hodierno die.*
To death. *Capĭtis ;* to condemn to death, *capĭtis damnāre.*
To-morrow. *Cras, crastĭno die.*
Tomb. *Tumŭlus, i,* m.
Torquatus. *Torquātus, i,* m.
Treachery, treason. *Proditio, ōnis,* f.
Trojan. *Trojānus, a, um ;* subs. *Trojanus, i,* m.
Troy. *Troja, ae,* f.
Try, attempt. *Tento, āre, āvi, ātum.*
Tullius. *Tullius, i,* m.
Turn, turn to or upon (*trans.*). *Converto, ĕre, ti, sum.*
Twelve. *Duodĕcim,* indecl.
Twenty. *Viginti,* indecl.
Two. *Duo, ae, o.*
Two hundred. *Ducenti, ae, a.*
Two years, space of two years. *Biennium, i,* n.
Tyrant. *Tyrannus, i,* m.
Tyre. *Tyrus, i,* f.

Tyrian. *Tyrius, a, um;* subs. *Tyrius, i, m.*

U.

Uncertain. *Incertus, a, um.*
Understand. *Intellĭgo, ĕre, lexi, lectum.*
Undertake. *Suscipio, ĕre, cēpi, ceptum.*
Unfavorable. *Non aequus, a, um; inīquus, a, um.*
Union, concord. *Conspiratio, ōnis, f.*
United. *Foederātus, a, um.*
Unlearned. *Indoctus, a, um.*
Unless. *Nisi.*
Untouched, unharmed. *Intactus, a, um.*
Unwilling. *Invītus, a, um.*
Unworthy. *Indignus, a, um.*
Upon, on, in. *In* with abl.
Use, make use of. *Utor, uti, usus sum.*
Useful. *Utĭlis, e.*
Useless. *Inutĭlis, e.*

V.

Valerius. *Valerius, i, m.*
Very. Often indicated by the *superlative* of the *adjective;* very powerful, *potentissĭmus.*
Vespasian. *Vespasiānus, i, m.*
Victim. *Victĭma, ae, f.*
Victorious, a victor. Expressed by *victor, ōris,* m., in apposition with the noun.
Victory. *Victoria, ae, f.*
Village. *Vicus, i, m.*
Violate. *Vĭŏlo, āre, āvi, ātum.*
Virgin. *Virgo, ĭnis, f.*
Virginia. *Virginia, ae, f.*
Virginius. *Virginius, i, m.*
Viriathus. *Viriāthus, i, m.*
Virtue. *Virtus, ūtis, f.*
Visit, go to. *Adeo, īre, īvi* or *ii, ĭtum.*
Vitellius. *Vitellius, i, m.*

Voice. *Vox, vocis, f.*
Volscian. *Volscus, a, um;* subs. *Volscus, i, m.*
Voluntary. *Voluntarius, a, um.*
Voluptuousness, pleasures. *Delīciae, ārum, f. pl.*

W.

Wage, carry on *as war.* *Gero, ĕre, gessi, gestum; infĕro, inferre, intŭli, illātum.*
Wait for, await. *Opperior, īri, perītus* or *pertus sum.*
Walk. *Ambŭlo, āre, āvi, ātum.*
War. *Bellum, i, n.*
Watching, keeping awake. *I ervigilia, ae, f.*
Wealthy. *Dives, ĭtis; locŭples, ĕtis.*
Wear out, weaken. *Confĭcio, ĕre, fēci, fectum.*
Weariness. *Lassitūdo, ĭnis, f.*
What, which (*interrog. adj.*). *Qui, quae, quod?*
When. *Quum;* interrog. *quando.*
Where. *Ubi,* when not interrog. generally with the correlative *ibi* in the principal clause.
Whether. *Utrum;* whether—or (in double questions), *utrum—an;* (in other cases) *seu—seu; sive—sive;* whether in dependent questions, *num, ne, nonne; num* is more common than in direct questions and here does not necessarily expect the answer *no.* (177, R. 2.)
While. *Dum.*
Whither. *Quo, quonam.*
Who, which, what. *Quis, quae, quod* or *quid?*
Whole. *Totus, a, um.* (F. B. 113, R.)
Whose. *Cujus, a, um; cujus, quorum.*
Why. *Cur.*
Wife. *Uxor, ōris,* f.; *conjux, ŭgis,* f.
Winter. *Hiems, ĕmis, f.*

Wisdom. *Consilium, i,* n.; *sapientia, ae,* f.
Wise. *Sapiens, entis.*
Wish. *Volo, velle, volui.* (F. B. 410; A. & S. 178.)
With. *Cum* with abl.; also indicated by the *abl. alone.*
Withdraw, come off (from battle). *Discēdo, ĕre, cessi, cessum.*
Without. *Sine* with abl.
Withstand. *Sustineo, ēre, ui, tentum.*
Witness, see. *Specto, āre, āvi, ātum.*
World. *Orbis, is,* m.; *orbis terrārum.*
Worthy. *Dignus, a, um.*
Wound (*subs.*). *Vulnus, ĕris,* n.
Wound (*v.*). *Vulnĕro, āre, āvi, ātum.*
Write. *Scribo, ĕre, psi, ptum.*

X.

Xanthippus. *Xanthippus i,* m
Xerxes. *Xerxes, is,* m.

Y.

Year. *Annus, i,* m.
Yesterday. *Heri; hesterno die.*
Yet. *Tamen.*
You. *Tu, tui,* &c.
Your. *Tuus, a, um* (in reference to one person); *vester, tra, trum* (in reference to more than one).
Yourself. *Tu ipse, tui ipsīus,* &c.; sometimes particularly as object, *tu, tui.*
Youth, a young person. *Adolescens, entis,* m. and f.

HISTORICAL AND GEOGRAPHICAL INDEX.

☞ The numerals accompanying the proper names in the following Index refer to one or more paragraphs in the Latin where those names occur.

A.

A. An abbreviation for *Aulus*, a man's name; 46, 85.
Acca, ae, f.; *Acca Laurentia, ae,* f. The wife of Faustulus, and nurse of Romulus and Remus; 7.
Achaia, ae, f. Achaia, an important province in the northern part of the Peloponnesus. After the destruction of Corinth all southern Greece was reduced to a Roman province with the name of Achaia; 90.
   Achaeus, a, um; Achaïcus, a, um, adj. Achaean, 156; subs. *Achaeus, i,* m., an Achaean; 97, 155.
Actium, i, n. A promontory and town at the entrance of the Ambracian Gulf on the western coast of Greece; celebrated for the victory of Augustus over Antony and Cleopatra; 82.
Adherbal, ălis, m. Son of Micipsa and cousin of Jugurtha. Micipsa left the kingdom of Numidia to his two sons, Adherbal and Hiempsal, and his nephew Jugurtha whom he had adopted as a son. Jugurtha, however, not satisfied with a share merely of the government, slew his cousins and became sole king of Numidia; 65.
Adrastīa, ae, f. A district and city of Mysia; 130.
Aeacīdes, ae, m. A patronymic denoting a descendant of Aeacus who was the grandfather of Achilles. The name is often applied to Achilles; Alexander the Great also claimed it for himself; 140.
Aegeus, i, m. One of the early kings of Athens, and the father of Theseus; 95.
Aegos flumen. Aegospotamos, a river and town in the Thracian Chersonesus, noted for the defeat of the Athenians by Lysander; 115.
Aegyptus, i, f. Egypt; 78.
   Aegyptius, a, um. Egyptian; subs. *Aegyptius, i,* m., an Egyptian; 95, 133.

Aemilius, i, m. The family name of several distinguished Romans L. *Aemilius*, surnamed *Paullus*, fell in the battle of Cannae; 49 Another of the same name conquered Perseus and reduced Macedonia to a Roman province; 59, 154.

Aenēas, ae, m. A Trojan prince who after the destruction of Troy is said to have fled into Italy and formed a settlement; 2.

Aequi, ōrum, m. pl. A warlike people of Latium in Italy; 31.

Aetōlus, a, um. Aetolian; subs. *Aetōlus, i,* m., an Aetolian; 145, 154, 155.

Africa, ae, f. Africa; 44, 46.

Africānus, a, um. African. Also the surname given to the two most distinguished Scipios for their achievements in Africa during the Punic wars; 56, 61.

Africus, i, m. (sc. *ventus*). Southwest wind, as blowing from Africa; 132.

Agis, ĭdis, m. A king of the Lacedaemonians in the time of Alexander the Great; 136.

Agrigentum, i, n. A large and wealthy town in Sicily; 52.

Agrippa, ae, m. A family name among the Romans. *Menenius Agrippa* induced the people who had revolted at Rome and taken up their quarters upon *Mons Sacer*, to return into the city; 27. *Herōdes Agrippa,* son of Aristobulus prince of Judea, was educated at Rome with Drusus, the son of Tiberius. He gave offence to Tiberius, and was thrown into prison, but on the accession of Caligula was set at liberty; 83.

Agrippīna, ae, f. (1) The wife of Germanicus and mother of the emperor Caligula; 84. (2) The daughter of Germanicus and Agrippina (No. 1); she was the mother of the emperor Nero, and as her third husband was married to the emperor Claudius; 85, 86.

Alba, ae, f.; *Alba Longa, ae,* f. A city of Latium founded by Ascanius; 3, 14.

Albānus, a, um. Alban. *Mons Albānus,* a rocky mountain sixteen miles southeast of Rome; 3. *Lacus Albānus,* the Alban *Lake* west of Mount Albanus; 4.

Albānus, i, m. An Alban, a citizen of Alba; 5, 14.

Alcibiădes, is, m. An Athenian general in the Peloponnesian war; 109, 110, 112, 113, &c.

Alcmaeon, ŏnis, m. The last of the Athenian archons appointed for life; 99.

Alexander, dri, m. The most distinguished of this name was the son and successor of Philip, king of Macedonia; 127—141. A second by the same name was king of Epirus and son-in-law of Philip; 127. A third was the son of Perseus, the last king of Macedonia; 154.

Alexandrīa, ae, f. Alexandria, a celebrated city of Egypt built by Alexander the Great; 78, 79.

Allia, ae, f. A small river a few miles north of Rome; 33.

Alpes, ium, f. The Alps, a high range of mountains north of Italy; 48, 75.

Ammon or *Hammon, ōnis,* m. An appellation of Jupiter as worshipped in Africa; 133.

HISTORICAL AND GEOGRAPHICAL INDEX. 345

Amphictyon, ŏnis, m. One of the early kings of Athens; 95.
Amphipŏlis, is, f. A city of Macedonia, now *Emboli;* 123.
Amulius, i, m. Son of Procas, king of Alba; he was the brother of Numitor; 5, 6, 8.
Anaxarchus, i, m. A philosopher of Abdera, who accompanied Alexander into Asia; 139.
Anchīses, ae, m. Anchises, the father of Aeneas; 2.
Ancus, i, m.; *Ancus Marcius, i*, m. The fourth king of Rome; 15, 17.
Andriscus, i, m. A Macedonian who claimed to be the son of Perseus, and was accordingly called *Pseudophilippus*, i. e., False Philip; 62.
Anio, ēnis, m. A small river of Italy, a tributary of the Tiber; now *Teverone;* 27, 34.
Antigŏnus, i, m. One of Alexander's generals; 143.
Antiochīa, ae, f. The chief city of Syria, founded by Seleucus and named by him in honor of his father Antiochus; 73.
Antiŏchus, i, m. Antiochus the Great, king of Syria, long engaged in war against the Romans, and finally defeated by Cornelius Scipiŏ near Magnesia; 58, 150.
Antipāter, tri, m. One of Alexander's generals; after the death of Alexander he received the government of Greece and Macedonia; 136, 142.
Antonia, ae, f. Paternal aunt of Nero, by whom she was put to death; 86.
Antonius, i, m. Ántony; *M. Antonius* formed a triumvirate with Octavius and Lepidus; 80, 81, 82. *C. Antonius* was the colleague of Cicero in the consulship; 74.
Apollo, ĭnis, m. The god of divination; 98, 107, 145.
Appius, i, m.; *Appius Claudius, i*, m. One of the *Decemviri;* 30.
Apulia, ae, f. A province in southern Italy; 49, 70.
Arbēla, ōrum, n. A town in Assyria, famous for the victory of Alexander over Darius; 134.
Ardea, ae, f. A city of Latium, a few miles south of Rome; 21, 22.
Argos, n. (only in nom. and acc.), or *Argi, ōrum*, m. pl. The capital of the province of Argolis in the Peloponnesus; the name was often applied to the province itself, and poetically to all Greece; 42, 96.
Argīvus, i, m. An inhabitant or citizen of Argos; also a Greek; 96.
Argyraspĭdes, um, m. pl. A term applied to a company of Macedonian soldiers who wore silver shields; 137.
Aridaeus, i, m Brother and successor of Alexander the Great; 142.
Arimĭnum, i, n A town in Umbria, on the Adriatic; 77.
Aristobūlus, i, m. A king of Judea, who was taken by Pompey and carried as prisoner to Rome; 73.
Aristotĕles, is, m. A distinguished philosopher, and the teacher of Alexander the Great; 141.
Armenia, ae, f. A country of Asia, divided by the river Euphrates into two unequal parts, viz.: the eastern, called *Armenia Major*, and the western, called *Armenia Minor;* 71.
Armenius, a, um. Armenian; 71.

15*

Artaphernes, is, m. Nephew of Darius; 101.
Artaxerxes, is, m. Son and successor of Darius, king of Persia 119, 120.
Artemisium, i, n. A promontory of the island Euboea; 104.
Aruns, untis, m. Son of Tarquin the Proud; 24.
Ascanius, i, m. Son of Aeneas; 3.
Asia, ae, f. Asia; 101.
  Asiaticus, a, um. Asiatic; also a surname given to L. Cornelius Scipio for his achievements in Asia, especially his victory over king Antiochus; 58.
Asina, ae, m. A surname of *Cneus Cornelius,* who was the colleague of Duillius in the consulship in the early part of the first Punic war; 43.
Athēnae, ārum, f. pl. The capital of Attica; 95, 97, 112, 116.
  Atheniensis, e, adj. Athenian; subs. *Atheniensis, is,* m., an Athenian; 95, 100, 116.
Atilius, i, m. A family name among the Romans, as *M. Atilius* surnamed *Regulus;* 44.
Atreus, i, m. Son of Pelops; 99.
Attălus, i, m. One of Philip's generals and the uncle of his wife Cleopatra; 127.
Atthis, ĭdis, f. The daughter of Cranaus, who was one of the early kings of Attica; 95.
Attĭca, ae, f. An important province in Greece; 102, 108, 118.
  Attĭcus, a, um. Attic, Athenian; subs. *Attĭcus, i,* m., an inhabitant of Attica; 95.
Augustus, i, m. Surname of Octavius Caesar, the first of the Roman emperors; 81, 86. This surname was also often applied to the emperors generally.
Aurelius, i, m. Name of a Roman gens or family, as *L. Aurelius Cotta;* 69.
Aventīnus, i, m. The Aventine, one of the seven hills of Rome; 8

B.

Babylonia, ae, f. Babylonia, a province of Syria; also Babylon, the capital of Babylonia; 139.
Balbus, i, m. Balbus, *a man's name;* 247, 248.
Bacchantes, ium, pl. The votaries of Bacchus, the god of wine; 137.
Bestia, ae, m. A surname in the Calpurnian family at Rome; *L. Calpurnius Bestia* was consul when war was declared against Jugurtha; 65.
Bibŭlus, i, m. A proper name; *L. Bibulus* was Caesar's colleague in the consulship; 75.
Bithynia, ae, f. A fruitful province of Asia Minor; 69.
Boeotia, ae, f. A district of Greece north of Attica; 96.
  Boeotius, i, m. A Boeotian; 121.
Brennus, i, m. A distinguished Gallic leader; 147, 148.

HISTORICAL AND GEOGRAPHICAL INDEX. 347

Britannia, ae, f. Great Britain; 85, 86.
Britannicus, a, um. British; also a surname given to Germanicus, the son of the emperor Claudius; 75, 85.
Britannus, i, m. An inhabitant of Great Britain, a Briton; 75.
Bruttii, ōrum, m. A people in the south of Italy; also their country; 54.
Brutus, i, m. A Roman surname; *L. Junius Brutus,* one of the first consuls of Rome; 22, 23, 24; *M. Junius Brutus* and *D. Junius Brutus* acted prominent parts in the assassination of Caesar; 79, 81.
Byzantium, i, n. A city on the Bosporus, now *Constantinople,* 69, 90, 113.

C.

C. Abbreviation for *Caius; Cn.* for *Cneus, Cneius* or *Cnaeus,* names common among the Romans; 43, 46, 64, 72.
Cabīra, indecl. A town in Pontus; 71.
Cadmēa, ae, f. The citadel of Thebes in Boeotia, named after Cadmus, its founder; 120.
Cadmus, i, m. A Phoenician who is said to have been the inventor of alphabetic writing; 96.
Caecilius, i, m. A Roman name, as *Q. Caecilius Metellus;* 62.
Caepio, ōnis, m. A Roman consul; 63.
Caesar, ăris, m. A surname of the Julian family; *C. Julius Caesar,* a distinguished general and statesman; 75, 77, 83. The title or surname *Caesar* was applied generally to denote the Roman emperors; 88.
Caius, i, m. A Roman name.—*Caius Caligula, ae,* m. A Roman emperor, successor of Tiberius; 84, 86, 94. *Caius Augustus,* son of Germanicus; 83.
Calpurnius, i, m. (See *Bestia.*)
Camillus, i, m. A distinguished Roman general; 31, 32, 33.
Campania, ae, f. A province in Central Italy; 40, 51.
Cannae, ārum, f. pl. A village in Apulia, famous for the great victory of Hannibal over the Romans; 49.
Cannensis, e, adj. Of *or* belonging to Cannae; 53.
Capitolium, i, n. Capitol. This was the citadel of Rome, and was erected on the Capitoline Hill; 21, 33, 85.
Cappadocia, ae, f. A country of Asia Minor; 83.
Caprea, ae, f., or *Capreae, ārum.* An island in the Tuscan Sea; now *Capri;* 83.
Capua, ae, f. The chief city of Campania; 70.
Carrae, ārum, f. pl. A city near the Euphrates, famous for the defeat of Crassus by the Parthians; 76.
Carthāgo, ĭnis, f. An ancient city in Northern Africa; 47, 50.—*Carthago Nova.* New Carthage, a town in Spain; now *Carthagena;* 53.
  Carthaginiensis, e, adj. Carthaginian; subs. *Carthaginiensis, is,* a Carthaginian; 43, 44, 45, 46, &c.

HISTORICAL AND GEOGRAPHICAL INDEX.

Casca, ae, m. Surname of *Servilius,* one of the conspirators against Caesar; 79.

Cassander, dri, m. Son of Antipater and king of Macedonia after the death of Alexander; 143, 144.

Cassius, i, m. A Roman name. *C. Cassius,* one of the conspirators against Caesar; 76, 79, 81.

Catilīna, ae, m. (*L. Sergius*). The notorious conspirator against the Roman government; 74.

Catinensis or *Catiniensis, is.* A Catinean, a citizen of Catina a city in Sicily; 109.

Catti, ōrum, m. pl. A people in Germany; 94.

Catŭlus, i, m. Surname of *C. Lutatius,* a Roman consul at the close of the first Punic war; 46.

Caudīnus, a, um. Caudine; *Furcŭlae Caudīnae,* the Caudine Forks, a narrow defile near Caudium, in Italy; 37.

Cecrops, ŏpis, m. The most ancient king of Attica; 95.

Censorīnus, i, m. Surname of *L. Marcius,* a Roman consul in the third Punic war; 60.

Chaeronēa, ae, f. A town in Boeotia; 125.

Chalcēdon, ŏnis, f. A town on the Thracian Bosporus, opposite to Byzantium; 69.

Charops, ŏpis, m. The first decennial archon at Athens; 99.

Cicĕro, ōnis, m. The celebrated Roman orator; 74, 80.

Cilicia, ae, f. A province in the southern part of Asia Minor; 90.

Cineas, ae, m. A friend and favorite minister of Pyrrhus; 41.

Cinna, ae, m. A surname among the Romans. *L. Cornelius Cinna,* confederate of Marius in the civil war; 68.

Cirrhaeus, a, um. Cirrhaean, of or pertaining to Cirrha, a town near Delphi; 145.

Claudius, i, m. The fourth Roman emperor; 85, 90. *Appius Claudius,* one of the decemviri; 30. *M. Claudius Marcellus,* a Roman consul; 51.

Cleomĕnes, is, m. A king of Sparta; 150.

Cleopātra, ae, f. Queen of Egypt, 79, 82. Another of the same name was the daughter of Philip of Macedon; 127.

Cluentius, i, m. A leader in the Social war; 66.

Cnaeus or *Cneus* (abbrev. *Cn.*), *i,* m. A Roman name, as *Cnaeus Octavius,* 154; *Cn. Pompeius,* 72.

Cocles, ĭtis, m. (*Horatius*). A Roman distinguished in the war with Porsena; 25.

Collatīnus, i, m. Surname of Tarquinius, the husband of Lucretia; 21, 22, 23.

Commagēne, es, f. The northern province of Syria; 90.

Conon, ōnis, m. A celebrated Athenian general; 114, 115.

Corinthus, i, f. Corinth, a city of Achaia; 16, 62, 155, 156. *Corinthius, a, um.* Corinthian; subs. *Corinthius, i,* m., a Corinthian; 62.

Coriolānus, i, m. A surname given to *Qu. Marcius,* derived from *Corioli,* the name of a town which he had taken in war; 28.

Coriŏli, ōrum, m. pl. A town in Latium; 28.

Cornelius, i, m. The name of a distinguished Roman gens, or clan, including the *Scipios, Sulla,* &c.; 43, 48, 53, 66. (See also *Anno.*)
Corvīnus, i, m. Surname of *M. Valerius,* tribune of the soldiers; 35.
Cotta, ae, m. Surname of *M. Aurelius,* a Roman consul in the time of the Mithridatic war; 69.
Cranaus, i, m. King of Attica and successor of Cecrops; 95.
Crassus, i, m. Surname in the Licinian gens. *M. Licinius Crassus,* a Roman general defeated and slain by the Parthians; 76.
Cratěrus, i, m. A general in the army of Alexander the Great; 142.
Creměra, ae, f. A river of Etruria, in Italy; 29.
Cremōna, ae, f. A town of Cisalpine Gaul, on the Po; 88.
Creon, ontis, m. An archon at Athens; 99.
Creta, ae, f. The island of Crete; now *Candia ;* 96, 98.
Critias, ae, m. One of the thirty tyrants at Athens; 118.
Crixus, i, m. A leader in the war of the gladiators; 70.
Cures, ium, f. pl. The ancient capital of the Sabines ; 13.
Curiatii, ōrum, m. pl. Three brothers who were selected from the Alban army to engage in combat with the three Horatii, also brothers, from the Romans; 14. (See note on *Horatiōrum et Curiatiōrum,* 14.)
Cursor, ōris, m. Surname of *L. Papirius,* dictator in the Samnite war ; 36.
Cynoscephǎlae, ārum, f. pl. "Dogs' Heads," two hills in Thessaly ; 57, 151.
Cyprus, i, f. An island in the Mediterranean sea, near Asia Minor; 143.
Cyrus, i, m. Brother of Artaxerxes ; 114, 119.
Cyzǐcus, i, f., or *Cyzǐcum, i,* n. An ancient city in Asia Minor; 69.

D.

Dacus, a, um. Dacian, relating to Dacia, a province north of the Danube; subs. *Dacus, i,* m., a Dacian ; 94.
Danaus, i, m. Brother of Aegyptus and founder of Argos; 96.
Darīus, i, m. A celebrated king of Persia; 101, 103, 114, 131.
Datis, is, m. One of the generals of Darius ; 101, 102.
Deiotǎrus, i, m. A king of Galatia ; 73.
Delphi, ōrum. m. pl. A town of Phocis, celebrated for the temple and oracle of Apollo; 103, 107, 147.
Delphǐcus, a, um. Delphic; 98.
Demarātus, i, m. The father of Tarquinius Priscus ; 16.
Demetrius, i, m. The name of several Greeks, one of whom was the son of Philip V. and the brother of Perseus, the last king of Macedonia; 51, 57, 143, 152.
Demosthěnes, is, m. An Athenian general ; 111.
Deucalion, ōnis, m. An ancient king of Phthia, in Thessaly ; 95.
Domitiānus, i, m. A Roman emperor ; 94.
Draco, ōnis, m. A lawgiver of Athens ; 100.
Drusus, i, m. Son of Germanicus ; 83. *Drusus Caesar, ǎris,* m. Son of Tiberius ; 83.

Duillius, *i*, m. (*Caius*). A Roman commander and consul in the first Punic war; 43.

E.

Egeria, *ae*, f. A prophetic nymph from whom Numa professed to receive instructions; 13.
Eleusis or *Eleusin*, *ĭnis*, f. (accus. *Eleusin*). An ancient town of Attica; 95.
Elius, *i*, m. An Elean, native of Elis, in the western part of the Peloponnesus; 99.
Epaminondas, *ae*, m. A celebrated Theban general; 121.
Epīrus, *i*, f. A province in the north of Greece; 38, 42, 82.
Erectheus or *Erechtheus*, *i*, m. An ancient king of Athens; 95.
Eretria, *ae*, f. Important city on the island of Euboea; 102.
Eryxias, *ae*, m. The last of the decennial archons at Athens; 99.
Etruria, *ae*, f. A country of Central Italy; Tuscany; 16.
  Etruscus, *i*, m. An Etruscan; 25.
Euboea, *ae*, f. An island in the Aegean sea; 102, 104.
Euphrātes, *is*, m. A large river of Asia; 134.
Eurōpa, *ae*, f. The continent of Europe; 58. Also the name of the sister of Cadmus; 96.
Eurybiădes, *is*, m. A king of Sparta; 105.
Eurymĕdon, *ontis*, m. An Athenian general in the Peloponnesian war; 111.

F.

Fabius, *i*, m. The name of a distinguished Roman family; 29, 36.
Fabricius, *i*, m. A distinguished leader of the Romans in the war against Pyrrhus; 40, 42.
Falerii, *ōrum*, m. pl. A town of Etruria; 32.
  Faliscus, *a*, *um*. Of or belonging to Falerii; subs. *Faliscus*, *i*, m., a citizen of Falerii; 33.
Faustŭlus, *i*, m. A shepherd who brought up Romulus and Remus; 7.
Flaminius, *i*, m. (*C.*) A Roman consul defeated by Hannibal at the Lake of Trasimēnus; 48. *T. Quinctius Flaminius* or *Flaminīnus*, *i*, m., the conqueror of king Philip of Macedonia; 151.
Furcŭlae, *ārum*, f. pl. (See *Caudīnus*; 37.)
Furius, *i*, m. A Roman family name; as *M. Furius Camillus*; see *Camillus*; 32.

G.

Galatia, *ae*, f. A country of Asia Minor; 73.
Galba, *ae*, m. (*Sergius*). A Roman emperor; 87.

HISTORICAL AND GEOGRAPHICAL INDEX. 351

Gallia, ae, f. The ancient country of Gaul; 75, 81
  Gallĭcus, a, um. Gallic; 146.
  Gallus, i, m. A Gaul, a native of Gaul; 33, 34, 35, 48.
Gamăla, ae, f. A town in Palestine; 143.
Germania, ae, f. Germany; 90.
  Germanĭcus, a, um, adj. German; 88.
  Germanĭcus, i, m. Surname of several Roman generals who achieved victories over the Germans; *Germanĭcus Caesar* was the father of the emperor Caligula and the grandfather of Nero; 83, 84, 86.
  Germānus, i, m. A German; 75.
Gracchus, i, m. (*Sempronius*). A Roman general defeated by Hannibal at the river Trebia; 48.
Graecia, ae, f. The country of Greece; 42, 57, 96, 116, &c.
  Graecus or *Graius, a, um.* Grecian, 98; subs. *Graecus* or *Graius, i,* m., a Greek; 107, 119, 120.
Gylippus, i, m. A Spartan commander in the Sicilian expedition; 110, 111.

H.

Halys, yos, m. A river in Asia Minor; 134.
Hamilcar, ăris, m. The father of Hannibal; 44, 47.
Hammon, ōnis, m. (See *Ammon.*)
Hannibal, ălis, m. A celebrated Carthaginian general in the second Punic war; 29, 47, 51.
Hanno, ōnis, m. A Carthaginian general in the second Punic war; 55.
Hasdrubal, ălis, m. Son of Hamilcar and brother of Hannibal; 48, 50, 54. Another of the same name was the brother-in-law of Hannibal, and the founder of New Carthage, in Spain.
Hellespontus, i, m. The straits of the Dardanelles; 106, 113, 134.
Hercŭles, is, m. A hero of antiquity, celebrated for his great strength and his wonderful achievements; 99.
Herennius, i, m. The father of Pontius Thelesinus, who conquered the Romans at the Caudine Forks; 37.
Herōdes, is, m. (See *Agrippa.*)
Hiempsal, ălis, m. Son of Micipsa and cousin of Jugurtha; 65. (See *Adherbal.*)
Hiĕro, ōnis, m. A king of Syracuse at the time of the first Punic war; 43.
Hierosolўma, ae, f., or *ōrum,* n. pl. Jerusalem, the capital of Judea; 73, 90, 91.
Hispania, ae, f. Spain; 48, 53, 81, &c.
  Hispānus, a, um. Spanish; subs. *Hispānus, i,* m., a Spaniard; 53.
Horatii, ōrum, m. pl. (See *Curiatii;* also note on *Horatiōrum et Curiatiōrum,* 14.)
Horatius, i, m. (See *Cŏcles* and *Pulvillus.*)
Hostilius, i, m. A Roman name; *Tullus Hostilius,* the third king of Rome; 14. *C. Hostilius Mancīnus,* a Roman consul; 64.
Hyphăsis, is, m. A river of India, a tributary of the Indus; 138.

I.

Ibērus, i, m. A river of Spain; now *the Ebro;* 46.
Ilium, i, n. Ilium *or* Troy; 129.
Illyrĭcus, a, um, or *Illyrius, a, um.* Illyrian, of *or* pertaining to Illyria, a country on the northeastern coast of the Adriatic; 141, 146. Subs. *Illyrĭcus* or *Illyrius, i,* m., an Illyrian; 123.
Inăchus, i, m. The first king of Argos; 96.
India, ae, f. India, an extensive country of Asia, deriving its name from the river Indus; 137.
Ionia, ae, f. A country in the western part of Asia Minor; 113, 114.
Iōnes, um, m. pl. The Ionians; 101.
Iphītus, i, m. A king of Elis, who revived the Olympic games, and may almost be regarded as their founder; 99.
Ister, tri, m. The river Danube. This name is applied to the lower part of the river, the upper part usually taking the name *Danubius;* 101.
Italia, ae, f. The country of Italy; 38, 46, 81.
Italĭcus or *Itălus, a, um,* adj. Italian · subs. *Itălus, i,* m., an Italian; 1.

J.

Janicŭlum, i, n. A hill on the west side of the Tiber, not one of *the seven* hills of Rome, though included within the wall built by Aurelian in the third century; 1.
Judaea, ae, f. The country of Judea; 73.
Judaeus, a, um. Jewish; subs. *Judaeus, i,* m., a Jew; 73.
Jugurtha, ae, m. A king of Numidia, conquered by the Romans; 65 (See *Adherbal.*)
Julius, i, m. (See *Caesar.*)
Junius, i, m. (See *Brutus.*)
Jupĭter, Jovis, m. The king of the gods; 4, 21, 133.
Juvencius, i, m. A Roman general; 62.

L.

L. An abbreviation for *Lucius,* a Roman name; 22, 36, 49, 58, 60, &c.
Lacedaemon, ŏnis, f. The city of Lacedaemon *or* Sparta, the capital of Laconia; 111.
Lacedaemonius, a, um. Lacedaemonian *or* Spartan; subs. *Lacedaemonius, i,* m., a Lacedaemonian *or* Spartan; 44, 57, 98, 102, &c.
Laconia, or *Laconĭca, ae,* f. A country of the Peloponnesus; 97, 108.
Laco or *Lacon, ŏnis,* m. A Laconian; 120.
Laevīnus, i, m. A Roman family name; *P. Valerius Laevīnus,* a Roman consul; 38, 39. *M. Valerius Laevīnus,* also a Roman consul and a distinguished commander; 51, 52.
Lamăchus, i, m. An Athenian general in the Sicilian expedition; 109, 110.

Larissa, ae, f. A town in Thessaly; 123.
Latīnus, i, m. An ancient king of the Laurentians in Italy; 2.
Latium, i, n. Latium, a country of Italy containing Rome; 21.
 Latīnus, a, um, adj. Latin; subs. *Latīnus, i,* m., an inhabitant of Latium, a Latin; *pl.* the Latins; 15.
Laurentia, or *Larentia, ae,* f. (See *Acca.*)
Lavinia, ae, f. Daughter of Latinus and wife of Aeneas; 2.
Lavinium, i, n. A town in Latium, a few miles south of Rome, founded by Aeneas and named by him after his wife Lavinia; 2
Leonĭdas, ae, m. A Spartan king who fell at Thermopylae; 104.
Lepĭdus, i, m. One of the triumvirs with Octavius and Antony; 80.
Leuctra, ōrum, n. pl. A small town in Boeotia; 121.
 Leuctrĭcus, a, um. Leuctrian; of *or* belonging to Leuctra; 122.
Libănus, i, m. Mount Lebanon in Syria; 132.
Liber, ĕri, m. A name sometimes applied to Bacchus, the god of wine; 137.
Licinius, i, m. A Roman name. *P. Licinius,* a Roman consul and commander in the war with Perseus; 59. *L. Licinius Lucullus,* a Roman consul in the time of the Mithridatic war; 69, 71.
Ligŭres, un, m. pl. The Ligurians, inhabitants of Liguria, in the western part of Italy; 46.
Lilybaeum, i, n. A promontory on the southwestern coast of Sicily; 46.
Livia, ae, f. The mother of Tiberius; 83.
Lucānus, i, m. A poet put to death by Nero; he was the nephew of Seneca the philosopher; 86.
Lucius, i, m. A name common among the Romans; as *Lucius Tarquinius Priscus,* 16; usually represented by the abbreviation *L.,* as *L. Brutus;* 22.
Lucretia, ae, f. The wife of Collatinus; 21, 23, 24.
Lucretius, i, m. The father of Lucretia; 24.
Lucullus, i, m. (See *Licinius.*)
Lusitania, ae, f. Lusitania; now *Portugal;* 63.
Lutatius, i, m. (See *Catŭlus.*)
Lycia, ae, f. The country of Lycia in Asia Minor; 90, 96.
Lycurgus, i, m. The great lawgiver of Sparta; 98. Another was king of Sparta, successor of Cleomenes; 150.
Lydia, ae, f A country in Asia Minor; 114, 119.
Lysander, ari, m. A celebrated Spartan general; 114, 115, 116.
Lysimăchus, i, m. One of the generals of Alexander the Great · 143, 144.

M.

M. An abbreviation for *Marcus,* a Roman name; 35, 44, 60, 74, &c.
Macedonia, ae, f. Macedonia, Macedon, a country north of Thessaly; 51, 62.
 Macĕdo, ŏnis, m. A Macedonian; 122, 125.
 Macedonĭcus, a, um, adj. Macedonian; 57, 154.

Magi, ōrum, m. pl. The Magi, the learned men among the Persians; 139.
Magnesia, ae, f. A city in Lydia, in Asia Minor; 58.
Magnus, i, m. Surname of Alexander, meaning *the Great*; 143.
Mancīnus, i, m. A Roman consul in the war with the Numantians; 64.
Manlius, i, m. (*M.*) A Roman consul in the third Punic war; 60. *T. Manlius*, a Roman youth, surnamed *Torquātus* for his achievements in the Gallic war; 34.
Mantinēa, ae, f. A city of Arcadia, in the Peloponnesus; 121.
Marăthon, ōnis, m. A town and plain in Attica, celebrated for the victory of Miltiades over the Persians; 102.
   Marathonius, a, um. Marathonian; of *or* belonging to Marathon; 103, 106.
Marcellus, i, m. (See *Claudius*.)
Marcius, i, m. (See *Ancus, Censorīnus*, and *Coriolānus*.)
Mardonius, i, m. A Persian general, defeated by Pausanias in the battle of Plataea; 107.
Marius, i, m. A distinguished Roman general, the conqueror of Jugurtha, and leader in the civil war against Sulla. He was consul seven times; 65, 67.
Mars, Martis, m. The god of war; sometimes put for war itself; 6, 115.
Marsi, ōrum, m. pl. A people of Latium; 66.
Maxĭmus, i, m. A Roman surname; as of *Q. Fabius*, the famous dictator in the second Punic war, who weakened the force of Hannibal by delay; 29.
Medius, i, m. A Thessalian, friend of Alexander the Great; 139.
Megarensis, is, m. and f. A Megarian, a native of Megara, in Sicily; 100.
Meleager, gri, m. A commander in the service of Alexander the Great; 142.
Memphis, is, f. A city in Egypt; 133.
Menenius, i, m. (See *Agrippa*.)
Metellus, i, m. (*Q. Caecilius*). A Roman consul and leader in the war against Jugurtha; 62.
Metius, i, m. (See *Suffetius*.)
Micipsa, ae, m. A king of Numidia, the father of Adherbal and Hiempsal, and the uncle of Jugurtha; 65.
Miltiădes, is, m. A celebrated Athenian general, conqueror at Marathon; 102.
Minerva, ae, f. Goddess of wisdom and patron divinity of Athens; 95.
Minor, ōris. (See *Armenia*.)
Minos, ōis, m. A king and lawgiver of Crete; 96.
Misēnum, i, n. A promontory and town in Campania, in Italy; 83.
Mithridātes, is, m. A celebrated king of Pontus; 67, 68, 69, 71.
   Mithridatĭcus, a, um. Mithridatic; of *or* belonging to Mithridates; 67.
Mucius, i, m. A Roman name. *Mucius Scaevŏla*, a Roman youth who attempted to assassinate Porsena; 26.

HISTORICAL AND GEOGRAPHICAL INDEX. 355

Mummius, i, m. A Roman general who destroyed Corinth; 62, 156.
Munychia, ae, f. A hill in the peninsula of Piraeus, at the foot of which lies the harbor of the same name; 118.
Mycăle, es, f. A high promontory or mountain of Ionia, in Asia Minor; 107.

N.

Nabis, is or *ĭdis,* m. A king of Sparta; 57.
Nasīca, ae, m. A surname in the Scipio family. *P. Scipio Nasīca,* a Roman consul in the war against Jugurtha; 65.
Neptūnus, i, m. The god of the sea; 9.
Nero, ōnis, m. The fifth Roman emperor; 86, 94. Another of the same name was the son of Germanicus; 83. Also a *surname* of *Tiberius* and *Claudius;* 83, 85.
Nicias, ae, m. An Athenian statesman and general; 109, 110.
Nicomēdes, is, m. A king of Bithynia; 69.
Nilus, i, m. The river Nile, in Egypt; 79, 133.
Nola, ae, f. An ancient city in Campania; 51.
Nova, ae, f. (See *Carthāgo.*)
Numa, ae, m. (*Pompilius*). The second king of Rome; 13, 15.
Numantia, ae, f. A city in Spain; 64.
  Numantīni, ōrum, m. pl. The inhabitants of Numantia, the Numantines; 64.
Numidia, ae, f. The country of Numidia, in Africa; 55.
  Numĭda, ae, m. A Numidian; 55, 65.
Numĭtor, ōris, m. A king of Alba, grandfather of Romulus and Remus; 5, 8.
Nysa, ae, f. A city in India; 137.

O.

Ocĕănus, i, m. The Ocean; often used also to denote the Atlantic, sometimes the Pacific; 75, 137.
Octavia, ae, f. The wife of the Emperor Nero; 86.
Octaviānus, i, m. (*Caesar*). The first Roman emperor, usually called Augustus after his victory at Actium; 80.
Octavius, i, m. (*Cnaeus*). A Roman commander in the war against Perseus; 154.
Oenomaus, i, m. A celebrated gladiator; 70.
Olympia, ōrum, n. pl. The Olympic games; 99.
Olympiăcus, or *Olympius, a, um.* Olympic; 141.
Olynthus, i, f. A city of Thrace; 120.
  Olynthii, ōrum, m. pl. The Olynthians; 124.
Orcădes, um, f. pl. The Orkney islands, near Scotland; 85.
Oriens, entis, m. The East, the countries of the East; 81, 129.
Orōdes, is, m. The king of Parthia, by whom Crassus was taken and slain; 76.

Ostia, ae, f. A town in Latium, at the mouth of the Tiber; 15.
Otho, ŏnis, m. A Roman emperor who reigned but a few months 87, 88.

P.

P. An abbreviation for *Publius,* a Roman name; 38, 48, 49, 59, &c.
Palaestīna, ae, f. Palestine; 90.
Palatium, i, n. The Palatine, one of the seven hills of Rome. The residence of Augustus was upon this; hence the term came to signify a *palace;* 86.
Pannonia, ae, f. A Roman province north of Illyria; 146.
Papirius, i, m. (See *Cursor.*)
Parmenio, ŏnis, m. A general in the service of Alexander the Great; 134, 135.
Parnassus, i, m. A high mountain in Phocis, whose two summits were sacred to Apollo and the Muses; at its base stood the city of Delphi; 147.
Parthi, ōrum, m. pl. A Scythian people in the vicinity of the Caspian, principally known as roving warriors; 76.
Paullus, or *Paulus, i,* m. A surname in the Aemilian gens or tribe. *L. Aemilius Paulus,* the name of two Roman consuls, one of whom fell in the battle of Cannae, 49; the other conquered Perseus at Pydna; 59, 154.
Pausanias, ae, m. The leader of the Spartans in the battle of Plataea; 107. Another of the same name murdered Philip of Macedon; 127.
Pelasgi, ōrum, m. pl. The Pelasgians, the earliest inhabitants of Greece; 97.
Peligni, ōrum, m. pl. A people of Central Italy; 66.
Pelopĭdas, ae, m. A celebrated Theban general; 120, 122.
Peloponnēsus, i, f. The Peloponnesus, a peninsula forming the southern part of Greece; now *the Morea;* 42, 96.
Peloponnesiăcus, a, um. Peloponnesian; 109.
Pelops, ŏpis, m. Probably a Phrygian, the son of Tantalus. He settled in the southern peninsula of Greece, which from him was called Peloponnesus, i. e. the island of Pelops; 96, 99.
Perdiccas, or *Perdicca, ae,* m. One of the most distinguished of the generals of Alexander the Great; 140, 142, 143.
Perĭcles, is, m. A celebrated Athenian orator and statesman; 108.
Persa, ae, m. A Persian; 102, 107, 114, 119, &c.
Perseus, i, m. The last king of Macedonia; 152, 153, 154.
Persĭcus, a, um, adj. Persian; 129.
Phalērum, i, n. The oldest harbor of Athens; often called *Phalerĭcus portus;* 107.
Pharnăces, is, m. Son of Mithridates; 72.
Pharsalus, i, f. A city in Thessaly, where Pompey was defeated by Caesar; 78.
Philippi, ōrum, m. pl. A city in Macedonia; 81.

HISTORICAL AND GEOGRAPHICAL INDEX. 357

Philippus, i, m. The name of several Macedonian kings, the most celebrated of whom was the father of Alexander the Great; 51, 57, 59, 122, 125, &c.
Philopător, ŏris, m. A surname, meaning *a lover of a father,* given in derision to Ptolemy, king of Egypt, who slew his father and mother; 150.
Phoebĭdas, ae, m. A Lacedaemonian commander, who treacherously got possession of the Cadmea; 120.
Phoenīce, es, or *Phoenicia, ae,* f. The country of Phoenicia, in Syria 96, 132, 143.
Phoroneus, i, m. Son of Inachus, king of Argos; 96.
Phyle, es, f. A castle in Attica; 118.
Picēnum, i, n. A district in the eastern part of Italy; 54.
Picentes, um, pl. The Picenes, the inhabitants of Picenum; 66.
Piraeeus, or *Piraeus, i,* m. The Piraeus, the celebrated port of Athens; 107, 118.
Pisa, ae, f. A city of Elis, in Greece; 96.
Plataeae, ārum, f. pl. Plataea, a city in Boeotia; 107.
Plataeenses, ium, m. pl. The Plataeans, the inhabitants of Plataea; 102.
Plautius, i, m. (*A.*) A Roman commander who subdued the southern part of the island of Britain in the reign of Claudius; 85.
Poenus, i, m. A Carthaginian; 43, 44, 45.
Pompeius, i, m. The name of a Roman gens. *Cn. Pompeius,* a Roman consul and a distinguished commander, defeated by Caesar at Pharsalia; 72, 73, 77, 78. *Q. Pompeius,* also consul and commander, defeated in several engagements by the Numantines; 64.
Pompeiānus, a, um, adj. Pompeian, of *or* belonging to Pompey; 79.
Pompilius, i, m. (See *Numa.*)
Pontius, i, m. (*Thelesīnus*). A general of the Samnites, who conquered the Romans at the Caudine Forks; 37.
Pontus, i, m. A province in Asia Minor, south of the Black sea; 67.
Porsĕna, ae, m. A king of Etruria, in Italy; 25, 26.
Postumius, i, m. The name of a Roman gens or clan. *A. Postumius,* a Roman in whose consulship the first Punic war was brought to a close; 46. *Spurius Postumius,* a Roman consul, defeated by the Samnites at the Caudine Forks; 37.
Praeneste, is, n. A town in Latium; 40.
Priscus, i, m. The surname of *Lucius Tarquinius,* the fifth king of Rome; 16, 18, 19.
Procas, ae, m. (*Silvius*). A king of Alba; 5.
Pseudophilippus, i, m. (See *Andriscus.*)
Ptolemaeus, i, m. Name of the kings of Egypt after Alexander the Great; 79, 143, 150. Another of the same name was the son of Pyrrhus, king of Epirus; 149.
Publicŏla, ae, m. Surname of *Valerius,* one of the first consuls at Rome; 23, 24.
Pulvillus, i, m. (*Horatius*). A Roman consul the first year after the banishment of Tarquin; 24.

Punĭcus, a, um. Punic, belonging to Carthage *or* the Carthaginians (*Poeni*); 46, 56, 57.
Pydna, ae, f. A town of Macedonia, celebrated for the victory of Paulus over Perseus; 59.
Pyrenaeus, i, m. The Pyrenees, a range of mountains between France and Spain; 48.
Pyrrhus, i, m. A king of Epirus; 38—42.
Pythia, ae, f. The priestess of Apollo, at Delphi; 103.

Q.

Q. or *Qu.* An abbreviation for *Quintus;* 26, 29, 62, &c.
Quinctius, i, m. (*T.*) A Roman general at the time when the city was taken by the Gauls; 34. (See also *Flaminius.*)

R.

Regŭlus, i, m. (*M. Atilius*). A distinguished Roman consul, taken prisoner by the Carthaginians in the first Punic war; 44, 45.
Remus, i, m. The brother of Romulus; 6, 8.
Rhadamanthus, i, m. Brother of Minos; 96.
Rhea, ae, f. (*Silvia*). Daughter of Numitor and mother of Romulus and Remus; 6.
Rhenus, i, m. The river Rhine; 75.
Rhodănus, i, m. The river Rhone, in Gaul; 75.
Rhodus, i, f. The island of Rhodes, on the coast of Asia Minor; 90.
Roma, ae, f. Rome; 16, 17, 19, 23, &c.
  Romānus, a, um, adj. Roman; subs. *Romānus, i,* m., a Roman; 9, 19, 24, &c.
Romŭlus, i, m. The founder of Rome; 8, 11, 13, &c. *Romŭlus Silvius,* an Alban king; 4.
Rulliānus, i, m. (*Q. Fabius*). Master of the knights *or* cavalry (*magister equitum*) under the dictator Papirius Cursor; 36.
Rutilius, i, m. A Roman consul, slain in the Social war; 66.

S.

S. An abbreviation for *Sextius* or *Spurius; Sp.* for *Spurius;* 24.
Sabīni, ōrum, m. pl. The Sabines, a people of Italy, bordering upon Latium; 13, 14, 91.
Saguntum, i, n. A town in Spain, on the Mediterranean; 47.
  Saguntīni, ōrum, m. pl. The Saguntines, citizens of Saguntum; 47.
Salămis, is or *ĭnis,* f. (acc. *Salamīna*), or *Salamīna, ae,* f. The island of Salamis, off the coast of Attica; 100, 103, 106.
Samnītes, ium, m. pl. The Samnites, the inhabitants of Samnium, in Italy; 36—38.
Samothracia, ae, f. An island near the coast of Thrace. 154

Samus, or *Samos*, i, f. An island on the coast of Asia Minor; 90, 112.
Sardes, *ium*, f. Sardis, the ancient capital of Lydia; 101.
Sardinia, *ae*, f. The island of Sardinia, west of Italy; 46, 139.
Sarmătae, *ārum*, m. pl. The Sarmatians, a people dwelling between the Vistula and the Don, i. e. in parts of Poland and Russia; 94.
Saturnia, *ae*, f. The town and citadel built by Saturn; 1.
Saturnus, *i*, m. Saturn, the most ancient king of Latium; 1.
Scaevŏla, *ae*, m. (See *Mucius*.)
Scipio, *ōnis*, m. The name of a distinguished Roman family; 48, 50, 58.
Scythia, *ae*, f. Scythia, an extensive country in the north of Europe and Asia; 101, 125.
Scythae, *ārum*, m. pl. The Scythians; 101, 125.
Sejānus, *i*, m. The prefect of the praetorian bands under Tiberius; 83.
Seleucia, *ae*, f. A city of Syria, on the Orontes; 73.
Seleucus, *i*, m. A general of Alexander the Great; 143, 150.
Sempronius, *i*, m. (See *Gracchus*.)
Sena, *ae*, f. A town on the coast of Umbria (*not Picēnum*), in Italy; 54.
Senĕca, *ae*, m. A philosopher and rhetorician, put to death by the order of Nero; 86.
Senŏnes, *um*, m. pl. A powerful people in Gaul; 83.
Sergius, *i*, m. (See *Catilīna* and *Galba*.)
Servilius, *i*, m. (See *Casca*.)
Servius, *i*, m. A Roman name. *Servius Tullius*, *i*, m., the sixth king of Rome; 18, 19, 20.
Sicilia, *ae*, f. The island of Sicily; 43, 52, 108, 109, &c.
Silvia, *ae*, f. (See *Rhea*.)
Silvius, *i*, m. The name of several kings of Alba, the first of whom was the son of Aeneas; 3, 4, 5. Also a surname of Otho; 88.
Solon, *ōnis*, m. The celebrated lawgiver of Athens; 100.
Sparta, *ae*, f. The capital of Laconia, in the Peloponnesus; also called Lacedaemon; 98, 121.
Spartānus, *a*, *um*, adj. Spartan; subs. *Spartānus*, *i*, m., a Spartan; 98, 108, 116.
Spartăcus, *i*, m. A celebrated gladiator who waged war against the Romans; 70.
Spurius, *i*, m. (See *Postumius*.)
Suffetius, *i*, m. (*Metius*). Dictator of the Albans. Having been summoned to aid the Romans against the Veientines, he drew off his forces at the very moment of battle and awaited the issue of the engagement. For this perfidy he was put to death by order of Tullius Hostilius; 14.
Sulla, *ae*, m. A distinguished Roman dictator and general; 66—68.
Sulpicius, *i*, m. A Roman consul; 154.
Superbus, *i*, m. The surname of Tarquin, the last king of Rome; 20, 21.
Surēnas, *ae*, m. A general of the Parthians who defeated Crassus; 76.
Sutrīni, *ōrum*, m. pl. The inhabitants of Sutrium, in Etruria; 31.
Syphax, *ācis*, m. King of Numidia at the time of the second Punic war; 55.

Syracūsae, ārum, f. pl. A city in Sicily; 43, 52, 110.
   Syracusāni, ōrum, m. pl. The Syracusans, the citizens of Syracuse; 109, 110.
Syria, ae, f. A country in Asia, on the Mediterranean; 132.
   Syriăcus, a, um, adj. Syrian; 58.

T.

T. An abbreviation for *Titus;* 34, 37, 57.
Tanăquil, ĭlis, f. The wife of Tarquinius Priscus; 16, 18, 19.
Tantălus, i, m. The father of Pelops; 96.
Tarentum, i, n. A town of Lower Italy; 42.
   Tarentīni, ōrum, m. pl. The Tarentines, the inhabitants of Tarentum; 38.
Tarpeia, ae, f. A Roman maiden who betrayed the citadel of Rome to the Sabines; 10.
Tarpeius, i, m. One of the seven hills of Rome, also called *Capitolīnus.* The Capitol was erected upon it; 11.
Tarquinii, ōrum, m. pl. An ancient town of Etruria; 16.
Tarquinius, i, m. Tarquin, the name of the fifth king of Rome and of his descendants, as *Tarquinius Superbus,* the last king of Rome; and *Tarquinius Collatīnus,* the husband of Lucretia; 16, 18, 19, 21, 23, &c.
Taurus, i, m. A range of mountains forming the southern limit of the high table-lands of Central Asia; in a more restricted sense the term usually denotes only the mountain-chain in the south of Asia Minor; 58.
Terentius, i, m. (See *Varro.*)
Thaebae, ārum, f. pl. The capital of Boeotia, in Greece; 96, 120.
   Thebănus, a, um, adj. Theban, 121; subs. *Thebānus, i,* m., a Theban; 120, 121, 125.
Thelesīnus, i, m. (See *Pontius.*)
Themistŏcles, is, m. A celebrated Athenian commander; 103—107.
Theramĕnes, is, m. One of the Thirty Tyrants of Athens; 117.
Thermopỹlae, ārum, f. pl. The famous defile *or* pass between Locris and Thessaly where Leonidas fell; 104, 105.
Theseus, i, m. An ancient king of Athens, son of Aegeus; 95.
Thesprotius, i, m. A Thesprotian; a native of Thesprotia, in Epirus; 97.
Thessalia, ae, f. The country of Thessaly, in Greece, south of Macedonia; 78, 95, 97, 124.
   Thessălus, a, um, adj. Thessalian, 123; subs. *Thessălus, i,* m., a Thessalian; 139.
Thessălus, i, m. A native of Thesprotia, in Epirus, who is said to have formed a settlement in Thessaly, and to have given his name to the country; 97.
Thessalonīca, ae, f. A city of Macedonia; 149.
Thracia, ae, f. The country of Thrace, east of Macedonia; 90, 124.
Thrasybŭlus, i, m. An Athenian who liberated the city from the Thirty Tyrants; 118.

HISTORICAL AND GEOGRAPHICAL INDEX.

Tibĕris, is, m. The river Tiber, in Italy; 6, 7, 15.
Tiberius, i, m. The second Roman emperor; 83, 84, 94.
Ticīnus, i, m. A river in Cisalpine Gaul, famous for the victory of Hannibal over the Romans; 48, 53.
Tigrānes, is, m. Son-in-law of Mithridates and king of Armenia; 71.
Tigranocerta, ōrum, n. A city of Armenia, built by Tigranes; 71.
Tissaphernes, is, m. A distinguished Persian satrap of Lower Asia, under Darius; afterwards general in the service of Artaxerxes; 114.
Titus, i, m. A Roman emperor; 91, 92.
Torquātus, i, m. Surname of *T. Manlius* and his descendants; 34.
Trasimēnus, i, m. A lake in Etruria; 48.
Trebia, ae, f. A river in Cisalpine Gaul; 48.
Triptolĕmus, i, m. A king of Eleusis who was regarded as the inventor of agriculture; 95.
Troezen, ēnis, f. (acc. *Troezĕna*). An ancient city of Argolis; 103.
Troja, ae, f. The city of Troy; 2, 86.
Trojāni, ōrum, m. pl. The Trojans; 2.
Tullia, ae, f. The daughter of Servius Tullius and wife of Tarquinius Superbus; 20.
Tullius, i, m. (See *Servius* and *Cicĕro.*)
Tullus, i, m. (See *Hostilius.*)
Tuscia, ae, f. Tuscany, in Italy, the same as Etruria; 48.
Tuscŭlum, i, n. An ancient town of Latium; 26.
Tyrus, i, f. The city of Tyre, in Phoenicia; 132.
Tyrii, ōrum, m. pl. Tyrians, the inhabitants of Tyre; 132.

V.

Valerius, i, m. A Roman name. (See *Publicŏla, Corvīnus, Laevīnus.*)
Varro, ōnis, m. (*C. Terentius*). A Roman consul defeated at Cannae; 49.
Vecta, ae, f. An island off the southern coast of Britain; now *the Isle of Wight;* 90.
Veientes, um, or *Veientāni, ōrum,* m. pl. The Veientians, the inhabitants of Veii, in Etruria; 29, 32.
Vespasiānus, i, m. The emperor Vespasian; 89, 90, 92.
Vesta, ae, f. Vesta, the goddess of the hearth, to whom a perpetual fire was kept burning; 6.
Vestālis, e, adj. Vestal; 6.
Veturia, ae, f. The mother of Coriolanus; 28.
Veturius, i, m. (*T.*) A Roman consul defeated by the Samnites at the Caudine Forks; 37.
Virginia, ae, f. The daughter of Virginius, slain by her father to save her from the designs of Appius Claudius; 30.
Virginius, i, m. (*L.*) A distinguished Roman centurion, father of Virginia; 30.
Viriāthus, i, m. The leader of the Lusitanians in their war with the Romans; 63.

Vitellius, i, m. A Roman emperor; 88, 89.
Volsci, ōrum, m. pl. The Volsci *or* Volscians, a people of Latium; 28, 31.
Volumnia, ae, f. The wife of Coriolanus; 28.

X.

Xanthippus, i, m. A Spartan commander who took Regulus prisoner in the first Punic war; 44.
Xerxes, is, m. A celebrated Persian king; 103—107.

Z.

Zama, ae, f. A town of Numidia, in Africa, famous for the victory of Scipio over Hannibal; 56.

www.ingramcontent.com/pod-product-compliance
Lightning Source LLC
Chambersburg PA
CBHW031420230426
43668CB00007B/372